1988

# Public Speaking
# for College and Career

# Public Speaking
# for College and Career

*Hamilton Gregory*

Asheville-Buncombe Technical College

*Random House*
New York

To my mother
*Rachel Smith Gregory*

**Cover Photos:** Top left, Michal Heron/Woodfin Camp & Associates; top right, Ellis Herwig/ The Picture Cube; bottom left, R. Gabe Palmer/The Stock Market; bottom right, K. Bendo.

**Chapter Opening Photos:** Chapter 1, Random House photo by Kathy Bendo, courtesy of Pace University; Chapter 2, Owen Franken/Stock, Boston; Chapter 3, Random House photo by Kathy Bendo, courtesy of Pace University; Chapter 4, Ellis Herwig/Stock, Boston; Chapter 5, Barbara Alper; Chapter 6, Hazel Hankin; Chapter 7, Random House photo by Elyse Rieder, courtesy of Pace University; Chapter 8, Joseph Nettis/Photo Researchers; Chapter 9, Alan Carey/The Image Works; Chapter 10, Hazel Hankin; Chapter 11, John Maher/EKM-Nepenthe; Chapter 12, Frank Siteman/The Picture Cube; Chapter 13, Random House photo by Elyse Rieder, courtesy of Pace University; Chapter 14, Jeff Dunn/Stock, Boston; Chapter 15, Hazel Hankin; Chapter 16, Peter Southwick/Stock, Boston; Chapter 17, Robert Pacheco/EKM-Nepenthe.

First Edition
9876543
Copyright © 1987 by Hamilton Gregory

**Library of Congress Cataloging-in-Publication Data**

Gregory, Hamilton.
   Public speaking for college and career.

   Includes index.
   1. Public speaking. I. Title.
PN4121.G716 1987   808.5′1      86–29727

ISBN 0-394-34296-8

Book Development: Domenig and Henry; Acquisitions Editor: Roth Wilkofsky;
Text Design: Suzanne Bennett; Cover Design: Nadja Furlan-Lorbek

Manufactured in the United States of America

# Preface

Those of us who teach public speaking are faced with two important challenges: How can we show our students the basic principles of speech communication? And how can we teach them to apply those principles to the speeches they must give in the classroom, in their careers, and in their communities?

In *Public Speaking for College and Career*, I have tried to meet these challenges. While presenting thorough coverage of basic principles, drawn from contemporary research and from the accumulated wisdom of over 2,000 years of rhetorical theory, I have endeavored to show students the real-life applicability of those principles by providing copious examples from classroom, career, and community contexts, and by presenting models of good speeches.

To give students a perspective on public speaking in America today, I conducted a survey of 34 professional speakers, including such national figures as Dr. Henry Heimlich, the Ohio surgeon who invented the Heimlich Maneuver for aiding persons who are choking. (I refer to the speakers as "professional" because all of them, having achieved success in business or professional life, now make their living by speaking to conventions, workshops, and professional meetings.) Their suggestions and experiences are sprinkled throughout the chapters and in Tips for Your Career, a special feature placed at the end of each chapter.

I also interviewed business and professional leaders to find out what communication skills they considered important on the job. Not surprisingly, their views reinforce, rather than contradict, the basic concepts that public speaking instructors have been teaching for years. I discovered, for example, that they all dislike hearing speeches that are read from a prepared manuscript and that they consider audience analysis to be an essential ingredient in speech preparation.

In addition, I drew from my own experiences during the past 10 years in giving speeches to civic clubs, professional organizations, college for-

*129,353*

ums, and parent-teacher associations on such topics as "How Mentally Retarded Citizens Can Be Integrated into the Work Force," "Using a Computer for Writing and Editing," and "How Parents Can Help Their Children Develop Effective Study Skills."

The major themes of this book are the same ones that most public speaking instructors stress in the classroom. For example, audience-centered communication is emphasized throughout the book: how to analyze the listeners; how to be sensitive to their needs and interests; and how to talk *to* and *with* them, not *at* them. Students are urged to communicate ideas to real people rather than merely stand up and go through the motions of "giving a speech."

A rule of thumb in American seminaries is that ministers should spend an hour in the study for each minute in the pulpit. Since this ratio is a good one for any speaker, this book devotes 10 chapters to showing students how to systematically go through the preliminary stages—analyzing the audience, selecting a topic and specific purpose, devising a central idea, finding verbal and visual support material, organizing the material into a coherent outline, and practicing effectively.

At every stage of preparation and delivery, students are encouraged to engage in critical analysis, asking themselves such questions as these: "What are the attitudes and interests of my audience?" "How can I adapt my subject to their special needs and concerns?" "How can I make my ideas understandable and persuasive?" By the time students finish this book, they will realize that they have been trained not only in public speaking but in critical thinking as well. These skills will be useful to them in the future as tools for their own speeches, and as a means for analyzing the persuasive appeals of politicians and advertisers.

Because many students are troubled by a lack of self-confidence, I have tried to show how speakers can possess and project confidence in themselves and in their ideas. Chapter 3 provides a reassuring discussion of nervousness, and shows students how to turn their nervousness into an asset by using it as constructive energy.

## OVERVIEW OF THE BOOK

Most instructors have their own ways of organizing and presenting information for this course. I have tried to make each chapter as self-contained as possible so that it can be adapted to any instructor's syllabus.

Part 1, Foundations of Effective Communication, sets forth basic introductory material. Chapter 1 describes the benefits of a public speaking course, including advantages in the job market. It also explains the speech communication process and discusses speakers' responsibilities toward their audiences.

Chapter 2 guides students in improving their effectiveness as listeners and discusses the listener's responsibilities toward the speaker.

Chapter 3 is a comprehensive treatment of nervousness, with suggestions on how speakers can convert their nervous tension into positive energy. Students should find reassurance in the examples given of famous persons who suffer from stage fright.

Part 2, Preliminary Stages, guides the students through the difficult, but crucial, tasks of choosing and refining a topic and gathering materials. Chapter 4 emphasizes a major theme of the book—the need to focus on the listeners at every stage of preparation and delivery. Students are shown how to analyze the audience and how to adapt their remarks accordingly.

Chapter 5 is a practical guide to selecting a topic and narrowing it to manageable proportions. For students who have trouble finding topics, there are two worksheets—one for exploring personal interests, the other for brainstorming—that are explained and illustrated. After students refine their topics, they are shown how to devise a general purpose, a specific purpose, and a central idea.

Chapter 6 explains how to research a topic using several sources, including personal experiences, libraries, computer databases, and interviews. It also discusses taking notes and finding the right materials quickly and efficiently.

Chapter 7 discusses verbal materials that can be used to support ideas: definitions, description, examples, narratives, comparison and contrast, testimony, and statistics. Special attention is given to the use and misuse of statistics.

Chapter 8 examines visual supports for ideas. Various types of visual aids—graphs, charts, drawings, photographs, computer graphics, objects, and models—are discussed, along with media for visual aids: chalkboards, posters, flip charts, handouts, overhead transparencies, slides, films, and videotapes. Also included are nine guidelines for using visual aids effectively.

Part 3, Organizing the Speech, explains time-tested methods for arranging materials for a speech. Chapter 9 deals with the body of the speech: how to select main points and organize them in a logical pattern. Attention is also drawn to using transitions to carry the listener from one part of a speech to another.

Chapter 10 focuses on introductions and conclusions. Introductions are explained as a two-part process—first, capturing attention and interest and second, preparing the audience for the body of the speech. In the section on conclusions, emphasis is placed on reinforcing the central idea.

Chapter 11 provides a step-by-step guide for developing an outline and then preparing speaking notes based on the outline. Included in the chapter is a full-length sample of a student's outline and speaking notes, followed by a transcript of the speech as it was delivered.

Part 4, Presenting the Speech, examines verbal and nonverbal dimensions of speechmaking. Chapter 12 deals with the need for speakers to use language that is appropriate, accurate, clear, and vivid. One section also shows the differences between oral and written language.

Chapter 13 is a comprehensive treatment of delivery, including how to practice. It also discusses how to handle question-and-answer periods.

Part 5, Types of Public Speaking, focuses on the major kinds of speeches that students are likely to give in the classroom and in their careers. Chapter 14 provides guidelines on informative speaking. A sample informative speech, with commentary, is printed at the end of the chapter.

Chapter 15 is devoted to persuasive speaking. Two popular types of persuasive speeches, the speech to influence thinking and the speech to motivate action, are examined, followed by a discussion of the elements of persuasion. A sample persuasive speech, with commentary, is featured at the end of the chapter.

Chapter 16 covers special types of speeches, including the entertaining (or after-dinner) address, as well as speeches of introduction, acceptance, tribute, and inspiration.

Chapter 17 deals with group discussions, with special emphasis on the reflective-thinking method for solving problems, and team presentations (symposium and panel).

Appendix A gives pointers on how to speak in front of a camera. In many different college courses, students are apt to produce or participate in videotaped demonstrations or discussions. Also, more and more businesses and professions are using videotapes for instructions, sales pitches, and in-house communications.

Appendix B is a selection of sample speeches that illustrate and reinforce concepts taught in the text.

## RESOURCES FOR INSTRUCTORS

An ancillary material, *Supplementary Readings*, which is available to instructors who adopt this text, provides valuable extensions to this book. A handout on speech phobia, for example, gives tips for self-therapy to those students whose fear goes far beyond the normal range discussed in Chapter 3. This handout has proved valuable in my school in encouraging phobic students not to drop out of public speaking class. The other handouts include "Quick Guide to Public Speaking" (to help students with their early speeches), "Self-Introduction Speech," "Evaluating Speeches," "Using a Personal Computer for Research," "Oral Interpretation of Literature," "Handling Job Interviews," and "Voice Production."

The instructor's manual provides dozens of worksheets and forms for use in the classroom, including two handouts that list over 100 topics for informative and persuasive speeches, worksheets for discovering library materials, and exercises to practice outlining. The manual also gives tips on how instructors can videotape student speeches and suggestions on how student speeches can be evaluated. A reproducible transcript of Dr. Martin Luther King's famous "I Have A Dream" speech is reprinted in the manual for those instructors who would like to use it as a model for their students.

## ACKNOWLEDGMENTS

In writing this book, I received valuable suggestions from the following people, who reviewed various stages of the manuscript: Martha Bergeron, Vance-Granville Community College; Vincent L. Bloom, California State University, Fresno; Marjorie Brody, Bucks County Community College; Jeanne W. Creech, Dekalb Community College; Steve Collins, Modesto Junior College; Sandra F. Davis, Pikes Peak Community College; Fran Franklin, University of Arkansas at Monticello; G. Jack Gravlee, Colorado State University; Marion Gans, University of Connecticut; Anne Grissom, Mountain View College; Charlene Handford, Louisiana State University, Shreveport; Jim Hasenauer, California State University, Northridge; Harry P. Kerr, University of Maine at Farmington; Anne Marcus, Edison Community College; Marjorie McGregor, Central State University; Martha W. Moore, Murray State University; C.R. Newman, Parkland College; Jon F. Nussbaum, The University of Oklahoma; David Payne, The University of Texas at Austin; William R. Rambin, Northeast Louisiana University; Lloyd Rohler, University of North Carolina at Wilmington; Bob G. Sampson, Central Piedmont Community College; Monika Sutherland, Edgecombe Technical Institute; Jim Towns, Stephen F. Austin State University; Forrest D. Tucker, The University of Southern Mississippi, and Gretchen E. Wheeler, Chadron State College.

In the movies, behind-the-scenes people like producers and directors get top billing in the screen credits, along with the screenwriter. It's a shame that books don't have the same tradition because if they did, the name of my principal editor at Random House, Kathleen Domenig, could be emblazoned in big letters on the cover of this book. Such tribute would be fitting: without her astute editing, wise counsel, and unflagging sense of humor, this book could not have been written. I also wish to acknowledge, with gratitude, the valuable assistance of others on the staff at Random House: Roth Wilkofsky, Suzanne Thibodeau, Carolyn Viola-John, Tina Barland, Lorraine Hohman, Dorothy Bungert, and Kathy Bendo.

I am also grateful to the following individuals: Dr. Olin Wood, for urging me to write this book; Tom Gaffigan and Dr. Celia Miles, for giving me encouragement and support; Emily Gean Bergere and Sandy Cagle, for supplying ideas on teaching public speaking; Billie Dalton, Maretta Hensley, Terry Holt, and Peggy Kyle, for ordering research materials for me; Randy Barnett, for lending me a wealth of Toastmasters' publications; Richard Babb, Alan Willcox, C.L. Satterfield, and Jim Cavener, for providing ideas in the early stages of the book; D. Michael Frank, past president of the National Speakers Association, for giving me an entrée to most of the professional speakers who contributed to this book (for their names, see the acknowledgments page in the back of this book); attorney Paul Rifkin, for putting me in touch with Mr. Frank; Nido Qubein of Creative Services, Inc., for supplying me with back issues of his newsletter; Bob Sampson of Central Piedmont Community College, for contributing two of his class handouts to the instructor's manual; Dr. G. Michael Shehi of Highland Hospital, for providing me with information on speech phobia; Larry Schnoor, executive director of the Interstate Oratorical Association, for giving permission to reprint speeches from *Winning Orations.*

I am indebted to the hundreds of students in my public speaking classes over the years who have made teaching this course a pleasant and rewarding task. From them I have drawn most of the examples and samples of classroom speeches.

And for their support and patience, special thanks to my wife Merrell and to my children, Jess, Jim, and June.

Hamilton Gregory

# Contents

# Part 4
# Presenting the Speech                                           249

# Part 1

# Foundations of Effective Communication

# Chapter 1

# Introduction to Public Speaking

**Benefits of a Public Speaking Course**

**The Speech Communication Process**
  Speaker
  Listener
  Message
  Channel
  Feedback
  Interference
  Situation
  The Speech Communication Process in Action

**The Speaker's Responsibilities**
  Respect Your Audience
  Take Every Speech Seriously
  Be Ethical

Lee Iacocca, chairman of Chrysler Corporation, is considered by many people to be one of the most dynamic and successful communicators in America. He took command of Chrysler when the Detroit automobile firm was nearly bankrupt; a few years later the corporation was rolling up record profits, thanks in large part to Iacocca's communication skills: he inspired Chrysler employees to work hard and put out reliable products, and he persuaded American consumers (via TV commercials) to buy his cars.

Iacocca is much in demand as a public speaker. He receives over 3,000 speaking invitations each year and accepts about 45 of them. "He devotes enormous energy" to each speech, says *Time* magazine. "At the 1983 University of Michigan graduation exercises, the audience was not hot for him at first." The seniors seemed to be expecting just another dull, stodgy commencement speech. But Iacocca set his audience on fire. "When he finished with the graduates 45 minutes later," reported *Time*, "some 14,000 people were on their feet, cheering and stomping."[1]

How did Iacocca learn to be such an effective communicator? He attributes his success to a public speaking course he took at age 25. Before that, he says, he was a "terrible" speechmaker.[2]

This book and the public speaking course that you are embarking upon may not turn you into an Iacocca, but they are designed with one goal in mind: to help you deliver effective speeches with confidence and vigor— not only in college but in your career as well.

# Benefits of a Public Speaking Course

After leaving school, many college graduates look back upon all the courses they took in college and say that public speaking was one of the most valuable.[3] Here are some of the reasons why this course is considered so important:

1. *You learn how to speak to a public audience.* Knowing how to stand up and give a talk to a group of people is a rewarding skill to have for the rest of your life. It makes you more valuable as an employee than someone who refuses or shies away from the task. It can also help you in situations when you are away from the job. For example, imagine yourself in the following public speaking scenarios:

☐ In court you explain to a jury why a particular traffic accident was not your fault.
☐ At the monthly meeting of your club, you give a treasurer's report.
☐ You talk to a gathering of neighbors about your ideas for curbing crime in the neighborhood.
☐ You teach softball techniques to thirty boys and girls on the team you coach.

**A citizen speaks out at a town meeting. No matter where people live, there are times when they must speak in public.** *(Hazel Hankin)*

Throughout your life you will encounter many such occasions that require public speaking ability.

2. *You learn skills that apply to one-on-one communication.* Though the emphasis of this course is upon speaking to groups, the principles that you learn also apply to communication with individuals.[4] Throughout your lifetime you will be obliged to talk in situations such as these:

☐ In a job interview, the personnel manager says, "We've got fifty applicants for this job. Why should we hire *you?*" If you know how to give a reply that is brief, interesting, and convincing, you obviously improve your chances of getting the job (assuming, of course, that your qualifications are as good as those of the other 49 applicants). In a public speaking course, you learn how to organize and present such a persuasive message.

☐ You sit down in front of a bank executive to ask for a loan so that you can buy a new car. The skills of nonverbal communication (eye contact, facial expression, etc.) that you learn in a public speaking class should help you convey to the executive that you are a trustworthy and reliable person who can be counted upon to repay the loan.

After taking a public speaking course, many students report that their new skills help them as much in talking to one person as in addressing a large audience.

3. *You develop the oral communication skills that are prized in the job market.* When you go out to seek a job, which of the following factors is most likely to influence the employer when he or she decides whether to hire you?

a. The reputation of your school
b. Your grade-point average
c. Your letters of reference
d. Your technical knowledge of the field you are entering
e. Your oral communication skills—speaking and listening
f. Your written communication skills—reading and writing

Research shows that *e* is the correct answer.[5] Employers generally rank the ability to speak well and listen intelligently as the most highly prized of all skills when it comes to hiring—and promoting—employees.

The answer to the above question is surprising to many students. Surely *d* (technical knowledge of the field) is the most important factor for jobs in science and technology, isn't it? Not according to employers. Take engineering, for example: engineers work mainly with numbers, designs, and materials, so one might assume that communication skills would be less important than technical skills. But according to a survey by *Engineering Education* magazine, 500 leaders in engineering said that the most important capability for civil and electrical engineers was communication skills. *All the technical skills were ranked second in importance.*[6]

In the same survey, the leaders evaluated the recent engineering graduates and rated 59 percent of them as "inferior" in communication skills.[7] This means that the most highly prized skill for engineers—communicating effectively—is lacking in the majority of engineering graduates. Thus, if you are a competent engineer who also possesses good communication skills, you have a big advantage over many other engineers in getting a good job and in gaining promotions.

The same holds true for most other professions as well. For example, alumni of the University of Minnesota Business School ranked oral communication at the top of a list of skills needed for job success.[8]

While being a good communicator can help you get a job or a promotion, the opposite is also true: being a *poor* communicator can block you from being hired or promoted. When 170 business and industrial firms were asked to list the most common reasons for rejecting job applicants, the most frequent replies were "inability to communicate" and "poor communication skills."[9]

Why are communication skills so highly regarded? From an employer's point of view, good communication prevents costly mistakes, improves employee morale, and raises productivity. Consider the case of a General

Motors automotive plant that provided classes for its 6,000 employees on how to improve their communication skills. As a result of the classes, the plant showed an improvement in employee morale, a decline in absenteeism, and a decrease in production errors. In a two-year period, the program netted a savings for the company of $7 million.[10]

What does a public speaking class have to do with these oral communication skills? The most highly regarded of the skills—speaking and listening—are developed and practiced in a public speaking class. You learn how to analyze and understand your listeners, how to develop and support your ideas, how to organize your message, and how to deliver it with confidence and power. You also learn how to listen intelligently.

"No one who aspires to success in any profession," says Jack Valenti, president of the Motion Picture Association of America, "can neglect the art of communication. The role of communicator has become dominant in the careers of business [executives], professors, union [leaders], politicians—of anyone who must try to convince others of a point of view . . . It is not enough to be intellectual, gorged with facts, smart, competent in administration or in designing strategy. You must be able to speak reasonably, believably, engagingly. . . ."[11]

4. *You practice and gain experience in an ideal laboratory.* Effective communicators say that they became adept at communicating by learning certain skills and then practicing them—the way carpenters become masters of their trade by learning woodworking skills and then practicing them. The classroom is an ideal laboratory for practicing your skills because (1) it is an unthreatening setting—no one will deny you a job or a raise based on how you perform in class, and (2) your audience is friendly and sympathetic—made up of students who must go through the same experience.

If you have never given speeches before, this class will give you valuable experience. When your boss asks you to give a talk to a group of employees, you will not be giving your first speech—you will be giving your fifth or sixth, thanks to the speeches you gave in the classroom. If you are already experienced in giving speeches, you will still find this course helpful in fine-tuning your skills.

Extremely valuable to you are the critiques given by your instructor (and, in some cases, by fellow students). If, for example, you have the habit of saying "er" or "uh" between every sentence, you can get help in eliminating it from your speech. If you have difficulty organizing your thoughts into coherent form, you can learn strategies for constructing ideas logically.

5. *You gain self-confidence.* One of the greatest benefits of this course is helping you gain confidence in yourself and in your speechmaking ability. Giving a public speech is one of the most difficult tasks in life; so if you learn to do it well, you gain an extraordinary amount of self-confidence.

It is similar to Outward Bound, the program that teaches urban citizens to climb mountains and survive in the wilderness. "After Outward Bound," one graduate of the program told me, "everything else in life is small potatoes. I can take on any challenge." Many students have the same feeling of pride and self-worth after completing a public speaking class.

# The Speech Communication Process

A mistake made by some speakers is to think that when they have given a speech, communication has *necessarily* taken place. It often does take place, of course, but it sometimes does not, for this reason: *Speaking and communicating are not the same thing.* You can speak to a listener, but if the listener does not understand your message in the way you meant it to be understood, you have failed to communicate.[12] Here's an example of what I'm talking about.

When I was in basic training in the Army, my company spent a week out in the wilderness on "bivouac"—that is, living in a tent encampment. One morning, as the company prepared to hike out of camp for maneuvers, the company commander ordered me to stay behind and "police" the camp. "Yes sir," I said happily, glad to be free of a long hike in the blistering August heat. My job, as I saw it, was to act as a security policeman, making sure no intruders trespassed in our camp. I was proud to have this assignment because I had heard rumors that trainees from rival companies might try to slip in and knock down our tents, thereby hurting us in competition for an award as best company on bivouac.

I rested under a shade tree at the top of a hill, keeping an eye on our encampment until late afternoon, when two jeeploads of high-ranking officers roared up. A colonel, two majors, and several captains got out of the jeeps and strode through the camp, inspecting our tents, latrines, and field kitchen. After a while, the colonel walked over to me. I could tell by his demeanor that he was furious. I snapped to attention and saluted.

"Private," he demanded, "weren't you ordered to police this camp?"

"Yes sir," I replied.

"Well, how come there's trash all over the place?" he said angrily.

Suddenly I realized my mistake: while the verb *police* means to guard and protect, it also has a special military meaning—to clean up. When my company commander ordered me to police the camp, I temporarily forgot the military definition and reverted to civilian usage. It was a stupid blunder because I had heard the Army's definition every morning for six weeks when I and my fellow trainees were ordered to "police up" cigarette butts and other trash outside our barracks.

As I tried to stammer out an explanation, the colonel stared at me as if I were the dumbest trainee ever inducted into the U.S. Army. As punishment, he put me on KP (kitchen police), washing pots and pans, for two weeks.

This incident illustrates that speaking and communicating are not synonymous. The captain (playing the role of speaker) gave me instructions, but true communication failed to take place because I (the listener) failed to interpret his message correctly.

This same lesson applies to speechmaking, as we will see by using Figure 1.1 as our model and by examining how each element in communication actually works.

## *Speaker*

When you are a *speaker,* you are the source, or originator, of a message that is transmitted to a listener. Whether you are speaking to one individ-

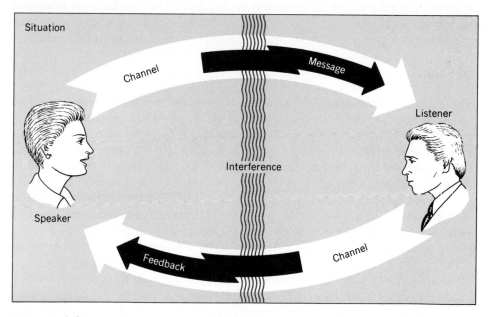

**FIGURE 1.1**
A model of the speech communication process. In the context of a particular *situation,* the *speaker* sends a *message* via a *channel* to the *listener,* who in turn gives *feedback* via a *channel* to the *speaker. Interference* is whatever impedes the flow back and forth.

ual or to an audience of 500, you bear a great responsibility for the success of the communication. The key question that you must constantly ask yourself is not "Am I giving out good information?" or "Am I performing well?" but rather, "Am I getting through to my listeners?"

## Listener

The *listener* is the recipient of the message sent by the speaker. As we saw in my Army story, the true test of communication is not whether a message is delivered by the speaker, but whether it is accurately received by the listener. Professional speaker David W. Richardson says, "A speech takes place in the minds of the audience."[13] In other words, no matter how eloquent the speaker, no matter how dynamic the speaker's delivery, if the listeners' minds do not receive and interpret the message correctly, the desired communication has failed to take place.

Who is to blame for such failure—the speaker or the listener? Depending on the situation, the blame could be placed on either, or both. While speakers share part of the responsibility for communication, listeners also must bear some of the burden. They must try hard to pay attention to the speaker, fighting off the temptation to daydream or think about personal concerns. They must listen with an open mind, avoiding the tendency to prejudge the speaker or discount a speaker's views without a fair hearing.

## Message

The *message* is whatever the speaker communicates to the listeners. The message is sent in the form of *symbols*, either *verbal* or *nonverbal*.

Verbal symbols are words. It is important for you to recognize that words are not things; they are *symbols* of things. If you give me an apple, you transfer a solid object from your hand to mine. But if you're making a speech and you mention the word "apple," you are no longer transferring a concrete thing. You are transferring a symbol, which may be interpreted by your listeners in ways that are quite different from what you had in your mind. When you say "apple," one listener may think of a small green fruit, while another conjures an image of a big red fruit. One listener might think of crisp tartness, while another thinks of juicy sweetness.

Nonverbal symbols are what you convey with your tone of voice, eyes, facial expression, gestures, posture, and appearance.

*Everything that you express in a message is in the form of symbols.* For example, if you want to tell me about your headache, you cannot transfer the ache and pain from your head to mine. You must transmit a symbolic description of it. The symbols you use might be verbal ("My head feels as if it's splitting apart") and nonverbal (a grimace).

When listeners receive messages, they must interpret the symbols—

that is, make sense out of the speaker's verbal and nonverbal symbols. This can cause misunderstanding and confusion because symbols are only an approximation of reality. The listener who hears of your headache might interpret the words "My head feels as if it's splitting apart" in a way that you did not intend. For example, listeners who have never had a headache (there are a few such lucky people in the world) might have trouble imagining the pain. Some listeners might misinterpret the symbols "splitting apart" and think that you had a psychotic break with reality.

As a speaker, you should strive to use symbols that will cause the listener to arrive at a meaning that is as close as possible to the one in your mind. For example, do not say, "Smoking may cause you a lot of trouble." The verbal symbols at the end of the sentence—"a lot of trouble"—might be interpreted by some listeners to mean "coughing," by others to mean "stained teeth," or by still others to mean "cancer." Be specific: "Smoking may cause lung cancer."

When you use abstract words like *socialism*, *feminism*, and *censorship*, you must be especially careful to define precisely what you mean because listeners often have their own widely varying interpretations of such verbal symbols. The term *censorship*, for example, might mean "stamping out filth" to some listeners, or "total government control of the press" to others.

Ideally, the two types of symbols, verbal and nonverbal, are harmonious, but if they are not, the listeners receive a mixed message. For example, suppose you say to an audience, "I'm delighted to be here tonight," but as you say these words, your face has a mournful expression and your tone of voice is regretful. The listeners are getting a mixed message. Which will they believe, your words or your nonverbal behavior? In most instances of mixed messages, listeners accept the nonverbal behavior as the true message. In this case, they will believe that you are *not* delighted to be there. This is an example of how your *intended* message is not always the same as the *actual* message received by listeners.

The solution to this problem is to always make sure that the nonverbal part of your message reinforces, rather than diminishes, the verbal part. In other words, smile and use a friendly tone of voice when you say, "I'm glad to be here tonight."

## *Channel*

The channel is the medium used to communicate the message. A speech can reach you by means of a variety of channels: radio, television, a public-address system, or direct voice communication.

For public speaking in the classroom, you have the best channel of all—direct face-to-face contact. For some speeches in the community, you may have a public-address system. This can be a very effective channel (if the system works well and the acoustics in the room are good) because you can speak in an easy, conversational style without having to raise your voice.

## Feedback

Feedback is the response that the listeners give the speaker. Sometimes it is verbal, as when a listener asks questions or makes comments during a lecture. In most public speeches and certainly in the ones you will give in the classroom, the listeners refrain from giving verbal feedback until the question-and-answer period at the end of the speech.

Even if there is no verbal feedback during the speech itself, the listeners can still give powerful responses by means of their nonverbal behavior. If they roll their eyes and look at each other in disgust, they are giving feedback that might mean, "Oh, brother! Can you believe what an idiotic thing that speaker just said?" If they have puzzled looks on their faces, they may be saying nonverbally to the speaker, "I don't understand what you're talking about." If, on the other hand, they lean forward in their chairs and occasionally nod their heads in agreement, they are clearly signaling their approval and enthusiasm.

As a speaker, you should look for feedback from your audience, and adjust your remarks accordingly. If, for example, you explain a concept, but most of your listeners are shaking their heads and giving you looks that seem to say, "I don't understand," you should try again, using different words, to make your ideas clear.

When you are looking for feedback, some audience behavior is not easy to decipher. If a couple of listeners are sleeping through your speech, it does not necessarily mean that your speech is boring. It could mean that they stayed out all night at a party and are physically exhausted.

## Interference

Interference is anything that blocks or hinders the communication of a message. It could be horns honking outside the classroom or someone coughing loudly inside the room. It could be static and snow on a TV screen that makes it hard to view a videotape. It could be an air-conditioning breakdown that leaves the listeners hot and sticky and preoccupied with their discomfort.

Sometimes listeners will fight to overcome interference—for example, straining to hear the speaker's words despite a truck roaring down the street outside the room. At other times, however, some listeners will fail to make the extra effort, and no communication takes place.

Sometimes interference is "internal," that is, it can come from within the listeners: some of them might be daydreaming or worrying about a test in their next class. They may be tired or sleepy or hungry—and therefore disinclined to expend mental energy on listening. One of the worst forms of "internal" interference is jumping to conclusions: listeners block out what the speaker is actually saying because they are sure they already know what his or her message or conclusion will be. As a speaker, you can help listeners overcome internal distractions by making your speech so lively and interesting that the audience feels compelled to listen to you. In the rest of this book we will look at ways in which you can prepare and deliver lively, interesting speeches.

On other occasions, the speaker might be the cause of interference because he or she uses words that are unfamiliar to the audience, or uses words that are interpreted in a way that the speaker did not intend. If the speaker wears bizarre clothing, some listeners might scrutinize the attire instead of concentrating on the speech. When you are a speaker, you should obviously avoid being the cause of such interference: you should choose your words and clothes with great care.

When you are a speaker, you should watch for any signs of interference and if possible take steps to overcome the problem. For example, if a plane roars in the sky and you see your listeners leaning forward to hear your words, you can either speak louder or pause until the plane's noise has subsided.

## Situation

The situation is the context—the time and place—in which communication occurs. Different situations call for different behaviors on the part of both speaker and listener. For example, one who delivers a eulogy in the stately hush of a cathedral does not crack jokes. Nor does the audience respond to the speaker's remarks with boisterous joy. But these kinds of behavior would be quite appropriate for an entertaining after-dinner speech at a convention.

Time of day plays a part in how receptive an audience is. Many listeners, for example, tend to be sluggish and sleepy between 3 and 5 P.M.; if you gave a speech during that period, you would need to have an especially lively presentation, perhaps using colorful visual aids to "jazz" up your speech. If your speech is a long one, you could invite the listeners to stand up and stretch at the midpoint of your speech so that they can shake off their sleepiness.

The size of the audience and the seating arrangements are important factors in some kinds of speeches, such as the humorous after-dinner address. You are more apt to get laughter from listeners seated close together in a small room than from the same size audience spread out in a huge room. If the latter situation exists, most professional speakers will ask the listeners to move to the front and center of the auditorium so that they are seated side by side.

When you prepare a speech, it is important for you to find out as much as possible about the situation: Where will the speech be given, indoors or outdoors? What is the nature of the occasion? How many people are likely to be present? By assessing these variables in advance, you can adapt your speech to make it appropriate to the situation.

## The Speech Communication Process in Action

The speech communication process is a dynamic process in which speaker and listener constantly interact, depending upon each other to keep the process going. In the following story, you can see how the variables of the speech communication process interact in a successful speaking situation. Refer to Figure 1.1 as you study the variables.

       [*Speaker*]
Carl Braun,* a counselor for a drug-abuse hotline, was asked to speak at a

     [*Situation*]                 [*Listeners*]
workshop on drug abuse for about 200 high school students from throughout

                                    [*Situation*]
his city. When it was his turn to speak, it was mid-afternoon, the room was hot and stuffy, and the audience was already weary from having heard an hour's worth of public speaking. As Carl began his talk, speaking into a

                 [*Channel*]
microphone hooked up to a public-address system, he noticed the drooping

[*Feedback*]                        [*Responding to the feedback*]
eyelids of many of his listeners, so he said, "You've been sitting a long time. I'd like to ask everyone to stand up and shake hands with four different people." The audience responded with gratitude; the novelty of shaking hands instead of just stretching created a mood of good humor. After the audience had sat back down, Carl continued with his speech. Soon, however,

           [*Feedback*]
he noticed from the listeners' expressions that many of them still appeared

                      [*New channel*]
sluggish, so he abandoned the microphone and walked out into the midst of

                   [*Responding to feedback*]
the audience. His close presence and his occasional strolls from one part of the room to another seemed to increase the alertness of most of the listeners.

                      [*Interference*]
As he continued, however, he noticed that three students were smirking and whispering among themselves. Looking directly at them, Carl said, "I know

*Except in cases where written permission has been given, the names of community and student speakers cited in examples in this book have been changed to protect privacy.

[*Confronting interference*]

what some of you are thinking: What does this old guy know about drugs? Why should we listen to him?" By the look of embarrassment and surprise that flashed across the three students' faces, Carl figured that he had correctly guessed the nature of their reaction. Without denigrating the three, Carl said in a gentle, good-natured way, "I don't blame you for having that attitude. Indeed, how can I claim to know anything at all about the world

[*Message*]

of teen-age drug use?" He then went on to explain what he had learned as a counselor for the drug-abuse hotline. For the rest of the speech, Carl continued to interact dynamically with his audience. For example, he

[*Feedback*]

"revved" them up by throwing out questions and then asking for volunteers to answer them. Carl's speech was a success because he overcame formidable problems—an audience that was already weary of speeches, a room that was too hot, and a time of day (mid-afternoon) that was more conducive to drowsiness than to mental alertness—and nevertheless, he managed to reach the audience with information that was delivered with energy and genuine concern.

# The Speaker's Responsibilities

When a speaker stands before an audience, he or she has certain personal and ethical responsibilities which an honest person should accept. Here are some suggestions which I hope will help you develop an awareness of these responsibilities.

## *Respect Your Audience*

As a speaker, you should respect your listeners, no matter who they are or why they have come to listen to you.

A speaker who failed to respect an audience wrote the following account of his fiasco for the benefit of readers of this book:

> When I was a senior in college, I was older than most of my fellow students and had already spent five years as a full-time journalist. When I was asked to take the job of managing editor of the school paper, I agreed, even though it meant that I was stepping down from the glamorous arena of daily journalism into the lowly (as I saw it) world of college reporting. But I thought it would be fun to teach these college "kids" the hard realities of the cold, cruel world beyond the hallowed halls of ivy. At the first staff meeting, I played the role of the hard-boiled newsman, haranguing the fledgling reporters on what they could and could not do. I told them that I was a veteran writer who would not tolerate lateness and that I would ruthlessly edit poorly written articles. Then, with a parting admonition to work hard, I

gruffly dismissed them. A few hours later, the editor-in-chief approached me sheepishly and informed me that every single one of the 20 reporters had resigned. I was without a staff, and I had to step aside to make way for a new managing editor. I had utterly failed to consider the sensitivities of my audience. I had failed to give them the respect that should be given to *any* group of people. Deep down I had thought of them as wet-behind-the-ears dunces and they had correctly picked up on my attitude. The slap in the face they gave me by resigning *en masse* was a painful slap that I richly deserved.

The lesson to be learned from that experience is this: *respect your listeners.* A sour, negative attitude not only alienates your audience, but it also diminishes *you.* It deprives you of meaningful communication with your fellow human beings; it stunts your psychological growth.

You should never patronize your listeners or talk down to them. If you say, "I know I won't change anybody's mind today, but . . . ," it is almost the same as saying, "I know you idiots are all close-minded and won't listen to me intelligently. . . ." You are insulting your audience. One professor used to close each of his lectures by gathering up his notes and declaring, "Well, I've finished casting my pearls." The statement was clearly an insult, since it was an allusion to the Biblical verse, "Neither cast ye your pearls before swine." When you insult or antagonize listeners, you do more than make them angry or defensive; you shut off all possibilities of reaching them with your ideas.

Michelle Cuomo, a student speaker, tried to persuade her audience that smoking should be banned in restaurants. Since she knew that some of her listeners smoked, she could have given them a stern tongue-lashing: "Don't you smokers have any common decency? How do you think the rest of us feel when you blow your foul smoke into the air that we must breathe?" If she had berated her audience in this fashion, how do you think the smokers would have reacted? With anger and defensiveness, of course. Wisely, Michelle used a more respectful approach. She said, "I know that some of you smoke, and I know that when you go out to eat at a restaurant with your friends, it's very enjoyable to have a cigarette at the end of the meal. I normally would not want to do anything to take away from your enjoyment, except that I have asthma, and I'd like to explain what smoke does to me." Notice how friendly and reasonable Michelle was. She refrained from attacking the intelligence or morals of the smokers; she merely presented her case in a respectful, but assertive, manner that should have prevented any listener from getting angry or defensive. And who knows? She might have convinced some smokers to accept her views.

## Take Every Speech Seriously

Some students fail to take their speech assignments seriously because they view the classroom as not the "real" world. This is a mistake. I believe that you should take a speech before your public speaking class as seriously as you would a speech before a Joint Session of Congress. Here is why: (1) Speech class is an ideal place to practice, and as with any endeavor in life, you get the maximum benefit from practice if you exert yourself to the fullest. High jumpers who win gold medals in the Olympics do so by trying as hard in practice as they do in Olympic competition. (2) While the classroom is a laboratory for speechmaking, the speeches are not artificial. They deal with real human issues and they are given by real human beings. As a teacher, I look forward to classroom speeches, not only because they are interesting, but also because they are highly instructive. I learn a great deal from them. To cite just a few examples from recent years: I have learned how to save the life of a person choking on food, I have learned the correct way to cut down some decaying trees in my backyard, and I have modified my views on gun control because of the persuasive talents of several students.

Some speakers think that if an audience is small, or a great deal smaller than they expected, they need not put forth their best effort. This is a

**Audiences like to listen to speakers who are sincere and enthusiastic.**
**(Susan Lapides/Design Conceptions)**

mistake; you should try as hard to communicate with an audience of five as you would with an audience of 500. At conventions, there are usually a number of speakers scheduled at the same time in different meeting rooms. I have seen some speakers get so angry at seeing only a handful of people show up for their talk (while hundreds are crowding in to hear the speaker across the hall) that they let their disappointment color their speech. They give their speech in a peevish mood. It is ironic: they are irritated because of the people who did not come, but their negative "vibrations" go out to the people who honored them by attending. They impatiently hurry through their presentation; their attitude seems to be: why should I take pains with just a handful of people?

Now contrast that kind of speaker with Nido R. Qubein, a professional speaker who was scheduled to give a talk at a convention of the Associated General Contractors of America. Because of some last-minute scheduling changes, he found that his competition was none other than the President of the United States! Instead of having an audience of hundreds, he found himself with only about 30 listeners. "It would have been easy for me to assume that . . . it was a hopeless situation," he said. "But I realized that those people who came really wanted to hear my message, and I tried twice as hard to please them. I called them up to the front of the room, seated them around a large table, and we had a group discussion. They got so involved that it was hard to break it off at the appointed time."[14]

Professional speakers have learned to take every audience seriously, even if it is an audience of only one. James "Doc" Blakely, a professional speaker, tells of a colleague who traveled to a small town in the Canadian province of Saskatchewan to give a speech, but found that only one person had showed up to hear him. He gave the lone listener his best efforts, and later that listener started a national movement based upon the speaker's ideas.[15]

## Be Ethical

Being ethical means being honest and straightforward with your listeners, avoiding all methods and goals that are deceitful, unscrupulous, or unfair.[16]

As an ethical speaker, there are two important principles that you should follow:

1. *Be as well-informed as you possibly can.* You should speak on a subject only after you have thoroughly investigated it, finding out as much as you possibly can. If, for example, you are planning to speak on the incidence and causes of airplane crashes, you should carefully collect data and analyze the statements of the experts—both inside the air-traffic industry and outside it. Sometimes, of course, there will be gaps in your knowledge

of a subject; you should be willing to admit this to the audience (for example, "I couldn't find a figure on the number of crashes so far this year, but I do have the figure for last year . . . .").

2. *Be honest with facts and figures.* Do not fabricate information to prove a point. Refrain from distorting data to fit an argument. But, you might ask, isn't it all right to bend the facts if one's cause is noble and good? No, for the honest speaker, the ends never justify the means. It is unethical to be dishonest in the service of a good goal. For example, let's say that you sincerely believe that the controversial drug Laetrile is the miracle cure for cancer that the world has long awaited. You come across an article that reports that 12 out of the 16 doctors interviewed by the authors favored legalization of the drug on an experimental basis even though they all predicted that the medicine would prove to be worthless. Would it be ethical to say in your speech, "Three out of four doctors surveyed support legalization of Laetrile"? This would of course be an outrageous distortion of statistics. Your statement would make it sound as if three-fourths of all doctors in America favor legalization, when in fact only 16 doctors were involved in the poll. Furthermore, you would be withholding a vital piece of information from your audience: the fact that all of the doctors predicted that the drug would prove to be worthless. Even if you could get away with this kind of dishonest reporting (that is, not being challenged by anyone in the audience), it would be unethical to pursue it, regardless of how admirable you think your goal is.

## Summary

A public speaking course helps you develop the key oral communication skills (speaking well and listening intelligently) that are highly prized in business, technical, and professional careers. You should gain both confidence and experience as you practice these skills in an ideal speechmaking laboratory—the classroom—where your audience is friendly and supportive.

The speech communication process consists of seven elements: speaker, listener, message, channel, feedback, interference, and situation. Communication does not take place just because a speaker transmits a message; the message must be accurately *received* by the listener. When the speaker sends a message, he or she must make sure that the two components of a message—verbal and nonverbal—do not contradict each other.

As a speaker, you should hold your listeners in high esteem. You should respect them and treat them courteously, no matter who they are or how large the audience is. In every aspect of your speech, you should maintain high ethical standards, making sure that you are as well-informed as possible and that you are honest with your facts and figures.

## Review Questions

1. Why are communication skills important to your career?
2. Name five personal benefits of a public speaking course.
3. What are the seven elements of the speech communication process?
4. Why is speaking not necessarily the same thing as communicating?
5. If there is a contradiction between the verbal and nonverbal components of a speaker's message, which component is a listener likely to accept as the true message?
6. What are the three major responsibilities of a speaker, as discussed in this chapter?

# TIPS *for your career*

### Tip 1: Avoid the Five Biggest Mistakes Made by Speakers

In a survey of 34 professional speakers, I asked what they considered to be the most common mistakes made by public speakers in America today. Here are the mistakes that were most often cited:

*1. Failing to tailor one's speech to the needs and interests of the audience*
"The most common mistake of speechmakers," says professional speaker Philip D. Steffen of Marietta, Georgia, "is failure to educate yourself about the specifics of the audience to which you will be speaking, [such as] age, gender, the essential points of their business, what problems they are facing, challenges they face, what they do well, where they and their business are going, and objectives of the overall meeting."[17]

Steffen gives over 125 talks to American corporations each year on management, sales, marketing, and production. Before each presentation, he finds out everything he can about the company that he will address. He interviews company officials and gets his name put on the organization's mailing list. "Most of my presentations are booked months in advance," he says. "I keep a file folder on each client. When I run across something I feel might be appropriate for the group, I put it in the file. Thus I am constantly preparing for them."[18]

Most good speakers are like Steffen—they center themselves and their messages on the listeners, finding out everything they can about them and then striving to meet their needs and interests.

## 2. Being poorly prepared

Some speakers fail to devote enough time to researching their topic, organizing their material, or rehearsing their speech.

Roy Fenstermaker of Lakewood, California, won the 1983 Toastmasters' International Speech Contest championship with a rousing address entitled "Retirement, Never!" Listening to a tape of the speech, I was struck by how natural and spontaneous he sounded, as if he simply decided on the spur of the moment to stand up and speak from his heart. Was he in fact speaking off the cuff, or had he spent a great deal of time preparing his speech?

Fenstermaker says that he started working on his speech two years before it was delivered. To gather ideas, he tapped his own experience as a retired person, read about 15 books on retirement, and culled through his personal notebook of favorite quotations. He wrote 20 drafts of his outline before deciding upon the final version. Then, he practiced his speech many times, making sure that he stayed within the contest's strict time limits ($4\frac{1}{2}$ to $7\frac{1}{2}$ minutes).[19]

Fenstermaker's experience shows that a good speech does not just "happen." If you want to deliver a strong, effective speech, you must be willing to spend a lot of time preparing it.

## 3. Trying to cover too much in one speech

Some speakers are so enthusiastic and knowledgeable about their topic that they want to tell you everything they can. So they try to cram a huge amount of material into a short speech. As professional speaker Arnold "Nick" Carter puts it: "They try to put ten pounds of information in a one-pound bag."[20]

Covering too much material causes the listeners to suffer from "information overload." They simply cannot absorb huge quantities of information in one sitting. A wiser approach is to give the listeners one big idea with a few main points to back it up.

## 4. Failing to maintain good eye contact

Listeners tend to distrust speakers who do not look them in the eye. Yet some speakers spend most of their time looking at their notes or at the floor or at the back wall.

One good way to maintain eye contact with your listeners is to think of your speech as a conversation with them. Hope Mihalap, a professional speaker from Norfolk, Virginia, says that she tries to "make the audience feel that we're all sitting together in a living room, having a warm, one-on-one conversation."[21] Treating a speech as if it were conversation helps your eye contact because, in the words of another professional speaker, Rosita Perez of Brandon, Florida, "you tune in to the audience instead of to yourself."[22]

## 5. Being dull

A dull speech can be caused by poor content or by poor delivery. To avoid being dull, you should (1) choose a subject about which you are enthusiastic, (2) prepare interesting material, (3) have a strong desire to communicate your message to the audience, and (4) let your enthusiasm shine forth during your delivery of the speech.

# *Chapter 2*

# Listening

**How to Listen Effectively**
**The Listener's Responsibilities**

**B**ecause of some misunderstandings, a secretary who worked for an extremely busy executive began to suspect that her boss was so preoccupied with paperwork that he never truly listened to her. To verify her suspicion, she arrived late for work one morning, entered the boss's office, and said, "I'm sorry I'm late but I had to pick up my ticket to Brazil. You see, I've been embezzling company funds and now that I've reached my goal, I'm off to Rio."

The harried executive glanced up from the mound of papers on his desk and said, "Well, at least you're here. Can you get me the notes on the Thompson proposal?"[1]

This story illustrates the difference between hearing and listening. *Hearing* occurs when your ears pick up sound waves being transmitted by a speaker. *Listening* involves making sense out of what is being transmitted. The boss heard the secretary's voice, but he failed to listen to everything that she said. He apparently paid attention to the words, "I'm sorry I'm late . . ." but let his brain tune out the rest of her remarks.

We may snicker at the boss's gaffe, but most of us are just as ineffective at listening as the boss was.[2] According to Dr. Lyman K. Steil of the University of Minnesota in St. Paul, "Tests have shown that immediately after listening to a 10-minute oral presentation, the average listener has heard, understood, properly evaluated and retained approximately half of what was said. And within 48 hours, that drops off another 50% to a final 25% level of effectiveness. In other words, we quite often comprehend and retain only one-quarter of what is said."[3]

Society pays a heavy price for our poor listening, Dr. Steil says. "With more than 100 million workers in this country, a simple $10 mistake by each of them, as a result of poor listening, would add up to a cost of a billion dollars. And most people make numerous listening mistakes every week. Letters have to be retyped, appointments rescheduled, shipments rerouted. Productivity is affected and profits suffer."[4]

Poor listening also hurts us at home. Many marriages, for example, are weakened by the absence of real listening. "Most couples never truly listen to each other," says Dr. M. Scott Peck, a psychiatrist and author of several best-selling books on mental health. "When couples come to us for counseling or therapy, a major task we must accomplish . . . is to teach them how to listen."[5]

Effective listening is taught not only by marriage counselors but by many American businesses as well. Giant corporations such as 3M, AT&T, General Electric, and Sperry routinely send employees to special listening-skills classes. For example, thousands of salespersons are being taught "how to sell by listening."[6] In one class run by Xerox Learning Systems and attended by employees from 80 percent of the Fortune 500 industrial corporations, salespersons are trained to listen as much as they talk. Commerce Clearing House Inc., a publisher of tax information, found that salespersons who took the Xerox class showed a big improvement in later performance on the job, increasing their billings by 33.7 percent on the average while salespersons who didn't take the class improved by only 2.5 percent.[7]

If you know how to listen effectively, you enhance your chances of getting a job. A survey of California business leaders conducted by one university asked what skills they looked for in hiring employees. A majority of the executives felt that listening was *the most important skill* for a potential employee.[8]

Once you have a job, good listening can help you get ahead. "In most companies," one executive told me, "men and women who are good listeners are so rare that no matter what their job—blue collar or white collar—they are usually the ones who win promotions and raises. A company doesn't want to see them hired away by somebody else."

# How to Listen Effectively

If you are reading a book, you can put it aside when you become weary or distracted, and then come back to it later. If the book contains complicated material, you can reread passages until you extract the meaning.

While the printed page is stable and enduring, a speech is transitory and short-lived—"written on the wind," as someone once said. That is why listening is more difficult than reading. If you listen to a speech and you fail to get the message the first time around, there is usually no way to go back and retrieve it.[9]

Though listening is a difficult task, there are some skills that you can develop to maximize your understanding and retention of material. These skills are presented in the following discussion.

## *Don't Fake Attention*

If you are like most people, you have indulged in fake listening many times. You go to history class, say, and sit in the third row and look squarely at the instructor as she speaks. But your mind is far away, floating in the clouds of a pleasant daydream. Occasionally you come back to earth: the instructor writes an important term on the chalkboard, so you dutifully copy it in your notebook. Every once in a while the instructor makes a witty remark, causing others in the class to laugh. You smile politely, pretending that you heard the remark and found it mildly humorous. You have a vague sense of guilt that you are not paying close attention, but you tell yourself that you can pick up the material from the textbook or from a friend's notes. Besides, the instructor is talking about road construction in ancient Rome and nothing could be more boring. So, back you go to your private little world.

You should never fake attention, for two main reasons: (1) you miss a lot of information, and (2) you can botch a personal or business relationship. Writer Margaret Lane relates an embarrassing instance of such fakery:

> Years ago, fresh out of college and being interviewed for a job on a small-town newspaper, I learned the hard way . . . [that] the ability to listen and respond can make all the difference in any relationship . . . . My interview had been going well, and the editor, in an expansive mood, began telling me about his winter ski trip. Eager to make a big impression with a tale of my own about backpacking in the same mountains, I tuned him out and started planning *my* story. "Well," he asked suddenly, "what do you think of that?" Not having heard a word, I babbled foolishly, "Sounds like a marvelous holiday—great fun!" For a long moment he stared at me. "Fun?" he asked in an icy tone. "How could it be fun? I've just told you I spent most of it hospitalized with a broken leg."[10]

If you fake listening, you will rarely be so painfully exposed, but this does not mean that you can get away with deception most of the time. Many speakers are sensitive to facial cues and can tell if you are merely pretending to listen. Your blank expression, your unblinking gaze, and the faraway look in your eyes are the cues that betray your inattentiveness.

Even if you are not exposed, there is another reason for not faking attention: it is easy for this behavior to become a habit. For some people, the habit is so deeply ingrained that they automatically start daydreaming the moment a speaker begins talking on a subject that seems complex or uninteresting. Such a habit cuts them off from valuable communication with others, and causes them to miss a lot of interesting and valuable information.

## Be Willing to Expend Energy

When you listen to a comedian cracking jokes on TV, do you have to work hard to pay attention? No, of course not. You simply sit back in a comfortable chair and enjoy the humor. It is easy, effortless, relaxing.

If you are like many listeners, you assume that when you go into a room for a lecture or a speech on a difficult subject, you should be able to sit back and absorb the content just as easily as you do in listening to a comedian's jokes. This is a major misconception because the two situations are actually quite different. Listening to light, entertaining material requires only a modest amount of mental effort, while listening effectively to difficult, complex material requires arduous work. You must be alert and energetic, giving total concentration to the speech, with your eyes on the speaker, your ears tuned in to the speaker's words, and your mind geared to receive the message.

The more complicated the material, the more raw energy you must put forth. Dr. M. Scott Peck tells of attending a lecture by a man who spoke on some interesting, but highly abstract theories of psychology. "Throughout the hour and a half he talked, sweat was literally dripping down my face in the air-conditioned auditorium. By the time he was finished, I had a throbbing headache, the muscles in my neck were rigid from my effort at concentration, and I felt completely drained and exhausted." Was the effort worth it? Yes, concluded Dr. Peck, because the speaker rewarded his concentration by giving him "a large number of brilliant insights."[11]

Fortunately, most speeches do not leave us in such an exhausted state, but Dr. Peck's experience illustrates the strenuous nature of active listening. As Dr. Ralph G. Nichols, who did pioneering work on listening skills at the University of Minnesota, put it, "Listening is hard work. It is characterized by faster heart action, quicker circulation of the blood, and a small rise in body temperature."[12]

If you tend to drift away mentally whenever a speaker begins to talk about unfamiliar or difficult material, try to break yourself of the habit. Vow to put as much energy as necessary into paying attention.

## *Prepare Yourself*

Since listening to difficult material is hard work, you must prepare yourself as thoroughly as a runner prepares for a race.

Prepare yourself *physically*. Get plenty of sleep the night before. If necessary, exercise right before the speech or lecture. If, for example, you will be sitting in a warm room in mid-afternoon (and therefore likely to become drowsy and lethargic), you might want to take a brisk walk before entering the room to make yourself alert and keen-minded.

Prepare yourself *intellectually*. If the subject matter of the speech is new or complex, do research or background reading beforehand. In this way, the speech will be much easier to understand. As the American philosopher Henry David Thoreau once said, "We hear and apprehend only what we already half know." The truth of this statement is shown in the way one student prepared for listening:

Margaret Edney, a student nurse, planned to attend a lecture by an expert on Alzheimer's disease, a crippling disorder affecting many elderly persons. Margaret realized that unless she did some background reading, the lecture would probably be too difficult to understand because of the unfamiliar medical terms that would be used. So she went to the library and found two recent articles on the disease. As she read the articles, she looked up definitions of some of the more important clinical terms associated with the disease—*cholinesterase, acetylchlorine, physostigmine*, etc. Later, when she went to the lecture, she was able to make sense out of the expert's remarks—thanks to her advance research.

**Before attending a lecture or speech on a difficult subject, the listener should research the topic to acquire background knowledge. This helps the listener understand and remember the key points of the speech. *(Guy Gillette/Photo Researchers)***

This technique is of course what all good students do in preparing for their classes. They read the relevant textbook pages before attending a lecture so that they can gain maximum understanding of the instructor's remarks.

## *Resist Distractions*

Concentrating on a speech is always hard work, but the task is made even more difficult by distractions of all sorts. There are auditory distractions: a fly buzzing near your ear, an air conditioner that creates a racket, people coughing or whispering. There are visual distractions: cryptic comments on the chalkboard (from a previous meeting), a nearby listener who is intriguing to look at, birds landing on a window sill. There are also physical distractions: headaches or stuffy noses, seats that are too hard, rooms that are too hot or too cold.

On top of all these distractions, we are plagued by mental distractions such as daydreams, worries, and preoccupations. We think about tomorrow or evaluate yesterday when we should be paying attention to the present moment. Mental distractions are often caused by our minds running faster than the speaker's words. In most speeches, we as listeners can process information at about 500 words per minute, while most speakers talk at 125 to 150 words a minute. This means that our brain works three or four times faster than the speed needed for listening to a speech. This creates a lot of mental spare time. Says Dr. Nichols: "What do we do with our excess thinking time while someone is speaking? If we are poor listeners, we soon become impatient with the slow progress the speaker seems to be making. So our thoughts run to something else for a moment, then dart back to the speaker. These brief side excursions of thought continue until our mind tarries too long on some enticing but irrelevant subject. Then, when our thoughts return to the person talking, we find he is far ahead of us. Now it is harder to follow him and increasingly easy to take off on side excursions. Finally we give up; the person is still talking, but our mind is in another world."[13]

How can you keep your mind from wandering? Only by using rigorous self-discipline. Shortly before a speech, prepare yourself for active listening by arriving in the room a few minutes early and getting yourself situated. Find a seat that is free from such distractions as blinding sunlight or friends who might want to whisper to you. Make yourself comfortable, lay out paper and pencil for taking notes, and clear your mind of personal matters. When the speech begins, concentrate all your mental energies on the speaker's message. There are two things you can do to aid your concentration—listen analytically and take notes. We will discuss both of these techniques in the following sections.

## Listen Analytically

You should analyze a speech as it is being presented, both to help yourself concentrate and to help you understand and remember the speaker's message. There are two elements that you should examine analytically: the main points and the support materials. Let's examine each in turn.

### Focus on Main Ideas

Some listeners make the mistake of treating all of a speaker's utterances as being equal in importance. This causes them to "miss the forest for the trees," that is, spend so much time looking at individual sentences that they fail to see the "big picture," or larger meaning.

As you listen to a speech, try to distinguish the speaker's primary ideas from the secondary material—such as facts, figures, and stories—that are used to explain or prove the primary ideas. If a speaker tells an interesting story, for example, ask yourself, "Why is the speaker telling me this? What main idea is the speaker trying to get across to me by telling this story?"

In the following passage, taken from a classroom speech by Rick Ballard, see if you can identify the main idea:

Cocaine can kill you. Without warning, it can cause a fatal reaction at any time with any kind of user. Not just heavy users; also light, so-called recreational users who snort only at weekend parties and ingest only a small amount of cocaine during any given evening. Two years ago, one of these recreational users, a 20-year-old woman in Miami, went to a disco party, drank some wine, snorted some cocaine, and then told friends she needed to lie down. A few moments later she experienced a violent seizure—caused by cocaine, not by epilepsy. The seizure was so strong that it threw her off the bed. An ambulance was called, but before it arrived, she was dead. She had used cocaine on previous occasions; for some reason her body—without warning—had suddenly developed an intolerance for the drug. Drug-abuse experts say that there is no way of predicting who will die from cocaine—it could be a regular user or a first-time user. Miami, Florida, has two cocaine deaths each month. Washington, D.C., had 88 last year. We should all remember that cocaine is a poison; cocaine used pharmaceutically in hospitals has the familiar poison warning—a skull and crossbones—on the bottles.

After hearing the above passage in a speech, some unskilled listeners might remember only that cocaine bottles in hospitals have a skull and crossbones on them, or that a young woman in Florida died after using cocaine. But these items are *not* the main idea of the passage. A careful listener would concentrate on, and try to remember, one idea above all else: Cocaine can randomly kill any user—light or heavy—without warning.

## Evaluate Support Materials

Most speakers use support materials such as stories, statistics, and quotations to explain, illustrate, or prove their main points. As a listener, you should evaluate each support as it is being presented: Is it accurate? Are objective sources used? Is enough support given? Am I getting an accurate picture of reality or a distorted one?

As an example of how to evaluate support materials, let's suppose that a speaker tries to persuade us that all states should revoke the drivers' licenses of motorists over 75 who cannot pass a comprehensive vision and safety test every year. Let's evaluate the evidence as the speaker gives it to us:

Elderly drivers are sometimes a menace on our highways. According to *USA Today*, an 84-year-old Hesperia, California, man climbed into his station wagon last January and headed down the San Bernardino Freeway—going the wrong way. Police stopped him, drove him back to his house, and started paperwork aimed at lifting his license. The next day, the man got into his station wagon again and headed down the freeway—again driving the wrong way. This time he was stopped by a head-on collision with a car filled with teen-agers. The man and a 16-year-old girl were killed.

This story is tragic, but does it prove the speaker's point—that drivers over 75 should be rigorously tested every year? No, this could be just an isolated case that proves nothing about elderly drivers in general. We need more evidence.

Though people age at different rates, most people at about age 75 experience a dramatic drop-off in their visual acuity, reflex quickness, and muscular coordination.

This is interesting but a bit vague. If such a drop-off does exist, does it really affect one's driving all that much? We still need more evidence.

According to the National Safety Council's analysis of traffic fatalities, there are 55 fatalities for every 100,000 drivers over 75. That's more than twice the rate for middle-aged motorists.

Now we have some solid evidence, from a prestigious source, that drivers over 75 are a high-risk group. But will stringent annual testing of this age group cut down on accidents?

Two states—Hawaii and Iowa—have instituted comprehensive test requirements for the very old. Both states have reported a decline in the rate of traffic accidents by drivers over 75.

This last piece of evidence is quite compelling. The speaker's plan has been tried out in two states, and apparently it works. Unless we come across information that refutes these arguments, we will have to concede that the speaker has marshaled some very convincing support for the main point.

## Take Notes

I strongly urge you to take notes whenever you listen to a speech—for the following reasons:

1. *Note taking gives you a record of the speaker's most important points.* Unless you have superhuman powers of memory, there is no way you can remember all of a speaker's key ideas unless you take notes.

2. *Note taking sharpens and strengthens your ability to listen analytically.* When you take notes, you force your mind to scan a speech like radar, looking for main points and evidence. You end up being a better listener than if you did not take any notes at all.[14]

**Taking notes during a lecture or speech is an excellent aid in listening. It helps the listener pay attention, and it provides a useful record of the speaker's main ideas.** *(Susan Lapides/Design Conceptions)*

3. *Note taking is a good way to keep your attention on the speaker and not let your mind wander.* This is why I recommend taking notes on *all* speeches—not just on important lectures at school. A colleague explains why he takes notes at every meeting he attends, even though he usually throws them away soon afterward:

> I take notes at any talk I go to, whether it's a business briefing, a professional seminar, or an inspirational speech. I usually review the notes right after the meeting to solidify the key points in my mind. Afterwards, I may save the notes for my files or for some sort of follow-up, but usually I drop them in a trash can on my way out of the room. This doesn't mean that I had wasted my time by taking notes. The act of writing them helped me to listen actively and analytically. It also—I must confess—kept me from daydreaming.

When you take notes, don't try to write down the speaker's exact words as he or she says them. Most speakers do not speak slowly enough for you to take down every word, anyway, but even if they did, you still should not try to record every word because you could easily fall into the habit of transcribing without evaluating. The message would go straight to your pad without being analyzed and understood. As much as possible, try to put the speaker's ideas into your own words, so that you can make sure that you are understanding what is being said.

There are many different ways of taking notes, and you may have already developed a method that suits you. Whatever system you use, your notes should include major points, with pertinent data or support materials that back up those points. You may also want to leave space for comments to yourself or questions that might need to be asked. One effective method for taking notes is to list your main ideas in one column, support materials in a second column, and listener responses in a third column. Here's a sample of the top of a sheet as it would look at the beginning of a speech:

**Main Ideas**          **Support Material**       **Response**

Using this method, let's examine a passage from a classroom speech by Stella Baldwin:

> Why do some men physically abuse their wives? There are many contributing factors, but the two most frequent causes are, first of all, stress in the man's life and secondly, abuse of alcohol or other drugs. Let's talk about stress for a moment: things go wrong in some area of his life. It's often his job. For example, he's involved in an ongoing dispute with his boss. He can't punch the boss (which is what he'd like to do) because he would lose his job. So what does he do? He comes home, full of rage, and takes it out on his wife. If he loses his job and can't find work, the stress is even worse. His self-esteem is badly damaged. Unemployment is probably the biggest stressor in our society today. Figures compiled by Helpmate, an agency that assists battered women, show that as unemployment goes up, so does the incidence of wife beating. After a General Motors plant was closed in Fremont, California, a few years ago, a task force appointed to study the effects of the closing on workers found a dramatic increase in the number of phone calls to the police because of violence in the home.
>
> Abuse of alcohol and other drugs often goes hand in hand with stress. Frustrated by problems in their own lives, some men turn to alcohol or some other substance for relief. The problem is that these chemicals often rip away their inhibitions, and men who would normally never strike their wives (or their children) suddenly become violent. Nancy Presson, drug abuse coordinator for San Francisco County, says that alcohol and other drugs play a part in 60 to 80 percent of wife-beating cases.

Now let's examine some notes based on the above passage:

| **Main Ideas** | **Support Material** | **Response** |
| --- | --- | --- |
| Two main reasons for wife beating: | | |
| (1) Stress in the man's life | Anger on the job— can't punch the boss | Why can't these men learn to release anger in less destructive ways? |

| Main Ideas | Support Material | Response |
|---|---|---|
| | Unemployment a major stressor | |
| (2) Alcohol/drug abuse | "Chemical" relief for stress | |
| | Takes away normal inhibitions | |
| | One county—60-80% of wife beating involved alcohol/drugs | Does our county have same situation? |

The response column is designed to help you interact with the speaker and ask questions that arise in your mind during the speech. When the question-and-answer period begins, you can scan the response column and ask questions. If a question that you jotted down gets answered later in the speech itself, no harm has been done; having raised the question will cause you to listen to the explanation with extra-special interest. The response column also enables you to plan follow-up research (for example, a response note for a classroom lecture might be a reminder to yourself: "Look up additional info in library").

If you have taken notes on a class lecture or some other complex presentation, review your notes soon afterward and expand them if necessary while the speaker's words are still fresh in your mind. If any parts of your notes are vague or confusing, seek help from another listener (or the speaker, if available).

## Avoid Prejudgments

Some people reject a speaker even before he or she stands up to speak. They dislike the speaker's looks or clothes or the organization the speaker represents. Let's say, for example, that a Catholic priest speaks on marriage; some people in the audience might say to themselves, "Why should I listen to him? What does a priest, who is celibate, know about marriage?" What is unfortunate about this reaction is that such listeners cut themselves off from gaining skills and insights. A priest might offer some excellent advice based on years of counseling couples.

Do not reject speakers because their delivery is ragged or because they seem shaky and lacking in confidence. Their ideas might be worth paying attention to. Professor Wayne Austin Shrope gives a good example of the value of concentrating on the message rather than on delivery:

When I was in college I took a history class from an instructor who was generally considered a very dull lecturer. He sat behind his desk and read his notes in a dull monotone. The other students I knew approached the lectures with the attitude that they would be bored by his dull delivery, and that they would learn nothing. This turned out to be a self-fulfilling prophecy: they *were* bored, and they *did* learn nothing. I, on the other hand, approached the lectures determined to get something from them—perhaps because I found that if I listened carefully I didn't have to read the text. At any rate, I found the lectures to be the best organized I have ever heard, and I thought the examples, details, facts, and language were fascinating. I liked the course better than any history course I ever took. I learned a great deal about history and particularly the people who made it. My classmates, who apparently listened only to the monotone and nothing else, were amazed at how well I did in the course despite little time spent studying, just by listening well in class.[15]

When you listen to a speech, try to concentrate on the message rather than on a speaker's looks, dress, or delivery. Give every speaker a fair chance.

## Don't Mentally Argue with the Speaker

Some people avoid prejudging a speaker, but as soon as he or she starts talking about a controversial topic, such as sex education or gun control, they immediately have a powerful emotional reaction that seems to cut off intelligent listening for the rest of the speech. Instead of paying attention to the speaker's words, they "argue" with the speaker inside their heads or think of ways to retaliate against the speaker in the question-and-answer period. They often jump to conclusions, convincing themselves that the speaker is saying something that he or she really is not. Here is an example:

John Rafferty, a veteran and a businessman, gave a speech to a group on why he was opposed to the military draft. His main argument was that conscription weakens our armed forces because it brings in some people who are unmotivated and unsuited for military service. "The best military forces," he argued, "are those made up of volunteers who have high morale and a strong commitment to their training. I am against the draft because it would place unmotivated people into the ranks; it would weaken the morale of our armed forces. I want a strong military, and a volunteer system is the best way to achieve this goal." In the question-and-answer period at the end of the speech, some members of the audience accused Rafferty of wanting to weaken the armed forces and of being anti-military. These people had failed to listen to what Rafferty said; if they had listened, they would have known that he was opposed to the draft not because he was anti-military, but because he was pro-military. "Most of the audience heard me correctly," Rafferty reminisced, "but those people who didn't understand— they just floored me. I felt like saying, 'Are you deaf or retarded, or what?' "

When you are listening to speakers who seem to be arguing against some of your ideas or beliefs, make sure you understand exactly what they are saying. Hear them out, and *then* prepare your counterarguments.

# The Listener's Responsibilities

As we discussed in Chapter 1, the speaker who is honest and fair has ethical and moral obligations to his or her listeners.

The converse is also true: the honest and fair listener has ethical and moral obligations to the speaker. Let's examine three of the listener's primary responsibilities.

## *Avoid Rudeness*

If you were engaged in conversation with a friend, how would you feel if your friend yawned and went to sleep? Or started reading a book? Or looked at the floor the entire time? You would be upset by your friend's rudeness, wouldn't you?

There are many people who would never dream of being so rude to a friend in conversation, yet when they sit in an audience, they are terribly rude to the speaker. They fall asleep or read a newspaper or study for a test or carry on a whispered conversation with their friends. Fortunately, a public speaking class cures some people of their rudeness. As one student put it:

> I had been sitting in classrooms for 12 years and until now, I never realized how much a speaker sees. I always thought a listener is hidden and anonymous out there in a sea of faces. Now that I've been a speaker, I realize that when you look out at an audience, you are well aware of the least little thing somebody does. I am ashamed now at how I used to carry on conversations in the back of class. I was very rude, and I didn't even know it.

If you are seated in the audience and you turn to whisper to a friend, your movement is as noticeable as a red flag waving in front of the speaker's eyes. If you do more than whisper—if you snicker or grin—you can damage the morale and confidence of inexperienced speakers, for they may think that you are laughing at them.

A speech is *enlarged* conversation, and you should show the speaker the same politeness you would show your best friend during a chat.

## *Provide Encouragement*

As a listener, you should strive to provide the speaker with as much encouragement as possible. You can do this by giving your full attention, taking notes, leaning slightly forward instead of slouching back in your seat, looking directly at the speaker instead of at the floor, and letting your face show interest and animation. If the speaker says something you particularly like, nod in agreement or smile approvingly. (If the speaker says something that offends you or puzzles you, obviously you should not give positive feedback; I am not recommending hypocrisy.)

The more encouragement a speaker receives, the better he or she is able to speak. Most entertainers and professional speakers say that if an audience is lively and enthusiastic, they do a much better job than if the audience is sullen or apathetic. From my own experience, I feel that I always do better in giving a speech if I get encouragement. Maybe it is just a few people who are displaying lively interest, but their nods and smiles and eager eyes inspire me and energize me.

As listeners, we have a personal stake in the speaker's success. The better the speaker is, the easier it is for us to listen. So, if for no other reason but self-interest, we should try to give encouragement to help the speaker do a good job.

Another reason for giving encouragement is summed up in the Golden Rule of listening: "Listen unto others as you would have others listen unto you." When you are a speaker, you want an audience that listens attentively, courteously, and enthusiastically. So when you are a listener, you should provide the same response.

Listeners exert a tremendous power over the speaker. At one college, some psychology majors conducted an "experiment" to prove that professors can be as easily manipulated as laboratory rats by means of positive reinforcement. In one political science class, if the professor walked to the left side of the classroom during his lecture, the students would give him approving looks, nod their heads in agreement, and enthusiastically scribble notes in their notebooks. But when he stayed in the middle or walked to the right side of the class, they would lay down their pencils and look away from the professor with glum expressions on their faces. Before long the professor spent the entire hour standing on the left side of the room. Carrying their experiment a step further, the students "rewarded" the professor with encouraging looks and nods only if he stood on the left side next to the window and absent-mindedly played with the lift cord of the venetian blinds. Soon the professor was spending all his lecture time holding the lift cord, blithely unaware that he was the "guinea pig" in a behavior-modification experiment.

I tell this story not to suggest that you manipulate a speaker, but to show the power that you as a listener exert. Use that power wisely. Use it to encourage and uplift the speaker.

## Find Value in Every Speech

There will be times when you are forced to hear a speech you feel is boring and worthless. Instead of tuning the speaker out and retreating into your private world of daydreams, try to exploit the speech for something worthwhile. Make a game of it: see how many diamonds can be extracted from the mud. Is there any new information that might be useful to you in the future? Is the speaker using techniques of delivery that are worth noting and emulating?

What if a speech is complicated and over your head? Listen anyway, and try to broaden your knowledge. Dr. Steil gives some good advice on this point:

> The listener who responds to complex material by "tuning out" can be missing a great opportunity to learn, to discover, to broaden himself. We have all had the experience of mastering a body of information, and then— when the material has become entirely familiar—using it as a foundation for understanding additional, even more complex information. It is a heady feeling—one of the joys of learning. And it can only be felt if we as listeners greet the arrival of complex information with anticipation. Not with anxiety.[16]

If a speech is so bad that you honestly cannot find anything worthwhile in it, you can always look for a how-not-to-do-it lesson. Ask yourself, "What can I learn from this speaker's mistakes?" Here is an example of how one business executive profited from a poor speaker:

> At a convention recently I found myself in an extremely boring seminar (on listening, ironically enough). After spending the first half-hour wishing I had never signed up, I decided to take advantage of the situation. I turned my thought, "This guy isn't teaching me how to run a seminar on listening," into a question: "What is he teaching me about how *not* to run a seminar?" While providing a negative example was not the presenter's goal, I got a useful lesson.[17]

"Turn your lemons into lemonade," some wise person once advised. If you look for value or a how-not-to-do-it lesson in every poor speech, you will find that the sourest oratorical lemon can be turned into lemonade. "Know how to listen," the Greek writer Plutarch said 20 centuries ago, "and you will profit even from those who talk badly."

## Summary

Listening effectively is often a difficult task, but it can be rewarding for the person who is willing to make the effort. The guidelines for effective listening include the following: (1) Avoid fakery. Do not pretend to be listening when in fact your mind is wandering; this kind of behavior can settle into a hard-to-break habit. (2) Be willing to put forth energy. Listening is hard work, especially if the material is new or difficult, so you must have a strong desire to listen actively and intelligently. (3) Prepare yourself for the act of listening. Do whatever background reading or research that is necessary for gaining maximum understanding of the speech. (4) Resist distractions, both external and internal. Use rigorous self-discipline to keep your mind concentrated on the speaker's remarks. (5) Listen analytically, focusing on main ideas and evaluating support materials. (6) Take notes, not only for a record of key points but as a way of keeping your mind from wandering. (7) Avoid prejudgments. Do not dismiss a speaker even before he or she starts the speech. (8) Do not mentally argue with a speaker, or you may think that the speaker is saying something that he or she really is not.

As a listener you have three important obligations to a speaker: to avoid all forms of rudeness, provide encouragement, and find value in every speech. The more support you give a speaker, the better the speech will be, and the more you will profit from it.

## Review Questions

1. What is the difference between *hearing* and *listening*?
2. Why is listening to complex material in a speech more difficult than reading the same material in a book?
3. List several ways in which you can prepare yourself both physically and intellectually to listen to a speech.
4. List five possible distractions that can keep a listener from concentrating on a speech.
5. What are the advantages of taking notes during a speech?
6. When you are a listener, how can you encourage a speaker?

# TIPS *for your career*

### Tip 2: Take Notes in Important Conversations and Small-Group Meetings

In any job that you may hold, take notes while your superiors and colleagues talk to you (either one-on-one or in a group meeting) about work-related matters. This not only enhances your listening ability, as we discussed earlier, but it also gains favorable attention for yourself. By taking notes, you show that you are a good listener who values the advice and opinions of the speaker. It is a nonverbal way of saying, "Your ideas are important to me—so important that I want to make sure I get them down correctly." Contrary to what some may think, taking notes does *not* signify to others that you have a poor memory.

One of the most common gripes of employees is that "the boss never listens to what we say." So, if you are ever in a supervisory position, take notes whenever one of your subordinates comes to you with a suggestion or a complaint. It shows that you are taking the employee's comments seriously and that you are preparing yourself to take action if necessary. Even if you are unable to take action, the employee's morale is boosted because you have shown you truly listen and truly care.

# Chapter 3

# Controlling Nervousness

ollywood actor George C. Scott, famous for his fierce, bulldog demeanor, has played such gruff characters as General Patton, the dictator Mussolini, and Charles Dickens's Scrooge. He is also known as a blunt, irascible person in real life. When actress Maureen Stapleton once complained to her director, Mike Nichols, that she was afraid of her co-star Scott, Nichols replied: "Don't worry. The whole world's afraid of George Scott."[1]

Yet, for all his intimidating ferocity, Scott confessed to a magazine reporter that "it's terrible when I have to make a speech. I really suffer. I'm a nervous wreck. When I get up, I shake all over like a dog shaking the water off." When Scott was asked why he was able to speak so effectively in films, he replied that while acting, he could "hide behind" whatever character he was playing, but in giving a speech "there's nothing to hide behind."[2]

George C. Scott is not the only person terrified of speaking in public. Various surveys in recent years have asked Americans to list their greatest fears; the fear of speaking to a group of strangers is cited more often than any other—surpassing fear of snakes, insects, lightning, deep water, heights, or flying in airplanes.[3]

# Reasons for Nervousness

Is it foolish to be afraid to give a speech? Is this fear as groundless as a child's fear of the boogieman? I used to think so, back in the days when I first began making speeches. Like Scott, I was a nervous wreck, and I would often chide myself by saying, "Come on, relax, it's just a little speech. There's no good reason to be scared." But I was wrong. There *is* good reason to be scared; in fact, there are *four* good reasons:

1. *Fear of being stared at.* In the animal world, a stare is a hostile act. Dogs, baboons, and other animals sometimes defend their territory by staring. Their hostile gaze alone is enough to turn away an intruder. We human beings have similar reactions; it is part of our biological makeup to be upset by stares. Imagine that you are riding in a crowded elevator with a group of strangers. Suddenly you realize that the other people are staring directly at you. Not just glancing. *Staring.* You probably would be unnerved and frightened because a stare can be as threatening as a clenched fist—especially if it comes from people you do not know. That is why public speaking can be so frightening. You have a pack of total strangers "attacking" you with unrelenting stares, while you are obliged to stand alone, exposed and vulnerable—a goldfish in a bowl, subject to constant scrutiny. As George C. Scott suggested, there's nothing to hide behind.

2. *Fear of failure.* Most speakers worry about botching their speech:

What if I make a fool of myself? What if my mind goes blank and I forget everything I was planning to say? What if I stumble or stammer? Any normal person, especially if he or she is an inexperienced speaker, is apt to have this fear. Indeed, a person who never has self-doubts is probably foolish and vain.

3. *Fear of rejection.* What if we do our best, what if we deliver a polished speech, but the audience still does not like us? It would be quite a blow to our ego because we want to be liked and yes, even loved. We want people to admire us, to consider us wise and intelligent, and to accept our ideas and opinions. We do not want people to dislike us, reject us, or worst of all, consider us a fool.

The most terrifying speaking situation of my life occurred in high school when I decided to telephone a girl to invite her to a dance. I was attending an all-boys' school, I was shy around girls, and it was my first date. Before I called her, I was afraid that I would fail to think of clever things to say, so I made note cards with sentences written out in full—things like "What is your favorite subject in school?" and "What kind of music do you like?" Even with these cue cards, I was choked with fear when I finally gathered enough courage to call her; my heart was thumping so furiously that it leaped up into my throat, and I could barely get my words out. She did say yes, but when I hung up the phone, I realized that I was now faced with a fresh terror: I would have to talk to her on our date, and I would have no cue cards to guide me through. What made this event so excruciating, of course, was my fear of rejection.

4. *Fear of the unknown.* Throughout our lives we are apprehensive about doing new things, such as going to school for the first time, riding a bus without our parents, or going out on our first date. We cannot put a finger on exactly what we are afraid of because our fear is vague and diffused. What we really fear is the unknown; we worry that some unpredictable disaster might occur. When we stand up to give a speech, we are sometimes assailed by this same fear of the unknown because we cannot predict the outcome of our speech. Fortunately, this fear usually disappears as we become experienced in giving speeches—we have enough confidence to know that nothing terrible will befall us, just as our childhood fear of riding in a bus by ourselves vanished after two or three trips.

All four of these fears are as real and as understandable as the fear of lightning. There is no reason why you should be ashamed of having them.

## The Value of Fear

Because the fears engendered by public speaking are real and understandable, does this mean that it is impossible to get rid of nervousness (which is also called butterflies, the jitters, or the shakes)? If you are like many of the students who come into my public speaking class, this is your primary concern: to completely eliminate all traces of nervousness. My response may surprise you as much as it surprises my students: *You should not try to banish all your fear and nervousness. You need a certain amount of fear to give a good speech.*

You *need* fear? Yes, fear energizes you; it makes you think more rapidly; it helps you speak with vitality and enthusiasm. Here is why: When you stand up to give a speech and fear hits you, your body goes on "red alert," the same biological mechanism that saved our cave-dwelling ancestors when they were faced with a hungry lion or a human foe and had to fight or flee in order to survive. Though not as crucial to us as it was to our ancestors, this system is still nice to have for emergencies: if you were walking down a deserted street one night and a crazed person tried to attack you, your body would release a burst of adrenalin into your bloodstream, causing fresh blood and oxygen to rush to your muscles, and you would be able to fight ferociously or run faster than you have ever run in your life. The benefit of adrenalin can be seen in competitive sports: athletes *must* get their adrenalin flowing before a game begins. There is one high school football coach who looks at his players' hands before the kickoff. Any player without sweaty palms is benched; he is obviously not fired up enough to play well. The great home-run slugger Reggie Jackson said during his heyday, "I have butterflies in my stomach almost every time I step up to the plate. When I don't have them, I get worried because it means I won't hit the ball very well."[4]

Public speakers often have the same attitude. Don Beveridge, a professional speaker, says, "I've been speaking professionally for 15 years. I have given speeches to [audiences consisting of] 4,000 Burger King franchisees, 3,000 AT&T managers, and 5,000 Century 21 salespeople. I've taught classes of 15 people at the University of Wisconsin and communicated one-on-one. No matter what the speaking situation, my hands sweat before each and every presentation, and frankly that's what makes me a good speaker . . . . The day my palms stop sweating, I'll quit!"[5]

In public speaking, adrenalin infuses you with energy; it causes extra blood and oxygen to rush not only to your muscles but to your brain as well, thus enabling you to think with greater clarity and quickness. It makes you come across to your audience as someone who is "alive" and vibrant. Elayne Snyder, a speech teacher, uses the term "positive nervousness," which she describes in this way: "It's a zesty, enthusiastic, lively feeling with a slight edge to it. Positive nervousness is the state you'll achieve by converting your anxiety into constructive energy . . . . It's still nervousness, but you're no longer victimized by it; instead you're vitalized by it."[6]

If you want proof that nervousness is beneficial, observe speakers who

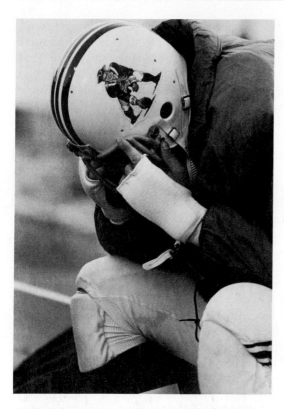

**Before entering a game, football players are often gripped by nervous tension, but when they are sent in, they concentrate on making their plays and their tension recedes into the background. Likewise, public speakers may be filled with anxiety before a speech, but if they concentrate their energies on communicating with the audience, they find that their anxiety moves to a back burner, where it provides ongoing energy. (Peter Southwick/Stock, Boston)**

have absolutely no butterflies at all. Because they are 100 percent relaxed and cool, they give speeches that are dull and flat, with no energy, no zest. Most good speakers report that if they do not have butterflies before a public appearance, their delivery is poor. One speaker, the novelist I. A. R. Wylie, said, "I rarely rise to my feet without a throat constricted with terror and a furiously thumping heart. When, for some reason, I *am* cool and self-assured, the speech is always a failure. I need fear to spur me on."[7] There is an old saying popular with some speechmakers: "Speakers who say they are as cool as a cucumber usually give speeches about as interesting as a cucumber." In sports, we all know of champion teams that got smashed by puny underdogs. Why? Because the champs were too relaxed and confident, while the underdogs were supercharged with strong emotions. This is why coaches get apprehensive if their teams have a perfect season going into their final game. The players may lose that vital nervous energy they need to win.

There is another danger in being totally devoid of nervousness. Some years ago, before I learned the value of controlled nervousness, I tried to talk myself into being completely relaxed for a speech. I told myself, "There's nothing to be afraid of. Be calm, play it cool." On one particular occasion it worked—for a while. I was an after-dinner speaker at a banquet. For once, I was able to eat food before a speech without having it taste like cardboard. I congratulated myself on being completely relaxed as I sat at the head table and listened to the master of ceremonies introduce me. There was not a single butterfly in my stomach. I got up confidently, strode to the lectern, looked out at my audience, and then— WHAM!—I was suddenly struck by a lightning bolt of panic. I got a huge lump in my throat, my heart pounded, and I had so much trouble breathing that every word had to be wrestled from my suffocating larynx and forced out of my mouth. My face turned red and I started sweating heavily. It was a nightmare. Somehow I got through the speech and sat down, humiliated and angry at myself. But I learned a lesson I would never forget: to avoid last-minute panic, I must be "psyched up." Nowadays I never go into a speech without encouraging my butterflies to flutter around inside, so that I can be poised and alert. Other speakers have come to the same conclusion: if they aren't "pumped up" for a speech, they either suffer the kind of panic that hit me, or else they give boring speeches that have no fizz and sparkle.

# Guidelines for Controlling Nervousness

We have just discussed how a complete lack of nervousness is undesirable. What about the other extreme? Is *too much* nervousness bad for you? Of course it is, especially if you are so frightened that you forget what you were planning to say, or if your breathing is so labored that you cannot get your words out. What you want to do is keep your nervousness under control, so that you have just the right amount—enough to energize you, but not enough to cripple you. How can you do this? Here are some ideas that have helped my students.

## *In the Days and Weeks Before Your Speech*

### Choose a Topic You Like and Know a Great Deal About

Nothing will get you more rattled than speaking on a subject about which you know little. If you are asked to talk on a topic you are not comfortable with, decline the invitation (unless, of course, it is an assignment from a boss who gives you no choice in the matter). Speaking on a topic you know a lot about will give you enormous self-confidence; if something terrible happens (for example, you lose your notes on the way to the meeting), you can always improvise because your head is filled with information about the subject. Also, you will be able to handle yourself well in the question-and-answer period after the speech.

## Prepare Yourself Thoroughly

Here is a piece of advice that is given by many experienced speakers: *The very best precaution against excessive stage fright is thorough, careful preparation.*[8] You have heard the expression, "I came unglued." In public speaking, the best "glue" to hold you together is good, solid preparation. Professional speaker Joel Weldon (who quips that he used to be so frightened of audiences that he was "unable to lead a church group in silent prayer") gives his personal formula for controlling fear: "I prepare and then prepare, and then when I think I'm ready, I prepare some more."[9] Weldon recommends five to eight hours of preparation for each hour in front of an audience.[10] That ratio is not unusual. Most good speakers will tell you that 75 to 90 percent of their total effort goes into getting ready for the actual delivery.

Preparation means gathering ideas and information, organizing them into a coherent outline, writing note cards, and then practicing delivery of the speech. If you put time and energy into your preparation, you will become the master of your material and will know it thoroughly. This will give you enormous self-confidence.

Be sure to leave plenty of time for practicing your delivery. Do not just look over your notes—actually stand up and deliver your talk in whatever way suits you: in front of a mirror, into a tape recorder, before a family member or friend. Do not rehearse just once; run through your entire speech at least four times. If you "give" your speech four times at home, you will find that your fifth delivery—before a live audience—will be smoother and more self-assured than if you had not practiced at all.

## Do Not Read or Memorize Your Speech

Never write out a speech in its entirety and then read it. This is the perfect way to put an audience to sleep.

If you memorize a speech, you are courting disaster. As a young man, Winston Churchill, considered one of the greatest orators of modern times, used to write out and memorize his speeches. Then one day, while giving a memorized talk to Parliament, he suddenly stopped. His mind went blank. He began his last sentence all over. Again his mind went blank. He sat down in embarrassment and shame. Never again did Churchill try to memorize a speech. This same thing has happened to many others who tried to commit a speech to memory. Everything goes smoothly until they get derailed, and then they are hopelessly off the track.

Even if you do not get derailed, there is another reason for not memorizing: you will probably sound mechanical, like a robot with a tape recorder in its mouth. In addition to considering you dull and boring, your audience will sense that you are speaking from your memory and not from your heart, and they will question your sincerity.

### Imagine Yourself Giving a Good, Strong Speech

Let yourself daydream a bit: picture yourself going up to the lectern, nervous but in control of yourself, then giving a forceful talk to an appreciative audience. Does this sound silly? It is a technique that has worked for many speakers and it might work for you. Whatever you do, do not let yourself imagine the opposite—a bad speech or poor delivery. Negative daydreams will add unnecessary fear to your life in the days before your speech, and sap you of creative energy—energy that you need for preparing and practicing. Actress Ali McGraw says, "We have only so much energy, and the more we direct toward the project itself, the less is left to pour into wondering 'Will I fail?' "[11]

Notice that the daydream I am suggesting includes nervousness. You need to have a realistic image in your mind: picture yourself as nervous, but nevertheless in command of the situation and capable of delivering a strong, effective speech.

In addition to picturing yourself as confident and in control, you need to imagine yourself reaching out to your audience. Try to focus as much *positive* mental energy as possible on the people who will be listening to your message. One professional speaker, James "Doc" Blakely, has an effective, audience-centered technique that he uses before each speech: "I learn everything I can about the organization I'm going to address as far in advance of the speaking date as possible. Then at least four hours prior to the actual speaking engagement, I review all the facts I know about the group, go over the points I want to make with them, and then concentrate on pouring positive thoughts into my mind about the group. I visualize them as accepting me as a friend, of being wildly enthusiastic about what I have to say to them, and I block out every negative emotion in my mind . . . . Concentrating totally on the needs and concerns of your listeners is great therapy for a speaker . . . ."[12]

Some speakers have trouble imagining success because deep down they do not really believe that they are capable of success. These speakers are often shy individuals who think that their shyness blocks them from becoming good speakers. Actor and speechmaker Steve Allen says it is a mistake for shy people to disqualify themselves from public speaking. "I tend toward shyness, particularly in the presence of strangers in small social gatherings," he says, noting that other Hollywood figures such as Johnny Carson and Dick Cavett are also shy and introverted, yet are excellent speakers.[13] "Like stutterers who have no trouble singing, we shy introverts often blossom when placed on stage, in front of a camera, or next to a microphone," he says. "So whether you personally are a life-of-the-party type or are inclined to sit and listen to others means little so far as . . . public speaking is concerned."[14] (To Allen's list of shy introverts in show business can be added Carol Burnett, Barbara Walters, and Michael Jackson.[15])

The truth of Allen's remark is demonstrated by Joe W. Boyd of Bellingham, Washington. "I used to stammer," says Boyd, "and I used to be petrified at the thought of speaking before a group of any size." Despite his shyness, Boyd joined a Toastmasters club to develop his speaking skills. Two years later, in 1984, he won the Toastmasters International Public Speaking Contest by giving a superb speech to an audience of over 2,000 listeners.[16]

### Keep in Mind That It Is Not Abnormal to Have Stage Fright

When you get the jitters, it should console you to know that you are not reacting in an abnormal way. Most great public speakers have suffered from stage fright before or during their speeches. When Churchill was prime minister of Great Britain, he said that every time he had to give a speech, he had a block of ice, nine inches by nine inches, in the pit of his stomach. Philosopher Bertrand Russell said he was so afraid of giving speeches that every time he had to leave home to deliver a speech, he hoped that he would break a leg so that he would not have to give his talk. General U. S. Grant played a major part in the Union victory over the Confederates in the Civil War, but he said giving a speech was more terrifying to him than leading troops into battle.

## *During Your Speech*

Here are some important things to keep in mind as you deliver a speech.

### Deal Rationally with Your Body's Turmoil

If you are a typical beginning speaker, you will suffer from some or all of the following symptoms when you begin your talk:

☐ Pounding heart
☐ Trembling hands
☐ Shaky knees
☐ Dry, constricted throat
☐ Difficulty in breathing

☐ Quivering voice
☐ Flushed face

You usually suffer the greatest discomfort during the first few minutes of your speech, but then things get better. If, however, your symptoms get worse as you go along, it might be because your mind has taken the wrong path (see Figure 3.1).

If you take Route A, you are trapped in a vicious cycle. Your mind tells your body that disaster is upon you, and your body responds by getting worse. This, in turn, increases your brain's perception of disaster. If you take Route B, however, your mind will help your body stay in control. You can remind yourself that your symptoms, rather than being a prelude to disaster, are evidence that you are keyed up enough to give a good speech.

### Concentrate on Getting Your Ideas Across to Your Audience

Let's go back a moment to our example of football players. Before the kickoff, they are nervous, tense, and filled with butterflies. But what happens when the game actually starts? Though nervousness is still present, it recedes into the background as the players concentrate on catching the ball or making a tackle. Jerry West, the former star of the Los Angeles Lakers professional basketball team, used to be so nervous before a game, according to *Time* magazine, that "in the dressing room his hands are wet with sweat, and waiting on the bench, he has even retched into a towel." But when the game begins, he "sets his long face in a stony mask and begins to release his tremendous store of nervous energy." West was such a good player under stress that he became known as "Mr. Clutch."[17]

Public speaking is similar: you are experiencing terrible anxiety at the beginning, but once you get into your speech, if you focus all your attention on communicating your ideas to your listeners, your nervousness will recede into the background (it does not go away, of course; it simply simmers on the back burner, where it can remain an ongoing source of energy).

Actress Ali McGraw says that before every performance, "I nearly pass out from anxiety. My heart pounds deafeningly, and I sometimes break out in a cold sweat." Yet, she says, "once I actually begin *doing* what I have to do, my fright subsides."[18]

When you concentrate on getting your message across to your listeners, instead of dwelling on your nervousness, you do more than quell your butterflies; you also give a better speech, as Hugh Downs, television commentator for ABC News, discovered in dealing with his own nervousness problem. "Somehow when you give full attention to subject matter and audience," he said, "you wind up looking and sounding better than when you're focused on yourself."[19]

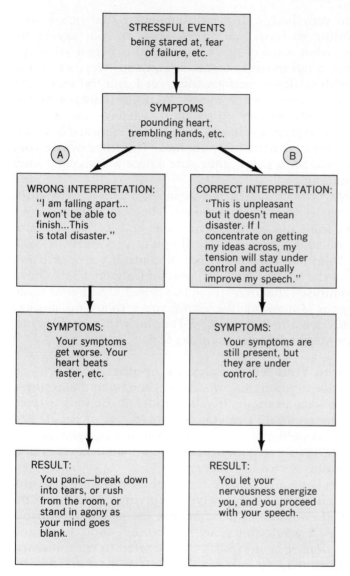

**FIGURE 3.1**
The alternative paths that a speaker might take.

## Remember: Most of Your Bodily Reactions Are Not Seen by Your Audience

Some speakers get rattled because they think the audience is keenly aware of their thumping heart and quaking hands. You, of course, are painfully aware of these symptoms, but believe it or not, your audience is usually oblivious to your body's distress. Remember that people are sitting out there wanting to hear your ideas. They are not saying to themselves, "Let's see, what signs of nervousness is this person displaying?" I have had students tell me after a speech that they were ashamed or embarrassed about their jittery performance, yet I and the other listeners in the class saw no signs of nervousness. We were listening to the ideas and failed to notice the speaker's discomfort. Various studies have found the same thing to be true: audiences simply are unaware of signs that the speakers think are embarrassingly obvious.[20] In other words, you are probably the only one who knows that your knees are shaking and that your heart is pounding.

Speaking of his own problems with nervousness, TV talk show host Dick Cavett says, "It varies from night to night. The best thing to do is tell yourself it doesn't show one-eighth as much as you feel. If you're a little nervous, you don't look nervous at all. If you're very nervous, you look slightly nervous. And if you're totally out of control, you look troubled. It scales down on the screen. Anybody who appears on a talk show should always remind himself that everything he's doing *looks* better than it *feels*. . . . Your nervous system may be giving you a thousand shocks, but the viewer can only see a few of them."[21] The same thing holds true for the public speaker: you look better than you feel.

### Never Call Attention to Your Nervousness or Apologize for It

Despite what I said above, there may be times when an audience does notice your nervousness—for example, if your hands are shaking as you hold your note cards. But so what? Everyone knows that most people get nervous when they talk in public, so why mention it or apologize for it? Whether or not your nervousness is noticeable, you should never make comments about it because of two big dangers.

First of all, you might get yourself more rattled than you were to begin with. I remember listening to a teacher who was giving a talk to a PTA meeting one night. In the middle of her remarks she suddenly blurted out, "Oh my god, I knew I would fall apart." Up to that time, I had not been aware of any discomfort or nervousness. She tried to continue her talk, but she was too flustered. She gave up the effort and sat down with a red face. I do not know what kind of internal distress she was suffering, of course, but I am certain that if she had said nothing about her nervousness, she could have dragged herself through the speech. When she sat down, I felt irritated and disappointed because I had been keenly interested in her remarks. How selfish of her, I thought, to deprive me of the second half of her speech simply because she was nervous. I know that my reaction sounds insensitive, but I wanted to share it with you so that I can underscore an important point: your listeners do not care about your emotional distress; they only want to hear your ideas.

The second risk you run if you mention your symptoms is this: Your audience might have been unaware of your nervousness before you brought it up, but now you have distracted them from your speech and they are watching the very thing you do not want them to scrutinize: your body's behavior. If you say, for example, "I'm sorry about my voice being so rough, but my throat is very dry," what do you think the audience will play close attention to—at least for the next few minutes? Your voice, of course, instead of your speech. Keep your audience's attention focused on your ideas, and they probably will not notice your emotional and physical distress.

## Do Not Let Your Audience Upset You

Some inexperienced speakers get rattled when they look out at the audience and observe that most listeners are poker-faced and unsmiling. Does this mean they are displeased with your speech? No, their solemn faces have nothing to do with your performance. This is just one of those peculiarities of human nature: in a conversation, people will smile and nod and encourage you, but when listening to a speech in an audience, the same people will wear (most of the time) a blank mask. The way to handle those stony faces is to remind yourself that your listeners want you to succeed; they hope that you will give them a worthwhile message. If you are lucky, you will notice two or three listeners who are obviously loving your speech; they are nodding in agreement or giving you looks of appreciation. Let your eyes go to them frequently, for they will give you courage and confidence.

If you are an inexperienced speaker, you may get upset if you see members of an audience whispering to each other. You may wonder, "Are these people making negative comments about me?" If the listeners are smiling, it's even worse: You ask yourself, "Did I say something foolish? Is there something wrong with my clothes?" If this happens to you, try to keep in mind that your rude listeners are probably talking about something other than the quality of your speech or your personal appearance. Most likely, they are just sharing some personal gossip. If by chance they *are* whispering about something you've said, it's not necessarily negative. The following story, told to me by an experienced speaker, illustrates this point.

> I was speaking to a group in El Paso, Texas, on why I, as a Vietnam veteran, was opposed to the [then-raging] war in Vietnam. It was a highly emotional issue, and I knew that many people in El Paso were staunch supporters of the war. So, even before I started my speech, I was apprehensive and defensive because I feared that my ideas would provoke anger and disagreement among some of my listeners. I began my talk and had said no more than three sentences when I saw a man in the back row turn to his companion

**Inexperienced speakers sometimes get upset when they look out at their audience and see solemn or stony faces. It is important to know that such facial expressions do not necessarily signify disapproval. The listeners are simply reflecting a peculiarity of human behavior: in conversation, people smile and nod at the person speaking, but when they are part of an audience for a speech, their faces often remain unanimated. (Susan Lapides/Design Conceptions)**

and grin and whisper something. I was sure that he was making some snide, derisive comment about me. I got very annoyed and I had trouble maintaining my composure. At the end of the speech, however, the man came up to me and said, "I was glad to hear you say you were from Chattanooga, Tennessee. I am, too." It turned out that we had grown up in the same part of town and had friends in common. His grin and his whispers during the speech had not been negative feedback, after all, but rather a positive reaction to the discovery that I was a fellow Chattanoogan.

If you ever see whisperers in your audience, your best approach is to assume that they are friendly rather than negative or hostile. After all, they may be whispering that they agree with you 100 percent.

## Do Not Expect or Demand Perfection of Yourself

You put enormous—and unnecessary—pressure on yourself if you think you *must* give a perfect, polished speech. When you try to be perfect, you concentrate your energies on yourself instead of on what should be your real target—your listeners. Remember that they do not care whether your delivery is perfect; they simply hope that your words will enlighten or entertain them. Think of yourself as merely a telegram messenger; the telegram is what the audience is interested in, not how well you handed it over.

## Additional Hints

Here are some extra tips that might be useful.

### Use Visual Aids

Many speakers find that they can keep their nervousness under control if they use such visual aids as slides or charts or a chalkboard. Visual aids can help you in two ways: (1) you shift the audience's stares from you to your illustrations, and (2) you walk about and move your hands and arms, thereby syphoning off some of your excess nervous energy.

Whatever illustrations you decide to use, make sure they are understandable and appropriate. There is nothing better than a visual aid that is right on target ("One picture is worth more than ten thousand words"), but there is nothing worse than a visual aid that does not make sense or is completely inappropriate.

### Check Arrangements in Advance

Long before you give your speech, inspect the place where the speech is to be delivered and anticipate any problems. For example: Is there an extension cord for the slide projector? Do the windows have curtains so that the room can be darkened for your slide presentation? Is there a chalkboard? Some talks have been ruined and some speakers turned into nervous wrecks because at the last moment they discover that the entire building lacks an extension cord.

Arrive early on the day of your speech and reinspect every aspect of the arrangements. Has the extension cord been laid out for you? Is there chalk in the chalkboard tray? Is there an eraser for the chalkboard? If you are using equipment for visual aids, set it up to make sure it is working. If there is a public-address system, test your voice on it before the audience arrives so that you can feel at ease with it.

### Devote Extra Practice Time to Your Introduction

The beginning of your speech is the time when you are apt to suffer the greatest amount of distress, so you should spend a lot of time practicing your introduction.

Most speakers, actors, and musicians report that if they can survive the first minute or two, their nervousness moves to the background and the rest of the speech is relatively easy. Madame Schumann-Heink, the famous singer, said, "I grow so nervous before a performance, I become sick. I want to go home. But after I have been on the stage for a few minutes, I am so happy that nobody can drag me off." Perhaps happiness is too strong a word for what you will feel, but if you are a typical speaker, you will find the rest of your speech smooth sailing once you have weathered the first few minutes of turbulent waters. So practice your introduction until you can stand up and give it with confidence.

### Get Acclimated to Your Audience and Setting

It can be frightening to arrive at the meeting place at the last moment and confront a sea of strange faces waiting to hear your talk. It is a good idea to arrive early so you can get acclimated to the setting and, if possible, chat with people as they come into the room. In this way, you will see them not as a hostile pack of strangers, but as ordinary people who wish you well.

Dr. Henry Heimlich, a popular lecturer and creator of the famed Heimlich Maneuver for rescuing people who are choking, says, "I am always a little nervous wondering how a particular audience will accept me and my thoughts. It is good to meet some of the audience socially before lecturing to them, in order to relate to their cultural and intellectual backgrounds. You are then their 'friend.' "[22]

Another professional speaker, Danielle Kennedy, says that when she began speaking 10 years ago, she was so nervous she would hide out in a bathroom until it was time for her to speak. Now, she says, she mingles with the listeners as they arrive and engages them in conversation. "This reminds me that they are just nice people like anyone else who wants to be informed. I also give myself pleasant thoughts. Things like: 'Can you imagine these people drove 100 miles just to hear me. I am so lucky. These people are wonderful.' I get real warm thoughts going by the time I get up there."[23]

### Breathe Deeply or Do Exercises to Release Tension

To drain off excessive tension, try taking a couple of deep breaths right before a speech. Inhale slowly and exhale slowly. Or try doing some exercises that can be performed quietly, without calling attention to yourself, while you are waiting to speak. Here are some examples: (1) Tighten and then relax your leg muscles. (2) Push your arm or hand muscles against a hard object (such as a desk top or chair) for a few moments, then release the pressure. (3) Squeeze your hands together in the same way: tension, release . . . tension, release . . . .

### Act Poised

To develop courage when you face an audience, you should act as if you already are courageous. Why? Because playing the role of the confident speaker can often transform you into a speaker who is genuinely confident and poised. In various wars, soldiers have reported that they were terrified before going into combat, but nevertheless they acted brave in front of their buddies. During the battle, to their surprise, what started off as a pretense became a reality. Instead of pretending to be courageous, they actually became so. The same thing often happens to public speakers.

## Pause a Few Moments Before Starting Your Speech

You will notice that all good speakers pause a few moments before they begin their talk. This silence is good because (1) it is dramatic, building up the audience's interest and curiosity, (2) it makes you look poised and in control, (3) it calms you, and (4) it gives you a chance to spread out your note cards and get your first two or three sentences firmly in mind.

Many tense, inexperienced speakers rush up to the lectern and start their speech at once, thus getting off to a frenzied, flustered start. In the back of their mind they have the notion that silence is a terrible thing, a shameful void that must be filled up immediately. To the contrary, silence is a good "breathing space" or punctuation device between what went before and what comes next. It helps the audience tune in to the speaker and tune out extraneous thoughts.

## Look Directly at the Audience As Much As Possible

If you are frightened of your audience, it is tempting to stare at your notes or the back wall or the window, but this adds to your nervousness rather than reducing it.

Force yourself to establish eye contact, especially at the beginning of your speech. Good eye contact means more than just a quick, furtive glance at various faces in front of you; it means "locking" your eyes with a listener's for a couple of seconds. "Locking" may sound frightening, but it actually helps to calm you. Maggie Paley, a writer, in an article about a public speaking course that she took, said, "When you make contact with one other set of eyes, it's a connection; you can relax and concentrate. The first time I did it, I calmed down 90 percent, and spoke . . . fluently."[24]

## Get Audience Action Early in the Speech

I said earlier that it's a bit unnerving to see your listeners' expressionless faces. In some speeches, you can change those faces from blank to animated by asking a question. (Tips on how to ask questions will be discussed in Chapter 10.) When the listeners respond with answers or a show of hands, they show themselves to be friendly and cooperative, and this obviously reduces your apprehension. When *they* loosen up, *you* loosen up.

## Use Bodily Actions to Dissipate Some of Your Nervous Energy

I mentioned earlier that adrenalin is a good thing, providing athletes and public speakers with wonderful bursts of energy. There is, however, a bad side to adrenalin. When your body goes on red alert, you get pumped up and ready for action, but you also get trembling hands, jittery knees, and a dry throat. If you are an athlete, this is no problem, because you will soon be engaged in vigorous physical activity that will enable you to drain off your excess nervous energy. But the public speaker lacks such easy outlets for these unpleasant symptoms.

Nevertheless, there are two tension releasers that you can try: (1) Let your hands make gestures. You will not have any trouble making gestures if you simply allow your hands to be free. Some speakers clutch their note cards or thrust their shaking hands into their pockets or grip the lectern until their knuckles turn white. If you let your hands hang by your side or rest on the lectern, you will find that they will automatically make gestures. You will not have to think about it at all. (2) Walk about. Though you obviously should not pace back and forth like a caged animal, you can walk a little bit. You can speak at the lectern for a while, then step to one side for a few moments, then return to the lectern. If you have visual aids, you can easily move about as part of your presentation.

Gestures and movement will not only syphon off excessive tension, but they will also make you a more exciting and interesting speaker than someone who stands frozen in one spot.

## Do Not Be Afraid to Make Mistakes

If you give enough speeches in your life, you are bound to make many mistakes. But do not worry; it happens to everyone. Even Prince Charles and Princess Diana, the future king and queen of England, got flustered during their wedding ceremony and made some (literally) royal goofs. The bride called her groom "Philip Charles Arthur George" instead of "Charles Philip Arthur George." When he, in turn, was supposed to pledge to share all his worldly goods with her, he forgot to say "worldly."[25]

If you completely flub a sentence or mangle an idea, you might say something like, "No, wait. That's not the way I wanted to explain this. Let me try again." If you momentarily forget what you were planning to say, do not let it defeat you. Pause a few moments to regain your composure and find your place in your notes. There is no need to apologize. In conversation, you pause and correct yourself all the time; to do so in a speech makes you sound spontaneous and natural.

If you make a mistake that causes your audience to snicker or laugh, try to join in. If you can laugh at yourself, your audience will love you—they will see that you are no "stuffed shirt." Some comedians deliberately plan "mistakes" as a technique for gaining rapport with their audience.

Most audiences are very generous. They will forgive any amount of bumbling if they are convinced that you are sincere. Sincerity is more important in a speech than all the polished oratorical skills put together. The late Senator Robert Kennedy often stumbled badly in his speeches and had an embarrassing stammer at times, but the crowds loved him because his earnestness and sincerity shone through.

**Welcome Experience**

If you are an inexperienced speaker, please know that you will learn to control your nervousness as you get more and more practice in public speaking, both in your speech class and in your career. You should welcome this experience as a way to further your personal and professional growth.

One student told her public speaking instructor at the beginning of the course that she just *knew* she would drop out of the class right before her first speech. She stayed, though, and developed into a fine speaker. She later got a promotion in her company partly because of her speaking ability. "I never thought I'd say this," she commented, "but the experience of giving speeches—plus learning how to handle nervousness—helped me enormously. Before I took the course, I used to panic whenever I started off a talk. I had this enormous lump in my throat, and I thought I was doing terrible. I would hurry through my talk just to get it over with." But as a result of the course, she said, "I learned to control my nervousness and use it to my advantage. Now I'm as nervous as ever when I give a speech, but I make the nervousness work *for* me instead of *against* me."

In your career, rather than shying away from speaking opportunities, seek them out. As the old saying goes, experience is the best teacher.

## Summary

The nervousness engendered by stage fright is a normal, understandable emotion experienced by most public speakers. Instead of trying to eliminate nervousness, you should welcome it as a source of energy. Properly channeled, it can help you give a better speech than if you were completely relaxed.

The best way to avoid excessive, crippling nervousness is to pour time and energy into preparing and practicing your speech. Then, when you stand up to speak, deal rationally with your nervous symptoms (such as trembling knees and dry throat); remind yourself that the symptoms are not a prelude to disaster, but instead are evidence that you are keyed up enough to give a good speech. Never call attention to your nervousness and never apologize for it; the listeners do not care about your emotional state—they just want to hear your message. Concentrate on getting your ideas across to the audience; this will get your mind where it belongs—on your listeners and not on yourself—

and it will help you move your nervousness to a back burner, where it can still simmer and energize you without hindering your effectiveness.

## Review Questions

1. Why are fear and nervousness beneficial to the public speaker?
2. Why does extensive preparation help a speaker to keep nervousness within bounds?
3. Why is delivering a speech from memory a bad method?
4. Why should you never call attention to your nervousness?
5. Does an audience detect most of a speaker's nervous symptoms? Explain your answer.

# TIPS *for your career*

### Tip 3: Don't Be Afraid to Ask Questions When You Are a Listener

Some members of an audience are shy and nervous about asking questions during the question-and-answer period at the end of a speech. This reticence seems to be based on the fear of asking "a dumb question."

To bolster your confidence in asking questions, follow these guidelines:

1. *Listen carefully to the entire speech.* If you spend time daydreaming or letting your mind churn with ideas over what you are going to ask the speaker, you may miss the very information you plan to ask about.

2. *Do not fear that you may be the only person who needs clarification or explanation.* If you have listened carefully to a speech and you are still confused or unsure on certain points, the chances are great that other listeners are in the same situation. Think for a moment: haven't there been many times in school when another student has asked the very question that you were reluctant to ask? And didn't you feel grateful to that student for being brave enough to speak up?

3. *Use notes for your question.* Jot down a few notes to remind yourself of exactly what you want to ask the speaker. This prevents you from faltering or drawing a mental blank when the attention of the audience suddenly focuses on you.

# Part 2

# Preliminary Stages

## Chapter 4

# Reaching the Audience: Analysis and Adaptation

**The Importance of Analyzing and Adapting**

**Attitudes**
 What Are the Listeners' Attitudes Toward the Topic?
 What Are the Listeners' Attitudes Toward the Speaker?
 What Are the Listeners' Expectations?

**Interest Level**

**Knowledge**
 Audiences That Know a Lot About the Topic
 Audiences That Know Little or Nothing About the Topic
 Mixed Audiences

**Demographic Variables**
 What Are the Listeners' Ages?
 Are Both Sexes Represented in the Audience?
 What Is the Educational Background?
 What Are the Occupations?
 What Are the Racial and Ethnic Backgrounds?
 What Are the Religious Backgrounds?
 What Is the Economic and Social Status of the Audience?

**The Occasion**
 What Is Your Time Limit?
 What Is the Purpose of the Occasion?
 What Other Events Will Be on the Program?
 How Many People Will Be Present?
 Will There Be a Question-and-Answer Period?

**Getting Information About the Audience**

**Adapting During the Speech**

**T**wo of the worst types of public speakers are what I call *Robots* and *Performers*. As I describe them, see if you have ever listened to either of them.[1]

*Robots.* These people have dull, uninteresting speeches, which they deliver without a trace of enthusiasm. They scarcely look at their audience because their eyes are focused on their notes or upon the manuscript from which they are reading. They convey information as if they were automatons programmed to produce data. They seem not to care whether the audience is wide awake with interest or half asleep with boredom. You get the impression this is merely a task they must endure—something to be gotten through with. Perhaps deep down inside they want to communicate their ideas, but they are not willing to expend the energy to reach out to the people in front of them. If you want to see these Robots in action, watch television proceedings of Congressional committee hearings; a large number of the experts and officials who testify are unbelievably dull as they read their prepared remarks (written, in many cases, not by themselves, but by professional speech writers). It is therefore no surprise that when the camera swings to the audience (the legislators), you are likely to see the lawmakers whispering among themselves rather than listening to the Robot.

*Performers.* At first, Performers seem like perfect speakers; they have good eye contact, a strong voice, and confident posture. But they talk *at* their audience, rather than *with* them. They perform rather than communicate, and they are oblivious to the listeners' needs and interests. I once knew a man who jumped at every chance to give a speech because he loved the sound of his own voice. It was indeed a deep, rich voice, and this man sounded brilliant with his grandiloquent phrases and poetic images. He always gave the same speech; I heard it several times, but I could never find any substance. It was all cream puff and no meat. Other listeners told me they came to the same conclusion; in the beginning of this man's speech, they would be astonished and delighted by his powerful, old-style oratory, but as he went on, the novelty would wear off and it would become obvious that he had nothing to say. He was just a show-off, a Performer. You can often see Performers give speeches on college campuses. If they are celebrities, they draw a big crowd, but the next day no one on campus can remember a single idea from the speech; the only thing that many of the listeners know is that they have sat in the presence of a famous person.

What Robots and Performers have in common is a low sensitivity to their audience. They lack a strong desire to reach the people sitting in front of them. This causes both types to be ineffective communicators.

When you stand up in front of an audience, what is your goal? To deliver a good speech and then sit down? If your focus is upon yourself or upon your speech, you will never be an effective speaker. Your goal should be to reach your listeners and change them, so that they walk away with new information or new opinions or a warm feeling in their hearts.

All good speakers are audience-centered. They truly want to make contact with their listeners—to inform, persuade, entertain, or inspire them. Carol Conrad, a student in one of my classes, typified this kind of speaker. In evaluating one of her speeches, another student said, "I had the feeling she was talking to me personally." How did Carol achieve this success? She composed her speeches carefully, selecting items that she knew would greatly interest her particular audience. And when she delivered a speech, she displayed a strong desire to communicate with her audience—she would look her listeners in the eye and speak directly to them. Her tone of voice and facial expression carried a clear message to the listeners: "I care about you and I want you to understand and accept my message."

In this chapter we will look at how you, too, can become an audience-centered speaker.

## The Importance of Analyzing and Adapting

To be an audience-centered speaker, you need to carry out two important tasks: (1) *Analyze* the listeners to find out exactly who they are and what they know. (2) *Adapt* your speech to meet their particular needs and interests. Analyzing and adapting should be done not only when you stand up to speak but at every step of your preparation—when you choose your topic, when you gather your materials, and so on.

When I was a freshman in college, I signed up for Introduction to Astronomy. At the beginning of the course I was very excited because I wanted to learn some basic facts about the universe, and this particular class was to be taught by a visiting professor, a highly regarded astronomer from a leading observatory. My enthusiasm soon dissipated, however, when I sat through the first lecture. The professor was brilliant—no doubt about that—but he came into class and spent an hour discussing complex ideas that only a graduate student in astronomy could have understood. We freshmen were hopelessly lost. Though his ideas were brilliant, the professor had failed in the most important task of any speaker: to communicate ideas in a way that can be understood by the listeners. He had concentrated on himself and his ideas rather than on his audience. He had wasted his time, and ours.

Now let's look at another astronomer, Dr. Carl Sagan, professor of Astronomy and Space Sciences at Cornell University and host of the television series, *Cosmos*, which has been viewed by 140 million people throughout the world. In one of the programs, Sagan is shown visiting an elementary school where he explains a few facts of astronomy to a class of sixth graders. He speaks in language the children can understand. For example, he draws an analogy that is beautifully clear but not insultingly simplistic: "A handful of sand contains about 10,000 grains, more than the number of stars we can see with the naked eye on a clear night. But the number of stars we can *see* is only the tiniest fraction of the number of stars that *are* . . . . The total number of stars in the universe is greater than all the grains of sand on all the beaches of the planet Earth."[2]

Notice the big difference in how these two astronomers handled analysis and adaptation. The first failed to analyze the audience to find out who we were, and he failed to adapt his ideas to our level of understanding. Dr. Sagan, on the other hand, shrewdly sized up his audience. He knew that to show sixth graders the richness of the universe, he would have to devise an analogy based on their own experience: every child has a good knowledge of a handful of sand, the size of a grain, the vastness of beaches, etc. Notice how he avoided the extremes of overestimating and underestimating his audience. In other words, he did not talk over their heads, nor did he talk down to them as if they were kindergartners. He pitched his remarks to their level.

Adapting does not mean being insincere or compromising one's principles. Suppose that you are strongly opposed to the use of all illegal drugs and you have been invited to talk on drug abuse to a class of eighth graders. Should you use the current slang of eighth graders to show that you are one of the gang? No, that is not what is meant by adapting. That would be phony, and the students would resent your chummy approach. Should you water down your beliefs, dropping your opposition to marijuana in order to win audience support for your stand against cocaine? No, that is not what is meant by adapting, either. Such a tactic would be foolish; you would lose respect for yourself, and weaken your credibility with the audience (if you are perceived as inconsistent). How, then, can you adapt your ideas to the eighth graders without being a phony? In the first place, use terms and concepts that all eighth graders can understand; for example, say "pep pills" instead of "amphetamines." Second, relate your ideas to their lives and interests; for example, "I know that sometimes you feel down in the dumps. Maybe you're making bad grades in one of your classes, or you're afraid that a certain person no longer likes you, or you're having constant hassles with your parents. In times like these, it's easy to be tempted by little pills that someone tells you will make you feel good."

When you carefully tailor your speech to a particular audience, you are showing your listeners a lot of respect. You are saying, in effect, "I care about you." One of my students gave a speech about her trip to the Middle East. While showing slides of the pyramids in Egypt, she said, "I know some of you are engineering students, so I thought you'd like to hear the latest theory about how the ancient Egyptians were able to construct the pyramids without sophisticated machinery." I am sure the engineering students were flattered and pleased by her acknowledgment of them and of their interests.

Some speakers shy away from analysis and adaptation because they think the whole thing smacks of manipulation. Though an unethical speaker could indeed use these techniques for devious purposes, the ethical speaker uses them for honorable ends. For example, one of the most honorable goals you can have is to avoid wasting your listeners' time. Most people are very busy, and they consider time as a precious asset. If you make a careful analysis of your audience, you can give them a speech that means time well spent, and they will love you for it. But if you waste their time, they will regret having listened to you. Not long ago, I was required to stay after work for two hours to hear a man speak on how to manage stress. When I went into the room, I was a bit negative. Was this man making me stay overtime for nothing? Was he planning to tell me stuff I already knew? As it turned out, his speech was very helpful. Though he was from out-of-town, he had arrived early and had interviewed some of my colleagues to get information on our particular problems; then he aimed his remarks at helping us overcome them.

Let us now look at the ways in which you can analyze your listeners and then adapt your speeches to their special needs.

# Attitudes

Attitudes are the emotional baggage—the favorable or unfavorable predispositions—that the listeners bring to your speech. Here are some questions that will help you understand and adapt to the audience's attitudes.

## What Are the Listeners' Attitudes Toward the Topic?

Are your listeners negative, neutral, or positive toward your ideas? If they are negative toward your ideas, you should design your speech with their opposing arguments in mind. Suppose, for example, that you want certain industries to stop spewing toxic wastes into the atmosphere. You advocate the passage of laws that would force the plants to clean up their emissions. As you prepare your speech, you anticipate that your listeners will say, "But won't the cost of cleaning up the emissions be so great that the plants will go out of business, throwing thousands of people out of work?" To counter this argument, you find information showing that similar plants in other states were forced to stop polluting, without causing economic harm to the companies.

Do not become disheartened if you fail to win the support of an audience that is negative toward your ideas. Sometimes your ideas may be so far removed from what the audience believes that you have no realistic chance of persuading all the listeners. In such cases, the best you can hope for is to soften their opposition. You give a speech, for example, in favor of raising the speed limit on interstate highways to 75 miles per hour. Everyone in the audience disagrees with you, but by the end of the speech many of the listeners admit that your argument has merit and that they will have to reassess their own position. In this instance, a "limited" victory might be the best you can realistically hope to achieve.

If your listeners are apathetic or neutral, try to involve them in the issue, and then win them to your side. For example, during times of peace, when there is no military draft, most listeners are neutral and apathetic about whether the country should bring back conscription. To win an audience to one side or the other, a speaker would have to paint a picture of imminent war and say something like, "Six months from now, all of you—male and female alike—could be standing in the ranks of the United States Army." Such a picture, if believed by the audience, could move them from neutrality and apathy toward the position you espouse. What you are trying to do, of course, is show that the issue is not a faraway abstraction but a real possibility that could affect their own lives.

If your audience is favorably disposed toward your ideas, your task is to reinforce their positive views and perhaps even motivate them to take action. For example, you give a pep talk to members of a political party in your community, urging them to campaign on behalf of the party's candidate in an upcoming election.

## What Are the Listeners' Attitudes Toward the Speaker?

Sometimes audiences will have a negative attitude toward you because they think you are unqualified to speak on a particular subject. You can sometimes overcome this attitude by establishing your credibility at the beginning of your speech. Bob Monroe, one of my students, gave a speech on CPR (cardiopulmonary resuscitation). Even though he was just out of high school, he proved his expertise (and gained the audience's confidence) by telling us of the lives he had saved using CPR as a volunteer firefighter/rescue worker in a rural community. This sort of reporting is not bragging; it is a way of saying, "You can trust me to give you reliable information because I've used this knowledge myself with good results."

If you are not an expert on a subject, you can sometimes enhance your credibility by explaining how you got your information. Francine DuBois, a 19-year-old single woman, gave a classroom talk on the secrets of a happy, successful marriage. She knew that some of her listeners might say to themselves, "What does a young single woman know about this?" So she said, "I realize that some of you may be wondering how I can claim to know anything about marriage. To prepare for this speech, I read four books and a dozen magazine articles on the subject, and I interviewed some people I know who have good, solid marriages. I don't claim to be an expert, but I have done a lot of research and I'd like to share what I've come up with." By telling of her preparation, Francine bolstered her personal credibility with the audience.

## *What Are the Listeners' Expectations?*

Is the audience expecting to be instructed, inspired, or amused? If you fail to act as expected, you may disappoint or anger them. For an after-dinner speech, for example, your audience would expect you to give a light, diverting talk. If instead you gave a tedious, highly technical speech, they would groan inwardly and tune you out.

Audiences also get upset if you talk about something completely different from what they were expecting. A well-known science writer was invited to speak at a large university a few years ago. Most of the people in the audience expected him to speak on science; when he talked instead on a controversial political issue, the audience was outraged. There were mutterings of discontent throughout the speech, and some people even walked out in disgust.

# Interest Level

As you choose and develop a topic, you need to ask yourself how much interest your listeners will have in your material. Consider the following example:

A student whom I'll call Calvin had an unusual hobby: collecting and firing muzzle-loading rifles, the kind used in George Washington's day. He gave a speech on how to clean such rifles. It was terribly boring; no one in the audience cared about technical things like patches and cleaning oil and ramrods. During the question-and-answer period, however, there was lively interest in the rifles: Why would anyone in the modern world want to fire antique rifles? Are they dangerous? Are they accurate? How quickly can you reload? It was clear that if Calvin had spoken on the rifles themselves, he would have had an interesting topic. He should have saved his "how to clean" speech for his fellow gun-club members, who would have loved all the technical lore.

Now contrast Calvin's failure with a successful speech:

Ray Dillingham, a student speaker, knew how to train horses and he planned to give a speech on how to train the Tennessee Walking Horse for competition. As he analyzed his audience, however, he realized such a specialized talk would be uninteresting to anyone but a horse trainer, so he switched his focus to horses in general. He spoke on the different breeds of horses, showing color slides to demonstrate their variety and beauty. The speech was well received by the listeners, who found it very interesting.

These two examples show that whenever you prepare a speech, you should ask yourself what aspect of your topic would be most interesting to your particular audience. In some cases, if your audience is not very interested in a topic before you speak, you can *generate* interest. Here is how one speaker generated interest by using a provocative introduction:

Student speaker Maxine Fletcher chose tattoos as her topic. The speech might have failed to stir much interest if she had not done something very dramatic during her introduction: she pulled up the sleeve of her sweater to reveal a large, colorful tattoo on her upper arm. It was the first time most of the students had ever seen a tattoo on a woman, and they became very interested, asking many questions at the end of the talk.

A good way to gain interest is to figure out which aspect of your topic would be most relevant to the personal lives of the listeners. Think back to your own experiences as a member of an audience. If you are like most people, you wanted to know, "What's in it for me?" In other words, did the speaker have anything to say that you considered useful in your own life? People like to hear speeches that will help them reach their personal goals. They want to be healthy, feel secure, have friends, make money, solve problems, enjoy life, and learn interesting things. If you can talk about such things in an appealing way, people will listen to you with great interest. Here is an example of how one student related her topic to her audience.

Brenda Gudger wanted to convince her audience to use bargaining techniques in buying a used car. She knew that many of her listeners might find the subject boring and unrelated to their own lives, so she began by saying: "A lot of people don't like to haggle over buying a car. They'd rather pay the sticker price than bargain with the salesperson. Well, a couple of months ago, I haggled over a used car, and I was able to get $500 knocked off the price of the car. Today I'd like to tell you how you can save yourself a lot of money by bargaining with salespeople."

By appealing to everyone's desire to save money, Brenda increased the audience's interest in her speech.

# Knowledge

As you analyze your listeners, find out what they already know about the topic. Do they know a lot? A moderate amount? Nothing at all? Here are some tips on handling the different kinds of audiences.

## *Audiences That Know a Lot About the Topic*

Your audience will be bored and resentful if you give information that everyone already knows. Suppose that you have been asked to talk on computers. Is your audience a group of business executives who already own personal computers? If so, you do not need to define such basic terms as "default" and "booting up." What you should do is give them new ideas and concepts.

## *Audiences That Know Little or Nothing About the Topic*

Here are some hints on how to handle the audience that does not know much about your topic:

1. Carefully limit the number of new ideas you discuss. People cannot absorb large amounts of new information in a short period of time. If you overwhelm them with too many concepts, they will lose interest and tune you out.

2. Whenever possible, use visual aids to help the listeners grasp the more complicated concepts.

3. Use down-to-earth language; avoid technical jargon. If you feel that you must use a specialized word, be sure to explain it.

4. Repeat key ideas, using different language each time.

5. Give vivid examples.

## *Mixed Audiences*

What do you do if some listeners know a lot about your subject and some know nothing? This is a tough problem. The ideal solution, of course, is to make both groups happy. How? By starting off at a simple level and adding complexity as you go along. Let's go back to the computer example. Suppose you have some members of your audience who know very little about computers and some who know a great deal. You can say something like this: "I hope the computer buffs here will bear with me, but I know that some people in the audience will be confused unless I

**The speaker should find out as much as possible about how much the listeners know about a topic. Do they know nothing? A little? A great deal?** *(Robert George Gaylord/EKM-Nepenthe)*

spend a few moments explaining what a disk drive is." The computer buffs will not be upset, because you have acknowledged their presence and their expertise, and they will not mind a little review session (they might even pick up something new). The computer novices, meanwhile, will love you for being sensitive to their inexperience.

# Demographic Variables

Making a demographic analysis of your audience will give you many clues to the foregoing items: attitudes, interest, and knowledge. Here are the basic questions you should ask.

## *What Are the Listeners' Ages?*

If you have a variety of ages represented in your audience (as is often the case in college classes today), you should be sensitive to the interests, attitudes, and knowledge of all of your listeners, giving explanations or background whenever necessary. For example, if you are talking about a musician who is popular only with young people, you may need to give some information about his music and life style for the benefit of older members of the audience.

Here is an example of insensitivity to the ages of listeners:

After World War II, America's colleges were filled with war veterans attending school on the GI Bill. Grant Hansen, a corporation president, recalled the commencement address of his college graduation shortly after the war. "The speaker had given the same speech for years. He told us about this great milestone—graduation—we had just achieved, and that soon we would be arriving at other milestones—our first jobs, then getting married, and soon having children. I looked up and down the row and saw all these war veterans, seated with their wives and children behind them, and thought this speaker hadn't done his homework very well. I myself had been divorced and remarried."[3] This reminiscence illustrates that you need to find out the ages of your listeners ahead of time—and then adapt your remarks accordingly.

Now let's turn to an example of effective adaptation:

William Edwards, a minister, was well known in his community for conducting a special service on Sunday mornings for families with small children. His sermon was usually in the form of a parable—a simple story with an easily grasped moral, such as the story of the Good Samaritan. He would tell the story in a dramatic fashion so that the children were captivated by the narrative; in the meantime he would subtly point out the deeper allegorical meanings to the adult listeners. Thus, Edwards succeeded in adapting his sermon to the wide age span of the audience; he reached the 4-year-old and the 44-year-old, without talking down to anyone, without boring anyone. People of all ages went away satisfied.

## Are Both Sexes Represented in the Audience?

The sex of your audience will give you some clues about their background knowledge. If, for example, you are talking on sex discrimination to an all-female audience, you might need to provide little or no explanation of what you mean by sex discrimination. They already know, some from firsthand experience, what you are talking about. If there are males in the audience, however, you might need to elaborate by giving anecdotes about the subtle ways in which women are sometimes treated unfairly.

## What Is the Educational Background?

Always consider the educational background of your listeners. Avoid talking over their heads, using concepts or language that they cannot understand. Likewise, avoid the other extreme: do not talk down to your listeners. Find the happy medium. Albert Einstein, considered by many to be the most brilliant scientist of the twentieth century, could present his incredibly complex theories to his scientific peers in language that was appropriately sophisticated for their level of understanding, yet he could also adjust his speech for the benefit of the 99.9 percent of us who cannot begin to comprehend his theories. For example, he once made part of his theory of relativity understandable to the average person by using this analogy: "Time is relative. If you sit on a park bench with your girl friend for an hour, it seems like a minute. But if you sit on a hot stove for a minute, it seems like an hour." Thus did Einstein humorously and simply illustrate part of his theory—that time seems to slow down in relation to other events.[4]

Define terms whenever you think that someone in the audience does not know what you are talking about. Fred Ebel, past president of a Toastmasters club in Orlando, Florida, says that to one audience, "I told a joke which referred to an insect called a praying mantis. I thought everyone knew what a praying mantis was. But I was greeted by silence that would have made the dropping of a pin sound like a thunderclap. Several listeners came up to me and asked, 'What is a praying mantis?' It came as a shock to me until I realized that not everyone had taken a course in biology."[5]

## What Are the Occupations?

Adapt your speeches to the occupational backgrounds of your listeners. The best examples of this kind of adaptation can be found near election time when politicians size up the needs and interests of each audience they face. With steelworkers, for example, the typical politician may discuss competition from Japanese industries; with farmers, soil erosion; with truck drivers, highway speed limits; and with bankers, credit regulations. None of this is necessarily manipulative or unethical; it is simply good audience analysis and adaptation: steelworkers do not want to hear about soil erosion, and farmers do not want to hear about Japanese steel imports.

## What Are the Racial and Ethnic Backgrounds?

Find out the racial and ethnic backgrounds of your listeners so that you can adapt your remarks to their needs and interests. For example, in many college classrooms (and in other audiences as well), you will find a sprinkling of foreigners. As much as possible, you should try to include them in your adaptation. One student speaker, Mark Hopkins, was planning a speech on "hot rod" automobiles. While conducting informal interviews with members of his speech class, he discovered that some of the foreign students did not know what a hot rod was. So he prepared a drawing of a hot rod on a large piece of poster board, and then displayed it at the beginning of his speech.

You should avoid material that might offend any racial or ethnic group. A little common sense can prevent you from making errors such as this: During the 1960s, one of the television networks tried to line up sponsors for a new series based on the experiences of Allied bomber pilots in World War II. It invited representatives from a few big companies, including Volkswagen, to attend an advance screening of the show. The film began with scenes of American bombers blasting their targets. Within two minutes the German-accented voice of the Volkswagen representative was heard muttering, "There goes our factory in Stuttgart." Soon afterward, the network team packed up its film and silently departed.[6]

While it is obvious that you shouldn't make racial or ethnic slurs that would anger any minority-group members of your audience, some people think that if there are no members of a particular race or ethnic group present, it is all right to make insulting jokes. It is *not* all right. Such slurs are offensive and un-funny to many men and women who don't happen to belong to the group being ridiculed, and they lose respect for the speaker.

## What Are the Religious Backgrounds?

Knowing the religious affiliations of your audience will give you some good clues about their beliefs and attitudes. Most Seventh-Day Adventists, for example, are very knowledgeable about nutrition because of the strong emphasis the denomination places on health; many Adventists are vegetarians and nondrinkers. If you were asked to speak to an Adventist group on a health-related issue, you could assume that the audience had a higher level of background knowledge on the subject than the average audience has; you would therefore avoid going over basic information they already know.

While religious background can give you clues about your audience, you have to be cautious. You cannot assume that all members of a religious group subscribe to the official doctrines. A denomination's hierarchy, for example, may call for a stop to the production of nuclear weapons, while the majority of the members of that denomination may not agree with their leaders' views.

## What Is the Economic and Social Status of the Audience?

You need to be sensitive to the economic and social backgrounds of your listeners so that you can adapt your speech accordingly. Suppose you are going to speak in favor of food stamps for the poor. If your listeners have low incomes, most of them will probably be favorably disposed to your ideas before you even begin. You might therefore want to aim your speech at encouraging them to support political candidates who will protect the food-stamp program. If they are upper-middle-class, however, many of them will be opposed to your ideas and you will have to aim your speech at winning them over to your way of thinking.

# The Occasion

You need to find out as much as you can about the occasion and the setting of your speech, especially when you are speaking in the larger community beyond the college campus. Here are some questions to ask; pay special attention to the first one.

## *What Is Your Time Limit?*

It is important that you find out how much time has been allotted for your speech, and then abide by the time restriction. I have seen several public occasions marred by long-winded speakers who droned on and on, oblivious to the lateness of the hour and the restlessness of the audience. Once I attended a banquet where a half-dozen speakers had been asked to speak for only five minutes apiece but four of the six exceeded the time limit by 30–45 minutes each. By midnight, most of the people at the tables were yawning and looking at each other in weary disbelief.

If you are a speaker in such a situation, you may want to pare your speech down, if at all possible. Your audience will love you for it. When I am invited to speak at events where there are several speakers, I have learned to prepare two versions of my speech—a full-length one to use if the other speakers respect their time limits, and a shorter version if the situation dictates that I trim my remarks. You might want to consider doing the same thing for occasions that are loaded with many speakers and activities.

Though many audiences will suffer through an interminable speech without being rude to the speaker, some will not. One speaker found this out the hard way when he gave a speech to a civic-club luncheon. At the hour when the meeting was supposed to be over, even though the speaker was still holding forth, the club members got up and walked out. It was explained later that all the members had to get back to their jobs by a certain time.

Some speakers have absolutely no concept of time. For a five-minute speech, some of my students talk for 20 minutes and then swear later that they could not possibly have talked for more than five—something must have been wrong with my stopwatch. As we will see later, practicing your speech at home will help you keep within time limits.

People who give long-winded speeches might desist from this terrible vice if they knew what misery they cause their audiences. The poor listeners are forced to undergo an agony of boredom, as they squirm and fidget, stifle their yawns, and yearn for release from this windbag who tortures them for what seems like an eternity. If you tend to be a garrulous speaker, you should follow the wise speechmaking formula of President Franklin D. Roosevelt:

> Be sincere.
> Be brief.
> Be seated.

## What Is the Purpose of the Occasion?

A leading television commentator, widely known for his probing questions during live TV interviews, was paid $25,000 to lead a panel discussion at a national computer show in Atlanta. His task, according to *PC Week* magazine, was to extract "pithy and provocative insights" from major computer-industry leaders. He failed to carry out this assignment, however, because he "evidently misunderstood the show's business orientation." Instead of asking probing questions about how businesses can use computers, he "repeatedly hammered on the subject of home computing, to the apparent confusion and irritation of the panelists."[7]

Avoid this commentator's mistake by finding out in advance what is the purpose of the meeting. Suppose you are something of an authority on the life and music of the late singer John Lennon, a member of the Beatles who was murdered by a deranged fan, and you are asked to give a talk at a club meeting. To prepare your speech, it would be crucial for you to know the purpose of the occasion. Is the club meeting devoted to remembering Lennon's tragic death? If so, you would obviously want to prepare a somber eulogy to Lennon. Or is the meeting devoted to a celebration of the Beatles' music? In this case, you might want to give an upbeat talk on Lennon's personality, interlaced with tape-recorded playings of his music.

## What Other Events Will Be on the Program?

Are there other speakers on the agenda? If so, what will they speak on? It would be disconcerting to prepare a speech on the life of Martin Luther King and then discover during the ceremony that the speaker ahead of you is talking on the same subject.

Even more disconcerting is to come to a meeting and find out that you are debating someone on your topic. Obviously you need to know such information in advance so that you can anticipate what the other speaker will argue and prepare your rebuttal accordingly.

**Audiences reflect a wide variety of backgrounds. The speaker should find out as much as possible about the listeners' needs and interests.** *(Alan Carey/ The Image Works)*

## How Many People Will Be Present?

It can be unsettling to walk into a room, expecting an audience of 20 but instead finding 200. Knowing the size of your audience ahead of time will not only help you to prepare yourself psychologically, but it will also help you to plan your presentation. Will you need extra-large visual aids? Will you need a microphone?

Where your listeners sit in relationship to others can be important. If you have 15 people scattered about in a large hall, it will be easier to make contact with them if you first have them move to seats at the front and center. Nightclub comedians are very sensitive to seating arrangements; they make sure tables are pushed close together because they know that patrons are more likely to laugh if they are jammed together in warm coziness. Some comedians would never dare tell jokes to an audience widely scattered in a large room; people feel isolated, and they are afraid that if they laugh, they will be conspicuous. (Have you ever noticed that funny movies are funnier if you see them in a packed theater than if you see them in a sparsely attended theater?)

## Will There Be a Question-and-Answer Period?

If there is a question-and-answer period, who will moderate it, you or the program chairperson? How long will it be? Will it come after each speech or after all the speeches?

In most speeches, the questions from the audience should come after the speech is finished. If they were to come during the speech, they could spoil the carefully organized flow of your remarks. Some questions could get you sidetracked onto issues that are not directly relevant to your subject. And of course some questions might be premature, bringing up points that you have not covered yet.

In classroom speeches, your instructor will establish rules for asking questions. In talks that you give out in the community, you might want to establish guidelines for your audience in the early part of your speech. For example, you could say, "If you have any questions during my talk today, please hold them until the end and I'll be happy to try to answer them."

## Getting Information About the Audience

Where can you get information about your audience? The best source is usually the program director (or whoever invited you to speak). Using the suggestions in this chapter, find out all that you can about the audience and the occasion. Ask, also: "Is there anything special about this group or this meeting that would help me prepare my speech?"

For classroom speeches, there are several ways to gain information. If your class has speeches in which students introduce themselves, you can make notes regarding their backgrounds, interests, and other features. Also, you can interview your fellow students directly or you can have them fill out a questionnaire.

When you have finished analyzing your audience, you need to make good use of your data. The best way to do this is to put yourself in the listeners' shoes at each step of your preparation. Play a game of imagination. Visualize yourself sitting in the audience, and ask yourself questions such as: Does this introduction attract my attention? Do I know the technical terms that are being used or do I need to have them explained? Are these visual aids helping me to understand the speech or do I find them confusing or irrelevant?

Here is something else you can do: when you rehearse your speech, do it in front of friends and relatives. Ask them to make notes of any parts of the speech that are unclear or clumsy. Ask them to make suggestions on how the speech could be improved. In this manner you get helpful audience feedback before you stand in front of your "real" audience.

## Adapting During the Speech

Adapting to your audience, so important during the preparation stages, must also take place during the actual delivery of the speech. You must be sensitive to their moods and reactions, and then make the necessary adjustments, if possible. Here is an example:

Using a portable chef's stove, Lester Petchenik, a student speaker, was demonstrating how to cook green beans *amandine*. At one point, he sprinkled a large amount of salt into his pan—an action that caused several members of the audience to glance at each other with looks of surprise. Noticing this reaction, Lester ad-libbed, "I know it looks like I put too much salt in, but remember that I've got three pounds of green beans in this pan. In just a moment, when you taste this, you'll see that it's not too salty." (He was right.)

Reading the mood of your audience is really no different from what you do every day with your friends. You tell them about the new "framas" that you've just bought; they say "Huh?" and give you a quizzical look. You then explain what a framas is. In like fashion, if you see people in your audience frowning when you mention a technical term, you need to add a definition.

Try to overcome any barriers to communication. John Naber, a professional speaker and former Olympic gold medalist in swimming, says that he once gave a speech in a room with poor acoustics. Realizing the audience would have trouble understanding him if he stayed at the lectern, he said, "I moved into the middle of the group and walked among them as I spoke."[8]

You should be especially sensitive to the mood of the listeners. Are they bored, drowsy, or restless? Sometimes they are listless not because your speech is boring but because of circumstances beyond your control. It is eight o'clock in the morning, for example, and you have to explain a technical process to a group of conventioneers who have stayed up partying half the night.

If you ever need to "wake up" a listless audience, here are some techniques you can use: (1) Invite audience participation (by asking for examples of what you are talking about, or by asking for a show of hands of those who agree with you). (2) "Rev up" your delivery (by moving about, by speaking slightly louder at certain points, or by speaking occasionally in a more dramatic tone). (3) Use visual aids.

Sometimes it is easy to "read" audience behavior. If people in the back of the room are leaning forward with a puzzled look on their faces, they are obviously having trouble hearing you, and you know that you need to speak louder.

In other cases, however, it is hard to interpret your listeners' faces. That man in the third row with a sour face—is he displeased with your speech? Before you jump to conclusions, pay heed to the astute observation of the well-known inspirational lecturer, Earl Nightingale:

I've seen people in my audiences many times who appeared to be outright hostile to what I was saying, who seemed to be trying to tell me by their expressions that I was a blithering idiot, yet I have learned over the years that it's often these same people who come up to the head table afterwards with the most profusive compliments and expressions of gratitude. They just happen to look like that. They wear customary frowns and their mouths turn down at the corners as though they had just bitten into a dill pickle. That's the way they look.[9]

What if the frowns do mean disapproval? Should you alter your speech to make everyone in the audience happy? No, of course not. While trying to be sensitive to the mood of the audience, you should never compromise your principles or violate your personal integrity simply to win approval. Besides, your goal in public speaking is not to have the audience like you, but to communicate your ideas to them as clearly and as effectively as possible.

## Summary

To be an effective speaker, you must concentrate your attention and energies on your audience, and have a strong desire to communicate your message to them. You must analyze the listeners beforehand and adapt your materials and presentation to their needs and interests.

You should analyze the listeners' attitudes toward you and your topic, their level of interest in your subject matter, and their degree of knowledge about your material. You should take into consideration a variety of demographic factors: age, sex, educational levels, occupations, racial and ethnic backgrounds, religious affiliations, and economic and social status. You should also analyze the occasion to gather details about the time limit, the purpose of the meeting, other events on the program, the number of people who will attend, and whether or not there will be a question-and-answer period.

Be prepared to adapt to the needs of the listeners during the speech itself. Try to be sensitive to the cues that indicate boredom, restlessness, or lack of understanding.

## Review Questions

1. Why are Robots and Performers considered ineffective speakers?
2. How should you deal with listeners who think you are unqualified to speak on a particular subject?
3. Why are listeners' expectations important?
4. What guidelines should be followed for a speech to an audience that knows little or nothing about your topic?
5. What demographic factors should you consider in analyzing an audience?
6. What aspects of the speech occasion should you examine before giving your talk?

# TIPS *for your career*

### Tip 4: Develop a Positive Attitude Toward Each Audience

There is an old comedy routine you have probably seen at least once on TV in one form or another. It goes something like this: a nervous young man is waiting for a blind date to appear at a prearranged spot. As he waits, he fantasizes how she will react to him. The TV camera captures the fantasies: when she approaches him, she looks at him with disappointment bordering on disgust. When he introduces himself, she laughs at his name and says it is stupid. When he suggests that they go to a particular restaurant for dinner, she ridicules his idea of good food. When he tries to make small talk, she laughs at his accent. The fantasy goes on and on, from one humiliation to another. Finally, the fantasies fade away as the real, live date appears on the scene. By now, however, the young man is so outraged that he screams at the date, "Well, I didn't want to go out with you, either!" and storms away, as the startled date stands alone, blinking her eyes in confusion.

In like fashion, some speakers indulge in fantasies of audience rejection and when they actually stand up to speak, they act very defensive, as if they just *know* that everyone in the audience is going to reject them and their ideas. Their "body language"—tone of voice, facial expression, posture—is defensive, sometimes even angry and sullen. I saw one such speaker argue in favor of the sport of hunting animals. He knew that some members of the audience were opposed to hunting. From start to finish, he acted as if the audience had just insulted him. "We are not sadistic people who enjoy watching animals suffer," he said angrily. Who said he was sadistic? Who said he enjoyed watching animals suffer? Like the young man waiting for his blind date, this speaker had worked himself into an unnecessary rage.

Do not prejudge your audience. Most listeners are kind and sympathetic to speakers. Even if they reject your ideas, they usually are respectful of you the speaker, as long as you are respectful of them.

Instead of nurturing gloomy fantasies, try to develop a positive attitude toward every audience you address. Professional speaker Rosita Perez of Brandon, Florida, attributes her success as a public speaker to her love and respect for her audiences. "The key to giving a good speech," she says, "is remembering that the audience is the single most important element there. When we tune in to them, and set aside our ego needs, some magical things happen because they *feel* our commitment."[10]

It helps to think of the audience not as an impersonal mass, but as a collection of individuals who are basically no different from you and your friends. "When I speak," says Perez, "I communicate to the audience in the most personal way I am able to. In an auditorium of 3,000, I speak as if to one."[11]

# Chapter 5

# Selecting Topic, Purpose, and Central Idea

**Selecting a Topic**
 Select a Topic That You Care About
 Select a Topic That You Know a Lot About (or Can Learn About)
 Choose a Topic That Is Interesting to the Audience
 Narrow the Topic

**The General Purpose**
 Informative Speech
 Persuasive Speech

**The Specific Purpose**
 Begin the Statement with an Infinitive
 Include a Reference to Your Audience
 Limit the Statement to One Major Idea
 Make Your Statement As Precise As Possible
 Make Sure You Can Achieve Your Objective in the Time Allotted
 Do Not Be Too Technical

**The Central Idea**

The best way to write a love letter, the Swiss-French philosopher Jean Jacques Rousseau once said, is to begin without knowing what you are going to say. Such a formula might be effective for the ecstatic outpouring of a love letter, but if applied to speechmaking, it is a recipe for failure. Yet I know a few foolhardy individuals who insist that they do not have more than a vague idea of what they are going to say to an audience until they stand up and "go with the mood of the moment" (as one of them expressed it). A couple of these people, I have to admit, are effective speakers, but most of them range from mediocre to devastatingly boring. Because their own minds are unfocused, their speeches are fuzzy. They ramble, repeat themselves, and get bogged down in irrelevant matters.

The best speeches I have heard were given by men and women who sounded as if they were speaking spontaneously but who had in fact spent hours and days in careful preparation. In this chapter we will examine some of the most important steps in preparing a speech—selecting a topic, a general purpose, a specific purpose, and a central idea.

# Selecting a Topic

For many of the speeches that you will give during your lifetime, your topic will be chosen by someone else. Your boss, for example, tells you to give a talk to your fellow employees on a new product. Or you are asked to speak to the Rotary Club on safe-driving skills because you are known in the community as an expert on the subject.

In most public speaking classes, on the other hand, students are permitted to choose their own topic, a freedom that causes some students a lot of grief. They spend days walking around with a dark cloud over their heads, moaning to friends, "I have to give a speech next week and I can't think of a *thing* to speak on." Do not let yourself get stuck at this stage. Choose your topic as far ahead of your speech date as possible because you will need to spend a great deal of time and energy on other important tasks, such as researching, outlining, and practicing. If you spend days and days stewing over which topic to select, you may find yourself without enough time to adequately prepare the speech.

As you read this chapter, keep a note pad handy and jot down ideas for topics as they come to you so that you will have a stockpile to draw from throughout the course. In the weeks ahead you can add to your list as you get more ideas.

Here are some important points to bear in mind as you look for a topic.

## *Select a Topic That You Care About*

Have you ever had something happen to you that was so exciting, you could hardly wait to tell your friends? That is the way your speech topic

**A police officer gives a safety talk to public school children. Speakers often use personal experiences as the source material for their speeches. (David S. Strickler/The Picture Cube)**

should be—something you care about and are eager to communicate to others. Are you angry over the air pollution in your town? Speak on air pollution. Are you excited about the wizardry of your personal computer? Speak on computers. Are you having so much fun baking pastries that you try a new recipe every evening? Speak on how to bake pastries.

Enthusiasm is contagious; if you are excited, some of your excitement will infect your listeners. If, on the other hand, you are unexcited about your topic, you are apt to do a lackluster job in preparing the speech, and when you deliver it, you will probably come across as dull and unconvincing.

Here are two examples that illustrate how enthusiasm, or the lack of it, can make the difference between a good speech and a poor one:

A student whom I'll call Bob had trouble coming up with a topic for his speech class. So at the last moment he grabbed a magazine article and used it as the basis for a talk on gun control. His speech was poorly constructed and tedious. Worst of all, he seemed to have no real emotion about his subject. Normally, when a student talks on gun control, there is a lively response from the audience during the question-and-answer period, but Bob's listeners seemed as listless as he was; they had no questions or comments for him.

Theresa Schmidt gave a talk on doll collecting and brought along some of the dolls from her own collection. I was afraid that her talk would be boring to an audience of grownups, but she started off by telling why she, as an adult, still collected dolls, then gave fascinating stories about how she got some of them from foreign countries, and told of particular dolls' names and personalities. Her speech was a success, not just because of her well-told stories and colorful visual aids, but because she herself displayed a consuming, passionate interest in her subject. While she was speaking, I glanced around at the students in the class; their animated faces showed that they were fascinated.

Now look at these two speakers. Gun control is one of the most highly emotional subjects in our society today, as likely as any topic you can name to capture an audience's interest. But Bob succeeded in making it dull because he had a ho-hum-I-don't-really-care attitude. Theresa, on the other hand, took a subject unlikely (at first glance) to appeal to adults, and made it into a wonderful speech, mainly because she was imbued with a contagious enthusiasm. She *cared* about her subject.

## Select a Topic That You Know a Lot About (or Can Learn About)

Make things easy for yourself. Speak on something you are already thoroughly familiar with—or can learn about through research. If your listeners realize they know more about the subject than you do, they lose confidence in you. This can be especially painful if your speech is followed by a question-and-answer period. When I was in college, I was asked to give an oral report on a particular issue in a sociology class; I had no interest in the subject and did little research. After I gave my report, a student in the class (who knew a great deal about the subject) ridiculed my omissions and errors. I felt like an absolute fool. But I learned an important lesson: a person should *never* give a speech unless he or she knows the subject matter extremely well.

Here are several ways to probe for topics that you know a lot about (or can learn about).

### Personal Experiences

There will be times in your life when you will be obliged, as I was in the sociology class, to speak on a topic chosen by someone else. If, however, you are permitted to choose your own topic, my advice is to start your search with the subject on which you are the world's foremost expert—your own life.

"But my life isn't very interesting or exciting," you might say. You are wrong. Maybe you are not an international celebrity, but there are dozens of aspects of your life that could make fascinating speeches. Let me give you some examples, all of them involving students:

Mike Gronowski gave a speech about the only job he had held in his life—bagger at a supermarket. At first glance this sounds like a dull job, and a boring speech. But Mike made it fascinating: he told about the fashionably dressed woman who tried to hide T-bone steaks in her overcoat, the surprisingly large number of customers who could not find their cars in the parking lot, and the fact that if a bagger got bitten by a dog while loading groceries into a car, the attacker was more likely to be a snippy little dog than a huge snarling Doberman Pinscher.

Susan Peterson went to her first rock concert and discovered that the rock fans were as interesting as the band. She gave a speech about the different types of fans she observed, using vivid descriptions that amused and fascinated her audience.

Carlos Gomez loved to jog every afternoon to dissipate the tensions of the day. He gave a speech on the mental and physical benefits of jogging, showing his listeners how they, too, could feel better if they took up this form of exercise.

Mitzi Stevens worked as a waitress in a restaurant. She gave a talk on the way customers treat waitresses, with some fascinating insights. She reported, for example, that the most generous tippers are parents of small children, who apparently feel guilty for the fuss and mess their kids create.

These four students were *ordinary* people who chose to speak on *ordinary* aspects of their lives, but their speeches turned out the way all good speeches should turn out—interesting. So when you are trying to come up with a topic, start with yourself and look for the interesting things in your own life. Figure 5.1 is an inventory that you can fill in to help you identify topics.

After you have filled in the inventory, go back and analyze the list for possible speech topics. If you are not sure which items would make good speeches, ask your friends for advice or consult your instructor. Figure 5.2 is an example of how one student, Karin Johansson, filled in the inventory.

In Karin's inventory, which items could make a good speech? All of them are potentially good speech topics. Which would be the best? That would depend on Karin's current state of enthusiasm; her rafting trip on the Colorado River through the Grand Canyon sounds exciting, for example, but if it turned out to be a disappointing trip and Karin is tired of telling about it, this would obviously be a poor topic for her.

## Exploring Interests

What if the personal inventory fails to yield a topic that you are happy with? Or what if you simply dislike talking about yourself? Do not despair. There are plenty of topics outside your personal life that can captivate your audience. Choose one that you have always wanted to know more

Name:

**Personal Inventory**

Jot down as much information about yourself
as you can in the categories below:

Work experience (past and present)



Special skills or knowledge



Pastimes (hobbies, sports, recreation)



Travel



Unusual experiences



School interests (academic and extracurricular)



Concerns or beliefs (politics, society, family, etc.)

**FIGURE 5.1**
This personal inventory can help you pinpoint speech topics from your own life.

about—something that intrigues you. The following case illustrates what I am talking about:

A few months before she enrolled in a public speaking class, Julia Lavagetto saw a television documentary on UFOs. This whetted her curiosity, and she yearned to read some books and articles on UFOs, but unfortunately she was too busy with her schoolwork. When she took the public speaking course, Julia realized that she now had the opportunity to meet her speech assign-

```
┌──────────────────────────────────────────────────┐
│                                                    │
│              Name:   Karin Johansson                │
│                                                    │
│           Personal Inventory                        │
│                                                    │
│   Work experience (past and present)                │
│                                                    │
│      Emergency medical technician (paramedic)       │
│      Ambulance driver                               │
│      Volunteer firefighter                          │
│      Waitress                                       │
│                                                    │
│   Special skills or knowledge                       │
│                                                    │
│      Cardiopulmonary resuscitation                  │
│      Rescue from burning buildings                  │
│      First aid                                      │
│                                                    │
│   Pastimes (hobbies, sports, recreation)            │
│                                                    │
│      Water skiing                                   │
│      Swimming                                       │
│      Cooking Chinese food                           │
│      Restoring antiques                             │
│                                                    │
│   Travel                                            │
│                                                    │
│      Quebec                                         │
│      Mexico                                         │
│      Colorado River (rafting)                       │
│                                                    │
│                                                    │
│   Unusual experiences                               │
│                                                    │
│      Rescuing two children from a burning house     │
│      Rafting through the Grand Canyon               │
│                                                    │
│   School interests (academic and extracurricular)   │
│                                                    │
│      Nursing courses                                │
│      Biology                                        │
│      Drama Club                                     │
│                                                    │
│                                                    │
│   Concerns or beliefs (politics, society, family, etc.) │
│      We need to stop child abuse                    │
│      Learning CPR should be a prerequisite for      │
│         getting a driver's license                  │
│      Curtail sale of handguns (but not rifles)      │
│                                                    │
└──────────────────────────────────────────────────┘
```

**FIGURE 5.2**
Personal inventory,
as filled in by one
student.

ment and satisfy her intellectual craving at the same time. She read books
and magazine articles on UFOs, and gave an interesting speech.

Some students use their speech assignment as a vehicle for gaining
vital information for their own lives. Here is an example:

Lloyd Feinberg still mourned the suicide of a close friend in high school. He
deeply regretted that he had been unable to dissuade his friend from taking

an overdose of pills. For his classroom speech, he decided to do research on suicide. He read books and magazine articles, and interviewed a suicide-prevention counselor. He ended up giving his talk on "How to counsel a person who threatens to commit suicide," a topic he chose because he wanted to know how to handle such a situation if it ever happened again. During his research he found tips and insights that were valuable not only for his audience, but for himself as well.

As you will notice in the two cases just cited, the main point of this section—select a topic you know a lot about—still applies. If you do not know a great deal about the subject now, you can do some research and make yourself knowledgeable. Perhaps you will not qualify as an expert, but you will at least know more about the subject than most of your listeners.

### Brainstorming

If the suggestions already discussed do not yield a topic, try brainstorming (so called because it is supposed to create a lot of intellectual thunder and lightning). In brainstorming, you write down whatever pops into your mind. For example, if you start off with the word "school," the next word that floats into your mind might be "homework" and then the next word might be "algebra," and so on. Do not censor any words. Do not apply any critical evaluation. Simply write whatever comes into your mind. Nothing is too silly or bizarre to put down.

Using a sheet of paper or the guide in Figure 5.3, jot down words as they come to your mind.

**Brainstorming Guide**

| | |
|---|---|
| People | Music |
| Places | Sports |
| Things | Current Events |
| Health | Social Problems |

**FIGURE 5.3**
A brainstorming guide can be helpful in finding topics.

When you finish brainstorming, analyze your list for possible topics. Do not discard any possibility until you have chosen a topic. Here is an example of how brainstorming might work: Under "Things," let's say you write "cars." Then you free-associate the following: car payments . . . trips . . . highways . . . accidents . . . drunk drivers . . . . When you analyze the list, perhaps the word "trips" leads you to choose a trip to Mexico as your topic. Or the term "drunk drivers" causes you to realize that you feel strongly about the need for stronger laws against driving while intoxicated, so you choose drunk driving as your topic.

Figure 5.4 is a sample of one student's brainstorming notes.

**Brainstorming Guide**

People
Dad
fishing
weekend trips
camping
great fun, no fish
excuses—fishermen

Music
guitar
how to play
country music
records
bluegrass bands

Places
gym
swimming pool
laps
backstroke
Olympics
East Germans

Sports
hockey
violence
boxing
wrestling
'rasslin'
villains
good guys

Things
money
greed
rat race
power
high finance
Wall Street

Current Events
nuclear war
disarmament
Russians
Russian paranoia
Paranoia in Islamic
  countries
Iran
Middle East
Israel
Atomic attack on
  Israel

Health
vitamins
nutrition
vegetables
vegetarians
red meat

Social Problems
pollution
crime
juvenile delinquency
drunk driving
legal age for drinking
age for voting
age for military duty

**FIGURE 5.4**
One student's entries on a brainstorming guide.

In Figure 5.4, the student's brainstorming under most categories was fairly straightforward. It is easy to see his train of thought. But under "Places," he made some interesting jumps (which is okay; writing down whatever comes to mind is the way the "game" is played). He started with a place, the gym, which reminded him of the gym's swimming pool. This made him think of the laps he liked to swim every day, and this led him to think of the backstroke. Then his mind leaped to some Olympics trials he had seen on TV, and this made him think of East German prowess in swimming competition. As it ended up, the list gave him a lot of choices for topics: swimming for exercise, competitive swimming, Olympic competition, East German participation, etc.

Based on his brainstorming under "Current Events," this student chose to give a speech on Israel's vulnerability to an atomic bomb ("Israel is only one bomb wide," he said) and what that nation can do to protect itself. He could have easily picked another topic from his list: "Paranoia in Islamic countries" could have led to a speech on why some Islamic fundamentalists view the United States as a bastion of evil.

The other categories could have also yielded many topics. His brainstorming under "Sports," for example, could have led to a talk on the good-versus-bad symbolism of professional wrestling on TV. He also could have made speeches on other items suggested by the list: boxing, hockey, violence in sports, etc.

You may be wondering why you should put all this down on paper. Why not just let all these ideas float around in your mind? The advantage of writing items down is that you end up with a document that can be analyzed. It helps you focus your thinking.

### Library Search

If the techniques previously discussed fail to yield a topic, there is another method you can use: go to the library and look through magazines or an encyclopedia or the *Readers' Guide to Periodical Literature* until you find something that appeals to you and should also appeal to your audience. Here is an example:

> Roosevelt Evans went to the library and picked up the most recent copies of several popular magazines. As he leafed through the magazines, he spotted an article on the foods one should eat in order to avoid cancer. This subject was so interesting to him that he read other articles on the same topic and decided to give his speech on it.

## *Choose a Topic That Is Interesting to the Audience*

Some students are unsure of their ability to determine whether a topic is worthwhile. "How do I know," they say, "what will be interesting to the audience?" Here are four ways to assess the interest level of a topic:

1. Analyze the audience as thoroughly as you can, as suggested in Chapter 4. This should enable you to make good educated guesses about the topics that would be ideal for your audience.

2. Consult your teacher for his or her suggestions.

3. Ask your friends how much interest they would have in the subject if they were part of the audience.

4. Make sure that *you* find your topic interesting. In choosing a topic, says professional speaker Danielle Kennedy, "I try to stay away from things I find boring. If I'm bored, the audience will be, too. Even if your topic takes a lot of research, pick something you have a natural curiosity about."[1]

**A student journalist is enthusiastic about a story she has just written. When choosing topics for a speech, speakers should consider talking about things they find interesting and exciting. (Bob Daemmrich/Texa-Stock)**

## *Narrow the Topic*

Once you find a topic, you often need to narrow it. Suppose you want to give a speech on crime in America; five minutes—or twenty—is not enough time to adequately cover such a broad topic. How about limiting yourself to just crimes of violence? Again, five minutes would be too short to do justice to the topic. How about one type of violent crime—rape? This subject perhaps could be handled in a five-minute speech, but it would be advisable to narrow the topic down even more—to one aspect of the subject: How to fight off a rapist. Or: Why some men rape.

Here are some examples of topics that can be narrowed:

*Too broad:* Politics in America
*Better:* My stint as a volunteer campaign worker in a congressional election

*Too broad:* Relations between parents and children
*Better:* How some parents unwittingly display higher expectations for sons than for daughters

The most important way to narrow your topic is to formulate a specific purpose, which will be discussed later in this chapter. But first, let's take a look at your general purpose.

# The General Purpose

Once you have a topic, your next step is to decide your general purpose in giving the speech. Most speeches have one of the following purposes:

To inform

To persuade

There are other purposes—to entertain, to inspire, to stimulate, to introduce, to create goodwill, and so on—but the two above are the most common. Let's take a closer look at them.

## *Informative Speech*

In the informative speech, you are concerned about giving new information to your listeners, not with winning them to your way of thinking. The informative speech can take a variety of forms, such as defining a concept (feminism, for example), explaining a situation (why TV soap operas are so popular), or demonstrating a process (the correct way to ski cross-country).

Your main concern in this kind of speech is to have your audience learn and remember new information. You are in effect a teacher—not a preacher, nor a salesperson, nor a debater. Here is a sampling of informative topics:

> How to complain—and get results—when you receive poor products or service in a store
> The use of computers in the home
> Soccer—the world's most popular sport
> The life of Martin Luther King
> How to design and create a leather belt

## Persuasive Speech

Your aim in the persuasive speech is to convince the listeners to come over to your side, to adopt your point of view. You want to *change* your listeners in one or both of these ways: (1) to change their minds (for example, persuade them to believe that the nuclear arms race should be ended), and/or (2) to change their behavior—get them to *start* doing something they normally do not do (such as using seat belts) or get them to *stop* doing something they normally do (such as sprinkling salt on their food).

Here are some examples of persuasive topics:

> Colleges should abolish letter grades and give only "pass" or "fail."
> Married couples should not go into debt on anything except a home.
> Every person should travel to a foreign country at least once in his or her lifetime.
> Congress ought to cut off all military aid to repressive dictatorships.
> The summer Olympic games should be held at a permanent site in Greece from now on.

# The Specific Purpose

After you have determined your general purpose, your next step is to formulate a specific purpose, expressing precisely what you intend to accomplish in your speech. The specific purpose serves two important functions: (1) it helps you narrow down your topic to something that can be covered comfortably and effectively in the time allotted, and (2) it forces you to put your ideas into sharp focus. For example, if your topic is "life on other planets," and your general purpose is "to inform," your specific purpose might be: "To inform my listeners of the three main reasons why some astronomers think that life exists on other planets."

Let's take another example. Suppose you start out with the following:

*Topic:* Television

What if you stopped at this point? You might make the mistake of talking about a lot of different things on TV, failing to develop any of your ideas very well. But imagine that you continue with the following:

> *General Purpose:* To inform
> *Specific Purpose:* To explain to my audience the reasons for the popularity of TV soap operas

Now you have a sharp focus for your speech. You have wisely limited yourself to something that can be covered adequately in a short speech. Here are some guidelines for writing a specific purpose statement.

## *Begin the Statement with an Infinitive*

An infinitive is a verb preceded by "to"—for example, *to write, to read.* By beginning your purpose statement with an infinitive, you clearly state your intent.

> *Poor:* Hiking in the mountains
> *Better:* To inform the audience of the health and recreational benefits of hiking in mountain terrain

For informative speeches, your purpose statement can start with such infinitives as "to explain," "to show," "to demonstrate." For persuasion speeches, your purpose statement can start with infinitives such as "to convince," "to prove," and "to get the audience to believe."

## *Include a Reference to Your Audience*

Your specific purpose should include references to your audience, by means of such phrases as "to my listeners" or "to the audience." This may seem like a minor matter, but it is important for you to keep your listeners in mind at every stage of your speech preparation. Writing them into the specific purpose helps remind you that your goal is not to stand up and talk, but rather to communicate your ideas to real flesh-and-blood human beings.

> *Poor:* To explain how fast-food restaurants use colors and music to stimulate sales
> *Better:* To explain to my listeners how fast-food restaurants use colors and music to stimulate sales

## *Limit the Statement to One Major Idea*

Avoid the temptation to try to cover several big ideas in a single speech. Limit yourself to only one.

*Poor:* To convince the audience that scenes of explicit sex and violence in prime-time television shows should be censored, and that local TV stations should be encouraged to expand their local coverage
*Better:* To convince the audience that scenes of explicit sex and violence in prime-time television shows should be censored

In the first example, the speaker tries to cover two major ideas in one speech. While it is true that censorship and local news both pertain to TV, they are not closely related and should be handled in separate speeches.

*Poor:* To demonstrate to my audience how to take care of their cars by changing the oil and oil filter, tuning the engine, adjusting the carburetor, flushing out the radiator, and properly inflating the tires
*Better:* To demonstrate to the audience how to change the oil and oil filter in a car

The first example covers too much territory. If you tried to compress all that information into a five-minute speech, you would have to race through so fast that your listeners would be unable to keep up with you.

## Make Your Statement As Precise As Possible

You should strive to have a statement that is clear and precise.

*Poor:* To tell my audience about cancer
*Better:* To tell my audience the six warning signals for cancer

The first statement is too broad and ill-defined for a speech; you would need hours and hours to cover the subject. The second statement shows one of the ways in which you can narrow your focus so that you can adequately cover one aspect of the topic in a short speech.

*Poor:* To help my audience brighten their relationships

This statement is fuzzy and unfocused. What is meant by "to help"? What is meant by "brighten"? And what kind of relationships are to be discussed—marital, social, business? Here is one possible improvement:

*Better:* To explain to my listeners four techniques people can use to communicate more effectively with loved ones

## Make Sure You Can Achieve Your Objective in the Time Allotted

Do not try to cover too much in one speech. It is better to choose a small area of knowledge that can be developed adequately than to select a huge area that can only be covered sketchily.

> *Poor:* To give my listeners a history of the Roman Empire
> *Better:* To explain to my audience the ancient Romans' views on marriage and divorce

The first example would require at least twenty hours to discuss adequately; the second example could be easily and effectively handled in a five-minute speech.

### *Do Not Be Too Technical*

You have probably sat through a speech or lecture that was too technical or complicated for you to understand. Do not repeat this mistake when you stand at the lectern.

> *Poor:* To explain to my listeners the different types of golf clubs and their uses

This is too technical for the average classroom audience. Some listeners have never played golf and probably never will. The speaker should shift to some aspect of golf that will appeal to *all* listeners. Here is one possibility:

> *Better:* To tell my audience why golf is an enjoyable sport for millions of Americans.

# The Central Idea

"When we ministers preach a sermon," a clergyman friend told me, "we like to think everyone in the congregation understands everything we're saying. And we like to think that when they leave the church, they carry our eloquent words with them in their hearts and in their minds." But unfortunately, he confessed, it does not always work out that way. "They remember our human-interest stories, but they either don't understand the point behind the stories or they soon forget it. It's always disappointing to have someone shake your hand after the service and say, 'Just what *were* you driving at this morning?' "

If people ask this question after you have given a speech, you have failed to accomplish your most important task—to communicate your *central idea.* The central idea is the basic message of your speech expressed in one sentence. It might be helpful for you to know that the central idea is the same thing as the *thesis sentence* or *controlling statement,* terms you have probably encountered in English composition courses. If you were forced to boil your entire speech down to one sentence, what would you say? That is your central idea. Or think of it in this way: one month after you have given your speech, if the audience remembers only one thing, what would you like it to be?

Let's imagine for a moment that you decide to give a speech on the incompetence of some teachers. You plan to cite cases of certain elementary school teachers who cannot write coherent sentences and some high school math teachers who cannot solve algebra problems. You bring up these cases because you believe that teachers should not be employed in the public schools unless they can pass a competency test. The specific purpose statement for your speech might look like this:

> *Specific Purpose:* To persuade my audience to support mandatory testing of all teachers in grades K through 12.

Next, you develop your central idea by asking yourself, "What is the key idea I want my audience to retain if they forget everything else?" Your central idea might look like this:

> *Central Idea:* All teachers in grades K through 12 should be required to pass a competency test on basic reading, writing, and math skills before being allowed to teach in public schools.

You have probably noticed that the specific purpose and the central idea are similar, and you may be asking whether there is any significant difference between them. The answer is yes. The specific purpose is written partially from your point of view—it is what *you* set out to accomplish. Your central idea is written entirely from the listeners' point of view—it is the message *they* go away with.

Every speech should have only one central idea. Why not two? Or three? Because you are doing well if you can fully illuminate one big idea in a speech. And if you try to handle more than one, you run the risk of overwhelming the listeners with more information than they can comfortably absorb.

Devising a central idea is helpful because it keeps you from rambling in your speech. It prevents you from being the kind of speaker who never quite gets to the point. It is especially important that you write down your central idea—at the top of your outline. Writing it down gives you a path to follow and a clearly defined destination. As you prepare your outline, you can evaluate every potential item in light of the central idea. Does Fact A help explain the central idea? If yes, keep it. If no, throw it out. Does Statistic B help prove the central idea? If yes, keep it. If no, throw it out.

In some cases, the central idea will provide a miniature outline, as in the following example:

*Topic:* Problem drinking
*General Purpose:* To inform
*Specific Purpose:* To tell my audience how people can determine if they have a serious drinking problem
*Central Idea:* There are four early warning signs of a serious drinking problem: frequent desire for drink, an increase in consumption, unusual (often embarrassing) behavior, and the inability to remember what happened during a drinking bout.

This central idea gives the speaker an outline in a nutshell. The four items constitute the four Roman numerals of the outline (we will discuss outlines in detail in Chapter 11).

Here are a few more examples:

*Topic:* Artificial turf
*General Purpose:* To persuade
*Specific Purpose:* To convince my audience that artificial turf should not be used on athletic playing fields
*Central Idea:* Artificial turf should not be used on playing fields because it causes serious, sometimes permanent, injuries to athletes.

*Topic:* Bonsai trees
*General Purpose:* To inform
*Specific Purpose:* To explain to my listeners how to train trees to grow small
*Central Idea:* Anyone can grow bonsai (miniature) trees by taking three easy steps.

*Topic:* TV censorship
*General Purpose:* To persuade
*Specific Purpose:* To convince the audience that scenes of explicit sex and violence in prime-time television shows should be censored
*Central Idea:* TV shows that appear during "prime time" should not be allowed to contain scenes of explicit sex and violence because of the large numbers of impressionable children who watch during these hours.

The time you spend formulating the items discussed in this chapter—specific purpose, central idea, etc.—may seem like an extra burden of time and energy, but in reality, these items are shortcuts. Because they channel your thinking, they prevent you from scattering your efforts across too wide a field. They end up saving you time. More importantly, they help you give a better speech than you might otherwise.

## Summary
In choosing a topic for your speech, think of subjects that (1) you care a great deal about, (2) you know a lot about (either now or after you

complete your research), and (3) your audience will find interesting.

After you choose a topic, decide upon your general purpose in speaking (such as to inform or to persuade) and then formulate your specific purpose—exactly what you hope to accomplish in the speech. Next, write out your central idea: the one big idea that you want your audience to remember if they forget everything else in the speech.

Though they may seem time-consuming, these preliminary steps will actually save time in the long run and they will help you organize your ideas in a coherent, understandable form.

## Review Questions

1. When a speaker is enthusiastic about his or her ideas, how do listeners usually react?
2. How does one go about brainstorming ideas?
3. List three *general* purposes for speeches.
4. List the six criteria discussed in this chapter for writing a specific purpose statement.
5. What is the central idea of a speech?
6. What is the difference between the specific purpose and the central idea?

# TIPS *for your career*

### Tip 5: Be Yourself

It is ethical to study other speakers and borrow some of their ideas and methods, but you make a big mistake if you try to imitate them—if you try to make yourself over in their image.

Be yourself. Do not try to be someone else. I once knew a man who, whenever he gave a speech, tried to sound exactly like the famous evangelist Billy Graham. He succeeded in reaching his goal: if you closed your eyes, you would swear that Billy Graham himself was addressing the audience. But people considered this imitator an insincere fool and laughed at him behind his back. There is only one Billy Graham and there is only one you. This is not to say that you should not try to improve your speaking style. Just make sure the finished product is a polished you, not a polished imitation of someone else.

"You should always try to be *you*," advises professional speaker Arnold "Nick" Carter. "You should express how *you* think, feel, and believe. Imitation is suicide in public speaking."[2]

# Chapter 6

# Finding Materials

**Personal Experiences and Investigations**

**Library Resources**
  Getting Help from Librarians
  Consulting Reference Works
  Finding Books
  Finding Articles
  Finding Audiovisual Materials

**Computer Databases**

**Interviews**
  Preparing for the Interview
  Conducting the Interview
  Following up on the Interview

**Other Resources**

**Finding the Right Materials Efficiently**
  Start Your Research Far in Advance
  Turn Your Specific Purpose Statement into a Research Question
  Establish a Research Strategy
  Evaluate All Sources

**Taking Notes**
  Prepare Bibliography Cards
  Make Note Cards

**Giving Credit**

A student, Marie DiBenedetto, decided to prepare a speech on how to handle a job interview successfully. Before writing her outline, she looked for and found some good "raw materials." First, drawing upon her own experiences as a job applicant, she jotted down a list of things she had learned during job interviews. Next, Marie went to the college library and found several books and magazine articles on job interviews; as she read the material, she wrote key information on note cards. Then, Marie interviewed the personnel managers of two large companies on what they looked for during job interviews.

When it came time to organize her speech into an outline, Marie had a wealth of material from which to draw. And when she stood up in front of the class, she was able to deliver a speech that was interesting, thorough, and well-substantiated.

A good speech should not be a bag of hot air, a collection of vague ideas and unsupported opinions; rather, it should be like Marie's—an interesting package containing a rich variety of solid, up-to-date information. To prepare such a speech, you need to allow yourself ample time to gather an abundance of materials. In this chapter I will give you some tips on where and how to find materials for your speeches.

# Personal Experiences and Investigations

Your personal experiences can be a gold mine of good material for your speeches. Listeners love to hear about other people's lives, and a story from your own life can be the most interesting part of a speech. Your personal experiences can be especially useful when they are used to supplement information you have gleaned from books or magazine articles, as in the case below:

> Student speaker David Rhodes gave tips on how to buy a good car at the lowest possible price. He presented information from *Consumer Reports*, supplementing it with first-hand knowledge he had gained in his job as a car salesman the previous summer. An example of his "insider's" knowledge: "When the car salesman gives you the price on a car," David advised, "tell him that you'll think about it and maybe call him the next day. Start to walk away. Before you leave the lot, the salesman will give you a lower price—he doesn't want you to get away."

You can also undertake personal investigations to gather material for a speech. For a speech on acid rain, for example, you can visit a mountaintop that has been ravaged by pollutants, making observations and perhaps even taking color slides. For a speech on prison conditions, you can visit a county jail or state prison and then tell your audience what you have seen. For a speech on animal overpopulation, you can tour a local animal shelter and interview the director.

Another type of investigation is to conduct public opinion surveys. One student polled her classmates on their views concerning the death penalty. This survey not only helped her analyze and adapt to her audience, but it also provided interesting data to include in the speech itself.

# Library Resources

A library is a wonderful treasury of resources for your speeches. Your campus library is the best place to begin, but do not forget that there are many other kinds of libraries. Your local newspaper has a *morgue*, a library of old news stories that are clipped and filed by subject matter. These clippings are usually limited to local and state affairs; no effort is made to collect national and international news articles. Most newspapers allow researchers to look at the files and photocopy any items they want. There are also specialized libraries maintained by historical societies, museums, professional associations, law firms, medical societies, and large businesses. To find the location of these libraries in your community, consult the *American Library Directory* (in the reference section of your college library), or ask people who are knowledgeable about the particular field.

## *Getting Help from Librarians*

If you were lost in a strange city, it would be silly to just wander around, hoping to locate your hotel. To find your way, you should ask advice from someone who lives in the city. Likewise, it would be silly to wander around a library, hoping to stumble upon good information for your speech. You can save yourself a lot of time and frustration if you seek the help of the librarians. (Some students are reluctant to ask librarians for help because they think that a librarian's work is limited to ordering, shelving, and checking out books. The truth is that an important part of a librarian's job is helping patrons find materials, and most librarians are friendly and helpful.)

When you start your research, introduce yourself to a member of the library staff and explain the nature of your project. A librarian will be designated to help you; in large libraries, there is usually a reference librarian whose sole job is to help people like you track down information.

One of the most helpful services that librarians provide is interlibrary loan. This means that if your library does not have the book or magazine article you need, the librarians can make a search (often very quick and computerized) of other libraries in your state until they find it and borrow it for you. It often takes less than a week to get the book. (You should not count on it coming quickly, however; some books are hard to locate and mail delivery can be slow.) Most libraries have this service; ask your librarian for details.

**Libraries offer a rich variety of materials for speeches. Librarians can be consulted for tips on how and where to find material.** *(Walter S. Silver/The Picture Cube)*

## Consulting Reference Works

The reference section of the library, with its encyclopedias, dictionaries, yearbooks, and other aids, is an important resource. In most libraries, reference books cannot be checked out, so you need to allow yourself ample library time when you delve into these books.

### General Encyclopedias

For some research projects, encyclopedias are a good place to begin because they can give you an overview of your subject—a general idea of the basic concepts and issues. They also list books and articles on your subject, saving you the time it would take to compile such a list on your own. If the library carries several editions of a particular encyclopedia, look for the most recent edition. Following is a list of some of the most popular encyclopedias:

*The New Columbia Encyclopedia*
*The New Encyclopaedia Britannica*

*Random House Encyclopedia*
*World Book Encyclopedia*

## Specialized Encyclopedias

Many specialized encyclopedias offer technical information written in language that a nonspecialist can understand. One of the best and most popular of these is the *McGraw-Hill Encyclopedia of Science and Technology,* a 15-volume set that includes an index. Here is a sampling from among the dozens of other specialized encyclopedias:

*Encyclopedia of Advertising*
*Encyclopedia of American History*
*Encyclopedia of Athletics*
*Encyclopedia of Psychology*
*Encyclopedia of Superstitions*
*Encyclopedia of World Art*

## Dictionaries

For definitions of currently used words in the English language, consult dictionaries such as *The American Heritage Dictionary, The Random House Dictionary,* or *Webster's Third International Dictionary.* For the history of a word, look at *The Oxford English Dictionary.* Also available are specialized dictionaries such as the following:

*Dictionary of American Slang*
*Dictionary of Scientific and Technical Terms*
*Dorland's Medical Dictionary*
*Sports Dictionary*

## Almanacs and Yearbooks

Because they are published annually, almanacs and yearbooks provide a great amount of updated facts and statistics. A few of the more popular are:

*Facts on File*
*Information Please Almanac*
*Statistical Abstract of the United States*
*The World Almanac and Book of Facts*

## Atlases and Gazetteers

Atlases contain maps and other geographical information; gazetteers are geographical dictionaries. Here are some of the most widely used:

*Britannica Atlas*
*Rand McNally Cosmopolitan Atlas*
*Times Atlas of the World*
*Webster's New Geographical Dictionary*

## Biographical Sources

Most libraries have many different biographical references, giving you information about the lives and careers of famous people, living or dead. Here is a sampling:

*Current Biography*
*Dictionary of American Biography*
*Notable American Women*
*Who's Who in America*
*Who's Who of American Women*

## Collections of Quotations

If it is appropriate and interesting, a quotation can enrich a speech. Here are some sourcebooks:

*Bartlett's Familiar Quotations*
*Dictionary of Quotations*
*Peter's Quotations*
*The Quotable Woman*

## *Finding Books*

To find a book in the library, you have two major resources—the librarians and the card catalog (sometimes called the public catalog), which tells you which books the library owns. It was once available only in the form of index cards in filing drawers, but now some libraries display the cards on microfiche, microfilm, or computer monitors.

The catalog lists books alphabetically by (1) author's last name, (2) title, and (3) subject. (In some libraries name and title cards are housed separately from subject cards.) Which type of card should you consult? It depends on your situation. If you do not know much about your topic, the subject cards are very helpful. For example, if you want to do research on lasers but you do not already know the titles of any books in that field, begin by looking under the subject heading "lasers." If, on the other hand, you know the name of an author in the field, you may want to go directly to that name in the "author" section and write down a list of his or her books. For example, if you know that Stanley Leinwoll is an expert on lasers, look under the author's last name, "Leinwoll." Finally, if you know of a book called *Laser Handbook* but you cannot recall the author's name, look for the title under "L" in the "title" section of the catalog.

Here are sample cards:

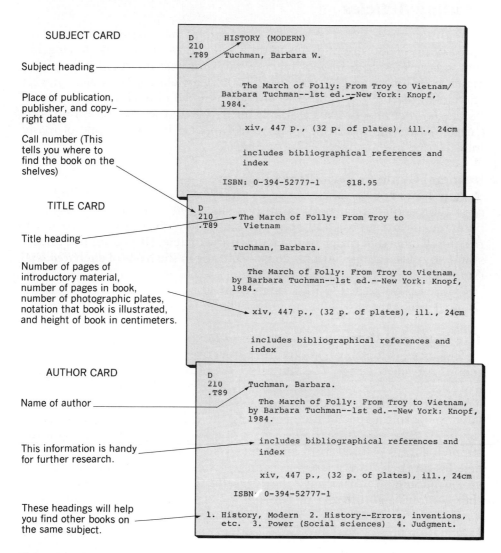

**FIGURE 6.1**
Subject, title, and author cards of a typical library book.

The most important item on a card is the call number in the upper left corner, for this tells you where to find the book in the library's stacks. The call number is usually derived from either the Dewey Decimal System or the Library of Congress System.

Most libraries have a chart or map showing how to locate books in the stacks. Or you can ask a librarian for help.

## Finding Articles

Sometimes magazine and newspaper articles are better sources than books because they are more up-to-date and may even contain information that will never appear in book form. What is the best way to find magazine articles? If, for example, you want to find articles on modern aircraft carriers of the U.S. Navy, should you get a bunch of back issues of *Armed Forces Journal* and browse through until you find an article on aircraft carriers? No, this would be a waste of time. Go instead to one of many indexes that are available in most libraries.

### Readers' Guide to Periodical Literature

Your library is certain to have the *Readers' Guide,* a general index of over 170 popular magazines published since 1900. Articles are listed alphabetically by author and subject. Each entry gives you all the information you need in order to track down the article. (If you do not understand any of the abbreviations, consult the key in the front of each *Readers' Guide.*)

Figure 6.2 on page 113 illustrates what you would find in the *Readers' Guide* if you wanted to look up an article on videotapes.

### The Magazine Index

This index, which is on microfilm, covers over 400 magazines—far more than the *Readers' Guide. The Magazine Index* provides coverage of the last five years; as a new month is added, the corresponding month five years ago is deleted. If you wanted to go back earlier than five years, you would have to consult a special file containing the deletions (see your librarian for help). *The Magazine Index* also provides "Hot Topics," a monthly supplement (in printed form and kept in a looseleaf notebook) of current articles on such timely issues as gun control, the arms race, and family violence. Some libraries have the *Magazine Collection,* a retrieval system that contains the full text of selected articles from *The Magazine Index.* To be able to identify which articles are available in this form, see the explanation of a typical entry in Figure 6.3 on page 114.

### Newspaper Indexes

Your library may have back issues of several newspapers on microfilm. Some newspapers are indexed, others are not; check with your librarian to find out what is available. If your library has only one newspaper on microfilm, it is likely to be *The New York Times* because of that publication's broad coverage of national and international events. *The New York Times Index* is a valuable resource because each entry contains a brief

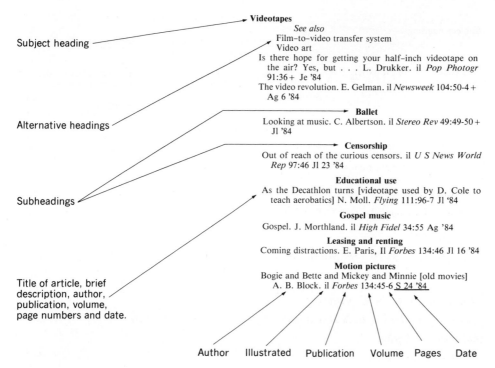

**FIGURE 6.2**
Sample entry from *Readers' Guide to Periodical Literature.*

abstract of the story; if you are looking for a single fact, you can sometimes find it in the *Index* without having to go to the issue cited. Another good resource is *The Newspaper Index,* which indexes *The Wall Street Journal, The New York Times, The Christian Science Monitor, The Los Angeles Times,* and *The Washington Post.*

## Special Indexes

If you need information from specialized publications that are not covered by the above indexes, there are a number of other indexes you can consult:

*Applied Arts Index*
*Applied Science and Technology Index*
*Art Index*
*Biological Abstracts*
*Biological and Agricultural Index*
*Business Index*

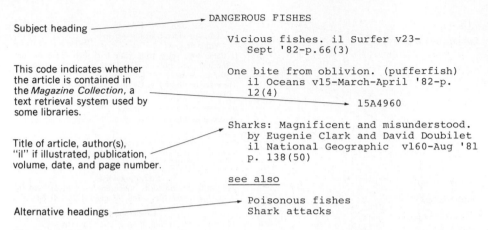

Subject heading ———————→ DANGEROUS FISHES

Vicious fishes. il Surfer v23–
Sept '82–p.66(3)

This code indicates whether
the article is contained in
the *Magazine Collection*, a
text retrieval system used by
some libraries.

One bite from oblivion. (pufferfish)
il Oceans v15–March–April '82–p.
12(4)
———————————→ 15A4960

Title of article, author(s),
"il" if illustrated, publication,
volume, date, and page number.

Sharks: Magnificent and misunderstood.
by Eugenie Clark and David Doubilet
il National Geographic  v160–Aug '81
p. 138(50)

see also

Alternative headings ———————→ Poisonous fishes
Shark attacks

**FIGURE 6.3**
An example from *The Magazine Index*.

*Business Periodicals Index*
*Cumulative Index to Nursing and Allied Health Literature*
*Education Index*
*Engineering Index*
*Environment Index*
*General Science Index*
*Hospital Literature Index*
*Humanities Index*
*Index Medicus*
*Psychological Abstracts*
*Social Sciences Index*

## *Finding Audiovisual Materials*

Most libraries have audiovisual materials that can be checked out or
played in the library. These materials include videotapes, 16mm films,
audiotapes, phonograph records, filmstrips, and slides. These items may
be listed in the card catalog or in a separate catalog. Ask your librarian
for help.

Sometimes audiovisual materials that help in your research can be
incorporated as aids into your speech (see Chapter 8).

# Computer Databases

Computer databases are vast storehouses of information. Some of them
duplicate what is already in libraries—complete encyclopedias, periodical

indexes, and reference works—while others offer information not available elsewhere. Your college library (or one in your community) might have computers that can tap into one of the more than 2,000 databases currently available in the United States. Even if your library has no computers, it might be able to order a computerized search by an outside source on your behalf.

Computers offer these advantages as research tools: (1) They provide the fastest search available. In minutes computers can find and compile information that might take several days of diligent labor in the library to locate. (2) Databases are updated more frequently than reference books; many receive new information daily. In some subjects, printed encyclopedias are out-of-date within two years of publication; their electronic versions are much fresher; the *Academic American Encyclopedia*, for example, is revised twice a year. (3) Databases provide access to more magazines and technical journals than most libraries could possibly afford to subscribe to. For example, *Biosis Previews*—just one out of the 200 databases offered by Dialog Information Services—provides research information about the life sciences from 9,000 medical and scientific journals published in the United States and abroad.

There are, however, a few disadvantages: (1) Making a computer search can be expensive (though not necessarily so; check with your library concerning fees because some libraries charge only a modest amount). (2) You usually get words only—no photos, drawings, or diagrams, which are often an important element in understanding an article. (3) Most databases go back no earlier than the 1970s. For most speeches this is not a problem because you want the most recent information available; but if you need to read articles written before the seventies (for example, if you want to find contemporary articles on hippies of the sixties), databases will offer no help.

Databases provide information in three forms (some databases offer only one of these types; some offer all three):

1. *Citations.* This is a basic bibliographic reference, which usually gives the name of the article, the author(s), the name of the magazine, volume number, issue number, page numbers, and date.

2. *Abstracts (or brief summaries) of an article.* An abstract is designed to give you enough information to decide whether you want to see the complete text of an article. Sometimes, however, the abstract itself gives you as much information as you need. For example, let's say you want to know if Laetrile can cure cancer; you see the abstract of an article in *The New England Journal of Medicine* which examines ten years of research on Laetrile and finds no efficacy in Laetrile. Without reading the entire article, you can say in your speech, "According to a recent article in *The New England Journal of Medicine,* Laetrile has been found to be ineffective in the treatment of cancer."

3. *Complete texts*. A few databases offer complete texts of articles. You usually have three options: (1) You can read the text on the screen, making notes on paper as necessary; (2) you can print out the text on a computer-linked printer; or (3) you can pay the database owner to print out the text for you and mail it to you.

To give you an idea of the incredible wealth of information at your fingertips, here is a sampling of what databases can do:

☐ If you are speaking on arms negotiations between the United States and the Soviet Union, you can get the latest United Press International news reports from The Source or the latest Associated Press dispatches from CompuServe.

☐ If you are interested in the ethical problems raised by genetic engineering, Georgetown University in Washington, D.C., has a database on bioethics issues that you can get free of charge.

☐ If you want to find articles related to financially troubled computer companies, you can type the words *bankrupt* and *computer* on the Dow Jones News/Retrieval database and retrieve articles about bankrupt computer companies from the pages of *The Wall Street Journal, Barron's,* and the *Dow Jones News Service,* dating back as far as June, 1979.

Many college and local libraries are hooked up to the 80 databases offered by BRS (Bibliographic Retrieval Services) of Latham, New York. These databases cover such subjects as mathematics, robotics, pollution, engineering, physics, drug abuse, alcoholism, psychology, religion, sociology, education, and marriage.

How can you find out what is available? Check with librarians at not only your college library but at public and specialized libraries as well. Or find a copy of *Online Database Search Services Directory* (Detroit: Gale Research Company, revised annually). This directory not only describes databases but lists those organizations, such as libraries, that will conduct information searches for the general public.

If you cannot find a library that offers computerized searches, there are other possibilities. If you own a personal computer or if you can borrow time on a friend's computer, you might want to tap the databases directly. All you need is a modem (telephone hookup) and telecommunications software. Some databases can be used free of charge; others charge a fee, ranging from modest to exorbitant. Many database services charge a much smaller fee if you make your search in the evenings or on weekends.

Once you start doing research on a computer, you may become so dazzled by the quickness and thoroughness of the process that you will never want to use any other technique. As the *Whole Earth Software Catalog* puts it, "you may never look at a card catalog again."[1]

# Interviews

While the library is an important source, do not overlook the possibility of conducting interviews with people who are knowledgeable about your subject. These individuals can often give you current information that is not yet available in magazines or books. In the world of computers, for example, change occurs so rapidly that a magazine article published three months ago on a particular kind of software can be hopelessly outdated today.

Who can you find to interview? The obvious place to start is your own college; some faculty members may have expertise in your area of interest. In the larger community beyond the campus you may find experts in many different fields. If you are speaking on snakebites, for example, and there is a nationally recognized herpetologist living in your community, you could obviously learn a lot from an interview. In some cases, you may want to interview fellow students. If you are preparing a speech on communication problems between males and females, for instance, you might want to collect the ideas, experiences, and observations of other students.

If you are lucky, there can sometimes be a wonderful bonus from an interview: you might develop a professional contact or personal friendship that will prove useful to you in later years. Consuela Martinez, an accounting major in one of my classes several years ago, interviewed an official at a local bank to get information for a speech. The official was so impressed with Consuela that when she graduated and returned to the bank to seek a job, he hired her. Another student, Skyler MacPherson, interviewed a well-known poet in his community; after the interview, the poet asked Skyler to come to his house for dinner, and a long-term friendship began, with the poet helping Skyler to get some of his own poems published.

Do not let fear of rejection deter you from asking for an interview. Some students have the idea that the knowledgeable persons they want to interview are so important and so busy, they will certainly have no time for questions from a "lowly" student. This is a mistaken notion. I have sent hundreds of students out for research interviews, and I have found that virtually everyone in the community *loves* to be interviewed. Does this surprise you? Think about yourself for a moment: when a friend asks you for advice (on such things as how to bake a cake or how to solve an algebra problem), don't you enjoy holding forth as an "expert"? The same thing is true of knowledgeable people in your community—they are flattered to be interviewed by a student.

Should an individual be interviewed in person or over the telephone? If you have only two or three short, easily answered questions, you could conduct your interview over the telephone, but if you want detailed answers to many different questions, you are more likely to get good responses if you conduct your interview in person. People tend to speak more freely and in greater detail during face-to-face encounters than they do on the telephone. There is also a greater chance of warmth and trust developing between you. Here are some guidelines for planning and conducting interviews.

## *Preparing for the Interview*

There are a few things you should be sure to do before you interview a person.

### Telephone Interviewee in Advance for an Appointment

Arrange a time that is convenient for the person you want to interview by telephoning beforehand. Do not just drop by and expect the person to agree to an interview on the spot; you may catch the person off-guard or during a hectic time of day. When you call to line up the appointment, explain briefly what you are trying to find out and why you think he or she can help you. Such an explanation gives the person time to get his or her thoughts together before talking to you.

### Conduct Research Before Interview

You need to read up on your subject *before* you go to an interview. Here is why: First of all, you need to know enough about the subject to ask intelligent questions. Suppose you are planning to interview a psychiatrist about schizophrenia. If you read articles and books on the mental disorder beforehand, you will know enough about the subject to ask an important question, such as, "Do researchers feel that they are close to discovering a cure?" In addition to helping you ask intelligent questions, research will also help you avoid asking embarrassing questions like, "How does the split in personality occur?" Such a question would be embarrassing because it would reveal your ignorance of what the term schizophrenia means. (It means a psychotic break with reality, not a Jekyll-and-Hyde split in personality.)

Second, if you find something in your reading that you do not understand, the interviewee might be able to explain it. Suppose that while you are doing your library research on schizophrenia, you come across the term *folie à deux*. You look up the term in a dictionary but cannot make sense out of the formal definition. In your interview with a psychiatrist, you ask for a plain-English explanation of what the term means (it is a psychotic delusion that one person persuades another person to share).

Finally, if you fail to find vital information in your library research, you can often get it from the interviewee. Suppose that you are investigating the effectiveness of automobile air bags in traffic accidents. You want to know, "Will air bags save a motorist's life if he or she is driving at 55 miles per hour and has a head-on collision with a car traveling at the same speed?" Your weekend spent in the library sifting through government studies failed to turn up the answer, but five minutes with a traffic-safety expert may give you what you are after.

## Prepare Questions in Advance

Decide ahead of time exactly what questions you want to ask, and write them down on a piece of paper, putting the most important ones first in case you run out of time.

## Decide How to Record Interview

You can capture the basic information from your interview by taking notes, by using a tape recorder, or by doing both. Let's examine each method in greater detail.

*Writing down key ideas.* Because human memory is highly fallible, you should take notes during *every* interview, even during an interview in which you are using a tape recorder. At first glance it may seem silly to take notes while getting everything down on tape, but I recommend it for these reasons: (1) A mechanical foul-up might cause you to lose your entire tape; having notes would give you a back-up record of the interview. (2) The act of making notes forces you to concentrate on the key ideas of your interviewee, thereby making you more alert in your questioning.

When you are jotting down notes, write key ideas only. If you try to write down every word the person is saying, you will concentrate on transcribing sentences instead of making sense out of what is being said. It is far more important to comprehend the interviewee's ideas than to get his or her exact words on paper.

*Using a tape recorder.* Before you decide whether or not you want to use a tape recorder, you should consider the following advantages and disadvantages. On the positive side: (1) You have a word-for-word record of the entire interview; you do not have to worry about forgetting key points or misquoting your source. (2) Some interviewees, knowing that they are being recorded, may try extra hard to be precise and accurate in giving information.

On the negative side: (1) You have to fuss with the mechanical details of running the machine at the beginning of the interview and when you change tapes; this can cause you to lose eye contact with the person, and also cause you to get distracted from giving full attention to the conversation. (2) Some interviewees may feel intimidated by the tape recorder and fail to speak as freely and as candidly as they might otherwise do. (3) You have to spend a lot of time afterward in analyzing and extracting information from the tape.

If you want to use a recorder, ask the interviewee for permission when you make the appointment. If the person prefers not to be taped, you should of course respect his or her wishes. Under no circumstances should you conceal a recorder and make a tape surreptitiously. It is unethical and in some cases illegal.

If you plan to take notes and make a tape recording simultaneously, you may want to have a friend accompany you to help with the recording. This frees you of all worry about starting and stopping equipment, changing tapes in the middle of the interview, etc.

## Conducting the Interview

Here are some tips on how to conduct the interview.

### Start Interview in a Friendly, Relaxed Manner

Before you begin your questions, you need to establish rapport with the interviewee. You can do so by making a statement of appreciation (for example, "Thanks for letting me come by to talk to you today") and by engaging in small talk on obvious topics (the weather, the beautiful painting on the wall, etc.). Small talk is an important lubricant in conversation, especially at the beginning of a dialogue, so you need not feel that it is a waste of time. You should also repeat the purpose of the interview; the person may have forgotten exactly what you are seeking. While these preliminary remarks are being made, you can set up your tape recorder (if you have previously received permission to use one).

### Get Biographical Information About Interviewee

The person you are interviewing is one of your sources, so you need to be able to tell your audience later why he or she is an authority on your subject. If you have not been able to get background information in advance, the early part of the interview is a good time to get it because it continues the building of rapport. You could say, for example: "Where did you get your doctorate?" Or: "How long have you been working on this problem?"

### Ask Both Prepared and Spontaneous Questions

Earlier we noted that you should decide ahead of time exactly what questions you want to ask. Make these questions as specific as possible. It would be ludicrous to walk into the office of an expert on robots and say, "Tell me what you know about robots." Such a question would probably draw a laugh and a comment like, "Have you got two months to listen?" A better, more specific question would be something like this: "Will robots someday replace all automobile assembly-line workers?"

There are two types of questions that can be prepared in advance:

1. *Closed* questions require only "yes" or "no" responses or short, factual answers. Examples: "Do Democrats outnumber Republicans in this state?" "What percentage of registered voters actually voted in the last

presidential election?" Closed questions are effective in getting specific data.

2. *Open* questions give the interviewee a wide latitude for responding. For example, "How do you feel about the nuclear arms race?" The advantage of such a broad question is that the interviewee can choose the points he or she wishes to emphasize—points that it may not have occurred to you to ask about. The disadvantage is that sometimes an interviewee can wander off the subject into irrelevant side issues.

There are two other types of questions that cannot be prepared in advance but may need to be asked spontaneously during the interview:

1. *Clarifying* questions are used when you are confused about what the person means. Do not write down a murky response and say to yourself, "I'll study this in my notes later and try to figure it out." If you cannot make sense out of it during the interview, there is not much chance you will succeed later. Ask a question like this: "Could you explain that a little more?" Or: "Correct me if I'm wrong, but I understand you to say that . . . ."

2. *Follow-up* questions are designed to encourage the interviewee to elaborate on what he or she has been saying—to continue a story or to add to a comment. Here are some examples: "What happened next?" "Were you upset about what happened?" "Could you give me some examples of what you're talking about?"

Try to make the interview more like relaxed conversation than interrogation. Though you have a list of prepared questions, don't slavishly follow it, going from #1 to #2 to #3, and so on. Be natural and spontaneous; follow the flow of the conversation. The interviewee may talk about #1, then skip to #7. That's fine. You can simply check off questions as they are answered. Toward the end of the interview, ask those questions that still have not been answered. Also, the person may bring up surprising aspects of your topic that you have not thought about; this should inspire you to ask spontaneous follow-up questions.

When the interviewee mentions things that are not on your check list, write them down, even if they seem inconsequential at the time, because you may find a use for them later. This advice would not apply if the person goes off on a tangent, telling you things that are totally unrelated to the subject. In such a case, you should steer the conversation back toward the pertinent topic.

## Ask Interviewee About Other Sources and Visual Aids

Interviewees may know of library resources that you are unaware of. They may have a pamphlet or a book that they are willing to lend you.

In some cases, they may even lend you a map or chart or some other kind of visual aid that you can use in your speech.

### Near the End, Ask If You Have Omitted Any Questions

When you have gone through all the prepared questions, ask the interviewee if he or she can think of any items that you have failed to ask about. You may find that you have inadvertently overlooked some important matters.

### End Interview on Time

Respect the amount of time that was granted when you set up your appointment; if you were allotted 20 minutes, stay no more than 20 minutes—unless of course the interviewee invites you to stay longer. If you still have questions when the time is up, you can ask for a second interview (perhaps a few extra questions can even be handled over the telephone).

## *Following up on the Interview*

After you leave the interview, you have two important tasks:

**Promptly expand your notes.** Immediately after the interview, go through your notes and expand upon them (by turning words and phrases into complete sentences) while the conversation is fresh in your mind. If you wait two weeks to go over the notes, they will be stale and you might puzzle over your scribbling or you might forget what a particular phrase means.

**Evaluate your information.** After you have expanded the notes, evaluate them to see if you got exactly what you were looking for. If you are confused on any points, or if you find that you need more information on a particular item, telephone the interviewee and ask for help. This should not be a source of embarrassment for you—it shows that you care enough about the subject and the interviewee to get the information exactly right.

# Other Resources

You can often get literature and visual aids from companies and agencies in your community. One student, Rhonda Murchison, visited an office of the American Red Cross and told them she wanted to give a talk on CPR (cardiopulmonary resuscitation); they lent her a portable dummy to use in her demonstration speech. Sometimes you can even get "freebies" from local sources. Student speaker Jerry Lipe was preparing a speech on stress; he went to a local mental-health agency and got brochures and 30 stress detectors—small color-coded dots that can be placed on the skin to determine how much stress a person is under at that moment. Jerry had enough tabs to give one to each listener at the end of his speech.

A vast amount of literature on a wide variety of subjects can be ordered at no charge (or for a very small fee) from thousands of corporations and associations. To get addresses of national groups, go to the library and consult reference books such as *The Encyclopedia of Associations* and *The Directory of Corporations*. Another good source is the United States government, which each year puts out 25,000 new publications on subjects ranging from rabid animals to gardening to solar heating. Your librarian can help you locate or order government documents.

An important note of caution: do not rely too heavily on requested material because they may not arrive in time for your speech. I remember one student telling me that she wrote for some interesting material, but they arrived *three months* after she gave her speech. Also, do not overestimate the value of material that you have not yet seen. One student felt certain that some pamphlets he ordered would give him all the information he needed for his speech; they arrived one day before his speech but turned out to be worthless. He had to race to the library to do some frantic research.

# Finding the Right Materials Efficiently

Many students fail to come up with good material because they spend most of their time in unproductive research. They either fail to find the right kinds of information or they get more material than they have time to process. Here are steps leading to productive research.

## *Start Your Research Far in Advance*

Running out of time is the most common reason students give for not doing adequate research. If you start your research well ahead of the speech date and budget your time sensibly, you should be able to do a thorough job. Keep in mind that most research takes longer than you anticipate. Leave yourself more time than you think necessary.

The worst thing about waiting until the last minute to do research is that most people do not think well under pressure. The anxiety engendered by the approaching deadline can lock up the gears of your brain, causing you to think less efficiently than you normally would.

## *Turn Your Specific Purpose Statement into a Research Question*

Your specific purpose should be decided before you start your research. Imagine that you had written the following specific purpose statement:

"To tell my audience how people can determine if they have a serious drinking problem." For research purposes, you can turn this into a question, "How can people determine if they have a serious drinking problem?" Why use a question? Because a question brings your research efforts into sharper focus than a statement does. If you write the research question at the top of the first page of your notebook or on your first index card—and keep it in front of you at each step of your research—it will be a constant reminder of precisely what you are searching for. It will prevent you from wandering off into areas that are not related. Let's say you pick up an interesting book on alcoholism. It contains fascinating charts on the physiological effects of alcohol and fact-filled chapters on such things as cirrhosis of the liver and delirium tremens. But you notice that nothing in the book answers your specific question. So you put it back. No sense wasting your time on a book that will not contribute to your speech. (After you prepare and deliver your speech, you can always go back and read this book at your leisure.)

## Establish a Research Strategy

Some people drift into the library, not knowing exactly what they are looking for, and then drift from place to place inside the library, hoping to stumble upon a helpful book or magazine. Rather than drifting, you should spend a few minutes devising a research strategy; here are two ways to achieve this.

1. *Talk to your librarians.* Explain your research question and get their advice. In your speech on alcohol, suppose that the librarian suggests that you start off by looking in the card catalog for some of the most current books on alcohol abuse with annotated bibliographies. These bibliographies might lead you immediately to the best materials. If this does not give you all that you need, the librarian might advise you to look in *The Magazine Index* because popular magazines often run check lists such as "How to Tell if You Have a Drinking Problem."

2. *Talk to an informed person on campus or in the community.* Suppose that you look in the Yellow Pages of the telephone directory and call the number of an alcohol abuse treatment center. The woman you talk to suggests that you come by and pick up some pamphlets on the subject. She also gives you the phone number of a member of Alcoholics Anonymous who has given talks in the community on warning signals of alcoholism.

By this point you should be able to devise a firm research strategy involving a series of tasks. Assign dates for completion of each task, leaving yourself plenty of time in case you run into a delay or get sick or have some unforeseen crisis.

Nov. 3   Call A.A. member to set up interview.

Nov. 4   Go to alcohol abuse treatment center and get pamphlets.

Nov. 5   Card catalog—alcohol abuse—look for books with annotated bibliographies.

Nov. 6   Look up the books and articles obtained from the above.

Nov. 7   If still need information, see *The Magazine Index.*

Nov. 9   Interview A.A. member

Post the schedule in a visible place in your room, or carry it around with you. Try to abide by it. With such a research strategy, you should be able to save time and avoid "drifting."

## Evaluate All Sources

Suppose that you find 12 books and 19 magazine articles for your speech on alcohol abuse. Should you read through all the books and articles? No, of course not. That would take too long. What you need to do now is sift through your potential sources, choosing those that will help you and discarding those that are irrelevant or unimportant. To assist you in your task, here are some questions to ask yourself.

*Is the source current?* In some fields, especially in the physical and social sciences, you need the most up-to-date material on a subject. If you were doing research on robotics, for example, a book published last year would be far more valuable than one published ten years ago because there have been hundreds of new developments in this field since the older book was published. Even in history and biography, more recent sources would generally be preferred because they might include previously undiscovered information; for example, a history of American Indians published this year might report new evidence concerning how humans first migrated to the Western Hemisphere.

*Is the source credible?* You should decide whether your particular audience will consider a source believable. If you are doing research on UFOs and you come across an article in one of the sensational tabloids (the kind sold at grocery-store checkout counters) with this headline: FLYING SAUCER ABDUCTS FARMER AND COW, you would be wise to ignore the article because most audiences would consider such a source to be laughably unreliable. If, on the other hand, you read an article in a prestigious journal such as *Aviation Week and Space Technology* on the possibility of flying saucers, your audience would most likely respect the source and therefore give serious consideration to the source's ideas.

*Is the source comprehensive?* If a magazine index shows that a particular article is only one page long, you may want to skip it and look for a longer article. Longer articles usually contain more information, and you can save yourself time by concentrating on them.

*Is the source understandable?* If you are researching volcanoes and you come across an article on the subject in *Journal of Earth Sciences,* you might find (unless you are a geology major) that parts of the article are too complicated for you to understand. You would be wasting your time if you tried to struggle with it. If, on the other hand, you find an article on volcanoes in *National Geographic,* you can be sure that it is written in language that is understandable to the nonspecialist.

*Can the source lead to other sources?* When you use the card catalog and you find a card for a promising book, look on the card to see if the book includes a bibliography (see Figure 6.1). A bibliography can save you an enormous amount of time if it cites the most important articles and books on your topic. Suppose you are interested in how people can interpret dreams. You find a book on the subject, and in the back is a long bibliography, giving you the names of dozens of magazine articles. You choose five of the most promising articles, look them up in the library, and subsequently find all the information you need for your speech. A bibliography can be especially helpful if it is annotated; that is, if the author gives a brief description of what is contained in each book or article cited. By the way, do not overlook your textbooks; they often have extensive bibliographies in the back.

# Taking Notes

As you hunt for materials in the library, you need to systematically record the key points that you find. Here are the steps you should follow.

## *Prepare Bibliography Cards*

As you go through catalogs and indexes, jot down the names of books and articles that sound promising. Use $3 \times 5$ index cards (because they are easy to shuffle and place in alphabetical order). These cards help you locate materials, and come in handy later when you put together the bibliography for your speech. In addition, if you need to consult a book or article again for clarification or amplification of facts, the data on your card should help you find it quickly. Figure 6.4 shows two sample bibliography cards.

Fill out a bibliography card for every book or article which you think might be helpful. You may end up with more sources than you have time to consult, but it is better to have too many sources than not enough. Leave space on each card for personal comments (see Figure 6.4), which can help you evaluate which sources are most likely to yield good information.

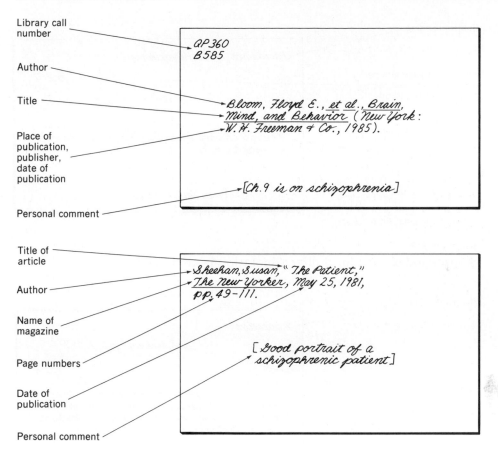

Library call
number

Author

Title

Place of
publication,
publisher,
date of
publication

Personal comment

Title of
article

Author

Name of
magazine

Page numbers

Date of
publication

Personal comment

QP 360
B 585

Bloom, Floyd E., et al., Brain,
Mind, and Behavior (New York:
W. H. Freeman & Co., 1985).

[Ch. 9 is on schizophrenia]

Sheehan, Susan, "The Patient,"
The New Yorker, May 25, 1981,
pp. 49–111.

[Good portrait of a
schizophrenic patient]

**FIGURE 6.4**
Sample bibliography cards for a book and a magazine article.

## *Make Note Cards*

As you read through books and articles, make notes of key ideas on large
cards (4×6 or 5×7). Using large cards will help you distinguish them
from the smaller (3×5) bibliography cards and also give you ample room
for note taking.

Put a subject heading on the top of each card, as shown in Figures 6.5
and 6.6 on page 128. These headings will be valuable when you finish
making your notes because you can group the cards into related clumps.
Identify each card with the author's name. There is no need to write down
full bibliographical information because those details are already on your
bibliography cards.

In making notes, follow these steps:

Subject heading

Author and page number
(Full details are available
on bibliography card)

Direct quotation

Personal comment (in brackets)

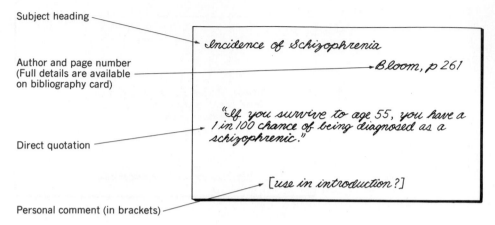

**FIGURE 6.5**
Sample index card for a direct quotation from a book.

Subject heading

Author and page number

Summary of author's ideas

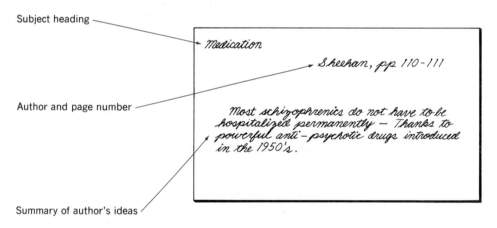

**FIGURE 6.6**
Sample index card for a summary from a magazine.

1. Quickly read through the material to see if there is anything worth noting.

2. If there is, reread the material, this time very carefully.

3. Try to summarize the key points in a few simple sentences. Avoid the temptation to copy down huge chunks of undigested information. Your task is to interpret, evaluate, and boil down ideas, not to convey a text verbatim.

4. While striving for brevity, you must make sure that summarized information is in a coherent form. If you jot down a phrase like "schizo-

phrenic—Jesus Christ or Napoleon," and then wait five days before organizing your notes, you may forget the meaning of that note. Write out a coherent sentence such as: "Schizophrenics who have delusions often think they are Jesus Christ or Napoleon."

5. Occasionally, you will find an arresting phrase or a short, vivid sentence which you will want to convey to your listeners in the form of a direct quotation. Be sure to put quotation marks around such passages in your note cards. Do not use too many direct quotations in your notes, however, because you may fall into the trap discussed above—copying down large blocks of text without proper evaluation and condensation.

6. Take more notes than you probably will need. It is better to have too much raw material than not enough.

7. Personal comments can be added to the bottom of note cards to provide ideas on how to use the note or how to connect it to other notes (see Figure 6.5). You can also express a personal reaction, such as "This sounds implausible—check other sources." Use square brackets or some other device to distinguish between your own comments and the text that you are summarizing.

8. Use a separate card for each idea. This will make it easy to sort your cards by subject headings.

# Giving Credit

If you have gathered information from sources, you should use oral footnotes in your speech; for example, "According to the **CBS Evening News** of March 15th of this year . . ." or "In the words of Thomas Jefferson . . . ." An oral footnote is the equivalent of a footnote in a written document and its purpose is the same: to give credit for information or ideas that did not originate with you. Oral footnotes also give credibility to your remarks. You are saying, in effect, "I didn't pull this out of thin air; I got this information from someone who is an authority on the subject."

If you got information from an interview, you could say something like this: "According to Elizabeth Smith, director of advertising for our city's biggest department store. . . ."

For material from books or magazines, you could say, "In an article in the latest issue of *Scientific American*, Dr. Paul Rhodes says that . . ." or: "The graph on this slide is based on data I found in the current edition of the *World Almanac*."

When you are quoting verbatim, use "oral" quotation marks such as the following: "To quote Abraham Lincoln . . ." or "In the words of Plato . . . ." Expressions like these are a little smoother than "Quote" at the beginning of a statement and "Unquote" at the end. A slight pause at the end of the quotation should be an adequate signal that you have finished quoting.

## Summary

Your quest for speech material should begin with yourself. What personal experiences or observations can you draw upon? After you have looked inward, you can look outward—at the books, magazines, and audiovisual holdings of college and local libraries. Some of these libraries may have computer databases that can be tapped for quick retrieval of a vast amount of information.

Interviewing knowledgeable people on your campus or in your community can yield valuable, up-to-date information in many fields. To prepare for an interview, do extensive research on the topic and then draw up a list of questions to be asked. Conduct the interview in a relaxed, conversational manner.

Whatever sources you draw from, start your research far in advance, devise a research strategy, and then carry out that strategy in a systematic way. Make all your notes on cards, with a subject heading at the top, and with only one idea per card. These cards can later be shuffled and arranged systematically as an aid to the writing of your outline.

## Review Questions

1. What is interlibrary loan and how can it help you?
2. What are three main advantages of using computer databases?
3. Why should you not feel hesitant about asking a local expert for an interview?
4. Why should most of your research be done *before* you call someone for an interview?
5. What are the advantages and disadvantages of using a tape recorder in an interview?
6. What steps should you take after an interview is completed?
7. In your research, why should you take more notes than you probably will need?

# TIPS *for your career*

## Tip 6: Develop a Lifetime Filing System for Important Ideas

Marie Judson, a computer programmer for a large manufacturing company, makes notes at every speech, training session, and seminar she attends and then files the notes under appropriate headings in her filing cabinet. She also clips and files articles from professional journals and newsletters.

Whenever Marie is required to write a memorandum or prepare a talk, her files provide a gold mine of good resource material. When her superiors want information about the latest developments in computers, they consult Marie first because of her extensive files. These superiors have come to regard Marie as an indispensable, "got-it-together" person who tries to keep up with developments in her field.

Like Marie, you should develop personal files on topics that are relevant to your career. Such files will obviously come in handy for preparing speeches and for writing memos and reports. Also, as in Marie's case, they can be useful in establishing yourself as an indispensable, up-to-date employee.

Even if you are not yet employed in your chosen field, you should still keep files so that when you do enter the field, you will have a wealth of professional information at your fingertips.

What should you file? In addition to clipping or photocopying articles, I suggest that you keep a pack of index cards or a legal pad handy so that you can jot down notes of important ideas that you encounter. These ideas may come from your own thoughts or they may come from books, TV programs, speeches, lectures, workshops, and interviews. Since many of your instructors are experts in their fields, you may want to file lecture notes from some of your college classes. Do not worry that you might accumulate too many notes. You can always go through your files later and discard deadwood.

How should you file information? Devise whatever method works best for you. A popular arrangement is to place items in manila file folders that are labeled by topic. You might want to start with some broad categories and then later create subcategories when a folder starts overflowing. For articles that you clip or photocopy, be sure to write down the name of the publication and the date. For notes of interviews or speeches, write down the speaker, date, place, and occasion. You can start off by putting your file folders in a cardboard box and later storing them in a filing cabinet.

## Chapter 7

# Supporting Your Ideas

In a classroom speech, a student, whom I'll call Sam, made an interesting point. "Violence on television," he contended, "causes some viewers to commit violent acts."

The reaction of the audience was undoubtedly skeptical. Some of the listeners were probably saying to themselves, "I don't believe it—prove it" or "Says who?" or "How do you know that?"

After making his assertion, Sam made these comments: "When people see violence night after night, they are going to become violent themselves. It's just common sense: seeing violence encourages people to act violently. How can you let impressionable children and teen-agers watch murder, robbery, and brutality every night and then expect them not to imitate what they see?"

Do you think Sam's remarks convinced the audience that TV violence causes some viewers to become violent? Probably not. His remarks did nothing to bolster his contention. He offered no proof, no illustration, no support. All he did was repeat his original point.

Now imagine how the audience might have reacted if Sam had substantiated his assertion with these items:

☐ Following the telecast of the film *The Deer Hunter*, which showed a character playing a game of Russian roulette with a revolver, 29 Americans killed themselves while "playing" Russian roulette, according to Dr. Jon M. Shepard, professor of sociology at the University of Kentucky.[1]

☐ A TV show depicted an alcoholic "bum" being doused with gasoline and set on fire; the next day three "winos" in three different American cities were murdered in similar fashion by youths who had seen the show, according to The Associated Press.[2]

☐ The National Institute of Mental Health evaluated 2,500 studies on TV violence conducted over a 10-year period and concluded that "violence on television does lead to aggressive behavior."[3]

These items, which are samples of *support materials*, help back up the contention that TV violence causes some viewers to commit violent acts. The first two provide vivid examples, while the last item brings in testimony from a prestigious source. If Sam had used these support materials, his audience would have seen that his argument had merit.

Examples and testimony are just two of the kinds of support materials that we will discuss in this chapter. The others are definitions, descriptions, narratives, comparisons, contrasts, and statistics.

# Reasons for Using Support Materials

Support materials enable you to move from general and abstract concepts, which are often hard for audiences to understand and remember, to specific and concrete details, which are easily grasped. Support materials add spice and flavor to a speech, but they are more than just seasonings; they are basic nourishment that is absolutely essential to the success of a speech. Below are five reasons why support materials are so important.

1. *Support materials develop and illustrate ideas.* In a classroom speech on sharks, Austin Fitzgerald pointed out that unlike most creatures of the sea, sharks behave unpredictably. To develop and illustrate his point, he said:

> In his book on sharks, Jacques-Yves Cousteau, the famous oceanographer, says that he has seen sharks flee from an almost naked, completely unarmed diver, but soon afterwards hurl themselves against a steel diving cage and bite furiously at the bars. Sometimes a diver can scare off a shark by waving his flippers at it, while at other times sharks are so determined to attack that they are not deterred by the sight of five divers with spears. The terrifying thing, Cousteau says, is that sharks never give clues as to what kind of behavior they will exhibit.

Without these examples, Austin's contention that sharks behave unpredictably would have been weak. With the examples, the listeners got a clear picture of sharks' volatile nature. Notice, too, that Austin enhanced the credibility of his remarks by attributing his information to a well-known authority.

2. *Support materials can clarify ideas.* Helping the listener make sense out of your ideas is one of the main reasons for using support material. Years ago I was taught a valuable fact about statistics by a professor who used a good example to make his point. He was trying to show the class why professional pollsters interviewed only 1,000 registered voters in all of America in order to predict a Presidential election. Why not interview 10,000? Or 100,000? Would not a larger sample produce a more accurate prediction? No, said the professor, a small sample is just as accurate as a large one. To make his idea clear and understandable, he gave us a hypothetical example: Imagine that you place 100,000 coins in a rotating drum. Of that number, 70,000 are gold coins and the remaining 30,000 are silver coins. In another rotating drum you place 1,000 coins, using the same proportion: 700 gold coins and 300 silver coins. You spin both drums, thoroughly mixing up the coins, and then you get a blindfolded man to reach in and randomly select 100 coins from each drum. The man will pull out 70 gold coins and 30 silver coins, or come very close to these numbers, every time he tries, even though one drum has a hundred times more coins than the other. This illustration, a type of support material, makes clear why a small sample in a public opinion poll can be as accurate as a large one.

3. *Support materials can make a speech more interesting.* In a classroom speech on how explorers from earth would experience life on Mars, Diane Weber said,

> Most of the time Mars is much colder than the coldest regions of earth, with summer temperatures dipping down as low as 126 degrees below zero and winter temperatures twice that cold. Sometimes, however, at the equator of Mars, the temperature does warm up to an earthly level of comfort. For a few minutes, the temperature can climb to a high of 68 degrees—like a pleasant October afternoon in New England.

Instead of merely reciting statistics, which would have been boring, Diane made her subject interesting by comparing and contrasting the climate of the two planets, using images (such as the October afternoon in New England) that her listeners could appreciate.

4. *Support materials help listeners remember key ideas.* I once heard Dr. Eldon Ekwall of the University of Texas at El Paso give a lecture on psychological tests. At one point he began discussing two important concepts: *reliability* (the consistency of test scores) and *validity* (whether a test measures what it is supposed to measure). These important terms are easily confused by many people, but Dr. Ekwall gave a hypothetical example that helped me remember the difference. He asked us to imagine that we devise an intelligence test based on the length of our thumb. We measure our thumb today and find that it is three inches long. We measure it again next year and it is still three inches. Our thumb-length intelligence test is *reliable* because every time we measure our thumb we get the same results. But is it *valid*? No, because the length of our thumb has nothing to do with our intelligence.

To this day, whenever I begin to get reliability and validity confused, I stop and think back to Dr. Ekwall's remarks. His example did more than just help me understand what he was saying; it also helped me remember the key idea.

5. *Support materials help prove an assertion.* When you want to prove a point, you must have evidence. If, for example, you wanted to prove that more counterfeiters are being caught today than ever before, you could quote a Secret Service official who states that the number of counterfeiting convictions this year is 10 times the number of convictions in any previous year. Such a statistic from a reliable source is solid proof of your statement.

But a note of caution: not all support materials constitute proof. Suppose that a speaker argues that flying saucers from alien planets visit the earth regularly, and to prove his claim, he cites 15 eyewitness accounts from different parts of the country. Is this proof? No. While it may be true that flying saucers do indeed visit the earth, the 15 eyewitness accounts do not constitute proof. Some of the people could have seen explainable phenomena, such as weather balloons or swamp-gas apparitions. Some of the people could have experienced hallucinations caused by drugs or psychosis.

# Types of Support Materials

In this chapter we will look at *verbal* support materials, reserving *visual* supports for the next chapter. The cardinal rule in using verbal supports is that they must be relevant; they must develop, explain, illustrate, or reinforce your message. They cannot be thrown in simply to enliven a speech.

Let's now examine the seven main categories of verbal supports.

## *Definitions*

One of the biggest obstacles to successful communication is the assumption that your listeners define words and phrases the same way you do. If you are speaking on gun control, it is not enough to say, "I'm in favor of gun control." Exactly what does gun control mean? To some members of your audience, it may mean that citizens must surrender all of their firearms. To some, it may mean that citizens must give up only their handguns. To others, it may mean that citizens can keep their guns if they register them with the authorities. If you say that you are in favor of gun control without giving your definition of the term, some listeners might misunderstand your position and angrily reject everything that you say on the subject. So define your terms at the outset; for example: "When I talk about gun control, I'm not talking about confiscation of all guns; I'm talking about citizens registering the serial numbers of their guns with the authorities." Now you and your audience have a common basis for an evaluation of your views.

You should also define any jargon or specialized words that some listeners might not know. Do not assume, for example, that everyone knows military lingo such as KP and AWOL. Even though there have been dozens of movies and TV shows about military life, some people might not know that KP means *kitchen police* and AWOL means *absent without leave*. If you are a computer buff, you must be careful to define concepts like RAM (random-access memory) and ROM (read-only memory) that are well known to you but not to the general public.

Avoid dictionary definitions, if possible. They tend to be tedious and hard to grasp. Instead, use informal definitions that can be easily understood by the audience. For example, *chutzpah,* a slang word that the English language has borrowed from Yiddish, is defined by the *Random*

*House College Dictionary* as "unmitigated effrontery or impudence." I once heard a speaker give a humorous, informal definition of the word: "Chutzpah is the kind of audacity and gall that a youngster would show if he killed both of his parents and then demanded that the court be lenient to him because he was an orphan." This informal definition drives home the point that chutzpah is more than ordinary gall; it is the *ultimate* form of gall. Such a definition is very effective because it not only helps the listeners understand the meaning of the word; it also helps them remember it.

## Description

One good way to support your speech is to use descriptions—verbal pictures that are created by using lots of details about specific, concrete objects or people. One of my students, Jacqueline Wilson, lived with her husband and child on a homestead in a remote rural area. To show the joys of using a woodburner as a means of heating a home, she painted the following word portrait:

> The woodburner in my kitchen crackles constantly from October until March, warming our home, our hands, and our hearts. The heat that radiates from it is constant, efficient, and—best of all—free. If you wanted to, you could make it spit out the heat so intensely you'd have to open the front door in February to keep from roasting. But heat isn't all the stove's good for. It cooks great pinto beans and chili on the top, and inside it bakes the best potatoes you'll ever eat. It can get the wettest laundry dry in nothing flat, too. And the smell—oh, the smell is what I love, like the leaves my daddy used to burn on a crisp fall day when I was a child. Every time I open the door to load the box, I get a blast from the past. The stove has also become a family gathering place. Especially in the mornings, when I've just kicked her up, there will be my little boy and my husband dressing for school and work, and warming themselves way up close to it. It warms more than just my body; it warms my soul. There is no better way to heat a home than with a good woodburning stove.

Notice that Jacqueline used specific details to paint her word picture. Details are the brush strokes that provide richness, color, and vividness.

## Examples

Examples are instances or facts that illustrate a statement or back up a generalization. In a classroom speech on counterfeiting, Bob Lanelli made the following point:

> Sophisticated counterfeiters are careful not to pass bills that are crisp and new-looking.

**Good speakers provide support materials such as narratives, quotations, and statistics to develop, illustrate, and clarify their ideas.** *(Random House Photo by Mary Schoenthaler, courtesy of Pace University)*

If Bob had said no more on the subject, he would have forced his listeners to guess for themselves just how counterfeiters go about aging their bogus money. Fortunately for the audience, Bob gave examples:

> To get their phony money to look old, counterfeiters might put the bills in a washing machine with a combination of water and coffee. Or they might run them through a homemade device that crinkles them up and rubs in dirt at the same time. Or they might crumple each bill by hand and tear off a corner.

Examples can be longer and more detailed than the preceding ones. In a classroom speech, Judy Korytowski made an unusual assertion which at first seemed absurd: on many occasions if you offer an item to people at no cost whatsoever, they will look down on it and consider it worthless, but if you put a price tag on the very same item, people will respect it and consider it valuable. If Judy had stopped at this point, her audience probably would have been skeptical. After all, her assertion sounded far-fetched. People are not so naïve as to scorn something just because it is free, are they? But Judy did not stop there; she quickly gave a detailed example which demonstrated that her observation had merit:

> Did you know that veterinarians in this city no longer give puppies away? Instead they *sell* them. They charge five dollars per puppy. Why? Not because they're money-hungry but because when they used to give puppies away, people wouldn't take proper care of them. Now, with the five-dollar charge, people take good care of the dogs, making sure they get rabies shots and a collar, making sure they're clean and well nourished. If a puppy is free, it must be a worthless mutt; if it costs five dollars, it's obviously a deserving pet.

In case this example was not enough to convince the audience, Judy gave another example:

> A caretaker at [a nearby] zoo told me that a few years ago, when admission was free, they had a lot of trouble—vandalism, littering, and mistreatment of animals. Then they heard about zoos in other cities solving their problems by charging a small fee. So they tried it here; they started charging fifty cents to get in. Now, the caretaker tells me, they have very little trouble. It's not that the fee keeps the riff-raff away. The same number of people come—and they look the same as patrons in previous years. It's just that paying a fee makes people think that the zoo is a place that deserves respect and good treatment.

Judy proceeded in this way, piling example on top of example. By the end of her speech she had convinced even the most skeptical of her listeners that in many circumstances people do indeed value an item more highly if it has a price tag on it than if it is free.

Judy used more than one example to make her point. How many should you use in your speech? In some cases, one illuminating, well-developed example is sufficient to develop an idea. In other cases, you may need a series of examples. Judy needed several examples because her assertion ran contrary to what the audience probably believed. She needed lots of reinforcement to make her case. To decide how many examples to use in your speech, you should analyze your listeners. Put yourself in their shoes, and ask, "If I were those people sitting out there, would I be convinced on the basis of just one example?"

## Narratives

Narratives, which are stories that explain or illustrate your message, are audience favorites, lingering in the mind long after a speech has ended. People *love* stories, and even a sleepy or distracted member of the audience finds it hard to resist listening. As with all support materials, narratives must be relevant to your message. Never tell a story, even though it is a spellbinding tale, if it fails to develop, explain, illustrate, or reinforce your key ideas.

Sharon Eklund, a student nurse, gave a speech in which she tried to persuade her listeners to stop driving a car whenever they became sleepy. She used a narrative to underscore her message:

> Have you ever been so sleepy, you could hardly keep your eyes open? That's the way I felt one morning two years ago as I was driving home from work. I had worked the graveyard shift at the hospital and that's always tiring, but this time was worse than usual because I had slept only three hours out of the last 48. I was really dragging. Even though it was a nice spring morning, there was a nip in the air so when my eyelids became thick, I rolled the window down to get some cool air on my face. This helped for a few minutes but my lids started getting heavy again, so I turned the radio on. Then I got to thinking: Why don't you try singing? If you have ever heard me sing, you'll know why I thought my singing would wake me up. Well, by the time the road had wound its way around beside the river, I had resorted to threats and was even slapping myself in the face. I told myself, "Now listen, dummy. You know you can't swim. If you fall asleep, you'll drown when this car hits the river."
>
> I made it past the river, however. I turned onto a back road and was almost home. My driveway was just beyond the next curve. Curve? What curve? I don't remember the curve for two good reasons: number one, I fell asleep, which meant that number two, I didn't make the curve. I woke up as my car smashed through several mailboxes, went over an embankment, jumped a ditch, and landed in an open field. I was shaken but unharmed.
>
> Thank God it was Saturday. If it had been a weekday, there would have been children waiting for a school bus at that very spot. . . . They would have been *my* children.

After telling this fascinating story, Sharon pleaded with her audience to act decisively (stop for coffee, pull over for a nap, etc.) if they ever became sleepy at the wheel. I doubt if anyone in the audience remained unmoved or unpersuaded by her argument.

Notice that Sharon's narrative was filled with details, giving you a sense of what it was like to fight desperately to stay awake. Details give richness and color to narratives. They paint a picture that the listeners can see.

While Sharon's story was factual, there are occasions when you may want to use a narrative that is *hypothetical*, that is, about an imaginary situation. Here is an example from a classroom speech by Coretta Johnson:

> You are riding along the highway when you see a two-car collision fifty yards in front of you. You pull over and park, and then run to offer help. You

realize that you're the first to arrive at the scene of the accident, and you hear a person inside one of the cars screaming for help. What should you do?

By means of this hypothetical story, Coretta made her point—that all citizens need to know what to do if they arrive first at the scene of an accident. By putting her listeners squarely in the middle of her narrative, Coretta increased the audience's curiosity and involvement. She proceeded to give the steps that should be taken: Do not move the victims unless there is an imminent danger of the car exploding, keep them calm and comfortable, administer first aid if they are bleeding or choking, and call an ambulance.

## Comparison and Contrast

Sometimes the best way to explain anything new or strange is to make a *comparison*, that is, show how it resembles something else. Here is a beautiful comparison of two species—ants and human beings—by Dr. Lewis Thomas:

> Ants are so much like human beings as to be an embarrassment. They farm fungi, raise aphids as livestock, launch armies into wars, use chemical sprays to alarm and confuse enemies, capture slaves. The families of weaver ants engage in child labor, holding their larvae like shuttles to spin out the thread that sews the leaves together for their fungus gardens. They exchange information ceaselessly. They do everything but watch television.[4]

By comparing ant behavior to human behavior with which we are all familiar, Thomas achieves his goal of demonstrating the amazing intelligence of ants.

While a comparison shows how things are similar, a *contrast* shows how they are different. Tony Rivas, a criminal-justice major, made an interesting contrast between how people view rich lawbreakers and how they view poor ones:

> One Saturday, while I was at work as a security guard for a department store, we managed to catch several people who were trying to steal merchandise from the store. One of the shoplifters was caught stealing some cologne. He was about 20 years old, not very well dressed, and definitely could have used a good bath. Employees who saw us take him to the security office later asked what that "crook" had stolen. They used words like "scum" and "low-life thief" in talking about him.
>
> Later that day, we had the opportunity to catch someone from the other side of the tracks. This woman was well-dressed, had plenty of money, and

had no excuse to be stealing from anyone. Once again the same employees saw us take her to the security office. What was their attitude toward her? "Did she really steal anything?" they asked. "She looks like too nice a lady to steal—she must be a kleptomaniac."

By means of this contrast, Tony was able to clearly demonstrate society's starkly different ways of viewing lawbreakers: poor thieves are "scum"; rich thieves merely suffer from a psychological illness.

Sometimes it is helpful to use both comparison and contrast. For example, comparing and contrasting Japanese and American cars could help the listener understand more fully the features of each.

## Testimony

Suppose for a moment that one of your fellow students gives a speech on America's jury system, and she tells you that the method of selecting and using jurors in most communities is inefficient, overly expensive, and demoralizing to the jurors. Would you believe her? Probably not, if all she gave was her personal opinion—after all, she is not a lawyer or a judge. But what if she quoted the Chief Justice of the United States Supreme Court saying the exact same thing? Now would you believe her? You probably would, because the Chief Justice is one of the nation's experts on what happens in our courts.

When you use what knowledgeable people have to say on your subject, you are using *testimony* to back up your assertions. The main advantage of using testimony is that it gives you instant credibility; quoting an expert is a way of saying, "I'm not the only one who has this idea; it has the backing of a leading authority on the subject."

There are three ways of using testimony:

1. *Quote verbatim.* Sometimes it is effective to quote a source word-for-word. For example, student speaker George Hassoun made the following point in a speech on the value of aerobic exercise:

> Aerobic exercise is the best preventive medicine you can find, according to Bob Anderson, sports physiologist and author of a national best-seller on exercise. He says: "If you don't find time for exercise, you'd better find time to be sick."

Quoting the expert verbatim was very effective because Anderson's statement was phrased in a colorful, yet authoritative tone that would have been weakened if it had been paraphrased.

2. *Summarize.* When a statement is lengthy, quoting it verbatim can bore the audience, so summarize any quotation that is more than one or

two sentences. In another part of George Hassoun's speech, he took a long quotation and boiled it down into one brief sentence:

> Anderson says that aerobic exercise decreases the risk of heart attack, helps control weight, relieves stress-induced tension, and alleviates anxiety and depression.

3. *Paraphrase.* If a quotation has archaic or technical language or is laced with jargon, you should paraphrase it. If, for example, you are speaking on computers and you want to quote an expert who says, "Don't buy a software package that doesn't have help menus," you can paraphrase this jargon into plain English by saying, "Don't buy a program for your computer unless it has lists of options on the screen to keep you from getting lost or confused."

Here are some guidelines for using testimony:

1. *Make sure quotations are accurate.* If you are not careful with a quotation, you can unwittingly change its meaning. For example, Ralph Waldo Emerson is often quoted as saying, "Consistency is the hobgoblin of little minds." That is an unfortunate misquotation. What he really said is quite different in meaning: "A foolish consistency is the hobgoblin of little minds." With the misquotation, consistency itself is damned, but with the correct quotation, only a *foolish* consistency is deemed stupid.

2. *Use testimony from unbiased sources.* Ethical speakers avoid using sources that are biased. Suppose you are researching the question of whether polygraphs (lie detectors) are accurate, and you come across glowing pro-polygraph statements by two "experts" who are on the payroll of a firm that manufactures polygraph machines. Could you expect such sources to be unbiased? Of course not. They would probably lose their jobs if they said anything negative about the machines. You should reject such "evidence" and look instead for statements by people who have no vested interest in the issue.

3. *Use testimony that your audience will respect.* As part of your prespeech audience analysis, ask yourself, "What kind of experts would this particular audience believe?" If you are speaking on foreign policy, for example, and you have a good quotation from a movie star, would your audience consider the star's views irrelevant? If so, quoting the star might weaken, rather than strengthen, your case.

4. *State the credentials of your source.* If you quote a famous person like Abraham Lincoln, you obviously do not need to give any background information about the person. But for authorities who are not well known, be sure to give some biographical data to establish their credibility. For example, "Jack Smithson, who spent 25 years as a research scientist for NASA, says that . . . ."

# *Statistics*

For a speech explaining the immense distances of space, Paula Schiller, a student speaker, began with some mind-boggling facts:

> Proxima Centauri, the star that is closest to our solar system, is only 4.28 light years away. That doesn't sound like a very great distance, does it? Is there any chance that we can reach that star—or one of its planets—in our lifetime? Before you start fantasizing about being the first human to travel to our nearest star, consider this fact: if you traveled to Proxima Centauri in the fastest spacecraft now in existence, it would take you *40,000 years* to make the trip.

Paula was using *statistics*, which are numerical ways of expressing information. As illustrated in this example, statistics do not have to be dry and boring. They can be made interesting and even exciting.

Statistics can be especially effective in persuading an audience to accept a particular point. In our society, people put a lot of trust in statistics. If a television commercial says that 78 percent of physicians prefer Cure-All pain reliever over all competing brands, many consumers will rush out to buy Cure-All.

In a speech in which she tried to persuade her audience to drive their cars less and walk more, Carol Morris wanted to prove that the fitness of Americans has been weakened by the automobile. She could have made a vague statement such as: "Because of the automobile, we Americans are getting soft and flabby." Instead, she gave a fascinating statistic to prove her point: "Since the advent of the auto, the average waistline of American adults has increased one inch every generation." That single statistic, short and surprising, was one of the most persuasive parts of her speech.

## Understanding Statistics

While statistics can provide powerful support for ideas, they also can be easily misused, either willfully or through carelessness or ignorance. Unfortunately, there is much truth in the old statement, "You can prove anything with statistics." To understand how statistics are used (and abused), let's look at several of the more popular varieties.

*Averages.* The most popular kind of statistic is the average. It can provide interesting views of a subject, as when one student speaker pointed out, "On an average day, 24 mail carriers in the United States receive animal bites." Giving the average in a case like this is much more interesting than simply stating the annual total.

Though averages seem like straightforward pieces of statistical data, there are pitfalls: most people are unaware that there are actually three different kinds of averages—the mean, the median, and the mode. Suppose a company is made up of a president with an annual salary of

$290,000; a vice president with a salary of $170,000; three managers with salaries of $50,000 each, and 20 workers with wages of $20,000 each. What is the average income of the people who work at this company? The *mean*, which is what most people use when they are asked to compute an average, is derived by totaling the salaries and dividing by 25. In this case, $40,400. The *median* is derived by listing the salaries in a column, ranging from highest to lowest, and then locating the salary that falls in the middle. In this case, the median is $20,000. The *mode* is simply the figure that occurs most frequently: $20,000.

Now suppose that the company had a labor-management dispute. In an interview with the press, the president could say, "I don't see what the workers are complaining about. The average income in this company is $40,400." And she would be correct, since she chose to use the *mean* as her version of average. A representative of the workers, on the other hand, could say "We are paid an average of only $20,000," and this would be correct, since the *median* is also a kind of average.

*Percentages.* Giving percentages can be a useful way to make a point. For example, suppose that you find that 2 percent of the 1,000 employees in a company are physically handicapped, and yet only 1 percent of the parking spaces has been designated for the handicapped. With these figures, you can make a good argument for increasing the number of spaces for the handicapped.

Unfortunately percentages can be misleading. A television commercial might say, "Eighty percent of the doctors interviewed said they recommend Feel Good medicated tablets for their patients." How many doctors were involved? If only 10 doctors were interviewed, and 8 of them gave the endorsement, the commercial is accurate (8 out of 10 amounts to 80 percent) but misleading.

The following statement is true: In one recent year Switzerland experienced a 50-percent jump in unemployment, causing that nation to rank number one in the world in the percentage increase of unemployed over the previous year. Sounds terrible, doesn't it? Sounds as if the prosperous little country is sliding toward economic catastrophe. But here is another way of reporting the facts: in the year cited, there were 51 jobless persons in Switzerland as compared to 34 in the previous year. This represents a 50-percent increase, but when you look at the actual number of people involved, there is obviously no reason for the Swiss to be alarmed.

*Correlations.* The term *correlation* is used to show the relationship between two sets of data. For example, when IQ scores are compared with academic performance, it is clear that there is a high correlation between the two; for most people in our society, the higher the IQ, the greater the level of academic achievement. By contrast, when shoe size is compared with academic achievement, there is no correlation at all.

Correlation is a handy statistical device because it can help us predict outcomes for individuals. Because we know that a high correlation exists between high IQ and academic success, we can predict that a person with a high IQ should be able to succeed in college.

Correlation, however, is often misunderstood and misused because some people think that it proves a cause-and-effect relationship. Just because two sets of data are correlated does not necessarily mean that one causes the other. For example, some medical researchers once thought that drinking milk might cause cancer because they found a high correlation between milk consumption and the incidence of cancer in some European countries, while finding a rarity of that disease in Asian nations where milk consumption is low. When the researchers analyzed their data, however, they found that a third factor was involved: cancer most often strikes people who are over 40; most of the people studied in the backward Asian nations did not live long enough to get the disease. So a correlation between milk consumption and cancer does exist, but there is no cause-and-effect relationship.

## Guidelines for Using Statistics

Here are some guidelines to consider when you are evaluating statistics for possible use in a speech.

*Use statistics fairly and honestly.* Sometimes a statistic is true but it is cited in such a way as to leave a false impression. A favorite ploy of unethical politicians is to make an accusation like this: "While my opponent has occupied the office of governor, state tax revenues have shot up 30 percent." To many voters hearing that statistic on TV (and seeing the accompanying graph), it sounds as if the governor has hiked their taxes. The truth is that tax revenues have gone up because they are tied to rising income—not because the tax *rate* went up. In reality, the governor should be cheered for the dramatic rise in personal income, but his opponent has used a clever 20-second TV commercial to discredit him. Notice that the statistic is true; the opponent cannot be charged with falsifying information.

When you prepare a speech, you should be sure to analyze a statistic for its true significance. For example, if you look at employment figures and notice a big drop in employment from December to January, does that mean the country is headed for depression and ruin? No, if you look at previous years, you will see that because of the Christmas shopping season, employment always goes up in December and then dips down in January. It would be unethical, then, for you to cite the one-month drop as an indication of economic decline.

Make sure that your sources for statistics are unbiased. If a pharmaceutical company comes out with a new drug which it claims is 100 percent effective in eliminating migraine headaches, you would be wise to treat the claim with skepticism. Look for an evaluation by a source that has no vested interest in the product—a university medical school, for example.

*Use statistics sparingly.* Too many statistics are hard for the audience to follow and to absorb. Be very selective, and choose only a few to make a point.

> *Poor:* China has a population of one billion, India has 730 million, the Soviet Union has 272 million, the United States has 240 million, and Indonesia 160 million. So these five countries have a combined population of two billion, 400 million. Contrast that with the entire world population, which is four billion, 800 million. That means these five countries have half the world's population.

> *Better:* There are four billion, 800 million people living on earth and one-half of them live in just five countries: China, India, the Soviet Union, the United States, and Indonesia.

The first version would be fine in a written essay, but in a speech it would be hard for the audience to get a handle on all those statistics. The second version, streamlined and simple, would be easier for the audience to absorb.

*Round off long numbers.* In print, a long number is no problem, but in a speech it is hard for the listener to absorb the information. A rounded-off number is easy to say and easy for the audience to grasp.

> *Poor:* Attendance at major league baseball games last year was 44,587,874.

> *Better:* Attendance at major league baseball games last year was about 45 million.

*Translate your statistics into vivid, meaningful language.* If you have a statistic that would be meaningless to most listeners, translate it into language they can understand. If you are explaining disk drives to a group of students who know very little about computers, do not just say, for example, that a particular fixed-disk drive has a storage capacity of 10 megabytes. Convert that into information the students can easily grasp: "On a 10-megabyte fixed disk, you can store the equivalent of over 5,000 doubled-spaced typewritten pages." The students can visualize 5,000 sheets of paper; now they understand that you are talking about a huge amount of storage space.

In a classroom speech on energy, Jack DuVall reported that a government experimental project, a giant windmill on a mountaintop near Boone, North Carolina, was supposed to produce 2,000 kilowatts of electricity. That statistic by itself would have meant nothing to most students, unless they happened to be well versed in electricity. Fortunately, Jack translated the statistic into understandable terms: he said that 2,000 kilowatts was enough electricity to satisfy the electrical needs of about 500 homes.

One student, Diane McDaniel, found a fascinating way to illustrate how cutting down on a few calories each day can result in substantial weight losses over the period of a year:

> If you want to lose weight, you don't have to go on a crash diet; you can shed a lot of pounds by altering your eating habits in very small ways. For example, if you eat just one pat less of butter every day, you will lose three and a half pounds in one year. If you cut out one piece of cake a week, you will lose five pounds in a year. If you omit two slices of bacon from breakfast each week, you will lose one and a half pounds in a year.

This interpretation of statistics was much more interesting to the audience than a recital of calories per food would have been.

*Adapt statistics to your particular audience.* Whenever possible, you should adapt your statistics to the needs and interests of your particular audience. Imagine that you are planning a speech on Alaska, and you want to give your audience an idea of that state's immense size. All you need to do is take a pocket calculator with you to the library, look up the areas of states in a reference work like the *World Almanac*, and make a few simple calculations. If you live in California, for example, you could give your audience a sense of Alaska's size by saying, "You can put three Californias inside Alaska's borders and still have room left over for Oregon."

*Relate statistics to familiar objects.* One way to make statistics dramatic is to relate them to something familiar. In a speech on bats, Sally Ingle wanted to give the audience an idea of the incredible smallness of one variety of bat. Instead of giving its weight in grams, which would have meant little to most of the audience, she said, "One variety of bat is so tiny that when it is full-grown, it weighs less than a penny." Knowing the lightness of a penny, the audience could easily get a notion of the smallness of the bat.

Everyone in America has a clear visual image of the width and length of a football field, so it is convenient to use the field as a point of reference for size and distance. To show that a baseball diamond uses more space than one would suspect from its appearance, you could say, "The distance that a home run hitter travels around the bases is 60 feet more than the length of a football field." To show the smallness of a basketball court, you could say, "A regulation court, if placed on a football field, will extend from the goal line to the thirty-one-yard line; its width will cover less than a third of the field."

## Summary

Verbal support materials are vital to the success of a speech. They develop, illustrate, and clarify ideas; they make a speech more interesting and meaningful, and they can help prove an assertion. Some of the more popular types of verbal supports are definitions, description, examples, narratives, comparisons, contrasts, testimony, and statistics.

Of all these types, the narrative (or story) is the favorite of most audiences. People love to hear stories and are more apt to remember them than most other parts of your speech. As with all support materials, you must make sure that a narrative explains, illustrates, or reinforces the message of your speech. Telling a story that is irrelevant to the subject is not appropriate in informative and persuasive speaking.

Statistics such as averages, percentages, and correlations can be useful in a speech, but you must be careful to use them accurately and fairly. Adapt statistics to your particular audience, making them as interesting and meaningful as possible.

## Review Questions

1. List five reasons why support materials are important in a speech.
2. Why are informal definitions usually superior to dictionary definitions in a speech?
3. "The human brain is like an incredibly sophisticated computer." Is this sentence an example of a comparison or a contrast?
4. What is the main advantage of using testimony in a speech?
5. The boss of a small firm has an annual salary of $100,000. Each of his 13 employees makes $12,000 a year. Give the average salary of the firm in terms of *mean, median,* and *mode*.
6. Whenever tar on asphalt roads gets hot enough to bubble on a summer day, the incidence of heat exhaustion among citizens goes up. In other words, there is a strong correlation between bubbling tar and heat exhaustion. Does the correlation prove that tar fumes cause people to pass out? Explain your answer.

# TIPS *for your career*

### Tip 7: Let Your Subconscious Mind Help You Prepare Speeches

Many speechmakers rely upon their subconscious mind to help them prepare speeches. The subconscious is the part of the mind that simmers beneath the surface of awareness. It is especially active at night, when it creates dreams, but it is also active during the day, when it occasionally floats an idea up to the surface of our minds. You probably have had the experience of wrestling with a problem, then later, while you are taking a walk or driving your car and not consciously thinking of the matter, a good solution suddenly appears in your mind like a flash of light—your subconscious mind had continued to work until it found a solution.

The subconscious mind can provide you with topics, support materials, and organizational patterns, but unfortunately it cannot be ordered to perform like a trained dog. It is unpredictable, often mysterious, and usually requires a lot of time. Nevertheless, there are four things you can do to take advantage of this creative process.

1. *Supply raw materials.* The subconscious cannot spin cloth out of thin air. You must fill your mind with information. Read, do research, conduct interviews.

2. *Allow time to elapse.* Sometimes you must allow a few days—or even a few weeks or months—to give the subconscious ample time to incubate your ideas. This is where the subconscious is most unpredictable: it's hard to forecast how long the process will take. (Note: in order for the subconscious to work for classroom speeches, you must choose your topic and carry out your research far in advance of your speech date.)

3. *Get away from deliberate mental activity.* For some reason the subconscious transmits its ideas when your mind is disengaged from rational, conscious work. In other words, don't sit at your desk and flog your brain for ideas. Go for a walk or take a ride in your car. Forget about whatever you've been working on. Once you "let go," you will often be happily surprised to have an idea suddenly well up from your subconscious. Relaxation seems to unlock the subconscious. Thornton Wilder, a Pulitzer Prize-winning playwright, reported that his best ideas came to him on hikes or in the shower but never at his desk.[5] Joe W. Boyd, a professional speaker from Bellingham, Washington, says, "I get my best topics when I'm exercising (running) or driving long distances. The topics just seem to flow into my mind."[6]

4. *Be prepared to record ideas.* Because ideas from the subconscious often come when you are climbing out of bed, driving to work, or walking across campus between classes, you should keep paper and pen with you at all times to get these ideas down. If you do not seize an idea at once, it might slip away and be gone forever.

Margaret McFadden, a business executive, uses her subconscious in a process she calls "living with" a speech. "As soon as I receive an invitation to speak," she says, "I choose my topic and do whatever research I need to do. Then I 'live' with my speech for a few weeks. Wherever I go—to work, to the store, to the beach—I find myself thinking about the speech. Not fretting or brooding, just playing with ideas. I carry a pad with me and jot down the ideas as they come to me. At the end of each day, I drop the notes into a manila folder. After a few weeks, I sit down at my desk, pull out the folder of notes, and organize my material into an outline. Usually everything just falls into place."

Everything falls into place because her subconscious mind has been busy for weeks, sorting and editing the materials.

# Chapter 8

# Visual Aids

**Reasons for Using Visual Aids**
**Types of Visual Aids**
    Graphs
    Charts
    Drawings
    Photographs
    Computer Graphics
    Objects
    Models
    Yourself

**Media for Visual Aids**
    Chalkboards
    Posters
    Flip Charts
    Handouts
    Overhead Transparencies
    Slides
    Films and Videotapes

**Guidelines for Using Visual Aids**
    Choose Visual Aids That Truly Support Your Speech
    Make Visual Aids Simple and Clear
    Do Not Let Visuals Become a Substitute for a Speech
    Do Not Use an Excessive Number of Visual Aids
    Practice with Your Visual Aids
    Make Sure Visual Aids Do Not Distract from Your Message
    Do Not Talk to Your Visual Aid
    Explain Visual Aids
    Plan for Emergencies

Imagine for a moment that you are driving across the country in a car and you stop at a gas station to find out how to get to a distant city. Which would you prefer to have? Oral instructions ("Drive north five miles, turn west on U.S. 25 . . .) or a chance to look at a clear, easy-to-follow map?

If you are like most people, you would choose the map because you know from past experience that when it comes to learning and remembering, your sense of sight is superior to your sense of hearing. A map gives you a mental "picture" which is easier to retain than five minutes of oral instructions. As the old expression has it, "One picture is worth more than a thousand words."

Even better than a map alone would be both the map and the oral instructions; that is, you look at the map while someone explains it. That is precisely what happens when a visual aid is used in a speech. The speaker shows visual information and explains it at the same time. Research carried out by Robert Craig, chief of the U.S. Public Health Service audiovisual facility, showed that people who were taught orally could remember only 10 percent of the information three days later, but people who were taught both orally and visually could recall 65 percent of the information three days later.[1]

Visual aids have always been important in speeches, but today, because of television, they are often expected. Television is the primary educator in our society (by the time the average student graduates from high school, he or she will have spent more hours in front of the television set than in the classroom) and people who have grown up with TV are conditioned to learn things by means of visual images. In business and professional life, you will find that visual aids are considered a vital part of most presentations, whether you are trying to convince the board of directors that your department is paying its own way and should not be axed, or whether you are trying to show customers why your product is superior to Brand X. The attitude throughout our society is: "Don't tell me, show me."

# Reasons for Using Visual Aids

While Chapter 7 dealt with *verbal* supports, this chapter will examine *visual* supports for a speech. Let us examine some good reasons for using visual supports.

*Visual aids can make your ideas clear and understandable.* Mary Callahan gave a classroom speech on how the United States government, when printing paper currency, uses complicated techniques that prevent counterfeiters from producing perfect imitations. Using a slide of a greatly enlarged dollar bill, she pointed out intricate designs and clever nuances that most people never would have dreamed existed. Without the blown-up dollar, her explanations would have been hard to follow. With the slide, her remarks were lucid and easy to grasp.

*Visual aids can make your speech more interesting.* Li Yang, a foreign student from Mauritius, showed slides to supplement his talk on his native country, which is an island in the Indian Ocean. To illustrate the geographical diversity of Mauritius, Li showed beautiful views of sparkling beaches and majestic mountains. To illustrate the racial and ethnic diversity of the island, he showed slides of citizens in a marketplace. There were also pictures of wind surfing and dancing. All in all, the slides took the audience on a vicarious trip to an exotic land and enhanced the speech.

*Visual aids can help the audience remember facts and details.* Research shows that visual aids help a listener retain ideas.[2] During his speech on Mauritius, Li showed a map of the world, on which he pinpointed his tiny country's location in the Indian Ocean. As we all do with visual aids, I took a mental snapshot of the map, which will help me remember where Mauritius is located.

*Visual aids can make long, complicated explanations unnecessary.* If you watch professional basketball on TV, you see a coach call a time out to set up one last play, with only seconds remaining in the game. He does not have time to explain to each player the complex pattern of the play, but he uses a miniature basketball court with little magnetic buttons representing the players. He moves the buttons about to show the players where they should run and what they should do. The players nod their assent, walk out onto the court, and execute the play as they saw it on the miniature board. The coach's visual aid saves time and makes a long, complicated explanation unnecessary.

*Visual aids can help prove a point.* A representative of Leica, the German camera manufacturer, once gave a talk to a group of photographers. He maintained that the body of the Leica (not the lens) could be dropped on a concrete floor without suffering any damage; in fact, he said, it could be dropped out the window (the group was on the third floor) to the sidewalk below and it would still function as well as ever. To prove his point, he sent the entire audience down to the sidewalk. The group formed a semicircle and watched as he dropped the camera from the third floor to the sidewalk. Sure enough, the camera was undamaged. He challenged the photographers to take pictures with the camera if they doubted his claim. Most speakers do not have such dramatic visual aids, but even simple aids like graphs and drawings can help prove a point. As the old saying goes, "Seeing is believing."

*Visual aids can add to your personal credibility.* Your listeners will be impressed if it is obvious that you have expended time and energy on visual aids to make your speech interesting and understandable. Researchers have discovered that if you add visual aids to your speech, audiences are apt to rate you as being more trustworthy and more intelligent than they would if no visual aids were used.[3] But some other research also needs to be mentioned as a warning: If listeners think that your visual aids are poor, their confidence in you falls off.[4] In other words, you are better off using no visual aids at all than poor ones.

# Types of Visual Aids

## *Graphs*

Graphs help audiences understand and retain statistical data. The *line graph* should be a familiar form to all college students because it is widely used in textbooks. It uses a horizontal and a vertical scale to show the

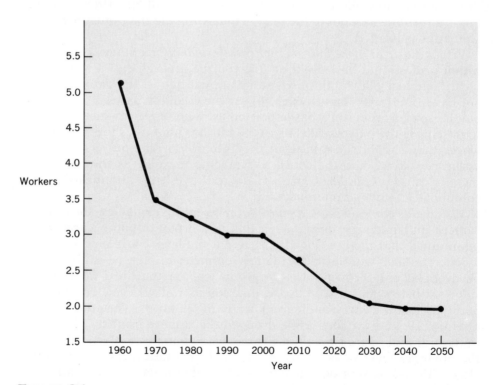

**FIGURE 8.1**
In America, workers pay Social Security taxes to finance Social Security benefits for people over 65. This graph shows the ratio of workers per Social Security dependent. In 1960, there were five people working for every person over 65 receiving Social Security benefits. By the year 2030, there will be only two workers for every Social Security retiree. Thus the tax burden on those two workers is expected to be very heavy. (Source: U.S. Commission on Population Growth)

relationship between two variables, as in Figure 8.1.

The bell-shaped curve for normal distribution is a feature known to many people through such statistical graphs as IQ scores in the general population. This curve can be used in symbolic ways (instead of in strictly mathematical terms), as Figure 8.2 demonstrates.

A *bar graph* is an easy way to show a great deal of data in a clear, easily comprehended manner. This kind of graph enables you to show comparisons within groups, as in Figure 8.3.

A *pie graph* is a circle representing 100 percent. It is easy for the audience to understand as long as there are not too many different "pieces" of pie. A textbook could have a pie graph with 20 different pieces because the reader would have ample time to analyze them, but a pie graph in a speech should have no more than six or seven pieces. Figure 8.4 shows a pie graph with only three pieces.

Of all graphs, a *pictorial graph* is perhaps the easiest to read, because

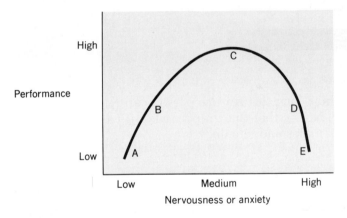

**FIGURE 8.2**
This is a graphic representation of the Yerkes-Dodson Law in psychology. One speaker used this graph to discuss the anxiety that students experience in taking tests. At Point A, people are asleep—no nervousness or anxiety, no mental performance. At Point B, people are alert because they have a small amount of tension; their performance on tests is moderately good. At Point C, people have a medium amount of nervousness so their performance is at its peak. At Point D, the nervousness is getting acute and the test-taking performance is beginning to falter. At Point E, panic and mental disorganization have set in and performance is zero. The purpose of the graph is to show that a moderate amount of nervousness or anxiety while taking a test is desirable. (This graph could also be used to demonstrate the point made in Chapter 3: a moderate amount of nervous energy during a speech is ideal for effective speechmaking.)

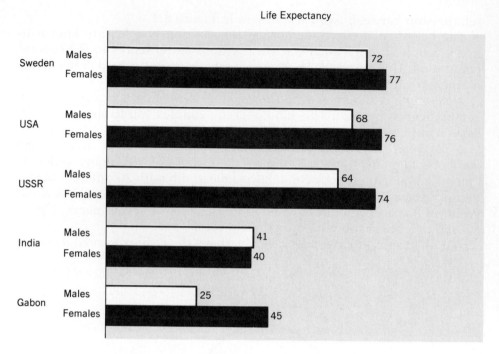

**FIGURE 8.3**
This bar graph shows how long the average person can expect to live in
five different countries. Notice that this graph makes it easy to show
comparative figures for males and female.

it visually translates information into a picture that can be grasped in-
stantaneously. Figure 8.5 is an example of a pictorial graph.

You need not be an artist to create a pictorial graph. Anyone can draw
a representation of human figures, even if they are as primitive as those
shown in Figure 8.6.

## Charts

Charts provide information in a compact, easily digested form. An *information chart* can show the main points of your speech or list the steps in
a process. In Figure 8.7, the speaker put five steps in a process on a poster.

An *organization chart* can be used to show a hierarchy in a business or
agency. We are familiar with charts that show the president of the company at the top and lines of authority going downward. This kind of chart
can also be used to organize information, as in Figure 8.8, which shows
how the body's nervous system is organized.

Where Americans Live

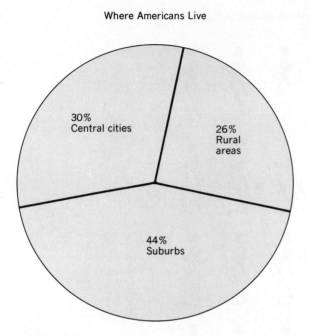

**FIGURE 8.4**
This pie graph shows at a glance the percentage of Americans living in central cities, suburbs, and rural areas.

A *flow chart* shows the flow or sequence of related events. (See Chapter 3, Figure 3.1, for a flow chart showing two possible sequences of events that can happen to a nervous speaker.) Figure 8.9 shows a flow chart involving personal computers.

## Drawings

Drawings make good visual aids because they can illustrate points that would be hard to explain in words. For example, telling an audience how to cut down a tree would be very difficult without a drawing, such as that in Figure 8.10.

Some students shy away from using drawings because they consider themselves unartistic. You need not be an artist to make a simple drawing such as the ones in Figure 8.10 and in Figure 8.11.

One kind of drawing that is highly effective is a map. By sketching a map yourself, you can include only those features that are pertinent to your speech. If you were speaking on the major rivers of America, for example, you could outline the boundaries of the United States and then

Napoleon's Invasion of Russia, 1812

422,000 Soldiers invaded Russia

Only 10,000
returned

**FIGURE 8.5**
Napoleon invaded Russia in 1812 with 422,000 soldiers, but only 10,000
survived the military battles and the bitter Russian winter. When the
speaker points out that each figure in this pictorial graph represents
10,000 soldiers, the audience can easily see the immensity of Napoleon's
disaster.

**FIGURE 8.6**
These simple pictorial representations of human beings illustrate that artistic ability is not required to create a pictorial graph. Figures such as these could have been used in Figure 8.5 if the speaker had lacked access to more sophisticated graphics.

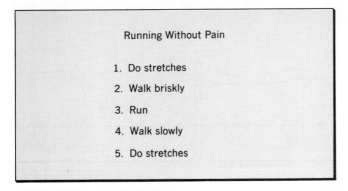

**FIGURE 8.7**
An information chart listing the steps in a process can make it easy for the audience to absorb the information.

draw heavy blue lines for the rivers, leaving out extraneous details, such as cities. Figure 8.12 shows a drawing with one map superimposed upon another—an effective way to show comparative size.

## *Photographs*

Photographs have a high degree of realism; they are very good for proving points. Lawyers, for example, often use photographs of the scene of an

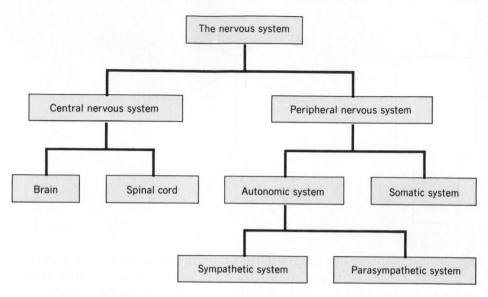

**FIGURE 8.8**
This organization chart shows subgroupings of the nervous system.

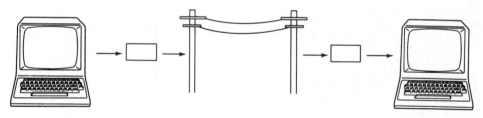

**FIGURE 8.9**
This flow chart shows how to send data from one personal computer to another, using telecommunications. There is no need to label the parts; the audience instantly recognizes all of the images except the rectangular box—the modem—which can be explained when the speaker discusses the chart.

accident to win a case. You should use photographs in a speech only if they are enlarged to poster size. If you have a small photograph that you think would make an important visual aid, have your school's audiovisual department make a 35-mm slide from it, if possible. A slide, of course, can be projected so that everyone in the audience is able to see it.

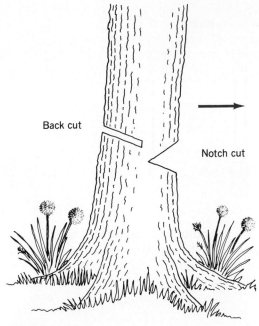

Back cut

Notch cut

**FIGURE 8.10**
This drawing shows how to make the cuts necessary for felling a tree.
This kind of illustration helps to explain to the audience the subtleties
of depth and angle.

## Computer Graphics

Computers can create all kinds of graphs, charts, maps, and drawings,
which can then be printed (sometimes in color) on either paper or on
transparencies for overhead projection. Slides can also be made from
computer graphics. Your college may have a computer that generates
graphics. More and more businesses are producing visual aids by this
means because computers can create graphics much more quickly than
an artist can. Such graphics are highly accurate and easily updated.[5]

## Objects

Three-dimensional objects make good visual aids, provided that they are
large enough for everyone in the audience to see. You could bring such
things as a blood-pressure gauge, a hibachi, handmade pottery, mountain-
climbing equipment, and musical instruments. Living objects could also
be used, but be sure to get your instructor's approval in advance. You

Rotating Tires

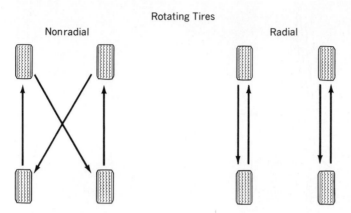

**FIGURE 8.11**
This drawing shows how to rotate both radial and nonradial tires.
Showing the illustration at the same time as explaining the process can
help the audience to understand and remember.

could use a friend, for example, to illustrate self-defense methods against
an attacker.

## Models

A model is a representation of an object. One student used a model of the
pyramids to discuss how the ancient Egyptians probably built their famous pyramids. If you were discussing space travel, you could use a model
of a space shuttle. One advantage of a model is that you can move it
around. If you had a model airplane, for example, you could show principles of aerodynamics more easily than if you had a drawing of a plane.
One student brought in a homemade "lung," the interior of which consisted of clean cotton. When cigarette smoke was sucked through a tube,
the lung turned from white to a sickening yellow-brown.

## Yourself

You can use yourself as a visual aid. You can demonstrate yoga positions,
judo holds, karate chops, stretching exercises, relaxation techniques, ballet steps, and tennis strokes. You can don native attire, historical cos-
tumes, or scuba-diving equipment. One student came to class dressed and
made up as a clown to give a speech on her part-time job as a clown for
children's birthday parties.

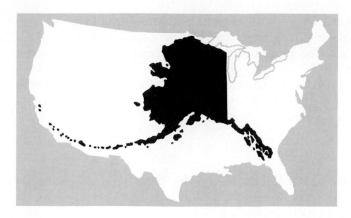

**FIGURE 8.12**
This drawing shows Alaska superimposed on the continental United States, vividly illustrating the huge size of the state and its long span from east to west.

# Media for Visual Aids

Some of the types of visual aids we looked at above—charts, graphs, drawings, etc.—can be conveyed to the audience by means of a variety of different media. Here are some of the more popular media.

## *Chalkboards*

A chalkboard is an ideal tool for visual aids if you have a few technical words that you need to write for your audience. If you use a big word like "transmogrification" (which means changing into a different, sometimes bizarre, form), you can step over to the chalkboard and write it down in big letters. A chalkboard is also effective if you have complex drawings that require constant insertions and erasures—for example, diagramming plays for a soccer team.

Otherwise, a chalkboard is usually not very desirable because if you put your visual—a graph, say—on the board during your speech, you have to turn your back on the audience; while you're drawing, their attention drifts away from you, and you may find it hard to regain it. Nor is it a good idea to put your graph on the board before the speech begins because the audience will be distracted by it; they will be scrutinizing it before you are ready to talk about it. (It would do no good to say, "Don't pay any attention to this until I get to it." Such an admonition would make the graph all the more interesting—and therefore distracting.) There is one solution: cover the part of the chalkboard on which you have written, but this can be awkward. You would have to find something large enough to do the job but not be distracting. Another problem is that speakers preceding you may also be planning to use the board and they might erase your visual aid.

Since people are so used to seeing chalkboards after spending years in school, there is not much novelty involved, so get chalk in different colors to add sparkle to your visuals.

## Posters

You can put many kinds of visual aids—graphs, drawings, charts, etc.—on posters. They do the same work as chalkboards, but they are usually a lot neater and more visually appealing.

The size of the poster will depend, of course, upon the size of the audience. Ask yourself: can the person in the back row see the words or artwork clearly? For huge audiences, posters obviously would be unsuitable; you would have to use slides.

Make sure there is a reliable place to put your posters. Propping them

**Statistics can provide strong support for a speaker's points. (Michal Heron/Woodfin Camp & Associates)**

against a chalkboard may cause them to fall to the floor during the middle of the speech. Taping them up on a wall may cause them to fall with a thud during the speech. Using thumbtacks might work if there is a suitable place for tacking. One technique is to put posters on a desk near the lectern and take one at a time from the pile and hold it up. If you follow this technique, be sure to hold your posters steady. The best, most reliable method is to put your poster on an easel (your school's audiovisual department may be able to provide one).

## Flip Charts

A flip chart is a giant writing pad glued or wired together at the top. It can be mounted on an easel. It is much like a chalkboard except that when you are through with a visual, you can tear off the page or flip it over the back of the easel.

With a flip chart, you can lightly pencil in your sheets at home; then during the speech, with a heavy marker you can trace over the lines. The audience is not aware that you are tracing, not drawing, and it makes you look efficient and professional. (With some flip charts, the paper might be so thin that ink will seep to the next page, so you might need to have a blank page between each drawn-on sheet.)

## Handouts

Handouts can be used to give the listeners key information to take with them for later use. As will be explained later in this chapter, handouts should never be passed out until the end of a speech. Figure 8.13 gives an example of a handout.

```
                    C A U T I O N

Early Cancer Symptoms:
Change in bowel or bladder habits
A sore that does not heal
Unusual bleeding or discharge
Thickening or lump in the breast or elsewhere
Indigestion or difficulty in swallowing
Obvious change in wart or mole
Nagging cough or persistent hoarseness
```

**FIGURE 8.13**
An example of a handout that can be given at the end of a speech on cancer, so that the audience will have key information for later use.

## *Overhead Transparencies*

Overhead projectors are light boxes that project images from transparencies onto a screen. There are five advantages in using overhead transparencies: (1) The transparencies are not hard to produce. (2) It is easy to make last-minute changes in artwork or statistics. (3) You do not need another person to operate the machine for you. (4) The room usually does not have to be darkened, so you and the audience can see each other at all times. (5) When you want to point to an item on your visual, you do not have to turn your back to the audience by going to the screen; you can simply point to the proper place on the transparency with a pencil or pen.

Prepare transparencies well ahead of time. You can reproduce photos or illustrations from magazines and books, or you can create original graphics. Using a variety of color pens, you can write directly on the film, or you can make a master copy on plain white paper, then use certain kinds of office copiers to make your transparency. (Your college's audio-visual department may be able to help you produce transparencies for a small fee, or a print shop in your community can make transparencies from your master copy.)

Make your artwork and letters larger than you think necessary. Do not try to use a typewriter to make the master copy because the letters are too small. Even large typefaces, such as IBM's Orator, are too small to be seen by people in the back of a room.

It is possible to write or draw on a transparency while you are projecting it on the screen, but I do not recommend doing so because you can lose your audience's attention while you write or draw. An exception to this would be using your pen to circle key words, draw arrows, or insert updated statistics.

When you create transparencies in advance, you must make sure that you use a marking pen especially designed for overheads. If you use an ordinary marker to prepare a transparency the night before your speech, the graphics might look fine at the time, but by the next day the ink may evaporate, leaving you with only thin traces. Avoid storing transparencies directly against each other. The ink may transfer from one to another. Put them in file folders or store them with a piece of paper between each one.

You can use a card or heavy paper to reveal one part of a transparency at a time. If, for example, you have four major points, you can cover up all but point #1 and discuss it; when you're through with point #1, pull the card down and show point #2, and continue in this way through the other points.

## *Slides*

Slides are very popular in business, government, and military presentations. They allow a great deal of flexibility: you can insert and delete slides quickly and easily, thus adapting a slide show to meet the needs of different kinds of audiences. As an example, if during a recent trip to Mexico you took 245 slides, including 35 at an ancient Mayan excavation site, you might want to show all 35 of the Mayan slides in a talk to an archaeological society. But if you are giving a talk to a civic club, you might want to show only three or four of those slides because a general audience would not be interested in detailed information on archaeology.

Slide projectors are easy to operate. You can set your own pace, lingering over a slide that requires long explanation, while hurrying through slides that need little or no commentary. If you have a remote-control device on a long cord, you can stand next to the screen and point out items without having to walk back and forth between projector and screen.

If you have a photograph, chart, drawing, magazine ad, or cartoon that is too small for the audience to see, consider making a slide of it. If you are making a slide of a graph or chart, limit yourself to only two or three bold, contrasting colors (too many colors would be garish) and do not use too many words. Keep the slide simple and vivid.

To be seen clearly, slides must be shown in a completely darkened room. This situation is both good and bad. It is good in that the attention of your audience is concentrated on one spot—the screen. This means there are no visual distractions that might cause the listeners' eyes to wander. The bad aspect is that you and your listeners lose eye communication with each other; you have to rely solely on your voice to make contact. To solve this problem, some speakers show slides in a semidark room, but this creates a new problem: the slides appear washed out and therefore are hard to see.

Once you have finished discussing a slide, do not leave it on the screen. If you are not yet ready to go to the next slide, project a light-colored blank slide on the screen while you talk, or turn off the projector and turn on the lights until you are ready for the next slide.

## Films and Videotapes

Films are awkward to use. Time is spent starting and stopping the projector (unless you have an experienced operator to run the machine for you). Furthermore, the projector makes noise and can block the view of some listeners. If you are thinking of showing a film as part of a classroom speech, you should get permission in advance from your instructor. Even if he or she approves, you want to guard against letting the film dominate the speech or take up most of your time. Outside the classroom, a film might be very effective if you are allotted, say, 45 minutes and the film could serve as an appetizer, something to whet appetites for the main course, your speech. If you have detailed, technical material to cover, you might use a film in the middle of your speech to break the monotony. Or you can use a film at the end if it will motivate the audience to take action on your proposals.

Always preview a film before using it. The title in a catalog might make it sound like something it is not. The film *Manhattan*, for example, is not a documentary about a borough of New York City; it is a Woody Allen social comedy. Even catalog descriptions cannot always be trusted; a film might be described as "sensitive, thought-provoking, and illuminating" but turn out to be hopelessly boring.

Videotapes are replacing 16mm films as the favorite type of motion picture. Not only are many commercially produced videotapes available, but many people can make their own tapes, using their own video-cassette recorders or ones borrowed from their schools or employers. Because of the ease in rewinding and advancing, videotapes are superior to films if you want to show only a small portion of a show. Furthermore, the playback machines for videotapes do not make a loud noise, as do 16mm projectors.

# Guidelines for Using Visual Aids

Here are some guidelines for effectively using visual aids in your speeches.

### Choose Visual Aids That Truly Support Your Speech

Before you use any visual aid, ask yourself this question: Will it help support an important idea in my speech? If the answer is "no," forget about using it. Your job is not to dazzle people with pretty colors on a screen or to impress them with your creative artwork. A beautiful drawing of an airplane, for example, would not really contribute to a speech on vacationing in Europe.

Beware of using a visual aid that is of poor quality. As we discussed earlier, a poor visual aid is worse than none at all because it can weaken your credibility with the audience. If you have taken slides to illustrate a point, look at them candidly and unsentimentally. Are they really worth showing?

### Make Visual Aids Simple and Clear

Each visual aid should have just one major idea which the listeners can quickly grasp. Too much information can confuse or overwhelm them. They might spend so much time and energy trying to make sense out of your visual that they stop listening to you.

If you take graphs or charts from books, be aware that some visual aids in books are jampacked with fascinating details which may not be suitable for a speech.

While visual aids should be appealing to the eye, they should also be clear, neat, and uncrowded. In aids such as graphs, make all labels horizontal (in a textbook, many labels are vertical because readers of a book can turn the visual sideways, but listeners should not be forced to twist their necks to read vertical lettering). You need not label every part of your visual, as you are there to explain the aid.

A common mistake made by speakers is to have visual aids that cannot be seen by everyone in the audience—for example, lettering that is too small to be read by people in the last four rows. A good rule of thumb is to make your letters and sketches much larger than you think necessary. Before the date of your speech, go to the room where you will be speaking, display your visual aid in the front of the room, and then sit in the back row and determine whether you can see it clearly.

It makes you appear amateurish when you show an aid that cannot be seen by everyone. If you have a multidimensional object, be sure to turn it during your talk so that everyone can see all sides of it. Before a speech, move any objects such as desks or tables that might block the view of some listeners.

## Do Not Let Visuals Become a Substitute for a Speech

Your visual aids cannot give your speech for you. This is especially important to remember for classroom speeches. Do not show a four-minute film on Denmark and then spend only one minute talking about your trip to that country. The aid is a supplement, a help, a clarifier—it is not a substitute for a speech.

## Do Not Use an Excessive Number of Visual Aids

How many visual aids should you use? Only the number necessary to make your points. No more, no less. It is not true that the more aids you have, the better off you are. If there are too many, the audience might get overwhelmed and even frustrated, wondering which aids are really the important ones.

## Practice with Your Visual Aids

When you practice your speech, do not forget to include your visual aids. It is especially important that you practice using unfamiliar equipment, such as overhead projectors or videotape machines, so that you can avoid fumbling or faltering during your speech. In order to have plenty of practice time, you obviously need to prepare your visual aids far in advance.

## *Make Sure Visual Aids Do Not Distract from Your Message*

Never let a visual aid draw the attention of your listeners away from your message. One speaker brought in a ferret to demonstrate what great pets they make. The only trouble was that the ferret did cute impromptu stunts all during the speech, causing the audience to laugh at the antics of the animal rather than listen to the speech. (A note of caution: some instructors disapprove of using animals in speeches; be sure to get permission before using an animal in a classroom speech.)

Inanimate aids can also be distracting. Drawings or graphs that are shown prematurely might cause the audience to scrutinize them rather than listen to you. For this reason, you should display only one visual aid at a time. Show it during the time you are talking about it—do not pull it out early or leave it on display after you have discussed it. If you have, say, five posters for your speech, displaying all of them at the same time would distract your listeners from following your remarks. Display poster #1 when it is time; then cover it up or turn it over; display poster #2 and talk about it, and so forth. If you have an object, keep it covered or in a box. (An object in a box, by the way, can be a great suspense builder. You can refer to the mysterious item in the box early in your speech, but not reveal what it is until the climax of your speech.) When you do bring the aid out, do not just show it briefly and leave the audience wishing for more time to see it. Let the audience have a good look before you put it away.

Do not circulate a visual aid among the audience because people will look at it instead of listening to you. And there's likely to be distraction, perhaps even whispered comments, as it is being passed from one person to another. Avoid doing anything that will take the eyes and minds of the listeners away from your speech. The best way to display the visual aid is to leave it in the front and invite the audience to see it after the speech. Or, if time is made available at the end of the question-and-answer period, you can pass it around. Some speakers try to handle this problem by walking from listener to listener, giving each person a closeup view of an object or photograph. This is a bad technique, however; the listeners who are not seeing the visual aid may get bored or distracted, or they may start whispering comments to their friends. Also, the listeners who are looking at the aid may ask questions that mean nothing to the rest of the audience. In a case like this, you can easily lose your audience's attention and interest.

You should also avoid distributing handouts during a speech. Even if everyone has a copy, some listeners will be tempted to read the entire handout, rather than paying attention as you go from point to point. If you have some good information that you want the listeners to take home with them, distribute the handouts at the end of the question-and-answer period. (But check with your instructor on this; he or she may prefer that you wait until the end of the class period; if you give out material at the end of your speech, students might read it instead of listening to the next speaker.)

## Do Not Talk to Your Visual Aid

Many speakers are so intent on explaining a visual aid that they end up looking at the aid instead of at the audience. This is a mistake because your eyes should be directed at the audience throughout most of your speech. The best approach is to stand to one side of your visual aid, face the audience, and use the hand nearest the aid to point out important features. Look at your audience most of the time, only occasionally glancing at the aid.

## Explain Visual Aids

No matter how simple your visual aid is, you should explain it to your audience. Some speakers slap transparencies of graphs onto an overhead projector, talk about them for a moment, and then whisk them off. To such speakers, the graph is simple and obvious; they do not stop to think that the listeners have never seen the aid before and need time to analyze and absorb the visual information.

As you discuss a part of your visual aid, do not wave your hand in the general direction of the aid and assume that the audience can figure out what feature you are pointing out. Be precise. Point to the specific part that you are discussing. If you have a small visual aid, you can use a finger to point; if your aid is large, you may want to use a ruler, pen, or extendable pointer.

## Plan for Emergencies

With visual aids, there is always a chance of a foul-up, especially if you are using electronic media, so you need to plan how to handle any problems that might arise. Sometimes the problem is simple but nevertheless frustrating. If you plan to sketch on the board, make sure there is chalk. It is disruptive to have to send someone to another room to find chalk.

Before you use any electronic media, you should talk with your instructor or the program chairperson to get his or her permission and to make arrangements (for darkening the room, getting an extension cord, etc.).

Be prepared for the unexpected—slides appearing upside down, the bulb in the slide projector burning out, videotape breaking in the middle of the program. Some of these disasters can be mitigated by advance planning. For example, you can carry a spare bulb for the slide projector; if the videotape breaks, you can be ready to fill in the missing information. If equipment breaks down and cannot be fixed quickly, continue with your speech as best you can. Try to keep your poise and sense of humor.

## Summary

Visual aids can enrich and enliven your speech in many ways: they can make your ideas clear and understandable, they can make your speech more interesting and memorable, they can help prove a point, and they can add to your personal credibility.

Whatever type of aids you choose, you should take into consideration the following guidelines: (1) Choose visual aids that truly support your speech. (2) Make your aids as simple and as clear as possible. (3) Do not let your visuals become a substitute for the speech. (4) Do not use an excessive number of aids. (5) Practice with your aids ahead of time. (6) Make sure the aids do not distract from your message. (7) Do not talk to your aids. (8) Explain each aid, regardless of how simple it is. (9) Plan for emergencies.

## Review Questions

1. List at least six types of visual aids.
2. List at least five media for visual aids.
3. Why is it a mistake to pass out handouts during your speech?
4. Why should a graphic in a speech be less complex than a graphic in a book?
5. What are the disadvantages of using a chalkboard for visual aids?

# TIPS *for your career*

### Tip 8: Use a Friend to Assist You

For speeches that you give on the job or in the community, you may want to consider using a friend to assist you. Here are some of the ways in which an assistant can be useful:

1. An assistant can help you set up and operate audiovisual equipment, turn lights off and on, or search for a missing extension cord. Such assistance will free you to concentrate on getting your message across to the audience.

2. If you are speaking to strangers, the presence of your friend can give you a nice psychological boost—you have an "ally" in the room.

3. An assistant might be able to handle any distractions or emergencies that arise. If, for example, a group of people start a loud conversation right outside the door of the room where you are speaking, the assistant can open the door and whisper a request for silence.

4. Your assistant can stand or sit in the back of the room while you are speaking and give you signals that the two of you have rehearsed. For example:
"Slow down—you're talking too fast."
"Speak louder—I can barely hear you."
"You're speaking too loud."
"You're looking at your notes too much."

5. An assistant can give you a critique of your speech afterward, so that you can learn from any mistakes you have made. Sometimes the assistant can mingle with the audience in the hall after your speech and pick up listeners' responses for you, so that you can learn about your areas of strength and weakness.

# Part 3

# Organizing the Speech

*Chapter 9*

# The Body of the Speech

**Selecting Main Points**
   Distinguish Between Main Points and Support Materials
   Limit the Number of Main Points
   Make Sure All Main Points Develop the Central Idea
   Restrict Each Main Point to a Single Idea
   Use Parallel Language Whenever Possible

**Organizing Main Points**
   Chronological Pattern
   Spatial Pattern
   Causal Pattern
   Problem-Solution Pattern
   Topical Pattern

**Selecting Support Materials**

**Supplying Transitions**
   Bridges
   Internal Summaries
   Internal Previews
   Signposts
   Spotlights

once heard a naturalist give a talk on why the leaves of hardwood trees change colors in autumn. As he talked (without notes), it was obvious that he had no coherent plan for his speech: he rambled from one item to another, without tying things together. He would talk for a while about the chemical makeup of leaves, then throw in a few comments about rainfall and temperature, then go back to chemistry. He gave his information in random order, not following a logical sequence. He backtracked a great deal ("Oh yeah, when I was talking about rainfall, I forgot to mention . . ."). For me, the speech was confusing rather than enlightening. I failed to get what I came for: an understanding of the chemical process by which leaves change colors. I think I would have understood the process, however, if he had organized his material in a logical, easy-to-follow pattern, such as: "Here's how leaves change colors: First . . . Second . . . Third . . .," and so on.

Organizing material logically and intelligently is important in all types of communication, but it is especially important in oral communication. If readers of an essay find themselves confused, they can easily go back a few paragraphs and study the material until they make sense out of it, but people who listen to a speech do not have this option. If they fail to understand what a speaker is saying, they are out of luck. There is no instant replay. What this means to you, the speaker, is that you must organize your ideas clearly and logically, so that your listeners will understand you. If your speech is rambling, illogical, and poorly constructed, the listeners may go away confused rather than enlightened. A well-organized speech has the following advantages over a poorly organized one:

1. *A well-organized speech is easier to understand.* As in the case of the naturalist, many speakers have interesting, important ideas, but their speeches are so poorly organized that the audience fails to grasp the ideas. Studies have shown that a well-organized speech is much easier for a listener to understand than a poorly organized one.[1]

2. *A well-organized speech is easier for the audience to remember.* Imagine that you need to remember to buy the following items at the store:

bagels
frozen spinach
milk
lettuce
rolls
frozen squash
butter
tomatoes
hamburger buns

carrots

frozen peas

yogurt

In a number of experiments, psychologists[2] have shown that your chances of recalling all the items increase if you revise your list to look something like this:

**Breads**

bagels

rolls

hamburger buns

**Frozen foods**

spinach

squash

peas

**Dairy products**

butter

yogurt

milk

**Fresh produce**

lettuce

tomatoes

carrots

The reason the second list is easier to remember is that items are grouped in meaningful clusters. You can, for example, get a mental picture of the bread section of your grocery store, and then tell yourself that you need to pick up only three things in that section—bagels, rolls, and hamburger buns. In a good speech, you should apply the same principle: group your ideas in meaningful clusters that are easy to comprehend and recall.

3. *A well-organized speech is more likely to be believed.* Studies show that if you present a poorly organized speech, your listeners will find you less believable at the end than they did at the beginning of the speech.[3] But if your speech is well-organized, you will come across as someone who is in full command of the facts, and therefore believable.

All good speeches are made up of three parts: introduction, body, and conclusion. You might think it logical to formulate your introduction first, but most speakers find it is easier to begin with the body of the speech and then prepare the introduction. If you stop and think about it, this makes a lot of sense: how can you introduce the body until you know its full nature?

In this chapter we will discuss how to organize the body of the speech. In the next chapter we will look at introductions and conclusions.

# Selecting Main Points

As discussed in Chapter 5, the central idea is your core message, the key concept that you want to get across to your audience. It is your speech boiled down to one sentence. The best way to get the central idea across to your audience is to firmly implant in their minds a few main points that are based on the central idea.

Suppose that you want to argue against the sport of boxing and you come up with the following purpose statement:

> *Specific Purpose:*   To persuade my listeners that the sport of boxing should be outlawed.

Next, you should ask yourself, "What is my essential message? What big idea do I want to leave in the minds of my listeners?" Your answer, of course, is your central idea. Here is one possibility:

> *Central Idea:*   Boxing should be banned because it is an uncivilized form of brutality.

Next, you do research on the subject and come up with a wealth of facts, statistics, anecdotes, and quotations. Then, you need to ask yourself the following question: "In order to get my audience to believe my central idea, what main points do I need to make?" Here are three main points that could be made:

> I. Boxing can cause permanent brain injury.
> II. Boxing sometimes leads to death.
> III. Boxing is the only sport in which inflicting injury is the primary goal.

To make these main points stick in the minds of your listeners, you would obviously need to back up each point with supporting materials such as narratives, examples, and statistics (as we discussed in Chapter 7). If you arrange a speech in this way, you will have an easy time getting your message across. Your listeners will know your central idea—that boxing should be outlawed because it is brutal—and they will know *why* boxing is brutal, thanks to your well-developed main points. (Later in this chapter, we will look at an outline with main points bolstered by support materials.)

Here are some guidelines for devising main points.

## Distinguish Between Main Points and Support Materials

It is important that you distinguish between main points and support materials. Main points are the key ideas that develop the central idea; support materials (as we saw in Chapter 7) prove, explain, clarify, illustrate, or reinforce the main points.

To return to our boxing example, can you determine what is wrong with the following arrangement?

    I. Boxing can cause permanent brain injury.
    II. One study shows that 87 percent of professional boxers suffer permanent brain damage.
    III. Boxing sometimes leads to death.
    IV. Some 421 boxers have died in the ring since 1918.

It should be obvious that the second and fourth items are not truly main points. They are support materials for the first and third points. Such materials are vital for the success of your speech because they develop and back up your ideas, but bear in mind that it is the main points, not the support materials, that you want to drive home. For example, long after your listeners have forgotten the statistic about 87 percent of boxers suffering permanent brain injury, they still should remember your point about boxing causing brain damage.

## Limit the Number of Main Points

A common mistake of public speakers is to cram too many points into a speech. They do this because they are approaching the speech from their own personal viewpoint and not from the viewpoint of the listeners. If you ask yourself, "How much information can I squeeze into the five minutes allotted?" you are approaching from your own viewpoint. To approach from the audience's viewpoint, you should ask, "How much information can the audience comfortably pay attention to, understand, and remember?" Remember that audiences simply cannot absorb too much new information. You should know this from your own experience; if you think for a moment, you probably can recall many speakers (including some teachers) who overwhelmed you with a barrage of ideas, facts, and figures. So do not be afraid to cut and trim your material.

Exactly how many main points should you have? In a short speech (five-ten minutes), you should limit yourself to two or three (or occasionally four) main points. That is as much as an audience can absorb. In a longer speech, you could have as many as five main points, but most experienced speakers cover only two or three, regardless of the length of their speech. It is a rare—and usually ineffective—veteran speaker who attempts six or more.

## Make Sure All Main Points Develop the Central Idea

You should make sure that all of your main points are truly based on the central idea. In the following example, one of the main points does not belong. Can you spot it?

*Specific Purpose:* To inform my listeners of the valuable lessons that humans have learned from the study of dolphins.

*Central Idea:* Humans have learned valuable lessons by studying dolphins.

*Main Points:*
I. People have learned how to construct faster boats by studying dolphins' skin.
II. People have learned to improve submariners' ability to "hear" underwater by studying dolphins' ears.
III. People have come to admire the intelligence and friendliness of dolphins.

The third main point fails to develop the central idea. It has nothing to do with lessons learned from dolphins, so it should be dropped as a main point (although it might be useful as part of the introduction).

## Restrict Each Main Point to a Single Idea

Each main point in a speech should focus on just one idea. The following example violates this rule.

*Specific Purpose:* To convince my listeners that country life is superior to city life.

*Central Idea:* Living in the country is preferable to living in the city.

*Main Points:*
I. Country life provides more privacy than city life.
II. Country life involves less stress than city life.
III. Country life involves less pollution, and there is little crime.

The third main point covers two different ideas. The discussion of crime should be made into a separate point or perhaps used as supporting material for the second main point.

## Use Parallel Language Whenever Possible

You should use parallel grammatical forms for your main points if at all possible. For example, suppose that you started off with the following:

*Specific Purpose:* To persuade my audience to swim for exercise.

*Central Idea:* Swimming is an ideal exercise because it dissipates nervous tension, avoids injuries, and builds endurance.

Now decide which set of main points would be most effective.

First set

    I. You can work out a lot of nervous tension while swimming.
   II. Muscle and bone injuries, common with other sports, are not a problem with swimming.
  III. Swimming builds endurance.

Second set

    I. Swimming dissipates nervous tension.
   II. Swimming avoids the muscle and bone injuries that are common with other sports.
  III. Swimming builds endurance.

The second set is superior because it follows a parallel grammatical form throughout (the noun "Swimming" followed by a verb). Parallel language is pleasant to hear, and it makes it easier for the listeners to understand and remember your points. With some speeches, this kind of consistent arrangement is not possible, but you should strive for parallelism whenever possible.

# Organizing Main Points

It is easier to understand information if it is presented in a sensible pattern rather than in an illogical manner. If, for example, someone tells you how to bake bread, you would expect him or her to tell you what to do first, then second, then third. It would be hard to follow if the person started off with oven temperature, then backtracked to kneading the dough, then went back to sifting flour. Likewise in a speech, your main points should be organized in a logical, easy-to-follow pattern. Let us look at five of the most popular patterns speakers use.

## *Chronological Pattern*

In the chronological pattern you arrange your main points in a time sequence. If, for example, you are describing a process or giving a demonstration, you can use this pattern to show how something is done step by step. Here is an illustration:

*Specific Purpose:* To tell my listeners how to cut down a tree safely and efficiently.
*Central Idea:* In three easy steps, people can cut down a tree without endangering themselves.
*Main Points:*
(First)    I. Determine the direction toward which the tree is leaning.

(Second)       II. Make a notch cut on the leaning side.
(Third)       III.  Cut through on the opposite side of the notch.

The chronological pattern is a logical choice for a speech dealing with periods of time in history. If, for example, you were speaking on the history of immigration in the United States, you could divide your subject into time periods—seventeenth century, eighteenth century, nineteenth century, twentieth century. Another way to deal with time is to discuss past, present, and future; if, for instance, you were speaking on society's changing attitudes toward women in leadership roles, you could discuss attitudes in the past, then talk about the situation in the present, and finally predict what will happen in the years ahead.

Another variation of the chronological pattern is before-during-after, as shown in this example:

*Specific Purpose:*  To tell my listeners how to run without suffering pain or injury.
*Central Idea:*  Running can be enjoyed without pain or injury if the runner takes certain precautions before, during, and after the run.
*Main Points:*
(Before)       I.  The runner should perform stretching exercises before every run.
(During)      II.  The runner should run in a balanced, but loose, position.
(After)      III.  The runner should perform stretching exercises after every run.

## Spatial Pattern

In the spatial pattern, you organize items according to the way in which they relate to each other in space—top to bottom, left to right, North to South, inside to outside, etc. If you were speaking on volcanoes, for example, you could start by telling about the magma (molten rock, minerals, and gas) under the earth's crust and then describe its ascent up the cone to the volcano's crater. If you were describing a marathon race, you could discuss the first 20 miles of "easy" running and then relate the agonies of the last stretch—6 miles and 385 yards. Here is a detailed example of the spatial pattern:

*Specific Purpose:*  To tell my audience how to inspect a used car before deciding whether to buy it.
*Central Idea:*  If a person examines a used car carefully and critically, he or she can avoid buying a "lemon."
*Main Points:*   I. Inspect the condition of the body of the car.
                II. Inspect the condition of the motor.
               III. Inspect the condition of the interior.

**A college professor discusses a point in economics. An important pattern for organizing material is the causal pattern, showing how causes lead to effects. *(Susan Lapides/Design Conceptions)***

Another example of this pattern, going from bottom to top:

*Specific Purpose:*   To explain to my listeners the four layers of the earth's atmosphere.
*Central Idea:*   The earth's atmosphere can be divided into four distinct layers.
*Main Points:*   I. The troposphere, the layer closest to ground, contains all our weather.
II. The stratosphere, the second lowest layer, is made up of dry, thin air.
III. The mesosphere, the third layer, includes high concentrations of ozone.

IV. The ionosphere, the top layer, contains a high concentration of electrically charged particles called ions.

## *Causal Pattern*

In some speeches, you are concerned with why something happens or happened—a cause-and-effect relationship. For example, some people refuse to ride in elevators because they have an inordinate fear of enclosed spaces. Their claustrophobia is the *cause* and their refusal to ride in elevators is the *effect*. Here is a sample of a cause-and-effect pattern for a speech:

*Specific Purpose:* To inform my audience of how Americans are responding to the bombardment of telephone calls by businesses, charities, and politicians.

*Central Idea:* Unwanted telephone solicitations by businesses, charities, and politicians are forcing many Americans to have unlisted telephone numbers.

*Main Points:*

(Cause)  I. More and more businesses, charities, and politicians are using the telephone to solicit the public.

(Effect)  II. A growing number of Americans are having the phone company change their telephone numbers from listed to unlisted.

Sometimes it is more effective to start with the effects and then analyze the causes, as in this case:

*Specific Purpose:* To explain to my listeners why people get headaches.

*Central Idea:* Most headaches are caused by tension, psychological frustrations and conflicts, excessive alcohol consumption, or too much caffeine.

*Main Points:*

(Effects)  I. Severe headaches create physical and psychological problems.
   A. They can make you short-tempered and irritable.
   B. They can keep you from sleeping.
   C. They can make you have difficulty thinking clearly.

(Causes)  II. Headaches are caused by a variety of things.
   A. A buildup of tension is a primary cause of headaches.
   B. Psychological frustrations and conflicts can lead to headaches.
   C. Excessive alcohol consumption can create headaches.
   D. Too much caffeine from coffee, tea, and soft drinks can cause headaches.

In the above pattern, putting the effects first is good strategy because the listeners can nod in agreement and say to themselves, "Yes, that's exactly what headaches do." This puts them in the proper frame of mind to hear the causes. Their unspoken response will probably be something like, "Now tell me what causes headaches so I'll know how to avoid them."

## Problem-Solution Pattern

A popular pattern in persuasive speeches divides the speech into two main parts: a statement of a problem and the solution. Here is an example:

*Specific Purpose:* To persuade my listeners to support mandatory safety devices in all new automobiles.

*Central Idea:* Thousands of lives could be saved each year if all new cars sold in the United States were required to meet basic safety standards.

*Main Points:*
(Problem)   I. Thousands of people are killed on American highways each year because of inadequate safety standards in cars.

(Solution)  II. Legislation should be passed requiring all cars sold in this country to meet basic safety standards.

This pattern has the advantage of simplicity. You convince the listeners that a particular problem exists, and then you tell them how it can be solved. Here is another example:

*Specific Purpose:* To convince my listeners that prison overcrowding can be solved by not incarcerating nonviolent offenders such as embezzlers.

*Central Idea:* Overcrowded conditions in prison can be eliminated if we require nonviolent offenders, such as embezzlers, to perform community service in their hometowns rather than spend time in prison.

*Main Points:*
(Problem)    I. Most American prisons are dangerously overcrowded.
(Solution)  II. Nonviolent offenders such as embezzlers can be required to perform community service in their hometowns rather than spend time in prison.

## Topical Pattern

In the topical pattern, you subdivide your central idea into main points, using logic and common sense as your guides. Thus, the federal government could be divided into three branches: *executive, legislative,* and *judicial.* You can subdivide according to whatever emphasis you wish to give; for example, politics could be divided into *international, national, state,* and *local;* or it could be divided according to the people who practice it: *liberals, moderates,* and *conservatives.* Here is an example of the topical pattern:

*Specific Purpose:* To inform my audience of the two kinds of sleep that all persons experience.
*Central Idea:* The two kinds of sleep that all persons experience at alternating times during the night are NREM (non-rapid-eye-movement) sleep and REM (rapid-eye-movement) sleep.
*Main Points:* I. NREM (non-rapid-eye-movement) sleep is the period in which a person does very little dreaming.
II. REM (rapid-eye-movement) sleep is the period in which a person usually dreams.

Another way of subdividing an idea is to show reasons for it, as in the following example:

*Specific Purpose:* To persuade my listeners to support the 55-miles-per-hour speed limit on interstate highways.
*Central Idea:* The 55-miles-per-hour speed limit should be maintained and enforced on America's interstate highways.
*Main Points:* I. The 55-miles-per-hour speed limit saves thousands of lives each year.
II. The 55-miles-per-hour speed limit conserves fuel.

When you use the topical pattern, you can arrange your main points in whatever order suits the purpose of your speech. In the persuasive speech above, the speaker chose to use the stronger of the two points—that the 55-miles-per-hour limit saves lives—at the beginning of the speech. In some speeches, on the other hand, you may want to put your least important points first and build up to your most important points. Here is such a case:

*Specific Purpose:* To persuade my listeners to buy a personal computer.
*Central Idea:* The personal computer offers the college student opportunities to have fun, keep financial records, and prepare school assignments.
*Main Points:* I. With a personal computer, a student can play mind-expanding games.

II. With a personal computer, a student can keep track of financial records quickly and efficiently.
III. With a personal computer, a student can prepare school assignments and papers with a huge savings of time and energy.

A note of caution: Some students make the mistake of thinking that the topical pattern is a formless bag into which anything can be dumped. Though you have a great deal of liberty to organize the points in whatever order you choose, you still must apply logic—for example, arranging points from least important to most important, or placing material under three major subdivisions.

# Selecting Support Materials

So far in this chapter, we have concentrated on main points, but main points by themselves are not enough for the body of your speech. As we discussed in Chapter 7, you also need support materials to develop and amplify your main points.

To see how support materials can be developed for main points, let us take a look at an outline by student Yolanda DeLeon:

*General Purpose:*  To persuade
*Specific Purpose:*  To persuade my listeners to volunteer their time to tutor illiterate adults.
*Central Idea:*  Illiteracy in America is widespread and harmful, but it can be eliminated if enough volunteers step forward to help.
*Main Points:*  I. Illiteracy is a major social problem in America.
II. Illiterates can learn to read and write if given proper instruction by volunteer tutors.

Yolanda uses the problem-solution pattern, but her first main point (problem) and second main point (solution) both need explanation and elaboration, as shown below:

COMMENTARY

The speaker uses *statistics* from prestigious sources to prove that illiteracy is a serious problem.

I. Illiteracy is a major social problem in America.
  A. Illiteracy is widespread.
    1. A U. S. Senate subcommittee estimates that 25 million American adults cannot read well enough to write a check, read a sign in a store window, or fill out a job application.
    2. The U.S. ranks 49th in literacy out of the 158 member nations of the United Nations.

The speaker uses vivid *examples* to demonstrate the human cost of illiteracy.

*Statistics* are used to show the price society pays for this problem.

*Testimony* from a leading authority lends credibility to the speaker's contention.

These *statistics* are impressive evidence that adults *can* be taught.

The speaker uses more *testimony* from an authority on the subject.

A *narrative* provides a bright picture of the prospects for eliminating illiteracy.

   3. The U.S. Navy found that 30 percent of its recruits were "a danger to themselves and to costly naval equipment" because they couldn't read or understand written instructions.
B. Illiteracy hurts individuals and society in general.
   1. A child was hospitalized in Syracuse, New York, after her illiterate mother mistook a pink dishwashing liquid for medicine.
   2. A worker in Chicago killed a herd of cattle because he couldn't read the word "poison" on a bag that he thought was feed.
   3. A Senate subcommittee estimated the social cost of illiteracy to be $225 billion a year in welfare checks, lost taxes, and crime costs.
   4. One half of all prison inmates are illiterate.
II. Illiterates can learn to read and write if given proper instruction by volunteer tutors.
A. Yale University Professor Jonathan Kozol, author of *Illiterate America* and a leading expert on the problem, says that illiterate adults are capable of learning to read and write, if they are given proper instruction.
B. The leading literacy organization, Laubach Literacy, teaches 60,000 adults to read and write each year.

C. Peter Waite, Laubach's national director, says that thousands of volunteer tutors are needed in each of the 50 states.

D. Lewis Meade was 43 years old when he learned how to read and write.
   1. He had masked his illiteracy in the Army by pretending to be unable to read "without my glasses."
   2. He had masked his illiteracy while employed as a salesman in a paint store by asking customers to point to the color they wanted on a paint chart, then using the corresponding number to fetch the correct can of paint.
   3. He heard a commercial for Laubach Literacy on the radio and went to an adult basic education course for training.
   4. Within six months he was able to read his favorite book—the Bible.

If possible, you should distribute your supporting materials evenly. In other words, don't put all your support under Point I and leave nothing to bolster Point II. This does not mean, however, that in your speeches you should mechanically place the same number of supporting points under every main point. In some speeches, it may turn out that you need five supports for one point and only two for another. You have to consider *quality* as well as *quantity*. One powerful anecdote may be all that is required to illustrate one point, whereas five minor supports might be needed for another point. In chart form, a typical speech might look like this:

Central idea

    Main point
        Support material
        Support material
        Support material
        Support material
        Support material

    Main point
        Support material
        Support material

    Main point
        Support material
        Support material
        Support material

When you are trying to decide how many supporting points to place underneath a main point, use this rule of thumb: have enough supporting points to adequately explain or bolster the main point, but not so many that you become tedious and repetitious.

# Supplying Transitions

Transitions are words, phrases, or sentences that show logical connections between ideas or thoughts. They help the listeners stay with you as you move from one part of your speech to the next. To get an idea of how transitions work, take a look at the following paragraphs and decide which is superior:

1. Mayor Smythe has been involved in graft for years. He is a capable administrator. I intend to vote for him.
2. Mayor Smythe has been involved in graft for years. Nevertheless, he is a capable administrator, so I intend to vote for him.

The second paragraph is obviously superior. The reason is that it contains two transitional words: *nevertheless* and *so*.

In a speech, transitions clarify the relationship between your ideas, thereby making them easy to comprehend. They serve as signals to help the listeners follow your train of thought. Here are just some of the many transitional words or phrases in the English language:

To signal addition: *and, also, besides, furthermore, moreover, in addition*

To signal time: *soon, then, later, afterward, meanwhile*

To signal contrast: *however, but, yet, nevertheless, instead, meanwhile, although*

To signal examples: *for example, to illustrate, for instance*

To signal conclusions: *in summary, therefore, consequently, as a result*

To signal concession: *although it is true that, of course, granted*

In public speaking, there are some special types of transitions that can be employed to help your listener follow your remarks. Let us look at five of them:

## *Bridges*

In crossing a bridge, a person goes from one piece of land to another. In giving a speech, the speaker can build bridges to tell the listeners of the terrain they are leaving behind and the terrain they are about to enter. It is a way of saying, "I've finished Thought A; now I'm going to Thought B."

Imagine that you had the following main points in an outline on professional wrestling:

I. The *Bad Guys* are the villains of professional wrestling.

II. The *Good Guys* are heroes who triumph over hatred, trickery, and diabolical enemies.

How can you go from Point I to Point II? You could simply finish with Point I and begin Point II, but that would be too abrupt. It would fail to give the listeners time to change mental gears. One way to bridge the two points is with a sentence like this: "Well, that's all I have to say about the Bad Guys; let me tell you about the Good Guys." Such a sentence is better than no transition at all, but it is clumsy and artificial. A smoother way to make a bridge is to refer back to the Bad Guys at the same time you are pointing forward to the Good Guys. Here is an example:

If you think that the Bad Guys are absurd exaggerations, you are right, of course, but what about their opponents, the Good Guys? Are they exaggerated to the same degree of absurdity?

This is a successful bridge because it smoothly and gracefully takes your listeners from Point I to Point II. It also has the virtue of stimulating their curiosity about the Good Guys.

Let us examine one more case: Assume that you are preparing a speech on child abuse. The first part of the speech deals with a description of the problem, and the second part deals with solutions. Here is one way to bridge the two parts:

> These examples [just given by the speaker] show that child abuse occurs in all social and economic levels of our society, but is the situation hopeless? Are there any possible solutions?

Now the audience is ready to hear the solutions.

## Internal Summaries

At the end of a baseball game, announcers always give a summary of the game. But during the game itself, they occasionally give a summary of what has taken place up to the present moment ("We're in the middle of the fifth inning; Detroit is leading Milwaukee 4 to 3 on a grand-slam homer by . . ."). Though this is primarily designed for the viewers who have tuned in late, it is also appreciated by the fans who have been watching the entire game because it gives them a feeling of security and confidence—a sense of knowing the "main facts." You can achieve the same effect in a speech. When you finish an important point or group of points, you may want to spend a few moments summarizing your ideas so that they are clear and understandable. This device, called an internal summary, is especially helpful if you have been discussing ideas that are complicated or abstract. An internal summary can be combined with a bridge to make an excellent transition, as follows:

> [*Internal summary*]:   So far we've seen that cocaine can kill a person if it is injected intravenously or if it is smoked as freebase. [*Bridge*]:   But are these the only ways in which cocaine can be deadly? How about the person who sniffs, or "snorts," cocaine?

Here is another example:

> [*Internal summary*]:   By now I hope I've convinced you that all animal bites should be reported to a doctor or health official immediately because of the possibility of rabies. [*Bridge*]:   While you're waiting for an ambulance or for an examination by a doctor, there is one other important thing you should do.

## Internal Previews

Internal previews can be used to tell your audience what lies ahead as you approach a main point or supporting points in your speech. You should not use it for every main point—it would become a cliché—but it is sometimes helpful to lead the audience from one area to another, especially if it is coupled with a bridge, as in this example:

> [*Bridge*]:   Though I've tried to show you the importance of intelligence, let me point out that raw cerebral power alone does not make a manager effective. [*Internal preview*]:   He or she also needs two other things—common sense and a high energy level. Let's spend a moment looking at each of these.

An internal preview can be achieved with a question, as in the following example:

> [*Bridge*]:   If the statistics I've just given you [about child abuse] are correct, we need to look for solutions. [*Internal preview*]:   What can be done to get parents to stop abusing their children?

## Signposts

Just as signposts on a road tell motorists their location, signposts in a speech tell listeners where they are or where they are headed. If you gave a speech on how to treat a cold, you could say, "Here are three things you should do the next time you catch a cold." Then the audience would find it easy to follow your points if you said, "First, you should . . . Second, you should . . . Third, you should . . . ." Using these signposts is much more effective than linking your points by saying, "Also . . ." or "Another point is . . . ."

Another way to enumerate points is to use repetition of phrases, as in this case:

> America is great for three reasons:
> America is great because . . .
> America is great because . . .
> America is great because . . .

## Spotlights

Spotlights are transitional devices that alert the listeners that something important will soon appear. Here are some examples:

> Now we come to the most important thing I have to tell you.

What I'm going to explain now will help you understand the rest of the speech.

Spotlights can build up anticipation and excitement: "And now I come to an idea that can mean extra money in your pocket . . . ." Or: "If you want to feel healthier and happier, listen to the advice of Dr. Jonas Knudsen . . . ."

When you choose transitional devices, remember that your listeners are totally unfamiliar with your speech, so try to put yourself in their place at each juncture. Ask yourself, "How can I lead the listener from one point to another in a way that is logical and smooth?"

## Summary

When you organize your speech, deal with the body first, leaving the introduction and conclusion for later. The best way to organize the body is to devise two or three (or sometimes four) main points based on your central idea. Arrange the main points in a logical pattern, such as chronological, spatial, causal, problem-solution, or topical.

Next, select support materials (as discussed in Chapter 7) to back up the main points, and then supply transitions to help the listeners stay with you as you move from one part of your speech to the next. Common types of transitions are bridges, internal summaries, internal previews, signposts, and spotlights.

## Review Questions

1. How many main points should you have in a speech?
2. How many ideas should be represented in each main point?
3. Which pattern of organization would be best suited for a speech on the solar system?
4. Why are transitions important in a speech?

# TIPS *for your career*

### Tip 9: Give Your Audience a Pretest on Your Main Points

Marcia Collins, an alcohol-rehabilitation counselor who gives talks in her community on drunk driving, has a method that she finds very effective in reinforcing her main points. She always starts by passing out a "test" with three questions that are tied to her three main points. "Let's make a game of this," she tells her listeners. "See how many of these questions you can get right."

Here are the questions:

1. *True or False?* An average-sized driver who has consumed three beers in the past two hours would probably fail a breathalyzer test (for intoxication) if stopped by police.

2. *True or False?* A driver's judgment (such as how fast one can safely drive on a certain road) can become impaired long before he or she shows obvious signs of intoxication (such as slurred speech or poor coordination).

3. *True or False?* Drinking several cups of coffee, taking a cold shower, or doing exercises can counteract the effects of alcohol and enable a drinker to "sober up."

The answers: #1 and #2 are true; #3 is false.

After the listeners take the test, Collins spends the rest of her talk going over the answers. The listeners have a keen interest in following her speech because they want to find out whether they answered correctly. Collins does not embarrass them by asking whether they missed a question, but from the looks of surprise that she sees when she gives the answers, she surmises that most listeners miss #1 and #3.

In her outline, here is the way the main points appear:

I. The legal threshold of intoxication in most states (.10% blood alcohol content) is achieved by a 150-pound person drinking three beers or three glasses of wine or three shots of whisky during a two-hour period.

II. A driver's judgment (such as how fast he or she can safely drive on a certain road) can become impaired long before he or she shows obvious signs of intoxication (such as slurred speech or poor coordination).

III. Only the passage of time—not drinking coffee, exercising, or taking a cold shower—will bring about the metabolism of alcohol.

# Chapter 10

# Introductions and Conclusions

**Introductions**

**Conclusions**

**Sample Introduction and Conclusion**

When Mike Palermo began his classroom speech, he held up a T-shirt with a brightly colored design emblazoned on the front. "This is a shirt that I printed last night," he said. "Designing and printing your own shirt is not difficult and it's not very expensive. Today I'd like to tell you how you can create a design and then print it on a shirt."

Mike then proceeded to outline the steps of the process, after which he concluded his speech by holding up another T-shirt and saying, "Printing shirts like this is not only easy—it's also a lot of fun. I hope you will consider trying it out yourself."

Mike's speech was a success; even people who had no desire to try the hobby were fascinated by his description of the process. Part of Mike's success was due to his interesting introduction and his graceful conclusion.

Some speakers give very little thought to what they are going to say at the beginning of a speech and at the end. Some wait until the actual hour of delivery, preferring to let the mood of the moment determine what they will say. Such inattention to the introduction and conclusion is a big mistake. A faltering or dull introduction can cause the audience to lose interest in both the speaker and the speech. A conclusion that is weak or clumsy can leave the audience with a bad opinion of what otherwise might have been a good speech.

Since both the introduction and the conclusion are crucial to the success of any speech, you should spend as much care and thought in devising them as you do in planning the body of a speech. This chapter will present some valuable guidelines.

# Introductions

The introduction to your speech has two parts: *attention material*, to get your audience's attention and interest, and *orienting material*, which prepares your audience intellectually and psychologically for the body of the speech. Here is a sample, from the beginning of a classroom speech by Virginia Ross:

**Attention Material**
Virginia grabs the attention and interest of her listeners by arousing their curiosity.

I. You may have wondered why some people go to such great extents to get their names in the *Guinness Book of World Records*. Michel Lotito of Evry, France, ate a bicycle—yes, a bicycle—in a period of only three weeks. He first reduced the bike to metal filings, then ate every piece. Henri La Mothe, a 75-year-old New Yorker, became the world's shallow-diving champion by jumping 40 feet from New York City's Flatiron Building into a wading pool filled with only 12 inches of water. He landed on his stomach and was unhurt.

**Orienting Material**
Virginia prepares her audience for the body of the speech. She poses an inter-

II. These are just two people out of thousands who risk their health and sometimes their lives in an effort to get their name in the *Guinness Book of World Records*. Why do these people do such stunts? According to psychologists, these risk takers feel that by

esting question, and then reveals the central idea of the speech. Next, she tells the audience what she will cover in the rest of her speech.

getting their names into the Guinness book, they gain a form of immortality. They insure that they will not die in obscurity—their names will live on. Today I'd like to show you why I think these psychologists are correct in their assessment of risk takers.

In the rest of her speech, Virginia developed her central idea, giving examples and psychologists' insights.

This introduction is fairly simple. For other speeches, there are many different variations and embellishments that can be worked into the introduction, so let's examine how to gain attention and interest (attention material) and how to orient your audience (orienting material) in greater detail.

## Gain Attention and Interest

If you were sitting in an audience, would you want to listen to a speech that begins with this statement: "I'd like to talk to you today about one of our state's most important crops"?

Crops? Who besides farmers and agricultural students would want to hear about corn or wheat or barley? If you are like most people, you would say to yourself, "I don't want to hear about crops . . ." and your mind would drift to something more interesting, such as the party you are planning to attend next weekend.

Now imagine that you had been sitting in the audience when Rex Kent, a student speaker, gave his speech on a crop. Rex began by raising a clenched fist and saying, "I'm holding in my hand something which no human being has ever seen before. And in a few moments, it will be transformed so that no human being will ever see it again." After pausing dramatically, he opened his hand and revealed a peanut in a shell. He cracked open the shell, ate the peanut, and said, "The lowly peanut may seem like an insignificant munchie to you, but it has hundreds of uses that most of you have never heard about. Did you know that peanuts are used to make explosives? And to make shampoos and shaving creams? Today I'd like to tell you about some of these amazing products."

The listeners were hooked. How could they possibly turn their attention away after such an interesting, dynamic beginning? Rex's technique was to use attention material as a lure, just as a fisher dangles bait in front of a fish.

A lure needs to be dangled in front of listeners because of an unfortunate fact: Audiences do not automatically give every speaker their full, undivided, respectful attention. As you begin a speech, you may find that some listeners are engaged in whispered conversations with their neighbors (and they do not necessarily stop in mid-sentence when you start speaking); some are looking at you but their minds are far away, floating in a daydream or enmeshed in a personal problem; some are shifting in their seats to get comfortable; others are thinking about what the preceding speaker said, or looking about the room to see who they know, or trying to figure out when they should slip out if you talk too long. So your task is clear: you must grab their attention when you start talking.

But grabbing their attention is not enough: your introduction must also *keep* their attention, so that they will want to hear your entire speech. Your introduction must deprive them of any possible excuse to sink back into their private thoughts and daydreams. If you simply say, "I'm going to talk about peanuts," you leave it up to the listeners to decide whether they want to listen to the rest of the speech. Do not give them a choice! Devise attention material that is so interesting that it is impossible for anyone *not* to listen to the entire speech.

Let us examine some common attention getters. Keep in mind that sometimes these can be combined.

### Tell a Story

Telling a story is one of the most effective ways to begin a speech because people love to listen to narrative accounts. If you begin a speech with these words—"While fishing early one summer morning, I heard a rustle in the brush behind me and then an awful buzzing sound; I knew instantly that it must be a rattlesnake"—who could resist listening to you? But do not make the mistake of thinking that you can tell an exciting story on one topic and then, once you have the listeners' attention, you can give a speech on a completely different topic. Such a strategy runs the risk of confusing the listeners, and it can make you seem unorganized. Whatever story you tell must be relevant to your central idea and it must provide an easy and natural entry into the rest of your speech.

Let us look at the attention material of Cathy Rogers, a student speaker who gave a talk on hypothermia, a precipitous and potentially fatal drop in body temperature:

> Some friends and I went on a long backpacking trip in mid-January two years ago. I still get chills when I think about the first day of our trip. It was late afternoon when my troubles started. We had been hiking all day and were looking for a campsite because it was getting dark. The wind was blowing hard and it had begun to snow. I was tired and anxious to set up camp, so I ran ahead to look for a good spot. My clothes became sopping wet with sweat. We soon found a level campsite, but it didn't offer much shelter from the wind. I remember rushing around trying to get my tent set up so I could get out of the wind. Since I wasn't running anymore, my body began cooling down rapidly. My feet felt numb and my hands were blocks of ice; I couldn't even tie a knot. My arms and legs hurt as if they had been beaten, and I was shivering uncontrollably. My thoughts seemed scattered

and I would forget what I was going to do next. Fortunately, one of my friends came over to help and noticed my shivering and incoherence. I must have faded out at this time because the next thing I remember is waking up in a tent, in a warm sleeping bag, with dry clothes on. If my friend had not recognized my symptoms and had not acted quickly to raise my body temperature, I probably would have died out there in the snow. I would have died as a victim of hypothermia, a condition in which the body loses heat quicker than it can be restored.

Cathy's story not only captured the audience's attention and interest, but it also provided a natural tie-in with the rest of her speech, which dealt with recognizing and treating hypothermia. Notice that while telling the story, Cathy gracefully inserted a definition of hypothermia, and she gave a preview of the symptoms, which she discussed in detail in the body of the speech.

One kind of story you can use is the hypothetical illustration, as demonstrated by Emily Gallagher in a classroom speech:

It is one year from today, and the United States is at war in the Middle East. You sit down in front of your TV to watch the evening news. The announcer reports the American casualties for that day: 55 men and 40 women have been killed in combat. How would it make you feel, to hear for the first time in American history that women were killed in combat?

In the rest of her speech she argued against the idea of women being drafted for combat duty in the armed forces.

## Ask a Question

Asking a question can be an effective way to intrigue your listeners and encourage them to think about your subject matter as you discuss it. There are two kinds of questions that you can use as attention material: rhetorical and overt-response.

With a *rhetorical* question, you do not want or expect the listeners to answer overtly by raising their hands or answering out loud. Instead, you want to trigger an inner curiosity. For example:

With powerful radio signals being beamed into outer space at this very moment, is there any realistic chance that during our lifetime we human beings will establish radio contact with other civilizations in the universe?

Such a question not only catches the attention of the listeners, but it also makes them want to hear more. It entices them into listening to your speech for the answer to the question.

With an *overt-response* question, you want the audience to reply by raising their hands or answering out loud. Here is an example:

Dave Rodriguez, a student speaker, began his speech by asking, "Other than swimming, what is the most dangerous sport or recreational activity in America, considering the number of people who lose their lives? Would anyone like to take a guess?"

The listeners were intrigued. "Football?" asked one student.

"No, it's not football."

"Mountain climbing?" asked another person.

"No, it's not mountain climbing."

"Hang-gliding?" asked a third student.

"No, it's not hang-gliding. Other than swimming, the most dangerous outdoor recreational activity in America is . . . bicycling. Last year, 1,200 Americans were killed while riding their bicycles."

Thus, Dave effectively launched his speech on the importance of bicycle safety. Note that he did not drag out the suspense too long. If listeners are forced to guess and guess and guess until the right answer is found, they might become exasperated, wishing that the speaker would get to the point.

Never ask embarrassing or personal questions such as, "How many of you have ever tried cocaine?" or "How many of you use an underarm deodorant every day?" An audience would rightfully resent such questions as intrusions into their private lives.

Do not divide your audience into opposing camps by asking "loaded" questions like this: "How many of you are smart enough to realize that capital punishment is an absolute necessity in a society based on law and order?" By phrasing your question in this way, you insult those who disagree with you.

With some overt-response questions, you can try to get every member of the audience to participate, but this can be very risky, especially if you poll the audience in this way: "How many of you favor the death penalty? Raise your hands. Okay . . . now, how many of you are opposed to the death penalty? Okay, thanks . . . how many of you are undecided or unsure?" What if three people raised their hands for the first question, five for the second question, ten for the third, while the remaining 67 people in the audience refused to cooperate? This can happen, and often does, much to the embarrassment of the speaker. Sometimes audiences are in a passive or even grumpy mood; this is especially true with audiences that are required (at work or at school) to listen to your speech. My advice is to refrain from asking questions that require the participation of the entire audience.

Make sure the audience is clear on whether you are asking a rhetorical question or an overt-response question. If you ask, "How long will Americans continue to tolerate shoddy products?" the audience knows that you are not expecting someone to answer, "Five years." It is clearly a rhetorical question. But suppose you ask a question like this: "How many of you

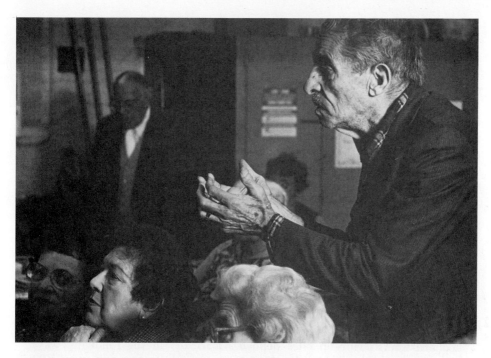

**Getting members of the audience to respond to a question is an excellent way to spark interest in a speech.** *(Deborah Kahn/Stock, Boston)*

have ever gone swimming in the ocean?" The listeners might be confused on whether you want them to raise their hands. Make it clear. If you want a show of hands, say so at the beginning: "I'd like to see a show of hands, please: How many of you have ever gone swimming in the ocean?" Alerting them in advance not only helps them know what you want, but it also makes them pay special attention to the question since they know that you are expecting them to respond.

## Make a Startling Statement

An opening remark that shocks or surprises the listeners can certainly get their attention. One student speaker began with the following:

> Some of you came to college straight out of high school. Some of you came to college straight out of the military. Well, I came to college straight out of prison.

The audience was electrified. Why had he spent time in prison? For murder? For armed robbery? For a lesser offense? The student went on to explain, "I spent two years in La Tuna, a federal prison near El Paso,

Texas, for trying to smuggle cocaine from South America into the United States." Then he used the rest of the speech to discuss the flow of illegal drugs into the United States. His dramatic introduction not only captured the interest of his audience, but it also established his credibility to speak on his subject.

A provocative statement can be made by taking a statistic, such as the fact that 25 percent of all Americans will be afflicted by cancer, and restating it in terms that will have an impact on the audience; for example:

> There are forty of you sitting out there in the audience. According to medical statistics, ten of you will someday be afflicted by that most dreaded of all diseases—cancer.

Such an opener is certain to draw your listeners in.

### Cite a Quotation

Quotations can provide a lively beginning for a speech. In a classroom talk on weight-reducing programs, Gail Zarefsky began by saying:

> Leonard Louis Levinson once defined Americans in the following way: "Americans are people who laugh at African witch doctors and spend 100 million dollars a year on fake reducing systems." It is true that many of us are suckers for a quick way to lose 10 pounds. How can we tell whether a weight-reducing plan is a scam or a legitimate method?

Quotations usually work best when they are short. Do not have a quotation that is so long that the listeners lose track of where the quotation ends and your remarks begin. The best way to indicate that you have finished quoting is to pause at the end of the quotation. The pause acts as an oral "punctuation" device, signaling the end of one thought and the beginning of another.

I do not recommend beginning with the actual quotation itself. Consider the following:

> *Poor:*  "Science has promised us truth. It has never promised us either peace or happiness." These words, by French psychologist Gustave Le Bon, offer a valuable insight into the nature of science.

> *Better:*  A French psychologist named Gustave Le Bon made an interesting observation about science. He said, "Science has promised us truth. It has never promised us either peace or happiness."

While the first version is better for a written composition, the second is better for a speech because the listeners need time to tune out distracting thoughts and tune in to you. If they fail to pick up the name of the French psychologist, no harm has been done; what you want them to get is the quotation.

If a quotation is too concise, it may go by so fast that the audience does not have a chance to absorb it. In such cases, it is a good idea to repeat it, as in this example:

> Bertrand Russell once said, "The opposite of love is not hate, but indifference." Think about that for a moment: "The opposite of love is not hate, but indifference."

In print, this repetition looks silly, but in a speech the audience is grateful for the "instant replay." It allows time for the idea to sink in.

### Arouse Curiosity

An effective attention getter is one that piques the curiosity of the audience. In a speech on common misconceptions about snakes and snakebites, student speaker Lynn Baker began by saying:

> When a person gets bit by a poisonous snake, some people think that the best thing to use is a tourniquet to tie around the injured limb, but they're wrong. Some people think the best thing to use is a knife to make an incision, but they're wrong. Some people think the best thing to use is a suction device to suck out the venom, but they're wrong. All of these devices have serious medical drawbacks, as I shall explain in a moment. So, what is the best thing to use?

Having aroused the curiosity of her listeners, Lynn picked up her purse; as she reached inside, she said:

> The best thing to have for a snakebite is a little item that all of you carry in your pocket or your purse. Here it is.

With a flourish, she displayed her car keys. Then she went on to explain that driving a snakebite victim to a hospital is more likely to save the person's life than giving first aid. At the hospital, the victim can be given an injection of antivenin, which she said is the best life-saving method of all.

### Provide a Visual Aid or Demonstration

Any of the visual aids we discussed in Chapter 8 could be used to introduce a speech, but you must be sure that while the aids get the audience's attention, they also are relevant to the main points of your speech. One student showed slides of sunbathers on a beach to begin a talk on sharks. Though there was a logical link (sometimes sunbathers who go into the water must worry about sharks), the connection was too weak to justify using these particular slides. In a case like this, it would be better to show a slide of a ferocious shark while describing a shark attack.

A demonstration can make an effective opener. Working with a friend, one student gave a demonstration of how to fight off an attacker, and then talked on martial arts. If you want to give a demonstration, you should get permission from your instructor beforehand. One note of caution about demonstrations: never do anything that might upset the listeners. Holding a revolver and firing a blank to start off a speech on gun control or suicide would upset some people and put them out of a receptive mood.

## Give the Audience an Incentive to Listen

At the beginning of a speech, many listeners have an attitude that can be summed up in these two questions: "What's in it for me? Why should I pay attention to this speech?" Such people need to be given an incentive to listen to the entire speech. So, whenever possible, you should state explicitly why the listeners will benefit by hearing you out. It is not enough to simply say, "My speech is very important." You have to *show* them how your topic relates to their personal lives and their own best interests. If, for example, you were giving a talk on cardiopulmonary resuscitation (CPR), you could say, "Everyone in this room may someday have a friend or loved one collapse from a heart attack right in front of your eyes. If you know CPR, you might be able to save that person's life." Now each person in the audience sees clearly that your speech is important to his or her personal life.

Sometimes giving the audience an incentive to listen is a technique that can be combined with some of the attention-getting devices already discussed in this chapter. Student speaker Pam Sluder, for example, gave a speech on anorexia nervosa, a pathological loss of appetite that some- times results in death. Pam started off with a heart-rending story of a 17- year-old victim of the disorder. Then, realizing that her listeners might feel that anorexia nervosa had no relevance to their own lives, she pro- vided them with a little extra motivation to listen to the rest of her speech: "You may never suffer from anorexia nervosa yourself, but someone you love may struggle with it someday. Will you know how to help?"

Be careful about promising too much. Do not say, "How would you like to live in perfect happiness for the rest of your life?" and then discuss the joys of the macrobiotic diet. Though you may be enthusiastic about such a diet, your listeners will distrust what you have to say because you have overstated your case.

If you know some listeners have probably heard most of your speech material before, you can try to use incentives especially designed for them. Professional speaker Joel Weldon gave a talk to over 700 business and industrial trainers at a national convention of the American Society for Training and Development. His speech consisted of tips on how to train people. In his introduction, he said:

> I know some of you are pros who have been involved in training for twenty years. When you hear some of these ideas you're going to say, "I've heard all this before." I'm sure you have. But as you say that to yourself, ask yourself these two questions: Am I using this idea? And how can I improve it?[1]

Weldon's technique was effective because he acknowledged the presence and the experience of the "pros," and then he challenged them to give his "old" ideas a fresh look. The incentive he dangled in front of the pros was the possibility of doing an even better job of training than they had done in the past—by using and improving the old ideas.

## Orient the Audience

Once you have snared the interest of your listeners by means of the attention material, you should go into the second part of your introduction, the *orienting material*, which gives an orientation—a clear sense of what your speech is about, and any other information that the audience might need in order to understand and absorb your ideas. The orienting material is a road map that makes it easy for the listeners to stay with you on the journey of your speech and not get lost and confused.

The orienting material does more than prepare the listeners intellectually for your speech; it also prepares them psychologically. It reassures them that you are well-prepared, purposeful, and considerate of their needs and interests. It shows that you are someone they can trust.

The three most common ways to orient the audience are: (1) preview the body of the speech, (2) give background information, and (3) establish credibility.

### Preview the Body of the Speech

Have you ever listened to a speech or a lecture and realized afterward that you had listened with the "wrong set of ears"—that is, your mental apparatus had been attuned to evaluating one thing when it should have been attuned to evaluating something else? I once heard a man speak on woodstoves. He plunged right into his speech, giving details about various woodstoves. Sitting out in the audience, I guessed that he was trying to show the advantages of wood as a heating source. I geared my mind to pick out those advantages. Halfway through the speech, however, I realized that I had guessed wrong. His real subject was safety features of woodstoves. Unfortunately I had not paid close enough attention to the safety features—I had listened with the wrong set of ears—so I failed to absorb some of his points. It was too late to retrieve the information, of course; in a speech, there is no instant replay.

To help your listeners use the "right set of ears," give them a preview of the body of the speech. In the example just cited, the speaker should have said something like this as orienting material: "Today I want to show you that woodstoves can be used in a safe way, so that your house doesn't catch fire. I plan to give you three tips to follow . . ." With such a preview, all the listeners would have known what to listen for.

Your instructor may have specific requirements for what you must put in your preview. Unless he or she advises you otherwise, I recommend that you include your central idea and/or main points.

1. *State the central idea.* Your audience can listen intelligently to your speech if you stress your central idea in the orienting material. For example, "Acid rain is killing all the trees on our highest peaks in the East. Today I'd like to give you evidence to back up my claim." (In some speeches, as we shall see in Chapter 15, you may want to delay giving the central idea until the end of the speech, but in most cases, it is best to state it in the orienting material.)

2. *State the main points.* In most speeches listeners appreciate being given a brief preview of your main points. For example, student speaker Barbara LeBlanc said, "I believe that passive-solar heating should be used in every home. Today I'd like to show you two reasons why you should consider using passive solar: First, it's easy to adapt your house to passive solar. Second, the energy from passive solar is absolutely free. Let me explain what I'm talking about." By stating the main points, Barbara not only helped the audience listen intelligently but she also gave them an incentive to listen: she mentioned the possibility of saving money.

Giving a preview by stating the central idea and/or main points reassures the listeners that you are not going to ramble. In other words, you give the audience a message that says, loud and clear, "I'm well-prepared; I know exactly what I'm going to say; I'm not going to waste your time." This last "message" is important, because audiences like speakers who don't waste their time, and they resent speakers who do.

### Give Background Information

Part of your orienting material can be devoted to giving background information—definitions, explanations, and so on—to help your listeners understand your speech. For example, in a classroom speech on hypochondriacs, Lucinda Howard used her orienting material to define the term:

Hypochondriacs are people who have a morbid preoccupation with disease. They usually think that they are ill in some way or another. I want to make clear that they are *not* malingering. Malingerers are people who fake illness; they know they're not really sick. Hypochondriacs, on the other hand, truly believe that they're ill.

Notice that Lucinda not only defined her term but she clarified her definition by contrasting hypochondriacs with malingerers to make sure that her audience did not confuse the two.

Sometimes it helps the audience if you explain the limitations of your speech. For example, assume that you are giving a speech on the notion that criminals should make restitution to their victims. If you are not careful, many people in your audience will reject your argument immediately by saying to themselves: "Restitution, baloney! How can a murderer make restitution to his victim?" So in your orienting material, you head off such objections by saying, "In this speech I will talk about criminals making restitution to their victims, but I'm only talking about nonviolent criminals such as swindlers, embezzlers, and bad-check writers. I'm not talking about rapists and murderers." By showing the boundaries of your subject, you increase the chances that the audience will listen with open minds.

## Establish Credibility

No one expects you to be the world's authority on your subject, but you can increase your audience's chances of accepting your ideas if you can give some credentials or reasons why you are qualified to speak on the subject. Here is how three student speakers established their credibility: In the orienting material of her speech on schizophrenia, Rachel Weintraub told of her experiences as a psychiatric assistant in a mental hospital. In the introduction of a speech arguing for better treatment of American Indians, William Lone Wolf briefly described his childhood on an Indian reservation. Before demonstrating the correct way to resuscitate a person who is in danger of drowning, Cynthia Cunningham related her experiences as a lifeguard. In all three of these cases, the students strengthened their speeches by establishing their credibility as part of the orienting material.

Do not be shy about giving your credentials or background; the audience appreciates information about your degree of interest and expertise. It helps them evaluate what you have to say. Be sure, however, to give this information in a way that is modest and tactful, rather than boastful and arrogant. Here are two ways of saying the same thing:

*Poor:* "I lived on the Mexican border for ten years, so I know more about the illegal alien situation than anybody in this room."

*Better:* "Before I moved here, I lived in a town on the Mexican border for ten years. I talked to a lot of illegal aliens and their employers during those years. I'd like to share some of the insights I gained from those conversations."

In the first example, the speaker would irritate the audience by the claims of superiority. The second example is preferable because the speaker is giving background experience in a way that is straightforward and inoffensive.

Sometimes it is helpful for audiences to know how you got your speech together. Consider the following examples:

> *Poor:* When I decided I wanted to speak on computers, I went to two different computer stores to get information and I couldn't find a thing that was helpful. All I got were a lot of sales pitches and a bunch of advertising brochures. Then I called up a member of a local computer club, and he gave me information that was over my head. I couldn't understand all that computer jargon. After that, I decided to hit the library, and I looked through a lot of books and finally came up with some pretty good information.

> *Better:* I want to tell you about a computer that actually talks to you in a humanlike voice. Sounds incredible? I thought it was incredible, too, until I went over to the computer lab and sat down for a fifteen-minute chat with a computer named Melvin.

The first example adds nothing to the content of the speech, and it does nothing to establish credibility. In the second example, the speaker's background information makes the rest of the speech more believable than it would otherwise be. It shows that the speaker is talking from personal experience, not on the basis of a science fiction story. The rule of thumb is: do not give any background information unless it will enhance your speech or your credibility.

## Guidelines for Introductions

Here are some points to keep in mind for introductions:

1. *Do not prepare your introduction first.* When you prepare a speech, it usually works best to complete the body of the speech and *then* work on your introduction. Once you have developed your main points, you are in a stronger position to decide how to introduce them.

2. *Make your introduction simple and easy to follow, but avoid making it too brief.* Your audience needs time to get into the groove of your speech. If the introduction is too short, it may go by too fast for the listeners to absorb. That is why effective joke tellers stretch out their introduction to give the listeners time to get "into" the joke. If the idea of stretching out an introduction sounds wrong to you, it is probably because you have been taught in English classes to write concisely. While it is a sin in

English composition to stretch out essays, it is a virtue to do so with a speech's introduction that might otherwise be too abrupt for an audience. A note of caution: do not let this tip cause you to go to the opposite extreme—being tedious and long-winded. Be brief, but not too brief. If you are unsure about whether you have achieved a happy medium, deliver your speech to relatives or friends and then ask them if your introduction was too long or too short.

3. *Make sure that your introduction has a direct and obvious tie-in with the body of the speech.* A common mistake is for speakers to give an introduction that has a weak or dubious link with the rest of the speech. This kind of introduction can be annoying and confusing to the listeners.

# Conclusions

When movies are made, the producers spend a lot of time and energy on getting a "perfect" ending because they know that if the ending is unsatisfying, the viewers will tend to downplay the film as a whole. As with the movies, the ending of a speech can either add to or subtract from the audience's opinion of the entire speech. So it is worthwhile to spend a lot of time working on your conclusion.

In your conclusion, you should do three important things: (1) signal the end of a speech to satisfy the audience's psychological need for a sense of completion, (2) summarize the key ideas of the speech, and (3) reinforce the central idea with a clincher. Let us discuss these points in greater detail.

## *Signal the End*

You should always give the audience some sort of advance signal that you are nearing the end of your speech. Do not come to an abrupt halt and then sit down. An abrupt ending jars the audience.

Imagine that you are listening to your favorite song on the radio and letting your mind float freely with the music. Then suddenly, before the song is finished, the disc jockey cuts in with a commercial or a news bulletin. You missed only the last 10 seconds of the song, but you feel annoyed. Why? Because most people need to experience a sense of completion. In listening to a speech, we have the same need for a sense of finality. We like to hear a conclusion that is psychologically satisfying, one that ties up all loose ends and wraps the speech into a nice, neat package. When a speaker ends a speech abruptly, we feel a vague dissatisfaction.

How do we know when a song or a speech is coming to an end? In the case of a song, we intuitively detect the techniques commonly used—the music builds to a rousing finish, or the sound gradually fades away.

Likewise in listening to speeches, we recognize the signals that speakers give to indicate that they are coming to the end of their speech. These signals can be placed in two categories: verbal and nonverbal.

*Verbal signals.* You can openly announce that you are coming to your conclusion by using such expressions as, "So, in conclusion, I'd like to say . . .," "Let me end by saying . . .," or "Let me remind you of the three major points I've been trying to explain today."

*Nonverbal signals.* Even if you do not use verbal signals, you can give two nonverbal cues: (1) say your conclusion with a tone of dramatic finality, and (2) subtly intensify your facial expression and gestures. These cues should come naturally to you, since you have observed numerous speakers use them in your lifetime. If you feel unsure of yourself, practice your conclusion in front of a mirror or, better yet, in front of a friend (who can give you feedback). You can also say it into a tape recorder and listen to see if you have the appropriate tone of finality in your voice.

## *Summarize the Key Ideas*

Because listening is often a difficult mental task, some people in the audience might get drowsy or inattentive toward the end of your speech. When you signal to the listeners that you are about to finish, you do more than provide them with the pleasant anticipation of an ending; you also increase their alertness. If they know they can rest soon, they may summon the mental energy required to stay alert for a few more minutes. Like runners near the finish line, they can bring forth an extra burst of energy.

This mental alertness of your listeners gives you a good opportunity to drive home your message one more time. One of the best ways to do this is to summarize your key ideas. There is a formula for giving a speech that has been making the rounds for years. Sometimes it is attributed to a spellbinding country preacher, sometimes to a savvy Irish politician. The true originator will probably never be known, but the formula is worth heeding:

Tell 'em what you're going to tell 'em.

Tell 'em.

Then tell 'em what you told 'em.

The first sentence refers to the introduction, the second to the body, and the third to a summary in the conclusion. The summary gives you a chance to restate the central idea and/or the main points.

If you are like a lot of people, you may say, "Why do I need to repeat my message? After all, in the body of my speech, I give the audience five minutes' worth of beautifully organized, forcefully delivered information.

If I hit this stuff again in the conclusion, won't I be guilty of overkill?" No, research shows that a restatement of your main points will increase the likelihood that the listeners will remember them.[2]

A summary should be brief. Do not get bogged down in explaining each point a second time; do all your explaining in the body of the speech. The following summary, for example, succinctly boils down the body of the speech into a few brief sentences, reiterating how a person can avoid being hit by lightning:

> So remember, if you're ever caught outside during a thunderstorm, you can avoid being struck by lightning if you follow the rules I've discussed: If you're on a bike or motorcycle, get off immediately. If you're in a car, stay there. If you're in the woods, crouch in a low area and stay away from lone trees. Wherever you are, don't touch metal.

Listeners do not mind hearing this kind of information again; it helps them retain it. I recommend that you try to combine a summary with at least one other technique, as discussed in the following section. For example, the summary of the rules regarding lightning could be followed by a brief story about a person who was killed by lightning because he or she did not know the rules.

## *Reinforce the Central Idea with a Clincher*

In addition to providing a summary, you should try to end your speech with a clinching statement that reinforces the central idea—a statement that drives home the main theme of your entire speech. Edward L. Friedman explains the process:

> It has been said that the speaker drives home his talk in the same way that the carpenter drives a nail into a floor. He begins with the introduction, which generally consists of a few preliminary taps to get the speech started right. Then he gets into the body of the speech, which is like delivering one hammer blow after another to drive the nail into its proper place with carefully executed strokes. In conclusion the carpenter executes a powerful, clinching blow. The experienced speaker also endeavors in his conclusion to deal a powerful, clinching blow.[3]

Use a clincher that is memorable, that leaves a lasting impression with the listener. You can find clinchers by using some of the techniques mentioned earlier in this chapter for the introduction (such as a rhetorical question or a visual aid), or by using some of the following techniques.

### Cite a Quotation

A good quotation can dramatize and reinforce a speaker's central idea. One of the best examples of this technique can be found in the closing words of Martin Luther King's famous "I Have a Dream" speech:

> When we let freedom ring, when we let it ring from every village and every hamlet, from every state and every city, we will be able to speed up that day when all of God's children, black men and white men, Jews and Gentiles, Protestants and Catholics, will be able to join hands and sing in the words of the old Negro spiritual, "Free at last! Free at last! Thank God almighty, we are free at last!"[4]

Eye contact is important at the end of your speech, so if you use a quotation, practice it so that you can say it while looking at the audience, with only occasional glances at your notes.

### Issue an Appeal or Challenge

In a persuasive speech, you can end by making an appeal or issuing a challenge to the audience. If you are trying to persuade the listeners to donate blood, you can end by saying:

> Next week the bloodmobile will be on campus. I call upon each of you to spend a few minutes donating your blood so that others may live.

If you are trying to convince the listeners that they should develop physical fitness, you can issue a challenge:

> Don't start exercising tomorrow or next week or next month. Start exercising *today.*

### Use an Illustration

An illustration is a popular way to reinforce the central idea of a speech. For example, Angela Di Napoli gave a classroom speech in which she urged her listeners to get an evaluation of any old coins they possessed, and she concluded with a true story that illustrated her point:

> Several years ago a woman in New England was rummaging through a trunk in her attic when she came across a box full of old coins. She took them to a coin dealer and got an evaluation. All of the coins were worthless except one. It was a five-dollar gold piece issued in 1849. The coin dealer informed the woman of its present-day value—*five thousand dollars.* So if you have some old coins lying around your house, take them to a reputable coin dealer for an evaluation. You, too, may be the owner of a very valuable coin.

You can close a speech with an example or narrative from someone else's life, as Angela did, or you can relate an event from your own personal experience.

### Refer to the Introduction

Using the conclusion to hearken back to something said in the introduction is an effective and graceful way to wrap up your speech. One way to do this is to answer a question asked at the beginning of a speech. Student speaker Daniel Hirata asked in his introduction, "Should we permit job discrimination on the basis of a person's weight?" In the conclusion, Daniel repeated the question and then answered it: "Should we allow job discrimination against overweight people? From what I've said today, I hope you'll agree that the answer is 'no'. To deny a person a job simply because he or she is overweight is as wrong as to deny a person a job because of skin color or ethnic background."

## *Guidelines for Conclusions*

There are four pitfalls to avoid in conclusions:

1. *Don't drag out the ending.* Some speakers fail to prepare a conclusion in advance. When they reach what should be the end of their remarks, they cannot think of a graceful way to wrap things up, so they keep on talking. Other speakers signal the end of their speech (by saying something like, "So, in closing, let me say . . ."), but then they drone on and on. This gives false hope to the listeners. When they see that the speaker is not keeping the promise, they feel deceived and become restless.

2. *Do not end weakly.* If you close with a statement such as, "I guess that's about all I've got to say," and your voice is nonchalant and unenthusiastic, you encourage your listeners to downgrade your entire speech. End with confidence.

3. *Do not end apologetically.* Earlier, we discussed the reasons why you should not apologize at the start of a speech. The same principles apply to the conclusion. There is no need to say: "That just about does it. I'm sorry I didn't have more time to prepare . . .," or: "That's it, folks. I guess I should have looked up more facts on . . . ." Apologies make you look bad. Besides, some people may not have noticed anything wrong with your speech or your delivery; you may have done better than you realized. So why apologize?

4. *Never bring in new main points.* It is okay to bring in fresh material for your conclusion; in fact, it is a good idea to do so, as long as the

material does not constitute a new main point. For an illustration, look at the following conclusions, which are based on a speech about the advantages of swimming.

> *Poor:*   So if you're looking for a good sport to take up for fun and health, remember that swimming dissipates your accumulated tension, it builds up your endurance, and it gives you a good workout without putting a strain on your muscles or joints. And, oh yes, another good reason for swimming: it can prevent you from developing back problems in old age.

> *Better:*   So if you're looking for a good sport to take up for fun and health, remember that swimming dissipates your accumulated tension, it builds up your endurance, and it gives you a good workout without putting a strain on your muscles or joints. I go over to the Y for a twenty-minute swim three days a week, and I always come out feeling healthy and invigorated. I wouldn't trade swimming for any other sport in the world.

The first conclusion is faulty because it lets a whole new point (the issue of back problems) slip in. Since this is the first the listeners have heard of the matter, it could confuse them. "Huh?" they may say to themselves. "Did I miss something that was said earlier?" Some listeners would expect you to elaborate on this new main point, but if you did, you would drag out your conclusion and spoil the sense of finality. The second conclusion has fresh material, but this material is not a new main point. It is merely a testimonial that underlines the message of the speech.

# Sample Introduction and Conclusion

To see how the principles discussed in this chapter can be applied to a speech, let us examine how one speaker, student Amy McGuffin, developed an introduction and a conclusion for a speech on lie detectors.[5]

## Lie Detectors

In preparing any speech, you should start with the specific purpose and central idea, and then develop the body. After the body has been fully developed, prepare your introduction and conclusion.

**Specific Purpose:** To persuade my audience to support legislation that would bar businesses from using lie detector tests in hiring and evaluating employees.

**Central Idea:** Businesses should be prohibited by law from using lie detector tests when they hire or evaluate employees.

**INTRODUCTION**

    I. How would you feel if you went for a job interview and were told that to be seriously considered for the job, you would have to permit yourself to be strapped to a lie detector machine and then asked a series of questions such as these:

        "Have you ever stolen money from anyone?"

**Attention Material**
The speaker starts off with a rhetorical question. No-

tice how effective it is to draw the listeners in by using the pronoun "you."

**Orienting Material**
The speaker gives some background information on her subject.

Notice how casually, but effectively, she introduces and defines the technical word "polygraph."

The speaker tells the audience precisely what will be covered in the speech, giving a preview of the three main points and her central idea.

"Have you ever had sexual relations with someone other than your spouse?"
"Do you change your underwear everyday?"
II. More and more businesses are using polygraphs—or lie detectors—to help them decide whom to hire, and also whether to fire the employees they already have. More than one million Americans take lie detector tests every year. Today I'd like to discuss lie detectors and try to answer these questions: Why do businesses use them? Are they reliable? Should we continue using them? By the time I'm finished, I hope you'll agree that businesses should be prohibited by law from using lie detectors.

[In the body of the speech, the speaker explains why some businesses use polygraphs to delve into the private lives of potential or present employees. She also uses psychologists' research to show that lie detectors are very unreliable in exposing lies; that many innocent people have been falsely accused by the machines, and that some criminals have learned how to cheat the machine. Then she outlines national legislation to bar the use of polygraphs.]

In the first part of the conclusion, the speaker summarizes the main points, but uses fresh language to do so.

In the final part of the conclusion, the speaker reiterates the central idea and appeals for audience action.

The final sentence is powerful because the speaker appeals to each listener's self-interest.

**CONCLUSION**
I. Though lie detectors sometimes smoke out the guilty, they are so unreliable that they endanger the innocent. I am sympathetic with the desire of businesses to prevent employee dishonesty and theft, but other means will have to be found—means that do not diminish the dignity of human beings, means that do not sometimes punish the innocent, means that do not use voodoo science.
II. Employees need to be protected from this voodoo science, and I urge each of you to support the legislation (which I discussed a moment ago) to bar businesses from using polygraphs. The innocent person whom you protect may be . . . yourself.

## Summary

Much of the success of a speech depends upon how well the speaker handles the introduction and conclusion. The introduction consists of two parts: attention material (to gain the audience's attention and interest), and orienting material (to prepare the audience intellectually and psychologically for the rest of the speech).

For attention material, you can use one or more of the following techniques: tell a story, ask a question, make a provocative statement, cite a quotation, arouse curiosity, provide a visual aid or demonstration, and provide the audience with an incentive to listen. For orienting material, you can preview the body of the speech, give background information, and establish your credibility.

The conclusion of your speech should signal the end, summarize your key ideas, and reinforce the central idea with a clincher. Examples of clinchers are any of the above techniques mentioned for attention material, plus a quotation, an appeal or a challenge, an illustration, and a reference to the introduction.

## Review Questions

1. Why is it necessary to have attention material at the beginning of a speech?
2. What is the purpose of the orienting material?
3. What is a rhetorical question?
4. Why is it a mistake to use a quotation as the first sentence of your speech?
5. Why is it a mistake to end a speech abruptly?

# TIPS *for your career*

### Tip 10: Use an "Icebreaker" to Start Off a Community Speech

You have probably noticed that many speakers at business and professional meetings start off by saying something like this: "I'm glad to have a chance to speak to you today." They are giving what I call an "icebreaker"—a polite little prologue to "break the ice" before getting into their speech.

In outline form, here is how an introduction with an icebreaker would look:

I. Icebreaker
II. Attention material
III. Orienting material

An icebreaker is helpful because it eases your nervous tension and it lets the audience get accustomed to your voice. You do not need an icebreaker for classroom speeches because your audience has already settled down and is ready to listen (besides, most instructors would disapprove of using one), but when you give speeches out in the community, you may want to use it.

I do not like "Hello, how are you?" as an icebreaker. It sounds too breezy and flip. It leaves a question as to whether the speaker wants the audience to roar a response like "Fine, thank you!" It is much better to say, "I appreciate the opportunity to speak to you tonight." But, you might object, phrases like this have been used so often, they are meaningless. Yes, they are. They are clichés. But they are also valuable aids to smooth social relationships. When you engage in small talk with your friends, you use sentences like, "Hi, how are you?" Such expressions are trite but they are necessary because they lubricate the wheels of human discourse.

In addition to expressing appreciation for the invitation to speak, you can include a thank-you to the person who introduced you or a reference to the occasion ("I'm delighted to take part in the celebration of Martin Luther King's birthday"). Some speakers also use the icebreaker to formally greet the audience. This custom, however, has fallen out of fashion. In the old days, orators would begin their speeches like this: "Madame President, Distinguished Members of the Paradox Society, Honored Guests, Ladies and Gentlemen, Greetings!" Such introductions are used today only in formal, traditional settings, such as a college commencement. In most of the speeches you will give in your life, a flowery greeting would sound pompous.

A note of caution: An icebreaker should be very brief—just a sentence or two. If you are too slow getting into your attention material, you may cause some listeners to tune you out.

*Chapter 11*

# Outlining the Speech

**Guidelines for Outlining**
    Use the Standard Outline Form
    Avoid Single Subdivisions
    Use Complete Sentences
    Use Cards for Preliminary Outlines

**Parts of the Outline**
    Title
    Purposes and Central Idea
    Introduction and Conclusion
    Body
    Transitions
    Bibliography
    Visual Aids

**Sample Outline**

**Speaking Notes**
    Sample Speaking Notes
    Using Speaking Notes

**Controlling Your Material**

**Speech as Presented**

In 1912, a new hotel was built in Baltimore—the New Howard Hotel. When the furnaces in the basement were fired up, a startling discovery was made. The builders of the hotel had failed to include chimneys![1]

This spectacular blunder illustrates the importance of using an architect's blueprint, or detailed plan, when constructing a building. The hotel builders had failed to follow a well-defined master plan.

Just as a blueprint helps a builder construct a building, an outline helps you construct a speech. An outline permits you to organize your thoughts into a logical sequence, and to see which points are irrelevant or improperly placed or poorly developed.

Some students dislike writing an outline because they consider it unnecessary, a total waste of time. As one student put it, "I know what I'm going to say—I've got the outline in my head." However, most people who shun written outlines discover sooner or later that their method hurts them. They may fail to present information in the clearest, most logical manner possible; they may annoy the audience with confusing or irrelevant material, or they may sit down after a speech and suddenly realize that they left out a very important point.

I strongly recommend that you use an outline not only for your classroom speeches but for any speech that you give in life. An outline will remind you to include "chimneys," and it will help you construct solid, livable hotels that your audience will enjoy staying in. In this chapter, we will examine how to prepare an outline, and then how to make speaking notes based on the outline.

# Guidelines for Outlining

Outlining is a common-sense way of organizing information in a logical pattern. Professional baseball, for example, can be organized in the following way:

  I. American League
 II. National League

Each league could be subdivided into its divisions; for example:

I. American League
  A. East Division
  B. West Division

Each division in turn could be subdivided by names of teams:

I. American League
  A. East Division
    1. Baltimore
    2. Boston

**Creating an outline for a speech is time well spent because it helps the speaker include key details and organize the points in a logical sequence.** *(Bob Daemmrich/TexaStock)*

    3. Cleveland
    4. Detroit
    5. Milwaukee
    6. New York
    7. Toronto
  B. West Division
    1. California
    2. Chicago
    3. Kansas City
    4. Minnesota
    5. Oakland
    6. Seattle
    7. Texas

Each team could then be subdivided into groups—staff, pitchers, infielders, outfielders—and then the groups could be broken down into individuals. Under each individual name, there could be subdivisions showing batting averages, etc.

Here are some important points to keep in mind as you prepare your outlines.

## Use the Standard Outline Form

In the standard outline form, you mark your main points with Roman numerals (I, II, III, etc.), then place the next level of supporting materials underneath in capital letters (A, B, C, etc.), then go to Arabic numerals, then to small letters, etc. Here is the standard form:

I. Major division
II. Major division
  A. First-level subdivision
  B. First-level subdivision
    1. Second-level subdivision
    2. Second-level subdivision
      a. Third-level subdivision
      b. Third-level subdivision
        (1) Fourth-level subdivision
        (2) Fourth-level subdivision
  C. First-level subdivision

Notice that each time you subdivide a point, you indent. For most speeches you will not need to break your material down into as many subdivisions as illustrated here.

## Avoid Single Subdivisions

Each heading should have at least two subdivisions—or none at all. In other words, for every heading marked "A," there should be at least a "B." For every "1" there should be a "2." The reason is obvious: how can you divide something and end up with only one part? If you divide an orange, you must end up with at least two pieces. If you end up with only one, you have not really divided the orange.

One problem that arises is how to show a single example for a particular point. Below is the *wrong* way to handle the problem:

A. Many counterfeiters are turning to items other than paper money.
  1. Counterfeit credit cards now outnumber counterfeit bills.
B. . . .

This is wrong because item "A" cannot logically be subdivided into just one piece. There are two ways to correct the problem. One way is to simply eliminate the single item and combine it with the heading above:

A. Many counterfeiters are turning to items other than paper money: counterfeit credit cards now outnumber counterfeit bills.
B. . . .

Another way to handle the problem is to not number the item but simply list it as "example":

A. Many counterfeiters are turning to items other than paper money.
   Example: Counterfeit credit cards now outnumber counterfeit bills.
B. . . .

## *Use Complete Sentences*

Unless your instructor tells you otherwise, you should use complete sentences. Here is why: (1) Writing complete sentences forces you to sharpen your thinking. You are able to go beyond fuzzy, generalized notions and think of the specific things you need to say. You are able to create whole, fully developed ideas—not half-baked fragments of thought. (2) If another person (such as an instructor) helps you with your outline, complete sentences will be easier to understand than mere phrases, thus permitting that person to give you the best possible critique.

The following is an example of a portion of an outline on suicide:

 I. Psychological theories
    A. Punishment
    B. Revenge
    C. Homicidal rage
II. . . .

Here is a better version of the outline on suicide:

 I. There are several psychological theories that attempt to explain why suicidal people want to kill themselves.
    A. They feel that they need to be punished because they are "failures" or "bad" people.
    B. They want to get revenge on someone with whom they have quarreled.
    C. They are filled with homicidal rage but turn the anger inward and "murder" themselves.
II. . . .

The second version is more precise than the first because the speaker's ideas are expressed logically and clearly. Speakers who rely on vague outlines, such as the first version, run the risk of thinking that they know what they mean by such terms as "homicidal rage," and finding out as they deliver the speech that they do not have a good grasp on the concept.

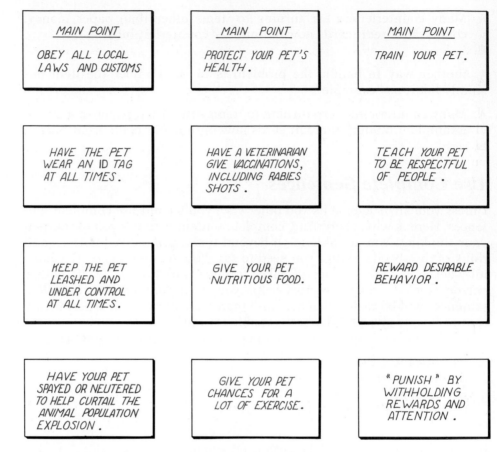

**FIGURE 11.1**
Note cards such as these can be used for a preliminary outline. This system provides flexibility, since you can add, delete, or rearrange cards before putting your outline into final form.

## Use Cards for Preliminary Outlines

One reason some students hate writing an outline is that they think they must sit down and write it all at once, then laboriously rewrite it whenever a change is made.

Here is a technique that can save you a lot of time and labor: For your preliminary work (before you write your final outline), use extra-large (4 × 6 or larger) cards, putting one point on each card. Sit at a desk or table and display the cards containing your main points (which we discussed in Chapter 9). Then underneath each main point, place those cards that support it. (If you want to get fancy, you can use a color code—yellow cards, say, for main points and white cards for supporting points.) Figure 11.1 shows examples of cards for an outline on how to take care of a pet.

With this system, you can move cards about to try different sequences. As you develop your ideas, you can add or eliminate cards.

After you have arranged the cards in logical sequences, you can number them according to the standard outline form, as discussed earlier in the chapter. Then you are ready to write out your final outline on a full sheet of paper. The cards in Figure 11.1 would look like this in the body of the outline:

I. Obey all local laws and customs.
   A. Have the pet wear an ID tag at all times.
   B. Have the pet leashed and under control at all times.
   C. Have your pet spayed and neutered to help curtail the animal population explosion.
II. Protect your pet's health.
   A. Have a veterinarian give vaccinations, including rabies shots.
   B. Give your pet nutritious food.
   C. Give your pet chances for a lot of exercise.
III. Train your pet.
   A. Teach your pet to be respectful of people.
   B. Reward desirable behavior.
   C. "Punish" by withholding rewards and attention.

This outline could be expanded easily. For instance, under item IIB, the speaker could give examples of what foods are recommended for pets.

# Parts of the Outline

The parts of the outline discussed below are keyed to the sample outline that follows this section. Your instructor may have requirements for your outline that deviate somewhat from the description in these pages.

## Title

Your outline should have a title, but you *do not actually say it in your speech*. In other words, do not begin your speech (as I have heard some speakers do) by saying, "How to Lose Weight Permanently" or "The title of my speech is 'How to Lose Weight Permanently.'"

If you should not say the title, why have one? For classroom speeches, your instructor may want you to write one simply to give you experience in devising titles. For some out-of-class speeches, a title might be requested so that your speech can be publicized in advance.

Your title should be brief and descriptive, that is, it should give a clear idea of what your speech is about. For example, "Why State Lotteries Should Be Abolished" is short and helpful. If you want an attractive, catchy title, you can use a colorful phrase coupled with a descriptive subtitle. For example:

A Lousy Bet: Why State Lotteries Should Be Abolished
Ouch! What to Do When A Bee Stings You
Are You Living Beyond Your Means? A Brief Look at Credit Cards

## Purposes and Central Idea

Having your general purpose, specific purpose, and central idea listed on your outline will help you bring into sharp focus the main points and supporting materials. Check with your instructor to find out where he or she wants these items placed.

## Introduction and Conclusion

As we pointed out in the previous chapter, the introduction and conclusion are so vitally important in a speech that they deserve special attention and care. Some speakers recommend that you write out both of these items in full so you can make sure that they are well developed. Both sections should have their own numbering system, independent of the body of the speech.

## Body

The body of the outline, which we discussed in Chapter 9, should be written in full sentences, with the main points keyed to Roman numerals. The body has its own numbering system, independent of the introduction and conclusion. In other words, the first main point of the body is Roman numeral I.

## Transitions

The transitional devices we discussed in Chapter 9 should be inserted in the outline at appropriate places. They are labeled and placed in parentheses, but they are not included in the numbering system of the outline.

While transitional devices should be placed wherever they are needed to help the listeners, make sure you have them in three crucial places: (1) between the introduction and the body of the speech, (2) between each of the main points, and (3) between the body of the speech and the conclusion.

## Bibliography

At the end of the outline, place a list of your sources—books, magazines, interviews, etc.—which you used in preparing the speech. Give standard bibliographical data; for a book, for example, give the author, title, publisher, place of publication, date of publication, and the specific pages that you used. If you used your own personal experiences, you should cite yourself as a source.

The bibliography is useful not only to give your instructor a list of your sources, but also to provide you with a record if you ever give the speech again and need to return to your sources to refresh your memory or to find additional information.

## Visual Aids

If you plan to use visual aids, give a brief description of them. This will help the instructor to give you guidance on whether the visual aids are effective.

# Sample Outline

Your outline should *not* include every word in your speech. It is merely the skeleton. Your actual speech will be longer.

Below is an outline by student speaker Laura Garcia.[2] Read it and then study the commentary in the left-hand column.

COMMENTARY

OUTLINE

Title is catchy and appealing. Note: it is not actually stated in the speech itself.

**"YOUR MONEY—OR YOUR LIFE!"**

Purposes and central idea should always appear at the top of outline to help bring content into sharp focus. Everything that comes below in the text of the outline should serve to develop the central idea.

**General Purpose:** To inform
**Specific Purpose:** To explain to my listeners how to handle themselves if they are ever the victim of armed robbery.
**Central Idea:** A person accosted by an armed robber should not resist but be cooperative and observant.

| | |
|---|---|
| Introduction is set off from the rest of the outline by its own heading and numbering system. | **INTRODUCTION** |
| Speaker grabs the listeners' attention with an exciting hypothetical narrative. Notice the use of "you" to draw the listeners in. | I. Imagine that you're walking to your car after seeing a late movie and suddenly a stranger appears. He's holding a gun and he demands your wallet or purse. |
| Using statistics and testimony from a leading expert lends credibility to the speech.

Speaker asks rhetorical questions aimed at making the listeners want to listen to the rest of her speech.

She previews the three main points, which also constitute the central idea. | II. This kind of crime could easily happen to you. Penny Harrington, police chief of Portland, Oregon, and the first woman to head a big-city police force, says that three out of every one hundred Americans—whether they live in cities, suburbs, or rural areas—are victims of assault every year. And one of the most common forms of assault is, of course, armed robbery. If you did have a gun poked into your ribs by a robber, what would you do? How should you handle yourself so that you increase the chances of coming out alive? Law enforcement experts like Harrington say that there are three steps that you should take: First of all, do not resist; second, try to appear cooperative; and third, be as observant as you possibly can. |
| By planning transitions, the speaker insures smooth passage from one part of the speech to another. Notice that transitions are placed in parentheses and are not part of the outline's numbering system. | (*Transition:* Let's look at these three suggestions a little more closely.) |
| The body contains the main points, marked by Roman numerals, and the supporting materials are placed under each main point.

Using an example is an effective way to illustrate and back up a point. | **BODY**<br>I. **Do not resist.**<br>  A. Resistance can frighten or anger the gunman.<br>    1. Many robbers are drug addicts and are very excitable and short-tempered. The drugs they are taking may make them violent and irrational.<br><br>    2. According to *Time* magazine, Thomas Mounce, the 51-year-old owner of a small business in Memphis, Tennessee, was held up in his store's parking lot at 6 P.M. by a gunman. Mounce grabbed for the gun, but the gunman shot and killed him. |

B. Even if you're carrying a weapon, don't try to use it.
1. A gun, knife, or a can of chemical mace can be turned against you.
2. By the time you reach into your pocket or purse, the gunman has time to kill you.
3. According to *Time* magazine, a 19-year-old secretary in Miami, Clarivel Benitez, was driving away from a supermarket when a man jumped into her car and tried to rob her. She tried to spray chemical mace at him, but he shot and killed her.

An example is powerful and believable when a speaker cites a reliable source and lists details such as name and age.

Testimony from a knowledgeable authority is interesting and convincing.

4. Penny Harrington, the Portland police chief, says she has never found chemical mace to be effective—even when she used it as an officer. All it does, she says, is make the assailant angry.
C. Don't try to use martial arts or other self-defense tactics.
1. Even experts in martial arts are not skilled enough to surprise a gunman.
2. Gerry Armstrong of Miramar, Florida, who has 19 years of experience as a martial arts instructor says, "If someone pulls a gun and tells me to hand over my wallet, he can have it. A bullet travels faster than my foot."
D. Do not scream.
1. The chances are great that no one will hear you.
2. Even if someone does hear you, your screaming might enrage the robber and make him more apt to shoot you.

When a quotation is colorful, it is best to quote it verbatim rather than paraphrase it.

The speaker uses "you" whenever possible—an effective technique for keeping the listeners' interest.

This transition provides a bridge, reminding the listeners where they've been while taking them over to the next point.

(*Transition:* So far, we've stressed the importance of not resisting, but how should you behave toward the robber?)

Progressive indentation dramatizes the relationship between main points and subpoints.

Under each main point, subpoints are marked with capital letters (A, B, C, etc.) and sub-subpoints with Arabic numerals (1, 2, 3, etc.).

II. **Try to appear cooperative.**
A. Remain calm.
B. Try to make the robber think that you are willing to give him whatever money or jewelry that he wants.
C. Do not make any sudden moves.
1. A quick reach for your wallet or purse might be misinterpreted by the gunman as a grab for a gun.
2. Tell the gunman in advance exactly what moves you are going to make.
D. Don't try to negotiate.

The speaker wisely anticipates objections that some listeners might raise and deals with them.

    1. The gunman may be nervous about being caught, and any delays can enrage him.
    2. Take the case of Steve Bostic, a 21-year-old autoworker in Detroit. After three strangers stopped and helped him jump-start his car, they demanded ten dollars. When Bostic tried to talk them down to five dollars, one of the men pulled a gun and killed him.
  E. Don't be ashamed of cooperating.
    1. All this advice may sound cowardly to you, but it's the best way to keep from being killed by an armed robber.
    2. There's no need to feel that you must be a hero. Law officers say that if you try to be a hero, you'll probably be a dead hero. Your wallet or your purse or your pride are not worth losing your life over.

This transition gives an internal summary and then prepares the listeners for the last main point.

*(Transition:* We've talked about not resisting and about trying to appear cooperative. If possible, there's one more thing you should do.)

III. **Be as observant as possible.**
  A. Try to notice as many features about the gunman as you can.
  B. Especially look for any peculiar facial features.
  C. When the robber leaves, try to see how he gets away without exposing yourself to any danger.
  D. Notify police as soon as you can safely do so and give them full details.

The final transition prepares the audience for the conclusion.

*(Transition:* It is hoped that the police will be able to arrest the robber, but even if they are not, you at least have the satisfaction of knowing that you've come through a terrible experience alive.)

The conclusion has its own label and numbering system.

**CONCLUSION**

The speaker unifies the speech by reminding the audience what was said in the introduction: the possibility of a listener being accosted.

I. I hope that you are never accosted by an armed robber, but if you are, I think you would be smart to follow the advice that I've given today. All of it is based on what law enforcement experts suggest.

The speaker reviews the three main points. In an essay, such a restatement would be repetitious, but in a speech, it is needed to help the listeners retain the information.

Remember: first, do not resist; second, try to appear cooperative; and third, be as observant as you can in order to help the police.

Testimony from a credible source drives home the central idea one more time and ends with a memorable phrase as a clincher.

II. To close, I'd like to share with you the advice of Captain Ephirne F. Leija of the Houston police department: "Stay as calm as possible. Try not to panic. Do the best you can under a difficult situation. Above all, don't try to be a hero."

The speaker lists all sources of information actually used in the preparation of the speech.

**BIBLIOGRAPHY**

Penny Harrington, "Crime: What You Can Do About It," *McCall's*, September, 1985, p. 98.

"If It Happens to You . . .," *Time*, March 23, 1981, p. 21.

Clarence M. Kelley and Carl A. Roper, *Security for You and Your Home* (Blue Ridge Summit, Pa.: Tab Books, 1984), pp. 272–273.

"The Plague of Violent Crime," *Newsweek*, March 23, 1981, p. 46.

The speaker describes the visual aids.

**VISUAL AIDS**

Three posters, each showing one of three main points.

# Speaking Notes

After you have devised an outline, what do you do with it? Do you use it to practice your speech? No. Do you take it with you to the lectern to assist you in the delivery of your speech? No. The outline should be used only for *organizing* your ideas. When it comes to *practicing* and then *delivering* the speech, you should use brief speaking notes that are based upon the outline.

What is so bad about using your outline to give the speech? Since your points are written in complete sentences, you might be tempted to read the outline, and nothing is duller than a read-aloud speech. As we will discuss in Chapter 13, you should deliver your speech extemporaneously, that is, in a conversational manner, looking at the audience most of the time, only occasionally glancing down at your notes. When you glance at your notes, you pick up ideas and then you convey those ideas in whatever words come to mind at the moment. Thus you end up sounding natural and spontaneous.

While an outline is undesirable for delivery, the other extreme—using no notes at all—is equally bad. Without notes, you might forget important points, and you might fail to present your ideas in a logical, easy-to-follow sequence.

Notes bolster your sense of security. Even if you are in full command of the content of your speech, you feel more confident and self-assured knowing that you have notes to fall back on in case your mind goes blank and you fail to recall your next point.

By the way, some people (I used to be one of them) have the idea that using notes is a sign of mental weakness or a lack of self-confidence. Most good speakers use them without losing the respect of an audience. After all, your notes represent a kind of compliment to your listeners. They show that you care enough about the occasion to spend time getting your best thoughts together in a coherent form. The kind of speaker that audiences *do* look down on is the windbag who stands up without notes and rambles on without making much sense.

Here are some guidelines for preparing notes. As you read them, you may want to refer to the sample speaking notes that appear in the next section.

1. Make indentations in your speaking notes that correspond to those in your outline. This will help reinforce the structure of the speech in your mind. You may also want to repeat the numbering system, but this is a matter of individual choice. (I personally prefer to use only the main—or Roman numeral—headings; I feel that putting in capital letters and Arabic numerals makes the notes too cluttered.)

2. Use only one side of a sheet of paper or note card because (1) you might forget to turn the paper or card over, and (2) flipping back and forth can be distracting to the audience.

3. Write down only the minimum number of words or phrases necessary to trigger your memory. If you have too many words written down, you might overlook some key ideas, or you might spend too much time looking at the notes instead of at the audience. An exception to this rule would be long quotations or statistics that you would need to write out in full for the sake of accuracy.

4. Write words in large letters that are neat and legible so that you have no trouble seeing them when you glance down during a speech.

5. Include cues for effective delivery, such as when to pause and when to use visual aids (see the sample notes that follow). Some speakers use black ink for their actual notes and red ink for delivery cues.

6. For speaking, use the same set of notes you used while rehearsing, so that you will be thoroughly familiar with the location of items on your prompts. I once practiced with a set of notes on which I penciled in so many editing marks that I made a fresh set of notes right before I delivered the speech. This turned out to be a mistake because the notes were so "new" that some of the key words failed to trigger my memory quickly, causing me to falter at several points. I should have stayed with the original notes. Even though they were filled with arrows and insertions and deletions, I knew them intimately; I had a strong mental picture of where each point was located. The new notes, on the other hand, had not "burned" an image in my brain.

# *Sample Speaking Notes*

The following speaking notes are based on the outline on pages 233–237.

COMMENTARY

These cues remind the speaker of the importance of looking at the audience and speaking slowly during the introduction.

The speaker uses only a few key words to trigger memory.

The speaker reminds herself to pause at this point. Pauses are effective transition devices because they signal that you are through with one idea and ready to begin another.

The speaker writes "Fingers" as a cue to hold up three fingers.

This cue reminds the speaker to show her first poster, on which is printed her first main point in large block letters.

The speaker puts enough key details to jog her memory.

**INTRODUCTION**

E Y E   C O N T A C T
G O   S L O W L Y

I. Imagine walking alone
   stranger . . . gun
   demands money

P A U S E

II. Could happen to you
    Penny Harrington
    —Portland, Ore.
    —1st woman
    3 of 100 assaulted
    —cities, suburbs, rural
    —of all assaults, robbery common
    What should you do?

P A U S E

   Three steps . . . [F I N G E R S]
      1. don't resist
      2. be cooperative
      3. be observant
(Let's look closer)

P A U S E

**BODY**

I. Don't resist [S H O W   P O S T E R]
   May frighten or anger
   —drug addicts
   —edgy, short-tempered
   —may be violent, irrational

   —Thomas Mounce (*Time*)
   ...51, Memphis, businessman
   ...store parking lot (6 P.M.)
   ...grabbed for gun/killed
   Even if have weapon, don't use
   —gun, knife, chem. mace...used against you
   —by time you reach...

—Clarivel Benitez (*Time*)
...19, secretary, Miami
...leaving supermarket
...robber jumped in car
...she tried mace/he killed her
—Penny Harrington
...chem. mace ineffective
...she used it as officer
...only result: makes him angry
Don't try martial arts
—Experts say no
—Gerry Armstrong
...Miramar, Fla.
...19 years, instructor

The speaker reminds her-
self to quote directly from
her notes. It is a good idea
to quote directly when you
have a particularly arresting quotation that would
lose some of its punch if
paraphrased.

Q U O T E   D I R E C T L Y

..."If someone pulls a gun and tells me to hand over my wallet, he
can have it. A bullet travels faster than my foot."
Don't scream
—no one hears you
—or might enrage

Transitions are included in
the speaking notes, just as
they were in the outline,
but of course they are
shortened.

(So far, don't resist . . . how behave toward robber?)
P A U S E
II. Try to appear cooperative [S H O W   P O S T E R]
Be calm
Show willingness
No sudden moves
—quick reach, misinterpreted
—tell your moves in advance
Don't negotiate
—may be nervous
—delays may enrage
—Steve Bostic
...21, Detroit autoworker
...3 strangers stopped
...helped jump start
...demanded $10
...Bostic said $5
...one man shot, killed him
No need to be ashamed
—may sound cowardly, but best way

Underlining key words
helps the speaker remem-
ber to emphasize them.

—try to be hero = <u>dead hero</u>
(So far, don't resist and do cooperate . . . one more thing)
III. Be observant [S H O W   P O S T E R]
Notice features

Especially note peculiarities, face
Observe route of getaway
Notify police
   (Even if no arrest, satisfaction of being alive . . .)
P A U S E

**CONCLUSION**
   I. Follow experts' advice
      Don't resist
      Try to appear cooperative
      Be observant
   II. Advice of Captain Ephirne F. Leija, Houston Police:
Q U O T E   D I R E C T L Y

"Stay as calm as possible. Try not to panic. Do the best you can under a difficult situation. Above all, don't try to be a hero."

## *Using Speaking Notes*

Your instructor may require you to use one particular kind of note system, but if you have a choice in the matter, I recommend that you use either of two popular types: note cards or a full sheet of paper.

### Option 1: Note Cards

Your speaking notes can be put on note cards, as shown in Figure 11.2.

Note cards (especially the 3 × 5 size) are compact and rather inconspicuous, and they are easy to hold (especially if there is no lectern to place notes on). Because of the smallness of the card, you are forced to write just a few key words rather than long sentences that you might be tempted to read. If you use cards, be sure to number each one in case you drop them and need to quickly reassemble them.

### Option 2: Full Sheet of Paper

If you use a full sheet of paper, your notes would look like the sample speaking notes on pages 239–241.

The advantage of this option is that you have your entire speech spread out in front of you. A short speech can usually fit on one side of a single sheet, so you do not have to do any shuffling, as you would have to do with cards.

There are, however, several disadvantages: (1) Because a whole sheet of paper is a large writing surface, many speakers succumb to the temptation to put down copious notes. This hurts them in their speechmaking because they end up spending too much time looking at their notes at the expense of eye contact with the audience. (2) I have found that a full sheet of paper can cause a speaker's eyes to glide over key points; it is as if the

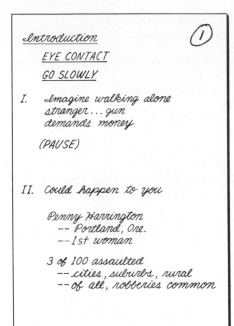
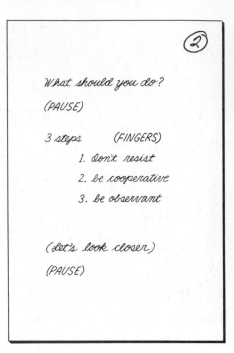

**FIGURE 11.2**
Here is how the speaker used note cards for the armed robbery speech. Each card is numbered so that if the speaker accidentally drops the cards, they can be put back into proper order very easily. (Only the first two cards are shown.)

"map" were too large to be scrutinized at a glance. (3) If sheets of paper are brought to the room curled up, they can curl up on the lectern, much to the speaker's dismay. (4) If no lectern is available, a hand-held sheet of paper tends to shake and rustle, causing a distraction to the listeners. (5) It is harder to make major corrections on paper than on note cards. With paper, you may have to rewrite all your notes, whereas with note cards, you simply delete the card containing the undesired section and write your corrected version on a fresh card.

# Controlling Your Material

While preparing an outline and speaking notes, it is important that you control your material, rather than letting the material control you. Here are two things you can do to make sure that you stay in control:

1. *Revise your outline and speaking notes whenever they need alterations.* Some students mistakenly view an outline as a device that plants their

**Asking a friend, relative, or instructor to critique an outline is a good way for a speaker to get feedback on weaknesses in a speech.** *(Bob Daemmrich/TexaStock)*

feet in concrete; once they have written an outline, they think that they are stuck with it—even if they yearn to make changes. An outline should be treated as a flexible aid that can be altered as you see fit. That is why I recommended earlier that you write your preliminary outline on large note cards—so that you can freely add, delete, or move points around. Whatever technique you use, feel free to make revisions at any stage of preparation.

Often an outline looks good on paper, but when you make your speaking notes and start practicing, you find that some parts are disharmonious, clumsy, and illogical. A speech needs a nice even flow, carrying the audience smoothly from one point to another. If your speech lacks this smooth flow, go back and alter the outline until you achieve a continuity that you are comfortable with.

2. *Make deletions if you are in danger of exceeding your time limit.* After you develop your outline and your speaking notes, you should practice delivering your speech while you clock yourself to see how much time it takes. If the speech exceeds the time limit (set by your instructor or by the people who invited you to speak), you must go back to your outline and speaking notes and trim them down.

Deleting parts of your outline can be a painful task, especially if you have worked hard to get a particular example or statistic. But it is a job that *must* be done. Be ruthless. Be brave. Even if you exceed the limit by only five minutes, you must cut. A speech that exceeds its allotted time can spoil a program that features other speakers or events in a tight time frame.

# Speech as Presented

The following is a transcript of the armed robbery speech as it was delivered by Laura Garcia. Note that the wording is not precisely identical to that used in the outline. The reason, of course, is that Laura was delivering the speech extemporaneously, using the speaking notes printed on page 242. If she had read from her outline or from a complete text, she might have sounded a bit stilted and artificial. By choosing her words as she went along, she made her speech vigorous, forthright, and easy to follow. If she gave this speech 10 different times, the wording would be different each time, although the ideas would remain basically the same.

## "Your Money—Or Your Life!"

Imagine for a moment that it's late at night, you've just seen the midnight showing of a movie downtown, and now you're walking to your car. Suddenly, out of the shadows, a stranger appears. He's holding a gun and he orders you to give him your wallet or your purse.

This could easily happen to you. Penny Harrington, who is police chief of Portland, Oregon, and the first woman to head a big-city police force, says that three out of every one hundred Americans are victims of assault every year. It doesn't matter whether they live in cities, suburbs, or rural areas. Three out of a hundred, assaulted each year. One of the most common forms of assault is, of course, armed robbery. If a stranger accosted you with a gun and demanded your money, what would you do? How should you handle yourself so that you increase the chances of coming out alive? Experts in law enforcement like Harrington say that there are three things you should do: number one, do not resist; number two, try to appear cooperative; and number three, be as observant as possible.

Let's take a closer look at these three suggestions. First of all, do not resist. If you struggle or fight, you might make the gunman angry or scared. A lot of robbers are drug addicts and this means that they are very edgy and short-tempered. The drugs they're using can sometimes make them irrational and violent—even homicidal. According to a cover story on crime in a recent issue of *Time* magazine, a 51-year-old businessman in Memphis, Tennessee, named Thomas Mounce was held up in his store's parking lot at 6 P.M. by a gunman. Mounce made a grab for the gun, but the robber pushed him back and shot and killed him.

Even if you've got a weapon in your pocket or your purse or your car, don't try to use it. Any weapon—whether it's a gun or a knife or a can of chemical mace—can be turned against you. Even if the weapon isn't used against you, you really won't get a chance to use it. While you're reaching for it, the gunman has time to kill you. According to *Time* magazine, Clarivel Benitez, a 19-year-old secretary in Miami, was driving away from a supermarket when a man jumped into her car and tried to rob her. She pulled out some chemical mace and was trying to spray him, but he shot and killed her. Penny Harrington, the police chief in Portland that I was talking about a minute ago, thinks that chemical mace is not very effective. She used it when she was making arrests as an officer and she said it wasn't very helpful. The only thing it really does, she says, is make the person mad.

Have you taken lessons in judo or karate? The experts say it's a mistake to try to use martial arts or other self-defense tactics. Even the pros say they aren't good enough to surprise a gunman. A Florida martial arts instructor with 19 years' experience, Gerry Armstrong, says, "If someone pulls a gun and tells me to hand over my wallet, he can have it. A bullet travels faster than my foot."

Should you scream? No, the chances are great that nobody will hear you, and even if they do, your screams might make the robber scared or angry enough to shoot you—long before help arrives.

So far, I've talked about why it's important to not resist. How should you behave toward the robber? Harrington and other law enforcement officials stress that you should try to appear cooperative. Not just be cooperative, but let the robber see and believe that you are cooperative. Remember what I said a moment ago—you may be dealing with a hothead on pills. So remain calm. Try to make him think that you will give him whatever money or jewelry he wants.

Don't make any sudden moves. If you make a quick reach for your wallet or your purse, he might think you're going for a gun. So move your hands slowly. Tell the gunman what you're doing. Say something like, "My wallet is in my back pocket. I'm going to pull it out, okay?"

Don't try to buy time or negotiate with the robber. He might be very edgy and nervous about getting caught, and if you slow him down, he might get angry enough to shoot you. Here's a true story that happened in Detroit, according to *Time*. A 21-year-old autoworker named Steve Bostic couldn't get his car started. Three strangers stopped and helped him start his car with jump cables. Then they demanded ten dollars. Bostic tried to talk them down to five dollars, and this made them so mad that one of the men pulled a gun and killed Bostic.

You shouldn't be ashamed of cooperating. All this might seem cowardly to you, but remember that it's the best way to keep from being killed. Don't feel that you ought to be a hero. Law enforcement people say that if you try to be a hero, you're very likely to become a dead hero. Nothing that you own—not your wallet, not your purse, not your pride—*nothing* is worth losing your life over.

So far, we've discussed not resisting and we've talked about trying to appear cooperative. If possible, there's one more thing you should do: be observant. Try to notice as many things about the robber as you can. Look for facial features—things like color of eyes, hair style, scars, and peculiarities. After the robber leaves, try to see where he goes if you can do so without exposing yourself to any danger. Call the police as soon as it's safe and give them as many details as you can. I hope the police can arrest the robber, but even if they can't find him, you can breathe a sigh of relief—you've come out of this experience alive.

I hope that you are never the victim of armed robbery, but if you ever are, I think you would be smart to follow the advice that I've given today. All of it is based on the suggestions of law enforcement experts. Remember: do not resist; try to appear cooperative; and be as observant as you can in order to help the police.

To close, I'd like to share with you the advice of Captain Ephirne F. Leija of the Houston police department: "Stay as calm as possible. Try not to panic. Do the best you can under a difficult situation. Above all, don't try to be a hero."

## Summary

An outline is as important to the speechmaker as a blueprint is to a builder. The outline provides a detailed plan to help the speaker organize thoughts into a logical sequence and to make sure nothing important is left out.

After you complete an outline, you should prepare notes based upon it. You have two options—note cards or a full sheet of paper. Whichever option you choose, you should avoid writing too many words because when you use notes in a speech, you want to be able to glance down quickly and retrieve just enough words to jog your memory.

## Review Questions

1. Why is an outline recommended for all speeches?
2. What is the advantage of using complete sentences in an outline?
3. What are the parts of an outline?
4. Why should each subdivision of an outline have at least two parts?

# **TIPS** *for your career*

## Tip 11: When No Time Limit Is Set, Speak Briefly

We have already discussed the need to abide by the time limits placed on a speech, but what should you do when no time limit is set—that is, you are invited to speak for as long as you like? The best advice I can give you is this: Be brief. Keep it short. In the words of Owen Feltham, a seventeenth-century English author, every person "should study conciseness in speaking; it is a sign of ignorance not to know that long speeches, though they may please the speaker, are the torture of the hearer."

How brief is brief? For a short speech, a good rule of thumb is to aim for about five minutes. Many clubs ask for five-minute talks; many executives ask for five-minute presentations, and all Toastmasters' clubs stipulate five minutes for their members' speeches. For longer speeches, such as after-dinner addresses, you would need to assess the audience and the occasion. I would recommend no more than 20 minutes, although some after-dinner speakers go 45 to 60. In any situation, if you go over 60 minutes, you will usually see the audience become fatigued and fidgety.

In general, audiences prefer—and are getting—shorter and shorter speeches, possibly because television has conditioned people to assimilate only short bursts of material. The demand for brevity is even being voiced in America's churches, which once featured sermons lasting well over an hour. Most ministers today preach for no more than 30 minutes. Donald Macleod, who teaches sermon preparation at Princeton Theological Seminary, tells his seminarians that 18 minutes is the maximum time for an effective sermon.[3]

Whenever you are in doubt about length, remember that if one must err, it is always best to err on the side of brevity. If, when you finish a speech, the listeners are still hungering for more wisdom from your mouth, no harm is done. They will probably invite you to come back and speak again. But if you speak so long that they become bored, weary and sleepy, they will resent you for wasting their time.

# Part 4

# Presenting the Speech

## Chapter 12

# Wording
# the Speech

The power of a single word is incredible. Take, for instance, the world of advertising. A book on automobile repair was once advertised under the headline "How to Repair Cars." When the advertising agency changed the headline to read, "How to Fix Cars," sales jumped by 20 percent.[1] Why is *fix* more likely to garner sales than its synonym *repair?* No one is sure exactly why—perhaps it sounds easier to fix a car than to repair it. Whatever the reason, ad agencies know that while the right word can help an ad, the wrong word can hurt it. David Ogilvy, an advertising copywriter, once wondered why one of his ads failed to lure buyers. He conducted a survey, which showed that he made the mistake of using the word "obsolete" in the ad's headline. The survey revealed that 43 percent of consumers in the group targeted had no idea what "obsolete" meant.[2]

The producers of television commercials know that the right word can be worth millions of dollars in increased sales. They have learned, for example, that the words "new" and "improved" in a commercial will boost sales significantly. That is why TV viewers so often hear a product touted as "the new, improved . . . ."

While finding the right word is obviously vital in advertising, it is also important in public speaking. The difference between the right word and the almost right word, Mark Twain once observed, is the difference between lightning . . . and the lightning bug.

The truth of Twain's remark can be seen in the following historical vignette: One of President Franklin Roosevelt's most famous speeches was his address to Congress asking for a declaration of war against Japan in the aftermath of the Japanese attack on the American fleet at Pearl Harbor. As written by an assistant, the speech began this way:

December 7, 1941: A date which will live in world history.

Before speaking, Roosevelt crossed out the words "world history" and substituted the word "infamy." Here is what he ended up saying:

December 7, 1941: A date which will live in infamy.

This has become one of the most famous sentences in American history, along with such memorable statements as "Give me liberty or give me death!" And yet, if Roosevelt had used the original sentence, it never would have become celebrated. Why? Because *infamy*—pungent and emotional—was the right description for the occasion; *world history*—dull and unemotional—was merely "almost right." Lightning . . . and the lightning bug.

In this chapter, we will look at ways in which you can choose the right words for your speeches.

# Using Appropriate Words

In choosing words for your speeches, your goal should not be to select the most beautiful or the most sophisticated, but to use the *right* words for the *right* audience. As you analyze your audience before a speech, you should ask yourself, "How can I best express my ideas so that the audience will understand and accept them?" A word that might be ideal for one audience might be inappropriate for another.

Dr. Martin Luther King, the brilliant leader of the civil rights movement of the 1960s, was a master at using the right words with the right group. To a highly educated audience, for example, he would employ sophisticated language and abstract concepts, such as this sentence from his Nobel Peace Prize acceptance speech:

> Civilization and violence are antithetical concepts.

Such a sentence, appropriate for an erudite audience, would have been incomprehensible if used in one of his speeches to poor, uneducated sharecroppers in Mississippi. For them, he used simple words and down-to-earth illustrations. For example, in defending himself against accusations of being allied with communists, Dr. King used a simple, but vivid comparison that could be grasped by the least educated of his listeners:

> There are as many communists in the freedom movement as there are Eskimos in Florida.

With either kind of audience, Dr. King was highly persuasive, but what did he do when he spoke to a group made up of both educated and uneducated people? He used inspirational messages designed to appeal to every listener. In his famous "I Have a Dream" speech, delivered to 200,000 people who had marched on Washington to demand equal rights for blacks, Dr. King used stirring words and striking images that appealed to everyone:

> I have a dream that one day on the red hills of Georgia the sons of former slaves and the sons of former slave owners will be able to sit down together at the table of brotherhood.

There was nothing phony about Dr. King's adaptation to his audiences. All good speakers pitch their language to the appropriate level for their audience.

In addition to choosing words that are appropriate to your audience, you should also use words that are appropriate to the occasion. If you speak at a fund-raiser, your words should be uplifting and encouraging; at a funeral, solemn and respectful; at a pep rally, rousing and emotional.

Always use words that are in good taste. Avoid political, religious, racial, ethnic, or sexual references that might alienate anyone in your audience. Ask yourself, "Is there any chance at all that what I'm planning to say might offend someone in the audience?" If you cannot decide whether a word is appropriate, do not use it.

In business presentations, where the speaker is trying to sell a product or a concept, you would expect presenters to avoid offending their audiences at all costs, but Thomas Leech, a communication consultant, has observed the following blunders committed during business presentations: (1) A male speaker began his answer to a female questioner with, "Well, honey . . . ." (2) A speaker made derogatory comments about the President of the United States to an audience that included many supporters of the President. (3) To a Navy audience, a speaker praised the way the Air Force had managed a program better than the Navy had done. In all of these cases, Leech said, "key members of the audience turned off or turned against the speaker."[3]

Avoid sex-related stereotypical expressions such as "little old lady," "broad," "chick," and "typical male brutality." Try to eliminate sexism from sex-linked occupational and organization terms. Here are some examples:

| Original | Preferred Form |
|---|---|
| workman | worker |
| stewardess | flight attendant |
| fireman | firefighter |
| policeman | police officer |
| mailman | mail carrier |
| man-made | artificial |
| congressman | member of Congress (or representative) |
| cleaning lady | housekeeper |
| foreman | supervisor |
| man's history | human history |

Before you give a speech, analyze your audience carefully (using the guidelines in Chapter 4) to learn everything you can about who they are. Having this advance knowledge should help you to use language that is appropriate.

# Using Words Accurately

To use words accurately, you need to be sensitive to two types of meanings—denotations and connotations—and also to the use of correct grammar.

## Use Precise Denotations

The *denotation* of a word is the thing or idea that it refers to—its dictionary definition. The denotation of *chair* is a piece of furniture for one person to sit on. Complications arise when a word has more than one denotation. The word *verbal*, for example, means "in words, either spoken or written." If I asked you to give a verbal report, you would not know whether I wanted your words spoken or written. I would have to come up with a more precise word; *oral*, for example, would be clear and unambiguous.

Another complication is that words sometimes change their denotations. Several years ago a middle-aged student was giving a classroom speech, in which he said, "When some people get intoxicated with alcohol, they become carefree and gay." The younger members of the audience reacted with laughter and looks of surprise. The speaker got flustered. What was wrong? Later he realized that when he was growing up, the word *gay* had no other meaning than "merry" and "exuberant"; to his youthful audience, *gay* had a different denotation—the word had become a synonym for homosexual.

Sometimes a word has different meanings in different parts of the nation. If, for example, you say, "In considering your nutritional needs, pay special attention to dinner," what time of day are you referring to? You would need to give an explanation because not all Americans use the word *dinner* in the same way. While most people think of dinner as the third and final meal of the day, some Americans, especially those from rural areas and from certain geographical regions, picture dinner as the meal served in the middle of the day.

You should never use a word, advises Dr. Kenneth McFarland, a professional speaker, "unless you know . . . that it means what you think it means." Dr. McFarland tells of hearing a county agricultural agent make a speech on the problems of the farm surplus. "A dozen times in his discourse he spoke of the 'dearth of wheat' and the 'dearth of corn.' At first his audience was bewildered but eventually it became obvious to most of the hearers that the speaker thought dearth meant abundance or surplus. [Actually, dearth means the opposite of surplus—it means scarcity.] The misuse of this one word killed the effect of what could have been a good speech."[4]

Do you see why the county agent wounded his credibility? From the audience's point of view, how could they accept the ideas of a man who was so sloppy with language that he used a word in a sense that was opposite its true meaning?

## Control Connotations

The *connotation* of a word is the emotional meaning that is associated with it. The words *slender, thin,* and *skinny* are synonyms; they have the same denotation, but the connotations are different: *slender* has a positive connotation, *thin* is neutral, and *skinny* has negative overtones. The words *fat*, *obese*, and *overweight* have similar denotations, but different connotations. Most fat people would prefer to be termed overweight, and if given a choice, they would rather be called fat than obese. Why? *Fat* sounds "fatter" than *overweight*, and *obese* suggests a gross fatness that is health endangering. Other synonyms like *chubby* or *plump* have special connotations—*chubby* is often used to refer to children and suggests a healthy condition; *plump* suggests a pleasing roundness.

As a listener and as a speaker, you should be aware of how connotations express a person's attitude. Let's say that some filmmakers produce a documentary on Senator Sally Jones. If they want to remain objective about the senator, they can describe her with a word that has a neutral connotation—*legislator*. If they want to convey approval, they can choose a word that has positive connotations—*national leader*. If they want to express disapproval, they can use a word that has negative connotations—*politician*. If they describe one of her campaign events, they could call it a *gathering* (neutral), a *rally* (positive), or a *mob* (negative). When she travels to Central America, the *trip* (neutral) could be called a *fact-finding mission* (positive) or a *junket* (negative).

With some synonyms, the connotations are so subtly different that you have to be especially thoughtful in selecting the right one. If, for example, you wanted to speak on the need for individuals to get away from other people occasionally and be by themselves, which word would have the more positive connotations—*loneliness* or *solitude?* When people hear the word *loneliness*, they often think of feeling sad, being friendless, craving companionship. *Solitude*, on the other hand, conjures images of peaceful serenity—walking alone on the beach, curling up with a book in front of the fireplace on a wintry night, or relaxing in a bathtub. Solitude, then, is the word you would want for describing the joys of being alone.

In exploring connotations, you do not have to rely solely on your own judgment. Many dictionaries have synonym notes, which are usually located after a word's definitions. While I have found that the best synonym notes are in the giant *Webster's Third New International Dictionary* (which most libraries have), you can also find helpful notes in many abridged dictionaries.

## Use Correct Grammar

Although I personally would never devalue a person for using incorrect grammar, there are many people who downgrade individuals if they make serious grammatical mistakes. To these people, bad grammar is as offensive as body odor or food stains on the front of a shirt. Recently, I was talking to a corporation executive who told me, "I just can't stand to be around people who use bad English. I would never hire a person who said things like 'I done it.' " And I know of a man who was passed over for a promotion (even though he was better qualified than the person who got the position) simply because he had the habit of saying "he don't" instead of "he doesn't."

Poor grammar hurts you because it makes you sound (to some people) as if you are not very intelligent. To make matters worse, people will usually refrain from telling you when your grammar offends them. A boss, for example, often is too ashamed to tell an employee that he or she uses unacceptable grammar; it is as embarrassing as telling someone they have bad breath. So the employee is never told the real reason why he or she is being denied a promotion.

Poor grammar can damage a speaker's credibility, according to Roy Fenstermaker, winner of the 1983 Toastmasters' International Speech Contest. "Careless syntax, ungrammatical expressions, or gross mispronunciation of common words," he said, are apt to be interpreted by listeners "as evidence of lack of education or disrespect for the standards of the audience."[5]

From my observations, the following mistakes seem to be the ones that are most likely to cause some people to downgrade you:

| Incorrect | Correct |
|---|---|
| He (or she) don't | He (or she) doesn't |
| You was | You were |
| I done it | I did it |
| Between you and I | Between you and me |
| I had went | I had gone |
| She's (he's) already went | She's (he's) already gone |
| I been thinking | I've been thinking |
| I've already took algebra | I've already taken algebra |
| hisself | himself |
| thcirself | themselves |
| We seen it | We saw it |
| Her and me went | She and I went |
| Him and me went | He and I went |
| I come to see you yesterday | I came to see you yesterday |
| She ain't here | She isn't here |
| She don't love me no more | She doesn't love me anymore |
| He be late | He is late |
| I had wrote it | I had written it |
| Give me them apples | Give me those apples |

If you make these or similar errors, I strongly urge you to learn how to correct your grammar and usage. Your school may have a tutoring service that can help you identify your grammatical mistakes and then

**Speakers who teach technical subjects such as computers should be careful to avoid jargon or technical terms that the listeners do not understand. (Bob Daemmrich/TexaStock)**

correct them. Or perhaps you can find a book in a library or bookstore on improving one's English.

# Achieving Clarity

To be clear in the words you use, you must first be clear in your thinking. Think about a word before you use it. Ask yourself, will it be clear to someone who is new to my subject? In this section we will examine how you can achieve clarity by using words that are simple, concrete, and precise.

## Use Simple Words

A speech writer for President Franklin D. Roosevelt once wrote, "We are endeavoring to construct a more inclusive society." President Roosevelt changed the wording to, "We're going to make a country in which no one is left out."[6]

Roosevelt obviously believed in the value of the old public speaker's maxim: "Never use a long word when a short one will do just as well."

Some people think the best way to convey complex ideas is to use complex language—big words and weighty phrases. This is nonsense. If you examine great works of literature, you will see that profound thoughts can be expressed easily and beautifully by simple words. Take, for instance, some of the greatest pieces of literature in the English language—the King James Bible and Shakespeare's works. In each of them you will see simple words used to convey big ideas. The Twenty-Third Psalm ("The Lord is my shepherd . . .") has 118 words, 93 of which consist of just one syllable. In Hamlet's famous soliloquy ("To be or not to be . . ."), 205 of the 261 words are of one syllable.

Some speakers are pretentious, trying to show off instead of making sure that their ideas are clear to the audience. In contrast, audience-centered speakers will choose the simple word whenever possible because they want their listeners to understand what they are saying. A pretentious speaker or an audience-centered speaker—which would you prefer to listen to? Which would you prefer to be? Here are some examples of the contrasting styles:

*Pretentious speaker:* It is incumbent upon the citizens of this country to find alternatives to the widespread distribution of discarded objects on the nation's roads and highways.

*Audience-centered speaker:* People ought to throw their trash some place other than on the streets.

*Pretentious speaker:* People who are experiencing intense negative emotions directed at a significant other would be well advised to disclose their condition to that individual.

*Audience-centered speaker:* If you're extremely angry at a loved one, don't keep it bottled up—tell the person how you feel.

As these examples show, communicating with your listeners is more important than showing off with big words.

## Use Concrete Words

Concrete words name or describe things that the listeners can see, smell, hear, taste, and touch—for example, *balloon, rose, gun blast, pizza,* and *chair.* They differ from abstract words, which refer to intangible ideas, qualities, or classes of things—for example, *democracy, mercy,* and *science.* While a certain amount of abstract language is necessary in a speech, you should try to keep it to a minimum. Instead, use concrete language because it is more specific and vivid, and therefore more likely to be remembered by your audience. Concrete words help you create the mental images that you want to convey to your listeners. Here are some examples:

| Abstract | Concrete |
|---|---|
| She is wealthy. | She makes $400,000 a year, has a winter home in San Diego and a summer home in Switzerland, and owns four different sports cars. |
| It was a stormy day. | The sky was gray and gloomy, and the cold, moist wind stung my face. |
| Rattlesnakes are scary. | A rattlesnake is ominous looking, with its beady eyes staring at you without ever blinking, and with its agile ability to slither through the brush without making a sound—until it suddenly coils and makes its terrible buzzing rattle. |

## Use Precise Words

The most commonly quoted authority in America is "they," as in the following sentences:

They say that too much salt is bad for you.

They say that the murder rate goes up during a full moon.

Who are *they?* Whoever they are, avoid using them as a source for information. Be specific. Be precise. For the first sentence above, find reliable sources: "Researchers at Johns Hopkins University have found that too much salt in one's diet can cause . . . . " For the second sentence, if you try to find who "they" are, you may discover, as did one student speaker, that reliable experts have concluded that the murder rate does *not* increase during a full moon, contrary to popular opinion. The mysterious *they* can be wrong.

Two kinds of word usage—jargon and euphemisms—rob a speech of precision. Let us examine each.

### Avoid Jargon

Can you understand everything being said in the following sentence?

During an attitude adjustment period, a government official explained to reporters that his department would effect a transformation in the preexisting regulations concerning domiciles for the lower socioeconomic bracket.

Translated into plain English:

During a coffee break, a government official told reporters that his department would change the regulations concerning housing for the poor.

The government official was speaking in jargon, the specialized language of a group or profession. When people use jargon in their work or in their academic studies, they sometimes mistakenly assume that everyone they talk to will understand their technical terms.

You may use jargon when you are talking to an audience made up entirely of people who share your specialty, but you should avoid jargon as much as possible in speeches to people of varying backgrounds. If you are forced to use a technical word because of the nature of your talk, you should always define it. One student speaker worked part-time in a hospital, and gave a speech on a medical situation that she had agonized over—dealing with "no code" patients. Much to the frustration of the audience, she failed to define "no code"—until she was asked about it during the question-and-answer period. It turns out that "no code" is the term written on a patient's chart to indicate that no artificial life-support measures should be used if his or her condition is determined to be hopeless. In other words, doctors and nurses should not make heroic efforts to keep such patients alive if they are comatose and irreversibly brain damaged. The speaker had failed to define "no code" because she assumed that everyone knew what it meant.

Be careful about using sports terms that the general public may not know. For example, if you argued for "a full-court-press against communist expansion," only people familiar with basketball would know that the term means trying to keep opponents from advancing.

Always explain abbreviations the first time you use them—even fairly well-known ones such as NATO and UNICEF. Some members of the audience may be unaware of what they stand for, and sometimes an abbreviation has several meanings. For example, CO is a popular military term that stands for commanding officer, but it also means conscientious objector, someone who refuses to participate in war. At one training seminar, a participant referred to his "PC" in a rather broad context, and it turned out that the other participants interpreted his abbreviation in four different ways: personal computer, program console, personal copier, and penal code.[7]

A friend who is a real-estate agent tells a story which may be fictional, but it illustrates why we need to explain abbreviations: A college student was hired to work as an intern at a real-estate agency for the summer. On the first morning of his new job, his boss sent him a message, "Mr. John Smith is in my office. Please get BLT for him." The young intern dutifully left the office, went down the street to a restaurant, and purchased a bacon, lettuce, and tomato sandwich. When he returned, he carried the sandwich into the boss's office, where the boss and Mr. Smith were conferring. "Here's Mr. Smith's BLT," said the young man. "Thanks," said the boss, laughing. "Now would you please go to the files and get Mr. Smith's Block, Lot, and Tract file?"

### Avoid Euphemisms

Refrain from using *euphemisms*—pleasant, mild, or inoffensive words that are used in place of blunt, direct words. Here are some examples of euphemisms:

- [ ] Instead of saying that Bill died, we say that he *departed* or *passed away*.
- [ ] Undertakers, who prefer to be called *funeral directors*, don't handle corpses; they deal with *cases* or *patients*.
- [ ] In many cities, public toilets are now called *comfort stations*.
- [ ] Nations that are poor and backward are termed *developing* and *emerging*.
- [ ] A used car is often advertised as a *pre-owned* automobile.

Sometimes euphemisms are harmless. If garbage collectors prefer to be called *sanitation engineers*, I may wince at the misuse of language but I cannot object too strenuously. If it makes them feel better about their valuable, but unglamorous work, if it increases their dignity and self-esteem, why should I criticize their euphemism?

But euphemisms become harmful when they mask a problem that should be dealt with. When a slum is called not a slum, but *substandard housing*, does this help the public turn its eyes away from a problem that needs attention?

# Using Vivid Language

Vivid words have the magical ability to paint pictures in your listeners' minds—clear, memorable pictures. Let us examine two techniques—imagery and rhythm—which can help you create these pictures.

## *Create Imagery*

You can bring an abstract idea to life by using precise, descriptive words to create images. For example, David Fields, a criminal-justice major who had visited several prisons, painted a chilling picture of prison life:

> Prison is a jungle. When you're inside, you're as vulnerable as a lion tamer who steps inside a cage with snarling lions. At any moment the prisoners might erupt in violence. You can find yourself with a dozen knife wounds as a result of an argument over something insignificant. For example, you get a box of chocolate-chip cookies from home, and another prisoner wants those cookies and will stab you with a crude, homemade shank if you don't hand them over. There is always noise in prison—even in the dead middle of night; you never have peace and quiet. Glaring lights are on all the time; you're never allowed the luxury of sleeping in the dark. And the place stinks with the odor of fear.

**Author Leslie Fiedler uses vivid language in his talks on American literature.** *(Joseph P. Schuyler/Stock, Boston)*

David's picture conveys the reality of prison life better than a long recital of dry statistics could ever convey.

Two devices that are especially effective for creating mental pictures are the *simile* and the *metaphor*. With a simile, you make a direct comparison of things that are dissimilar, using the words "like" or "as." For example, "The stars are like diamonds in the sky." Like a simile, a metaphor compares dissimilar things, but it leaves off the words "like" and "as." Thus, the simile just described can be changed into the following metaphor: "The stars are diamonds in the sky."

If fresh images are involved, similes and metaphors can be quite vivid. Here are some examples of the effective use of these devices:

> Marriage is a cozy, calm harbor where you are protected from the storms of the outside world. *(Pamela Smith, student speaker)*

> The snow covered up all the brown humps and furrows of the field, like white frosting on a chocolate cake. *(Joshua Burns, student speaker)*

> Manic-depressives are like passengers on an emotional roller-coaster that goes up, up, up to a high of exhilaration and then down, down, down to a low of despair—without ever stopping to let them off. *(Sarah Gentry, student speaker)*

Beware of *mixed metaphors*. These occur when the speaker combines two images that do not logically go together. Such an arrangement either confuses the listeners or leaves them smiling in amusement. President Dwight Eisenhower once said that "the Japanese have a tough row to hoe to keep their economic heads above water." This incongruous mixture of images paints the absurd picture of farmers scratching at the soil while struggling to keep from drowning. To correct the problem, one would have to say something like this: "The Japanese will have to swim vigorously to keep their economic heads above water."

Ernest Bevin, former foreign minister of Great Britain, once used this mixed metaphor: "If you let that sort of thing go on, your bread and butter will be cut out from under your feet." This ridiculous picture of people standing on their own food could be altered in the following way: "Your bread and butter will be snatched from your table."

Mixed metaphors are usually created by speakers who are not thinking of the images involved. They are simply stringing together clichés—trite, worn out words or phrases that have lost their freshness and vividness. Here are some metaphors and similes that have become clichés:

last but not least
stick out like a sore thumb
blind as a bat
beat the bushes
hit the nail on the head
like a bolt out of the blue
stubborn as a mule
mountains out of molehills
water over the dam

In your speeches, you should *work your fingers to the bone* and *move heaven and earth* to avoid clichés if you want to keep your listeners *glued to their seats*. And you should shun mixed metaphors because they are like *a rampaging elephant* that *climbs the ladder of success* in order to *hatch a new idea.*

## Use Rhythm

You can make your language vivid by taking advantage of rhythmic patterns. One such pattern is *parallel structure*, wherein words, phrases, or clauses are arranged in the same form. Here are some examples, placed in poetic form to emphasize the parallels:

Duty,
Honor,
Country.
These are the watchwords of the American soldier.

We want a government . . . of the people,
      by the people,
      for the people.

We need parents who will . . . praise honest efforts,

punish bad behavior, and

ignore inconsequential acts.

Parallel structure can intensify the speaker's emotions, as in this example by student speaker Georgia Adams:

> When I see fish dying in our streams because of acid rain, I am enraged. When I see trees dying on our highest peaks because of acid rain, I am enraged. When I see animal habitats destroyed because of acid rain, I am enraged.

In addition to using parallel structure, Georgia also used another effective rhythmic technique—*repetition*. Notice that by repeating "I am enraged," she conveyed the full measure of her anger.

In the next section of this chapter we will discuss repetition of key ideas to help the audience remember; here we are talking about repetition for its emotional, rhythmic effect. In the conclusion to a classroom speech on preventing nuclear war, Michael Browning repeated the words "we must work hard" over and over to dramatically challenge his listeners:

> Preventing a nuclear war will not be easy. We must all work hard. We must work hard to stop the arms race. We must work hard to create trust and understanding between ourselves and other nations. We must work hard to make sure that nuclear weapons are never used accidentally. We must work hard to keep new nations from joining the nuclear "club." It will not be easy. We must work hard.

If you go back and read Michael's conclusion out loud, you will *feel* the power of repetition.

# Oral versus Written Language

One of the biggest mistakes some speakers make is to treat oral language in a speech as being no different from written language. While the two forms of communication are similar, oral language has two significant requirements which you should be aware of:

1. *Oral language requires more amplification than written language.* If you are watching a football game on TV and you fail to see a key block that makes a touchdown possible, you have the luxury of watching an instant replay in slow motion. If you are reading a complicated passage in your chemistry text and you find yourself hopelessly confused, you can go back a few paragraphs and study the material again. Unfortunately, these opportunities are not available when you listen to a speech. If you fail to

understand what a speaker is saying, you are out of luck. There is no instant replay. There is no way to back up a few paragraphs.

Because of this handicap, oral language requires more amplification than is necessary in written language. If a statement is too terse, the audience has trouble absorbing it. Consider the following example, which is the opening sentence of an article about immigrants:

> The first generation tries to retain as much as possible; the second to forget, the third to remember.[8]

That terse sentence is excellent in an essay. The reader can study it at leisure if the meaning does not pop up immediately. But can you imagine sitting in an audience and immediately understanding it? It is too compact for easy comprehension. It would have to be spoken in an expanded form, such as this:

> When immigrants come to America, how do they treat their cultural heritage from the old country? The first generation of immigrants tries to retain as much as possible of the customs, cuisine, and language of the old country. But the second generation wants to forget all of that; these children of immigrants want to become "100 percent American," with no reminders of their foreign roots. But then along comes the third generation; these grandchildren want to celebrate the past, to find out all they can about their old-country heritage.

With this expanded version, the audience would be able to absorb the information.

A note of caution: Just because it is a good idea to amplify your spoken message does not mean that you should pad your oral language with meaningless or windy phrases. In spoken as well as in written communication, you should omit needless words. For example, don't say, "In terms of the future, the military expects to meet its recruiting goals." Leave off the unnecessary five words at the beginning and say, "The military expects to meet its recruiting goals." Don't say, "in the area of statistics." Say simply, "statistics."

2. *Oral language requires more repetition of key ideas than written language.* "If you have an important point to make," British Prime Minister Winston Churchill advised the young Prince of Wales, "don't try to be subtle or clever. Use a pile driver. Hit the point once. Then come back and hit it again. Then hit it a third time—a tremendous whack."[9]

One of the reasons Churchill is considered one of the greatest orators of the twentieth century is that he followed his own advice. For example, on the subject of resolution, he said:

Never give in! Never, never, never, never, never, never. In nothing great or small, large or petty—never give in except to convictions of honor and good sense.[10]

Too much repetition? For an essay, yes. For a speech, no.

One trainer of salespersons recommends that a sales message be repeated *six* times to prospective customers. Why? Because a week after you give a sales spiel *without* repeating your key ideas, the customers will remember only 10 percent of your message, but if you repeat the key idea six times, they will remember 60 percent of the message.[11] In a public speech, it is hard to predict how much information listeners will retain because there are many variables, such as how much they already know about the subject and how interesting the speech is. But the trainer's estimates do not sound far-fetched. In general, listeners do not remember ideas unless they are repeated by the speaker.

The trick is to repeat key ideas, but to do it without boring the audience. As an example, suppose that a speaker wanted to make the following point:

> When you're driving in late afternoon and it starts to get dark, turn on your lights so that other motorists can see your car.

While this sentence would be acceptable in an essay, it needs some elaboration and repetition if used in a speech. Here is the way student speaker Stanley Morgan made the point:

> When should you turn on your headlights in the evening? When it gets too dark for you to see other cars? No! That's too late. You should turn on your headlights at the first hint of darkness—not to help *you* see, but to make sure that the *other drivers* see you. I'm constantly amazed at the people who ignore this simple rule of survival. Next time you're driving at dusk, look at the other cars and you'll see what I'm saying is true. Some drivers wait until it's pitch black to turn on their lights. I think it's a matter of personal pride. They have the attitude, "Well, I can still see." The real question is, Can they be seen by other drivers? Remember what I'm telling you; it could prevent you from being in an accident—turn on your lights at dusk so that other drivers can see *you*.

In print, this passage looks too wordy—and it is. But in Stanley's speech, repeating his key idea (but using different words each time) was an effective way of driving home his point. If Stanley had limited himself to only one sentence, his point might have failed to stick in the minds of the audience.

## Summary

The words that you use in a speech should be chosen with care and sensitivity. Always use language that is appropriate for your particular audience and occasion, avoiding words that might be over the heads of the listeners or that might offend any member of the audience. To use words accurately, you must be sensitive to both denotations and connotations, and you must use correct grammar.

You can achieve clarity in your language by choosing words that are simple, concrete, and precise. You can achieve vividness by creating word images and by using rhythm.

Oral language and written language are similar in many ways, but there are two significant differences: (1) Oral language requires more amplification than written language, and (2) oral language requires more repetition of key ideas than written language.

## Review Questions

1. Why did Dr. Martin Luther King use different words with different audiences?
2. What is the difference between the denotation and connotation of a word?
3. Where can one find explanations of the synonyms of words?
4. Why is incorrect grammar a handicap for a speaker?
5. What are euphemisms? Give two examples.
6. What are the two major differences between oral and written language?

# TIPS *for your career*

### Tip 12: Be Sensitive to the Issue of Sexist Pronoun Usage

For centuries the masculine pronouns *he, his,* and *him* were used in the English language to designate an individual when gender was immaterial. In a sentence such as "Every driver should buckle *his* seat belt before *he* starts the engine," the pronouns *his* and *he* were understood to refer to drivers in general, both male and female. Today, however, according to Frederick Crews, a professor of English at the University of California, Berkeley, "many [people] find those words an offensive reminder of second-class citizenship for women."[12]

To avoid offending anyone in your audience, you can handle this pronoun issue in one of three ways:

1. *Use masculine and feminine pronouns in tandem.* In other words, use *he or she* (or *she or he*) when referring to an indefinite person. For example, "Every driver should buckle *his or her* seat belt before *he or she* starts the engine." A problem arises, however, in sentences like this: "Each participant should ask *himself or herself* whether *he or she* really needs *his or her* umbrella." If you continued in this way, the pronouns could become cumbersome, perhaps even distracting the listeners from your ideas. This problem has caused many people to prefer either of the two remaining alternatives.

2. *Use plural pronouns.* Say simply, "All drivers should buckle *their* seat belts before *they* start the engine." This alternative has the advantage of being simple, while offending no one.

3. *Use the pronoun "you."* For example, "Whenever you get behind the wheel, you should buckle your seat belt before starting your engine." For speeches, this is often the best of the alternatives because it is not only simple and inoffensive, but it also has the virtue of being direct and personal.

## Chapter 13

# Delivering the Speech

Roger Howard was one of the bravest speakers I have ever seen. A young man from New York City who had been addicted to heroin as a teen-ager, he founded a chapter of Narcotics Anonymous, which was devoted to salvaging the lives of drug addicts. He appeared at a government-sponsored symposium that dealt with the use and abuse of heroin. Though he was a high school dropout with limited public-speaking experience, he had the courage to stand before 300 highly educated people (government officials, professors, and journalists) and try to convince them that the government should provide funds to help victims of what he called the "heroin epidemic."

When Howard started speaking, his delivery was terrible: his eyes were cast downward at a spot on the floor in front of the first row; instead of standing up straight, he was hunched over the microphone; he used no gestures because his hands were too busy clutching the lectern as if it were a life raft; his voice was raspy and tremulous. He seemed shaky and unsure of himself—I'm certain that he was scared to death and wished to be a hundred miles from that room. Yet, at the same time, I sensed that he felt a strong compulsion to tell his story. And what a story it was—a harrowing tale of slavery to a narcotic habit that was so expensive that he had to commit crimes to get enough money for his daily fix. As he got into his story, I observed a remarkable transformation. He came out of his hunched-over position and stood up straight. His eyes looked directly at the listeners, imploring their understanding and support. His hands started moving with power and emphasis. His voice gained strength and confidence. The audience responded by listening with rapt attention. There was absolute stillness in the room. At the end of the speech, the listeners gave him a round of hearty, appreciative applause. His speech was a success.

As you read this chapter, I hope you will keep Roger Howard in mind because he exemplifies an important point: *The key to good delivery is a strong desire to communicate with the audience.* Though Howard started out with ragged, unpolished delivery, he had a burning desire to communicate with the audience, and before long he was unconsciously using good delivery techniques. I have observed this phenomenon time and time again: speakers who lack professional polish and training but who care deeply about conveying their ideas to the audience almost always do an adequate job with their delivery. A General Motors executive, R. T. Kingman, expressed it this way: "If a speaker knows what he wants to say, really wants to say it, and wants everybody in the room to understand what it is he wants to say, all the other things like looking people in the eye and using good gestures will just come naturally."[1]

The speaker's desire to communicate is emphasized so that you can put the ideas of this chapter into proper perspective. The dozens of tips about delivery in the pages that follow are important; you should study them carefully. But bear in mind that a strong desire to communicate with your audience is the dynamo of power that makes it possible for you to deliver a speech with strength and effectiveness.

# Methods of Speaking

There are four basic speaking methods used by public speakers today. You need to ask yourself which method is best suited for your particular audience.

## *Impromptu*

Speaking impromptu means speaking on the spur of the moment—with no chance to prepare. For example, without warning you are asked to give a talk to your fellow employees about your recent convention trip to New Orleans. In such a situation, you simply have to do the best that you can. If you get a few minutes' advance warning, jot down your central idea and as many supporting ideas as possible. Formulate your introduction and conclusion. If you have no advance warning at all, try to formulate your main idea as you stand to speak. As best you can, try to present your speech along the lines suggested in this book. The most important advice is this: be brief. When asked to speak impromptu, some speakers spend an hour saying the same thing over and over again because they are afraid of leaving out something important or of being unable to finish the speech smoothly. The sins of leaving something out or having a clumsy conclusion are minor compared to the wickedness of boring an audience for an hour. Brevity is almost always a virtue.

Try to foresee situations where you are likely to be called upon to speak impromptu, and prepare yourself accordingly. In other words, when you return from New Orleans and you are driving to work, rehearse in your mind what you will say if the boss asks you to make a little speech about the convention.

## *Manuscript*

A manuscript speech is written out and delivered word-for-word. It is primarily used in formal situations where precise wording is important. A biologist at a seminar attended by his or her colleagues might read a research paper in the interest of scientific precision. The President of the United States uses a manuscript in a major foreign-policy speech because every word will be scrutinized by reporters and officials in many different countries; if such a speech were delivered off-the-cuff, the President might say something that could be misinterpreted by people in other countries, causing them to react adversely. A manuscript speech is also used for a radio or television address because the words must fit precisely in a time slot.

There are two ways to deliver a manuscript speech. The first is to read it, the least effective of all speaking styles. Most speakers who read a manuscript fail to look at the audience, they speak in a monotone, and they read too quickly. Worst of all, there is no sense of communication with the audience, no reaching out to make contact. For all the good they do, they might as well pass out copies of the speech and let the audience read it at home.

The second way to deliver a manuscript speech is to use the written text but not actually read it. Here is how it works: You practice the speech over and over until you are thoroughly familiar with it. When you give the speech, you glance at the text to refresh your memory but most of the time you look at the listeners and speak to them as if the words were coming from the heart—fresh and newly minted. This technique is very effective, but I must warn you: it is much more difficult than it looks. Some actors, experienced politicians, and professional speechmakers use this method with great success, but most speakers—even ones with a lot of experience—fail to pull it off. They sound dull and lifeless, rather than natural and spontaneous.

Unless you are a veteran orator, do not use a manuscript. You might fail to maintain good eye contact with your audience, and your words—if they are read instead of spoken naturally—might be hard for the audience to absorb.


## *Memorized*

Memorizing a speech is a bad idea. Here is why:

1. You would be forced to spend an enormous amount of time in committing the speech to memory.

2. At some point in your speech, you might suddenly forget what comes next. This could cause you to become acutely embarrassed or even panic-stricken. Once derailed from your speech, you might be unable to get back on track.

3. Even if you remembered your entire speech, you would be speaking from your memory, not from your heart. This could cause you to sound remote, lifeless, unenergetic—more like a robot than a human being.

Memorizing does have one virtue: it lets you figure out your *exact* wording ahead of time. But this gain in precision fails to outweigh the disadvantages. Though a few popular speechmakers say that they memorize their speeches, I would not recommend this method for anyone. Certainly not for the inexperienced speaker.

**Though extemporaneous speakers spend a great deal of time in preparation, they appear as if they are speaking spontaneously; they are warm, direct, and conversational.** *(Sylvia Johnson/Woodfin Camp & Associates)*

## Extemporaneous

The extemporaneous method is the most popular style of speaking in America today. The idea is to sound as if you are speaking impromptu, but instead of giving the clumsy, faltering speech that many impromptu speakers give, you present a beautifully organized, well-developed speech that you have spent many hours preparing and practicing.

You speak from notes, but these notes do not contain your speech written out word-for-word. Instead they contain only your basic *ideas*, expressed in a few key words. When you speak, therefore, you make up the exact words as you go along. You glance at your notes occasionally to remind yourself of your next point, but most of the time you look at the listeners, speaking to them in a natural, conversational tone of voice.

This conversational tone is valued in a speech because it is the easiest kind for an audience to listen to, the easiest to understand, and the easiest to remember. When you speak conversationally, you are speaking directly, warmly, sincerely. You are speaking as closely as possible to the way you talk to your best friends: your voice is full of life and color; your words are fresh and vital rather than stale and warmed-over.

Though the extemporaneous method is popular and effective, it provides no guarantee of success. In fact, if you are not careful, it can lure you to failure. For this method to work, *you must spend a lot of time preparing and rehearsing your speech.* Mark Twain said, "It takes three weeks to prepare a good ad-lib speech." In other words, if you want to *sound* as if you are ad-libbing beautifully, you have to spend a lot of time in preparation and practice. Speakers who use the extemporaneous method correctly are like the Olympic divers you see on TV. These athletes make their high dives look natural and easy, but in reality they have achieved their graceful, "effortless" coordination through hours of hard practice. In public speaking, if you do not put forth time and effort in preparing and practicing, you are really no better off than if you give an impromptu speech. For example, if you fail to prepare a well-organized outline, you might find that your ideas do not hang together and your words are fuzzy and imprecise. If you fail to practice, you might find that your delivery is ragged, with awkward silences and many "uhs" and "ers."

Speaking extemporaneously permits more flexibility than reading from a written speech because you can adjust the speech to meet the needs of a particular audience. If, for example, you see that some of your listeners do not understand a point, you can restate your message in different words or you can insert additional explanations. If you are the last speaker of the evening at a banquet and you sense that your audience is about to go to sleep because of the long-winded speakers who preceded you, you can shorten your speech by cutting out some of your minor points.

# Voice

Some people think that to be an excellent speaker, you must have a golden voice, so rich and resonant that it enthralls anyone who listens to it. But this is not true. Some of the most famous speakers in history had undistinguished voices; for example, Abraham Lincoln's voice was considered harsh and unpleasant by many of his contemporaries, and Winston Churchill spoke with a slight lisp. In our own day, I have observed a popular evangelist whose voice is thin and weak, a successful TV commentator who talks in an irritatingly abrasive manner, and a leading politician who speaks with an unpleasant nasal whine. All three are in demand as public speakers. It is nice to have a rich, resonant voice, but there are other characteristics of the human voice which are of greater importance for effective speechmaking: your voice should have proper volume; it should be clear and understandable; and it should be expressive.

## *Volume*

The larger the room, the louder you have to speak. You can tell if your volume is loud enough by observing the people in the back row. Are they leaning forward with quizzical expressions as they strain to hear your words? Then obviously you need to speak louder. In some cases you may want to ask directly, "Can the people in the back row hear me all right?" There are some circumstances in which you may have to raise your voice to overcome unavoidable noises, such as the hum of air conditioners, the chatter of people in a hallway, the clatter of dishes and silverware during a banquet, or even the sound of a band blaring in the next room.

Speaking loud enough for all to hear does not mean shouting. It means *projecting* your voice a bit beyond its normal range. If you have never spoken to a large group or if your instructor tells you that you have problems in projecting your voice, practice with a friend. Find an empty classroom, have your friend sit in the back row, and practice speaking with extra force—not shouting—so that your friend can hear you easily.

If a speech requires the use of a microphone, go to the meeting site early and spend a few minutes testing your voice before the listeners arrive. Adjust it to your height; if someone readjusts it during the ceremonies, spend a few moments getting it just right for yourself. Your audience will not mind the slight delay. When you speak into a mike, it is not necessary to have your lips almost touching it; in fact, your voice will sound better if your mouth is 6 to 12 inches away from the mike. Position the mike so that you can forget that it is there. This frees you to speak naturally, without having to bend over or lean forward. At large meetings, I have heard speakers raise their voices while talking into a microphone; this makes their voice sound strident. A microphone means that you *don't* have to raise your voice. In fact, says professional speaker Arnold "Nick" Carter, "the invention of the microphone made it possible for me to speak to 18,000 people with a whisper."[2]

## Clarity

The words that you speak should be uttered clearly and understandably, with good articulation and correct pronunciation.

Here is the kind of dialogue you might hear on any college campus in America:

"Watcha doin?"
"Stud'n a liddle histry."
"Howbout that lass test? Wajagit?"
"Dunno, probly flunked."
"Jeatyet?"
"Nah."
"Lessgo getta pizza."

Most of us are lazy in our daily conversations; we slur sounds, drop syllables, and mumble words. Poor articulation is not a problem as long as our friends understand what we are saying, but in a public speech we need to enunciate our words crisply and precisely to make sure that everything we say is intelligible to our listeners. We should avoid going to an extreme, however, by enunciating in such an exaggeratedly precise way that we call attention to our way of speaking.

While poor articulation stems from sloppy habits, mispronunciation is a matter of not knowing the correct way to say a word. Here are some common pronunciation mistakes:

|  | **Incorrect** | **Correct** |
|---|---|---|
| recognize | reck-uh-nize | rec-og-nize |
| library | li-berry | li-brar-y |
| nuclear | nu-cu-lar | nu-cle-ar |
| picture | pitch-er | pic-ture |
| hundred | hun-derd | hun-dred |
| realtor | reel-a-tor | re-al-tor |
| perspiration | press-pi-ra-tion | per-spi-ra-tion |
| drowned | drown-did | drownd |
| athlete | ath-uh-lete | ath-lete |

If you are like most people, you use words which you have picked up from books but have never heard pronounced. If you rely on your own guess, it can sometimes cause embarrassment, as in the case of one student who had read all about the Sioux Indians, but apparently had never heard the tribal name pronounced. He called them the *sigh-ox* Indians. On other occasions you may confuse words that sound a lot alike. For example, one of my students said that a man and woman contemplating marriage should make sure they are compatible before they say their *vowels*. (One of the listeners couldn't resist the temptation to ask, at the end of the speech, whether consonants were also important for marriage.)

These kinds of mistakes should be avoided because if you mispronounce words, many listeners will downgrade you in their minds as someone who is incompetent and poorly educated. You can easily find out the correct way to say a word by looking up the pronunciation in a dictionary.

## *Expressiveness*

The most boring voices in the world are probably those of elementary school children when they stand on a stage for a holiday skit and mouth sentences they have been required to memorize, often using words whose meanings they are blithely unaware of. Their lines are uttered in a flat monotone, without any flair or meaning.

In sharp contrast, a dynamic speaker has a voice that is warm and expressive, producing a rich variety of sounds. Audiences find such a voice more interesting to listen to than a monotonous one, and therefore they are more likely to respond favorably to what the speaker says. To achieve expressiveness, one must make good use of the following elements.

## Pitch

The highness or lowness of your voice is called pitch. The ups and downs of pitch—called intonation patterns—give our language its distinctive melody. Consider the following sentence: *I was angry.* Say it in a variety of ways—with anger, with sarcasm, with humor, with disbelief. Each time you say it, you are using a different intonation pattern.

In conversation, almost everyone uses a variety of intonation patterns and emphasizes particular words, but in public speaking, some speakers fail to use any variety at all. They speak in a monotone—a dull, flat drone that will put many listeners to sleep. Even worse, they run the risk of appearing insincere. They may say, for example, something dramatic like "This is a terrible tragedy for America," but say it in such a casual, offhand way that the audience thinks they do not really mean it.

One of the problems with a monotone is that some words fail to receive the emphasis they deserve. For example, take a sentence like this: "Mr. Smith made $600,000 last year, while Mr. Jones made $6,000." Speakers who talk in a monotone will say the two figures as if there were no difference between $600,000 and $6,000. But listeners need help in *hearing* the disparity. A speaker should let his or her voice place heavy emphasis on the $600,000.

## Loudness and Softness

Besides having the proper volume, so that everyone in the audience can hear you, you can raise or lower your voice for dramatic effect or to emphasize a point. Try saying the following out loud:

(*Soft:*) "Should we give in to the kidnappers' demands? (*Switch to loud:*) NEVER!"

Did you notice that raising your voice for the last word conveys that you truly mean what you say? Now try another selection out loud:

(*Start softly and make your voice grow louder as you near the end of this sentence:*) Edwin Arlington Robinson's character Richard Cory had everything that a man could want—good looks, lots of money, popularity. (*Now make your voice switch to soft:*) But he went home one night and put a bullet through his head.

Changing from loud to soft helps the listeners *feel* the tragic discrepancy between Richard Cory's outer appearance and his inner reality.

## Rate

How quickly or slowly should you speak? The ideal speed for giving a speech is like the ideal speed for driving a car—it all depends on conditions. Driving a car at 55 miles per hour is fine for a highway but too fast

for a school zone. In similar fashion, a rapid rate of speaking is appropriate in certain conditions—if, for example, you are describing a thrilling
high-speed police chase. A slow pace, on the other hand, is preferred if
you are introducing a technical, hard-to-understand concept.

One of the biggest mistakes inexperienced speakers make is to speak
too rapidly. The audience simply cannot absorb their words. Students in
public-speaking classes who are graded down on this point are often
miffed because they swear that they do not speak as fast as the highly
paid professional communicators they see on TV who give the news or
announce a sports event. The students are right: they *don't* speak as fast.
But what they fail to consider is that speed itself is not so much the
problem as the lack of variety and rhythm in their voices. In other words,
they race through their speech without putting any variety into their
voice. If they said their words with expressiveness and meaning (as good
TV commentators do), their listeners probably could keep up with the
speed.

You can avoid speaking too rapidly by practicing your speech at home.
Use a tape recorder and listen to yourself. Have friends or relatives listen
to your speech; ask them to tell you frankly if you are speaking too fast
for easy comprehension.

Some people speak too rapidly because they write out all or most of
their speech on their note cards or a sheet of paper and then when they
rise to speak, they succumb to the temptation of reading rapidly from
their script. The solution is to have brief notes, not a written script, when
you stand up to speak.

It is especially important that you speak at a slow, deliberate rate
during your introduction (except in special situations, as when you lead
off with an adventure story). Have you ever noticed how TV dramas start
out very slowly? They do not divulge important details of the story until
you are three or four minutes into the show. One obvious reason for this
is to have mercy on the viewers who have gone to the kitchen to get a
snack and are slow in returning to the TV. But the main reason is to give
the viewers a chance to "tune in" to the story, to get adjusted to what is
happening on the screen, to get accustomed to the characters. If too much
action or dialogue takes place in the first minute, viewers are unable to
absorb the story. In like fashion, you need to give your audience a chance
to "tune in" to you, to get accustomed to your voice and subject matter.
If you race through your introduction, they might become lost and confused, and they might decide to spend the time daydreaming rather than
struggling to follow your race-horse delivery.

## Pauses

When you read printed material, you have punctuation marks to help
you make sense out of your reading—commas tell you when to pause,

periods when to stop, etc. In a speech, there are no punctuation marks; listeners must rely on oral cues to guide them. One of these cues is the pause, which lets your listeners know when you have finished one thought and are ready to go to the next. Audiences appreciate a pause. It gives them time to digest what you have said. And it gives you a moment to think of what you are going to say next.

A pause before an important idea or the climax of a story can create suspense. For example, student speaker Stephanie Johnson told of an adventure that happened while she was camping:

> It was late at night when I finally crawled into my sleeping bag. The fire had died down, but the moon cast a faint, spooky light on our campsite. I must have been asleep a couple of hours when I suddenly woke up. Something was brushing up against my sleeping bag. My heart started pounding like crazy. I peeked out of the slit I had left for air. Do you know what I saw? [*pause*]

By pausing at this point, Stephanie had the audience on the edge of their chairs. What was it? A bear? A human intruder? After a few moments of dramatic tension, she ended the suspense: "By the light of the moon, I could see a dark little animal with a distinctive white stripe. [*pause*] It was a skunk."

A pause can also be used to emphasize an important statement. It is a way of saying, "Let this sink in." If you were giving the following story in a speech, where would you insert pauses?

> Albert Einstein was once asked whether he thought that World War III would be fought with nuclear weapons. Einstein, the man who made possible the construction of the atomic bomb, gave this answer: "I don't know what weapons will be used for World War III, but I do know what weapons will be used for World War IV: sticks and stones."

There are several spots where pauses could be placed effectively. Here is how Erik Swensen delivered these words in a classroom speech:

> Albert Einstein was once asked whether he thought that World War III would be fought with nuclear weapons. [*pause to give the listeners a chance to think about the momentous nature of the question*] Einstein, the man who made possible the construction of the atomic bomb, gave this answer: "I don't know what weapons will be used for World War III, but I do know what weapons will be used for World War IV: [*pause to create dramatic tension and suspense*] sticks and stones." [*pause to let the audience reflect on the irony*]

Erik's dramatic pauses captivated his audience. Notice that his final pause gave the listeners time to reflect on Einstein's insight.

In some speeches you might find yourself pausing not because you want to, but because you have forgotten what you were planning to say next and you need to look at your notes. Or you might pause while searching your mind for the right word. Such a pause seems like an eternity, so you are tempted to fill in the horrible silence with "uh" or "er" or "um." Try hard not to make these sounds. There is nothing wrong with silence; there is no need to be embarrassed by it. The audience does not mind. In fact, a few such pauses can enhance your credibility, making you seem more conversational and natural, and less artificial and contrived. You look as if you are concerned about giving the audience the most precise words possible.

## Conversational Quality

Many inexperienced speakers give their speeches in a dull, plodding, colorless voice. Yet five minutes afterward, chatting with their friends in the hall, they speak with animation and warmth.

What they need to do, obviously, is bring that same conversational quality into their speeches. How can this be done? How can a person sound as lively and as "real" in talking to 30 people as in chatting with a friend? If this problem applies to you, here are two suggestions.

1. *Treat your audience not as an impersonal mass, not as a blur of faces, but as a collection of individuals.* Some students sound wooden and artificial when giving a speech, but during the question-and-answer period, they respond to questions in a natural, conversational manner. Why does this happen? One reason is that they are engaged in a conversation with the person who asked the question. They are now talking one-on-one. To capture this style of talking during the speech itself, here is a mental ploy you can use from the very beginning: look at one or two or three individuals in different parts of the room and act as if you are talking to them one-on-one. You should avoid staring, of course, but if you look at them briefly, it will help you develop a conversational attitude. As the speech goes on, you can add other faces to your "conversation."

2. *Be yourself—but somewhat intensified.* To speak to an audience with the same natural, conversational tone you use with your friends, you must speak with greater energy and forcefulness. We are not talking now about projecting your voice so that the people in the back of the room can hear you, but rather *intensifying* the psychological dimensions of your voice— the emotional tones and the vibrancy. How can you do this? Here are two ways.

First, let your natural enthusiasm come forth. If you have chosen a topic wisely, you are speaking on something you care a great deal about and want very much to communicate to the audience. When you stand in front of your audience, don't keep a lid on your feelings. Don't hold

**Most speeches feature question-and-answer periods at the end. Speakers should prepare for these questions as thoroughly as they prepare for the speech itself.** *(Frank Siteman/Stock, Boston)*

yourself back; let your voice convey all the enthusiasm that you feel inside. Many speakers are afraid they will look or sound ridiculous if they get involved with their subject. "I'll come on too strong," they say. But the truth is that your audience will not react this way; they will be impressed by your energy and zest. Think back to the speakers you have heard: Didn't you respond favorably to those who were vital and alive and enthusiastic?

Second, practice loosening up. Some novice speakers sound and look stiff because they simply have had no practice in loosening up. Here is something you can try: find a private location (such as a room at home or a clearing in the woods or an empty classroom late in the afternoon when no one else is around). For subject matter, you can practice a speech that you are working on, recite poetry, read from the morning newspaper, or simply ad-lib. Whatever words you use, say them dramatically. "Ham" it up. Be theatrical. Act as if you are running for President and you are trying to persuade 10,000 people to vote for you. Or act as if you are giving a poetry reading to 500 of your most enthusiastic fans. You will not speak so dramatically to a real audience, of course, but the practice of "letting go" will help you break out of your normal reserve. It will help you learn to be yourself, to convey your natural enthusiasm.

# Nonverbal Communication

Betty is at a party when one of her friends says solicitously, "Are you okay, Betty?"

"I'm fine," Betty replies with a weak smile. "Why in the world do you ask?"

The reason the friend asks the question is that all evening long, Betty has been unconsciously sending out nonverbal messages that say, loud and clear, that something is wrong; her shoulders are droopy, she sits in a dejected manner, her eyes betray sadness, the corners of her mouth are turned down. Betty says with words that she's okay, but her "body language" contradicts her. Which message will the friends believe? The nonverbal one.[3] And they are wise in doing so because the next day they all learn that Betty had broken up with her boyfriend just before the party but did not want to talk about it.

Nonverbal communication is a powerful language that we use every day, usually unconsciously. Most of the time, our words and our body language are in harmony (we say, "I'm fine" and our smile and shining eyes affirm our words). But occasionally, when there is a discrepancy between the two, the outside world usually accepts the nonverbal message as the true one.

In a speech, even if the verbal content of your speech is superb, you run the risk of damaging your credibility if you have poor body language— if, for example, you fail to look at the audience, if your facial expression says "I hate this; I don't want to be here talking to this group," and if your posture cries out that you are discouraged and bitter. What you need, instead, is positive nonverbal language: look your audience in the eye, stand poised, and let your face and body say, "I am confident in what I'm doing; I'm glad to be talking to you."

If you are truly enthusiastic about your speech and eager to share it with your audience, much of your body language will take care of itself, as we discussed at the beginning of this chapter. But you may be asking, "What if I don't really feel happy and confident? I can't lie with my body, can I?" This is a good question, because there are times in your life when you will resent having to give a speech, as when the boss orders you to give a presentation to the board of directors, or an instructor assigns you to give an oral report to the class. Also there are times when you simply do not feel like standing up in front of a group. Maybe you did not get much sleep the night before, and you have no zip, no spark. At times like these, what should you do?

Pretend. Yes, pretend to be confident in yourself and in your ideas. Pretend to be glad to appear before your audience. Pretend to be enthusiastic. But isn't this phony? Isn't this forcing the body to tell a lie? Yes, but we often must be "deceitful" in order to carry out life's tasks. We force ourselves to be cheerful and animated for a crucial job interview, for conferences with the boss, for an important date with someone we love, and for myriad other situations in life. By *acting* as if you are confident, poised, and enthusiastic, you will often find that after a few minutes, the pretense gives way to reality. You truly become confident, poised, and enthusiastic. Consider the comedians and talk-show hosts who appear night after night on TV. Do you think they are always "up"? No, they are like you and me. They have their bad days, their sluggish days, their down-in-the-dumps days, their head-cold and stomach-ache days, but they force themselves to perform; they pretend to be enthusiastic. After about 60 seconds (most of them report), the pretense gives way to reality, and they truly *are* enthusiastic. (A word of advice: If this transformation fails to happen to you—if you do not feel enthusiastic after a few minutes—you should still pretend.)

How do you carry out this pretense? How can you make the body "lie" for you? The answer is to be sensitive to the "signals" that the body sends out to show confidence and energy, and then to force yourself to use these signals. To familiarize yourself with these signals, take a look at the major nonverbal aspects of public speaking.

## Personal Appearance

Your audience will size up your personal appearance and start forming opinions about you even before you open your mouth to begin your speech. You should be clean, well-groomed, and attractively dressed.

Janet Stone and Jane Bachner, who conduct workshops for women executives, have some good advice for both men and women:

> As a general rule of thumb, find out what the audience will be wearing and then wear something yourself that is just a trifle dressier than their clothes. The idea is to establish yourself as "The Speaker," to set yourself slightly apart from the crowd, to show them that you are taking their invitation seriously enough to dress up a little for them, and yet to look enough like them to establish yourself as a person they can identify with.[4]

Your attire should always be appropriate. In other words, do not wear anything that would distract or offend the audience. A T-shirt with a ribald or controversial slogan printed on the front, for example, might direct attention away from the speech itself, and it might offend some members of the audience.

## Eye Contact

You should look at your audience 95 percent of the time while you are talking. The other 5 percent is for occasional glances at your notes. Having good eye contact with your listeners is important for three reasons: (1) It creates an important bond of communication and rapport between you and them. It is, in the words of professional speaker Jack Valenti, a "figurative handshake."[5] (2) It shows your sincerity. There's an old saying, "Don't buy a used car from a dealer who won't look you in the eye." We distrust salespersons and others who won't look at us openly and candidly. If you want your listeners to have confidence in what you are saying, look at *them*, not at a spot on the back wall. (3) It enables you to get audience feedback. Looking directly at your listeners makes you instantly aware of any lapses in communication. For example, did a number of listeners look puzzled when you made your last statement? Then you obviously confused them; you need to explain your point in a different way.

The biggest spoiler of good eye contact is looking at your notes too much. This is usually caused by one of the following: (1) Not being prepared. This can be corrected, of course, by rehearsing your speech so many times that you need only glance at your notes to remind yourself of what comes next. (2) Nervousness. Some speakers are well prepared and do not really need to look at their notes very often, but they are so nervous that they scrutinize their notes to gain security and avoid the audience. One way to correct this is to put reminders, in giant red letters, on your notes—LOOK AT AUDIENCE—to jog you out of this habit.

Eye contact is more than darting furtive glances at the audience from time to time. It is more than mechanically moving your head from side to side like an oscillating fan. You must have meaningful contact similar to the eye-to-eye communication you engage in with your friends. For a large audience, the best technique is to have a "conversation" with three or four people in different parts of the room (so that you seem to be giving your attention to the entire audience). Professional speaker James "Doc" Blakely explains how to do this:

> Many speakers, especially inexperienced ones, don't see an audience at all. To them, it is just a blur of faces. I have found that the real key in natural, conversational speaking is to pick out the friendliest faces in the audience and speak to them as if you were speaking only to that person. It's like everyone else is eavesdropping on the conversation. By shifting eye contact from one point to another scattered throughout the room, but still speaking to those friendly faces, you give the listeners the feeling that you are speaking to them as individuals.[6]

While picking out faces in different parts of the room is a good technique for large audiences, you should actually look at *every* listener when the audience is small. Professional speaker Danny Cox uses a technique called "locking" whenever he speaks to a small gathering:

> I learned something once from a piano player. I couldn't believe how she held an audience in a cocktail bar. It was so quiet in there you couldn't believe it. I realized one night what she was doing. She was looking at each person and as soon as she made eye contact with them, she smiled at them.

And then moved on to the next one, and smiled. She was "locking" everybody in. This is a good technique in public speaking—very simple, too.[7]

While the *quantity* of eye contact is important, the *quality* is also important. When you look at your listeners, do not give them blank stares, angry gazes, or frightened glances; instead give them friendly, confident looks. Your eyes are powerful communicators, capable of conveying a wide range of feelings, so let your eyes say to the audience: "I am glad to be here speaking to you, and I want very much to communicate my ideas to you."

## Facial Expressions

You should let your face express whatever emotion is appropriate at any given moment in a speech. A student told me he was planning to speak on how to perform under pressure; his primary example was the thrilling moment in high school when he kicked the winning field goal in the final seconds of a championship football game. When he described that triumphant feat, his face was suffused with excitement, but when he got up in front of the class and told the same story in his speech, his face was blank. Gone was the joy, gone was the exhilaration. By having a facial expression that was incongruous with the event he was describing, he weakened the impact of the story.

If you are speaking about sad topics, your face should not be grinning; if you are speaking about happy times, your face should not be grimacing. And whatever you are talking about, your face should not be devoid of any emotion at all—it should be expressive and natural. How can you let your face be expressive and natural? One way is to loosen up, as suggested previously in the section on speaking conversationally. (All aspects of vocal and nonverbal communication go hand in hand; if your voice sounds natural, your body will probably look natural.) Another way is to practice with a friend who can give you feedback on your facial expressions.

## Posture

Stand in front of your audience poised, with your weight equally distributed on your feet. Your body language should convey the message, "I am confident; I am in command of this situation." This does not mean that you should be cocky and arrogant, but simply that you should convey an appearance of relaxed alertness.

If you are speaking at a lectern, here are some things *not* to do: Do not lean on it. Do not slouch to one side of it. Do not prop your feet on its base. Do not rock back and forth with it.

Some speakers like to sit on the edge of a desk to deliver a speech. This posture is fine for one-hour classroom lectures because the speaker gets a chance to relax, and his or her body language bespeaks openness and informality. But for short speeches, especially the kind you are expected to deliver in a public-speaking class, stand up straight, primarily because it is easier to be alert and enthusiastic if you are standing up than if your body is in a relaxed sitting position.

## Movement

You do not have to stand in one place throughout your speech as if you were glued to the spot. Feel free to walk to the chalkboard and write a key word, or walk to your visual aid. Even if you do not have any visuals, you still may want to incorporate movement into your speech because of the following advantages:

1. Since nervousness can cause shaking hands and trembling knees, movement gives your body a chance to dissipate some of your nervous energy.

2. Movement can be used to recapture your listeners' attention if they are getting bored or tired. An animated speaker is easier to follow than an unanimated speaker who stays frozen in one spot.

3. Movement can be used to emphasize a transition from one point to the next. If you have three major points to make, you can make point 1 from your central standing position. When you are ready to make point 2, you walk two steps to the left, stop, make your point. When you are ready to make point 3, you walk back to your original place, stop, make your point.

4. Movement can be used to make a dramatic point. At a crucial point in your speech, when you want strong audience reaction, you can walk a few steps toward the listeners, speaking as you go. When you have finished this point, you can walk back to your original spot and continue.

Should you use a lectern to stand behind and place your notes on? For classroom speeches, you need to comply with whatever system your instructor prescribes. Out in the community, use a lectern if you think it helps you. Here is a technique that has become popular in the business world (but you should check with your instructor before trying it in a classroom speech): Using the lectern as "home base," walk a few paces to the left or the right of it each time you make a point. In other words, glance at your notes on the lectern to remind you of the point you want to make, move away from the lectern a few paces, make the point, then walk back to the lectern to pick up your next point. The idea behind this technique is to remove the physical barrier (the lectern) that separates you from your listeners so that you strengthen your bond of communication with them.

Any movement during your speech should be purposeful and confident—not random and nervous. You must also be careful not to move about too much. If you pace from one side of the room to the other, like a tiger in a cage, your audience may get distracted and even annoyed.

## Gestures

What should you do with your hands during a speech? The best advice is to let your hands be free to make gestures whenever you feel like making them. This, after all, is how you make gestures in conversation—naturally and without thinking. To make sure that your hands are free for gesturing, you can let them hang by your side, or allow them to rest on the lectern. Beware of doing things that prevent your hands from being free to gesture: (1) *Don't* grip the lectern with your hands. (2) *Don't* clutch your notes with both hands. (3) *Don't* stuff both hands into your pockets.

Gestures are good if they reinforce your message or help the audience to understand what you are saying; gestures are bad if they draw attention to themselves. If, to show anger, you slam your fist down on the lectern, knocking over a glass of water and scaring the audience, you have called attention to the gesture and distracted the audience from your message.

If you use a lectern, do not let it hide your gestures. Some speakers rest their hands on the lectern and make tiny, flickering gestures that cannot be seen by the audience. This is distracting to many listeners. Better no gestures at all than half-hidden ones.

Some speeches call for lots of gestures, some call for little or none. If you were describing your battle to catch a huge fish in the ocean, you would find your hands and arms constantly in motion. If you were giving a funeral eulogy, on the other hand, you might not make any gestures at all.

Most gestures should not be mechanically planned in advance because if you are not using gestures naturally, your timing might be off. One student gave a speech in which he planned ahead of time to slam his fist on the lectern at the climax of his remarks. He said to the audience, "We must close down all nuclear plants!" But then he waited a few seconds before he slammed his fist down on the lectern, as if he had forgotten to do it until he had seen the cue on his note cards. The effect was comical rather than serious.

Though most of the time you should not plan gestures in advance, there are a few occasions when this is appropriate. If you have three major points to make, you can practice in advance holding up the correct number of fingers to assist the audience in following your points. If you are discussing two contrasting ideas, you can hold up your left hand when you say "On the one hand . . . ," and then hold up your right hand when you say "On the other hand . . . ."

The larger the audience, the more sweeping your gestures. The evangelists who use windmill-like arm movements in addressing their multitudes in arenas are doing so for a good reason: they are able to establish a bond with people who are hundreds of yards away; small gestures would be lost in the vastness of the arena.

One last comment about gestures: if you are the kind of person who simply does not gesture much, don't worry about it. You have enough on your mind without having to add this item to your list of worries. Just be sure to keep your hands free (not clutching notes or the lectern), so that if a gesture wells up inside you and cries out for expression, you will be able to make it naturally and forcefully.

## *Beginning and Ending*

First impressions are important in many human events. The first impression we make on a person at a party, for example, often determines whether the person will want to spend much time chatting with us. In a speech, as one IBM executive told me, "You have only one chance to make a first impression." You make this first impression as you walk to the front and as you say your first few sentences.

When they are introduced, many inexperienced speakers rush forward and start speaking even before they get to the front. The problem is that the listeners are not ready. They need time to get settled, so that they can clear their minds of other things and tune in to you.

When you are called upon, you should walk confidently to the front, face your audience, and then pause a few seconds before speaking. Do not say a word—just stand in silence. Some inexperienced speakers are terrified by this silence; they view it as a horrible event that makes the audience think they are too frozen with fear to speak. If you have had this concern, relax. A brief period of silence is a very effective technique which all good speakers use. It is a punctuation device, separating what went before from what is to come—your speech. It creates drama, giving the audience a sense of expectancy. It is a dignified quietness that establishes your confidence and authority. In some cases, you may need to wait longer than a few seconds. If you are speaking to a civic club, for example, and a large number of people are arriving late, it is best to wait until the noise created by the latecomers has settled down. Or if many members of the audience are still whispering comments related to the previous speaker, you should simply stand and wait until you have their attention.

During these opening moments of silence, you have a chance to make sure your notes are in order and to review once again what you will say in your introduction. The next step is very important. Before you say a word, give your audience a friendly, confident look (if possible, smile) and then, continuing to look at your listeners instead of at your notes, say your first few sentences. You should have practiced your introduction thoroughly, so that you can say it without looking down at your notes. It is important to establish eye contact at this point. By looking at the listeners directly, your body language is saying, "I'm talking to you—I'm not up here just going through the motions of making a speech. I want to communicate. I want to reach out to you."

While first impressions are vital, final impressions are also important. Like your introduction, your conclusion should be well rehearsed (though not memorized), so that you can say it without looking at your notes. At the end of your speech, pause a few moments, look at your audience, and say, "Are there any questions?" or "I'll be happy to answer your questions now."

# Question-and-Answer Period

In classroom speeches, the question-and-answer period usually represents a small percentage of the total time spent in front of the audience, but in some presentations in business, professional, and technical fields, the question-and-answer period is *the* most important part. Your speech is just a prelude—a little warm-up to get the audience ready for the questions. In some sales presentations, for example, the speaker will talk for, say, 10 minutes and then the question-and-answer period will go on for over an hour, with the listeners getting down to the nitty-gritty ("Okay, you say this machine will never wear out, but what happens if . . . ").

Many listeners are so accustomed to listener-speaker interaction that they will interrupt during a speech to ask questions. In some technical presentations or classroom lectures, such interruptions might be appropriate and acceptable, but in other speeches, they are a nuisance. The continuity of the speaker's remarks is broken because listeners are prematurely asking questions that will be answered later in the speech. If you feel that your speech would be marred by interruptions, you should announce early in the orienting material of your introduction, "I know many of you will have questions. I'd like to ask you to hold them until I finish my presentation and then I'll be happy to try to answer them."

Here are some guidelines:

1. Find out ahead of time if the person planning the program will want or permit a question-and-answer period, and if so, how much time will be allotted.

2. Plan for the question-and-answer period as carefully as you plan for the speech itself. Jot down all the possible questions that you think might come from the audience, and then decide exactly how you will answer them if they are asked.

3. Try to regard the question-and-answer period as a blessing, not a curse. It is a blessing because it gives you valuable feedback—it helps you insure that the message you intended the listeners to receive is indeed the message that they end up with. If a misunderstanding has occurred, the question-and-answer period gives you a chance to clarify the matter. If you have unwittingly offended or angered some members of the audience, you have a chance to explain yourself and made amends.

4. Ask for questions as if you really wanted them. If you lean toward your seat and let your facial expression and tone of voice say, "Please don't ask me any questions," you won't get any—and the audience will be deprived of an opportunity to get clarification and amplification.

5. Do not feel defeated if you are not asked any questions. Some speakers fear that they will stand in embarrassment and defeat if no questions are asked. Not being asked a question might mean that you have covered everything so well that the listeners truly have nothing to ask.

6. Give the audience time to think of questions. Some speakers wind up their conclusion, hastily ask if there are any questions, impatiently wait three seconds, and then dash back to their seats. They do not really give the audience a fair chance. When you finish a speech, you should pause a few moments, ask for questions, and then pause for as long as ten seconds. If you get the feeling that no questions at all will be asked, you can say "Thank you" and sit down. But if you sense that the audience is simply shy (some listeners want to ask questions but are afraid that their question will be considered "dumb"), you may want to give them some encouragement. One way is to say, "While you're thinking of questions, let me answer one that a lot of people ask me . . . ."

7. When a question is asked, repeat it for the benefit of listeners who may not have heard it. Repeating it also gives you time to think of your answer. If a question is unclear to you, ask the listener to clarify it.

8. If you do not know the answer to a question, say so. Your audience will not think less of you for an honest admission of ignorance on a particular point. The audience *will* think less of you if you try to fake expertise on an issue.

9. If a listener points out a flaw in the logic of your argument, or calls into question some of your facts or figures, do not be defensive. If the listener seems to have merit to his or her point, say so. You can say

something like, "You've got a good point. I'm going to have to think about this some more." Or: "You may be right—that statistic could be outdated. I'll have to check it out. Thanks for mentioning it." Such a conciliatory approach is not only honest, it is also a good way to gain respect from the listeners. No one expects you to be perfect; if a listener finds an error in your speech, it does not mean that your whole effort has been discredited.

10. Do not let one listener "hog" the question-and-answer period, especially if a number of other people have questions. If a person persists in asking one question after another, deflect him or her by saying, "I want to give others a chance to ask questions, but I'll get back to you later if there's time." If a listener launches into a long monologue, you need to interrupt and gently ask, "What is your question?"

11. Decline to answer questions that are not appropriate for a discussion in front of the entire audience—for example, questions that are too personal or that would require a long, technical explanation that most of the listeners would find boring and tedious. You can deflect such questions by politely explaining your reasons; for example, "That's a little too personal—I'd rather not go into that," or "I'm afraid it would take up too much time to go into the details right now." In some cases, you might tell the questioner to see you afterward for a one-on-one discussion.

12. Don't let the question-and-answer period drag on interminably. If you have been allotted an hour, say, for both your speech and the question-and-answer period, end the session promptly at the end of an hour—even if some listeners still have questions. (As we have already discussed, it is important that you avoid going over your time limit.) If your speech is the last item on the program and you sense that some listeners would like to continue the question-and-answer period, you might want to say, "I'm going to end the formal part of my presentation now because I promised I would take up only one hour of your time and I know that some of you have other business to take care of. However, if any of you would like to stay, you can move to the seats here at the front and we'll continue with an informal question-and-answer period."

# Practice

After you have written your outline and made notes based on it (as discussed in Chapter 11), you should spend a great deal of time rehearsing your speech. Practice, practice, practice—it's a crucial step that some inexperienced speakers leave out. Practice makes you look and sound fluent, smooth, and spontaneous. Practice bolsters your confidence, giving you a sense of mastery and competence.

Here are some tips that might help you:

1. Start early. If you wait until the eve of your speech, you will not have enough time to develop and polish your delivery. Allow yourself at least four days of practice before your speech date.

2. Practice going through your entire speech at least four times, more if necessary. Space your practice sessions; in other words, do not do most of your practicing on a single day. You will find that you make greater progress if you have time intervals between practice sessions.

3. Learn your speech point by point, not word for word. Your goal should be to gain control of your ideas, not to memorize particular phrasing. In extemporaneous speaking, every time you say your speech (whether in practice or in delivery to an audience), the wording should be different. The ideas will be the same, but not the words.

4. Time yourself during practice sessions. If your speech exceeds the time limit set by your instructor or by the group that invited you, go back to your outline and notes and trim them down.

5. During most of your practice sessions, go all the way through the speech. Do not stop if you hit a problem (you can work it out later). Going all the way through helps you see whether your ideas fit together snugly, and whether your transitions from point to point are smooth.

6. Some speakers find it helpful to practice in front of a mirror or to use a videotape or audiotape recorder. Whether or not you use any of these techniques, you should practice at least once in front of a live audience—friends or relatives who can give you a candid appraisal of your speech. Most speakers find that they speak differently in front of real people from the way they speak in front of a mirror or videotape camera. For one thing, they are able to get feedback from their audience as they speak; the faces of their listeners give clues as to whether they are getting their points across.

7. Some speakers find it helpful to make a trial run in the very room in which they will give the speech. They practice, of course, when the room is empty. This would be an especially good idea if you have visual aids and equipment; you can practice the mechanics, for example, of showing overhead transparencies.

8. In addition to practicing the entire speech, devote special practice time to your beginning and ending. Getting started and winding things up are the two most difficult times of your speech.

9. Be sure that you don't put too many words down on your notes. Have just the bare minimum necessary to jog your memory. Practice from

the actual notes that you will use in the speech. Don't make a clean set right before the speech; the old marked-up notes are more reliable.

## Summary

You don't have to become a dazzling spellbinder to reach your audience. Think of yourself not as a *performer*, judged for your theatrical abilities, but as a *communicator*. In other words, you should concentrate not on making a good impression, but on getting your ideas across to the audience. If you respect your listeners and strive mightily to communicate with them, you will find that before long, your delivery takes care of itself.

There are four methods of delivering a speech: impromptu, manuscript, memorized, and extemporaneous. Of the four, extemporaneous is the most popular and usually the most effective because the speaker delivers a well-prepared, well-rehearsed speech in a lively, conversational manner.

In delivering a speech, your voice should be loud enough for everyone to hear; your words should be spoken clearly so that they are easily understood, and your voice should be expressive so that you sound interesting and lively.

Nonverbal communication is the message you give with your body by means of personal appearance, eye contact, facial expressions, posture, movement, and gestures. All of these elements should convey confidence and a positive regard for the audience. Of special importance is eye contact. You should look at your listeners during 95 percent of your speech to maintain a bond of communication and rapport with them and to monitor their feedback.

Practice is a vital part in the success of your speech. You should practice the entire speech over and over again—until you can deliver it with power and confidence.

## Review Questions

1. What are the disadvantages of impromptu, manuscript, and memorized speeches?
2. What ingredient is essential for the success of an extemporaneous speech?
3. Why is it a serious mistake to speak too rapidly at the beginning of a speech?
4. What are the characteristics of good eye contact?
5. What can speakers do with their hands to make sure that they are free for gesturing?
6. Why should a speech be learned and practiced point by point, instead of word for word?

# TIPS *for your career*

### Tip 13: Deal with Distractions in a Direct, but Good-Humored Manner

In classroom speeches you will have an attentive, courteous audience, but at some point in your career, you may encounter an audience that contains a few rude listeners who chat among themselves while you are trying to speak, thus causing a distraction for other listeners.

Professional speakers stress that you should *not* ignore the disturbance that the rude listeners are creating. You should confront these listeners, but do so in a calm, friendly, good-humored manner.

One technique is to simply stop your speech and look directly at the rude listeners (try to look friendly and not irritated). This nonverbal nudge is often all it takes to cause the persons to stop talking. Sometimes people sitting near the offenders will pick up on your cue and help you out by turning and saying "shh."

Professional speaker Rosita Perez of Brandon, Florida, says that you may lose the respect of your entire audience if you ignore the talkative few. "Confront them *kindly,*" she advises. "Say, 'It seems to me you must have a lot of catching up to do with your friends. I wonder if you would visit outside so I can continue?'" In most such cases, the listeners will stay in the room and give the speaker respectful silence for the rest of the speech.[8]

Speech consultant Sandy Linver says that in a large audience, "I take the trouble to gently zero in on . . . the chatterers and pull them back in. I say something like, 'Are you with me?' . . . If it's a small group, side conversations often are important to the subject at hand, so it is important not to ignore them. If I were speaking at a business meeting of fifteen people or so, I might say to the three people talking among themselves, 'That looks as if it might be important. Would you like to share it with the group?' Often they are discussing something I have said that needs clarification or elaboration, and the whole group benefits when they are encouraged to speak up."[9]

Some speeches are marred by the incessant crying of a baby. Even though members of the audience turn and give annoyed, disapproving looks, the parents of the baby sometimes refuse to take the infant out of the room. Actor and orator Steve Allen once handled this situation by saying, "As the father of four sons I've more than once been in the position of the parents of that child. Personally I could go on even if there were several children crying at the same time, but I know that most people are too distracted by that sort of thing to concentrate on what is being said. So if you wouldn't mind taking the child out—at least until he stops crying—I'm sure the rest of our audience would appreciate it." This remark, says Allen, prompted applause from the audience and "gracious cooperation from the parents."[10]

# Types of
# Public Speaking

## Chapter 14

# Speaking to Inform

At a shopping mall not long ago, I ran into Pete Gentry, a former student of mine. "Listen," he asked, "do you remember that speech Julie Parris gave about whatever-it's-called—the way you help a person who's choking on food?"

"Yes," I said, "the Heimlich Maneuver."

"Well," continued Pete, "it was a lucky thing I learned about it because a couple of months ago I used it on my kid brother. He got some food caught in his throat and was turning white as a sheet. I grabbed him and did what Julie taught us—made a fist on his stomach and forced the air up from his lungs. It worked—it cleared his windpipe. He could have died if I hadn't known exactly what to do."

Thus was a life saved because a speaker had presented information so clearly that a listener was able to remember it months later. Pete had forgotten the name of the technique, but so what? He had remembered the essence of Julie's speech—how to rescue a choking person.

Julie's talk on the Heimlich Maneuver is an example of an informative speech, one of the most popular kinds of speeches given in the classroom and in the community. In the informative speech your task is primarily to educate—to give new information to your listeners and help them understand it.

What you hope to achieve is what Julie achieved: having your audience remember the essence of your speech months later. To reach this goal, your speech must be interesting (so that the audience *wants* to listen) and it must be clear (so that the audience can understand what you are saying). In this chapter, we will look at four types of informative speeches and then discuss guidelines to help you create speeches that are clear, interesting, and memorable.

# Types of Informative Speeches

Informative speeches can be categorized in many different ways, with many different labels, but in this chapter we will concentrate on four of the most popular types: definition, description, process, and expository.

## Definition Speech

Suppose that one of your friends confides that she has dyslexia, but you do not know the meaning of this word. Obviously, then, you are going to say, "What do you mean by dyslexia?"

Your friend could give you a dictionary definition—"the impairment of the ability to read"—but that would not do much to satisfy your curiosity. You would want her to give examples such as this: "When I was in elementary school, I scrambled letters when I tried to read; the word *was* looked to me like *saw*." You would want her to relate how the affliction has affected her life: "I flunked first grade and I thought I was dumb. I had a terrible inferiority complex." And so on.

What your friend would give you is an *extended* definition, one that goes beyond the dictionary explanation. That is what a definition speech is all about—giving an extended definition of a concept so that the listeners get a full, richly detailed picture of its meaning. While a dictionary definition would settle lightly on the listeners' brains and probably vanish overnight, an extended definition is likely to stick firmly. Here are some sample specific purpose statements for definition speeches:

> To explain to my listeners the meaning of feminism in modern America.
>
> To explain to the audience my definition of an ideal marriage.
>
> To define astrology for my listeners.
>
> To explain to my audience what constitutes true intelligence.

In Chapter 7, we discussed various strategies for supporting your ideas, by using narratives, examples, etc. Any of those strategies can be applied to defining a topic. If you were trying to explain *biometrics*, for instance, you could use examples to define the term:

| | |
|---|---|
| *Specific Purpose:* | To explain to my listeners what biometrics is and how it works. |
| *Central Idea:* | Biometrics is an electronic way of identifying people through their unique physical characteristics. |
| *Main Points:* | I. Biometrics is used to scan fingerprints of persons trying to enter highly secured U.S. military installations. |
| | II. Biometrics is used with computers by law-enforcement agencies to match more than 500 fingerprints per second. |
| | III. Biometrics is used by some banks to detect forgery in the writing of signatures. |

Sometimes the best way to define a topic is to compare or contrast it with a similar item. If you were trying to define what constitutes child abuse, for example, it would be helpful to contrast abuse with firm, but loving discipline, as in the following outline:

| | |
|---|---|
| *Specific Purpose:* | To explain to my audience what constitutes child abuse. |
| *Central Idea:* | Child abuse, unlike firm discipline, damages a child's emotional growth. |
| *Main Points:* | I. Firm, but loving discipline is healthy for the child's emotional growth. |
| | A. It involves punishment that is fair and not excessive. |
| | B. It does not harm the child's self-esteem. |
| | C. It causes the child to feel protected and cherished. |

   II. Abuse is damaging to the child's emotional growth.
       A. It is harsh and extreme.
       B. It hurts the child's self-esteem.
       C. It causes the child to feel insecure, angry, and un-
          loved.

Contrasting abuse and discipline in this way helps the listeners see the line that separates the two.

One method of defining a topic is to break it down into logical subtopics. For example, here is one way of defining mental retardation:

*Specific Purpose:* To explain to my listeners the wide range of diversity among mentally retarded people.
*Central Idea:* The mentally retarded are a diverse group, ranging from the mildly retarded, who are capable of holding jobs, to the severely retarded, who require constant care.
*Main Points:* I. The highest functioning group of retardates is the mildly retarded, with IQs of 55 to 70.
II. The second group of retardates is the moderately retarded, with IQs of 40 to 55.
III. The lowest functioning group of retardates is the severely retarded, with IQs below 40.

By the time the speaker has finished analyzing the three categories of retardation, the listener has a good extended definition of retardation.

## Description Speech

Describing a person, place, object, or event is a technique that can be used in any kind of speech. In a definition speech on alcoholism, for example, you might include a description of an alcoholic. In some cases, however, you may want to devote your entire speech to description. Here are some specific purpose statements for description speeches:

To tell my listeners how a tornado looks, sounds, and feels.

To describe to my listeners the glories of the Grand Canyon.

To inform my audience about living conditions in an institution for autistic children.

To describe to my audience the highlights of the life of Margaret Sanger.

If you were describing an object or place, you might want to use the *spatial* pattern of organization. Here is an example as used in an outline on the Blue Ridge Parkway:

*Specific Purpose:* To describe to my listeners the Blue Ridge Parkway.
*Central Idea:* The Blue Ridge Parkway is a motor route through spectacular mountain and valley scenery.

Main Points:   I. The northern leg of the Parkway covers the highlands overlooking the Shenandoah Valley.
              II. The southern leg of the Parkway takes the motorist to the highest peaks east of the Mississippi.

The Parkway could also be described by means of another scheme of organization: the *topical* pattern. Here is one possible arrangement:

Main Points:   I. The roadway itself is a marvel of engineering.
              II. Spectacular scenery is visible from strategic overlooks.
            III. There are many campgrounds and off-road recreational sites.

Describing a person, living or dead, can make a fascinating speech. If you were describing a historical figure, you might want to use the *chronological* pattern; in a speech on Susan B. Anthony, for example, you could discuss the major events of her life, in the order in which they occurred, from birth to death.

For some descriptions of persons, you might prefer to use the *topical* pattern, as in the following outline:

Specific Purpose:  To describe to my audience the exploits that made Harry Houdini a famous and controversial figure in American history.
Central Idea:  Harry Houdini, the most famous magician of the early part of the 20th century, was best known for his amazing ability to escape from any bond imaginable and for his campaign to expose fraudulent "mediums."
Main Points:  I. Houdini was a magician who could extricate himself from any containment device then in existence—handcuffs, straitjackets, jail cells, and sealed coffins.
            II. Houdini tried to expose the trickery of "mediums" who claimed to have direct communication with the dead.

## Process Speech

In a process speech, you are concerned with explaining the steps or stages by which something is done or made. There are two kinds of process speeches. In the first kind, you show the listeners how to *perform* a process so that they can actually use the skills later (this is sometimes called a *demonstration* speech). Here are some examples of specific purpose statements for this kind of speech:

To teach my listeners how to apply first aid for snakebites.

To explain to my audience how to perform yoga exercises.

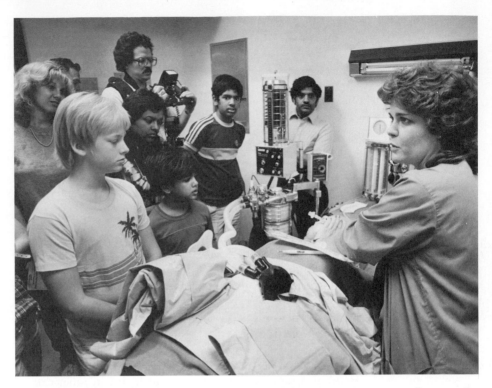

**A health professional demonstrates medical techniques at one hospital's open house for the public. Demonstration talks are frequently given in all kinds of professions.** *(Bob Daemmrich/TexaStock)*

To show my audience how to identify and pick nonpoisonous mushrooms.

To demonstrate to my listeners how to build kites.

In the second kind of process speech, you provide information on "how something is done" or "how something works." Your goal is to explain a process so that the listeners *understand* it, not necessarily so that they can perform it themselves. For example, let's say that you outline the steps by which counterfeiters print bogus money. You are showing these steps to satisfy the listeners' intellectual curiosity and also to teach them how to spot a counterfeit bill, not so that they can perform the job themselves. Here are some samples of specific purpose statements for this kind of speech:

To explain to my audience how magicians saw a person in half.

To tell my listeners how porpoises are trained to do out-of-water stunts.

To explain to my listeners how a hurricane is tracked.

To inform my listeners how a guitar makes music.

If your instructor consents, you may want to use humor to make serious points in a process speech. For example, if your speech purported to be on "how to flunk a test," you could discuss such items as "Be sure to party all night on the eve of the test." Though you do not state it explicitly, your true point, of course, is that a person should get plenty of sleep before taking a big test. One student gave a process speech on how to burglarize a house or apartment; by speaking tongue-in-cheek from the burglar's point of view, he effectively conveyed his real message—how to make sure your home is protected from burglars.

Here are some guidelines on preparing a process speech:

1. *Be sure to include all steps, even obvious ones.* A lawyer bought a huge aquarium for his new office and then went out and spent hundreds of dollars at a pet shop on an assortment of exotic tropical fish. He returned to his office, filled the aquarium with water, and dumped the fish in. When all the fish died, he called the pet shop and found out why: the directions for the aquarium had neglected to mention that tap water must sit 24 hours before fish are inserted so that all the chlorine can evaporate. Otherwise, the fish will die of chlorine poisoning. Whoever wrote the directions for the aquarium probably assumed that any fish lover would be familiar with this piece of information, but such an assumption was a mistake.

In a process speech, you should give all the steps involved, including the ones that are simple and self-evident. What seems obvious to you may not be obvious to some of your listeners.

2. *Use visual aids whenever possible.* Because processes are often complicated, you should use visual aids, if at all possible, to help the listeners understand and retain your points. One of the most effective visual aids is the demonstration, wherein you actually perform the process while talking. For example, if you wanted to teach cardiopulmonary resuscitation (CPR), you could demonstrate the steps on a dummy while you go through your explanations.

3. *Involve the audience in physical activity whenever possible.* If you involve the audience in a physical activity, you capitalize on more than just the listeners' sense of hearing and seeing; you also bring in touch and movement. There is an ancient Chinese proverb that says:

I hear—and I forget.
I see—and I remember.
I do—and I understand.

The wisdom of this saying has been confirmed by psychologists, who have found that of the three main channels for learning new information, the auditory is weakest, the visual is stronger, and physical action is strongest of all. The best approach is to bring all three together. For example, if you were explaining how to do stretching exercises, you could explain the techniques (auditory) as you give a demonstration (visual); then you could have each listener stand and perform the exercises (physical action). Some audience involvement can be accomplished while the listeners remain in their chairs; for example, if you are speaking on sign language, you could have the listeners practice the hand signals as you teach them.

Note of caution: Get your instructor's approval before you use any physical activity in a classroom speech. When you give a talk in the community beyond the college campus, use your best judgment. Make sure that you do not ask your audience to do something that would be embarrassing or awkward for some of the listeners. If, for example, there are physically handicapped people in the audience, would they be able to perform the task? One student, who was ecstatic about the hug-every-body philosophy of Leo Buscaglia, tried to get the entire audience to hug each other. Some of the students were embarrassed.

4. *Proceed slowly.* Always bear in mind that much of what you say might be brand-new to the listeners. If you are instructing on how to make leather belts, for example, you might be describing activities that are so easy for you that you could perform them blindfolded, but they might be completely foreign to some members of the audience. So talk slowly and repeat key ideas if necessary. Give the listeners ample time to absorb the points and form mental images.

5. *Give advance warning of difficult steps.* When you are ready to discuss especially difficult steps, you can use transitions to give the listeners a warning. For example, you can say, "The next step is a little tricky." Or: "This next step is the hardest one of all." This alerts the listeners that they need to pay extra-special attention.

## Expository Speech

An expository speech (also called an oral report or lecture) involves explaining a concept or situation to the audience. For this speech, your instructor may want you to choose a topic that you are not thoroughly familiar with and then conduct research (in the library and/or by means of interviews) to gain command of the subject.

The expository speech may contain many features of the definition, descriptive, or process speeches. For example, if you chose to speak on "how the bail system works," you would be explaining a process.

Here are examples of specific purpose statements for expository speeches:

To explain to my listeners the major causes of kleptomania.

To inform my audience of the courting customs of colonial Americans.

To explain to my listeners the effects of captivity (in zoos) upon wild animals.

To report to the audience on the condition of America's passenger trains.

To inform my audience of the opposing arguments for sex education.

Expository speeches are often organized in the *topical* pattern. As we saw in Chapter 9, you use the topical pattern to subdivide a central idea into main points, using logic and common sense as your guides. Here is an outline for an expository speech that uses the topical pattern:

*Specific Purpose:* To inform my audience about the dangers of quicksand.
*Central Idea:* Found in almost every state of the U.S., quicksand is a terrifying natural trap from which people can extricate themselves if they follow the correct steps.
*Main Points:*
I. Quicksand is as treacherous as the movies depict it.
   A. It has swallowed people.
   B. It has swallowed cars and trucks.
II. Quicksand is deceptive.
   A. The surface can appear as solid as the surrounding terrain.
   B. Underneath the surface is a sandy brew that is formed by water flowing upward from hidden springs.
III. If you step into quicksand, you can follow four easy steps that will save your life.
   A. Get rid of extra weight such as a backpack or coat.
   B. Throw yourself flat on your back and "float."
   C. Press your arms out onto the surface of the quicksand.
   D. Moving with snail-like slowness, roll your way to firm ground.

Notice that there are elements of description (Point I), definition (Point II), and process (Point III) in this outline.

One method of organizing an expository speech, which we have not discussed previously, is the *pro-con* pattern. Here is an example from an outline by a student speaker, Steve Ponder:

*Specific Purpose:* To inform my audience of the pros and cons of capital punishment.

*Central Idea:* Proponents and opponents of capital punishment disagree on whether the death penalty deters crime and what effect it has on society in general.

*Main Points:*

(Pro)    I. Proponents of capital punishment believe that the death penalty is necessary for the protection and well-being of society.

(Arguments)    A. The death penalty acts as a deterrent to crime.

B. The death penalty prevents a murderer from ever killing again—in prison or elsewhere.

C. The death penalty satisfies the public's need to see justice served and a fair retribution carried out.

(Con)    II. Opponents of capital punishment believe that the death penalty is unnecessary and uncivilized.

(Arguments)    A. The death penalty fails to deter crime.

B. The death penalty is sometimes enacted against people who later are found to be innocent.

C. The death penalty is a barbarous act of revenge unworthy of a civilized society.

In this speech, Steve was not trying to persuade his listeners to oppose or accept the death penalty; he was simply informing them of the primary arguments made by both sides in the debate. You may have noticed that Subsection A in Part I contradicts Subsection A in Part II. That's because both sides are able to cite statistics favorable to their respective positions—a reminder of the slippery nature of statistics that we discussed in Chapter 7.

If you use the *pro-con* pattern, try to give each side a fair and balanced treatment, even if you privately favor one side over the other. Your job in an informative speech is to act as a reporter, not as an advocate.

Another pattern is the *fallacy-fact* pattern (or it could be called *myth-reality*). In this pattern, the speaker cites a popular fallacy and then presents facts that refute it. Here is a sample outline from a speech given by student speaker Sarah Stepanovich, in which she refutes three popular misconceptions about sharks:

*Specific Purpose:* To refute common fallacies about sharks.

*Central Idea:* Sharks are not as dangerous to humans as most people think they are.

*Main Points:*

(Fallacy)    I. It is a widely believed fallacy that there are hundreds of shark attacks each year, most of which are fatal.

(Facts)    A. Worldwide, there is an average of 28 attacks each year.

B. Only three or four are fatal.

| | |
|---|---|
| (Fallacy) | II. It is a widely believed fallacy that when a shark attacks one person, it will attack anyone else who is nearby. |
| (Facts) | A. Sharks select a single person and ignore others. |
| | B. Rescuers are usually unharmed. |
| (Fallacy) | III. It is a widely believed fallacy that sharks attack people when they get hungry. |
| (Facts) | A. Very few attacks are made by sharks that are hungry. |
| | B. In most attacks, the shark takes one bite and then leaves. |

# Guidelines for Informative Speaking

Your goal in informative speaking is to have your listeners remember the essence of your speech. How can you get them to remember? First of all, your speech must be interesting so that they will want to listen to you; second, it must be clear so that they can understand you; and third, it must be conveyed in such a way that the key points stick in their minds. In addition to techniques already covered in this book, here are some guidelines that should be useful for informative speeches.

## *Relate the Speech to the Listeners' Self-Interest*

Many listeners seem to approach a speech with an attitude of: "Why should I care? Why should I pay attention? What's in it for me?" The best motivator in a speech, therefore, is something that relates directly to their self-interest, and has an impact on their lives in one way or another.

"When I was in the Navy," a friend recalls, "I was assigned to duty as a parachute packer. On our first day, we were given a talk on what people do to prepare themselves for jumping out of planes with a parachute. I didn't pay much attention because I figured my only contact with parachutes would be packing them. Then the next day they announced that in a few weeks *we* would have to parachute out of a plane! They wanted to make us appreciate—the hard way—just how important it is to pack a parachute correctly and carefully. When I heard this, I was scared, and I kicked myself for not paying attention to all that stuff they had said about getting ready for a jump."

Whoever gave that lecture failed to provide the audience with motivation to listen closely. The lecturer should have said something like this: "You may think your only contact with parachutes is packing them, but you're wrong. In a few weeks you will all jump out of an airplane with a parachute. Now here's how you do it . . . ." Hearing such a comment, my friend undoubtedly would have listened to the lecture with rapt attention.

Relate every speech you give to the listeners' self-interest, if at all possible. Show them that what you have to say is important to their individual lives.

## Do Not Overestimate What the Listeners Know

Here is a quick quiz; see how many correct answers you can get:

1. What were the last two states admitted to the United States?

2. True or False? When you vote in a national election, it is permissible to "split your ticket"—that is, choose a President from one party and a Senator from another party.

3. True or False? If you are out of town on election day, there's no way for you to cast a ballot.

4. True or False? Russia fought on America's side in World War II.

5. True or False? Canada has a larger population than Mexico.

Now for the answers: The correct response to Question 1 is Alaska and Hawaii—a fact known by only 3 percent of the 17- and 18-year-olds interviewed by the Gallup Poll. The answer to Question 2 is true; in the Gallup Poll, only 38 percent realized that it is legal to vote for both parties in a general election. The answer to Question 3 is false; in the poll, only 42 percent had ever heard of absentee ballots. The answer to Question 4 is true—a fact known by only 57 percent of the young people. The answer to Question 5 is false; only 39 percent realized that Mexico's population is over twice that of Canada.[1]

This poll demonstrates that when you speak to an audience, you cannot assume that everyone knows basic facts. Likewise, you cannot assume that everyone shares the same background of experiences. For example, almost one-half (47 percent) of American adults cannot swim,[2] and one-third of them have never flown in an airplane.[3]

To avoid overestimating what your listeners know, you should define words or explain concepts whenever you think some members of the audience may need this kind of help. How can you tell when you need to elaborate? The best way is to analyze your audience carefully, using the techniques we discussed in Chapter 4.

But, you may ask, how can I define words and explain concepts in a way that does not insult the intelligence of the listeners who already know the material? In some cases, you can give your information in a casual, unobtrusive way. For example, let's say you are planning in your speech to cite a quotation by Adolf Hitler. Most college students know who Hitler was, but there are some who do not. To inform the latter without insulting the intelligence of the former, you can say something like this: "In the

1920s, long before Adolf Hitler rose to power in Germany and long before he launched the German nation into World War II, he made the following prophetic statement . . . ." An indirect approach like this permits you to "sneak" in a lot of background information.

In other cases, you may need to be straightforward in giving definitions or explanations. For example, if you need to define *recession* for a speech on economic cycles, do so directly and clearly. Do not worry about insulting the intelligence of the listeners who already know the meaning. They will not be offended by a quick definition; in fact, they will probably welcome a chance to affirm the accuracy of their own understanding of the term.

## *Use the Familiar to Explain the Unfamiliar*

A few years ago an Israeli leader toured the United States to drum up support for increased military aid to Israel. Dorothy Sarnoff, an American consultant who was hired to help him prepare his speeches, gave him the following advice:

> If you describe Israel at its narrowest point by saying, "Israel is so narrow that we can be [easily] attacked," the Americans won't get it . . . Instead say, "Israel is so narrow that if you were driving on a[n] [American-style] highway, it would take you only twenty minutes to get from one side of Israel to the other."[4]

Sarnoff's advice was sound. When you want to explain or describe something that is unfamiliar to your audience, relate it to something that is familiar. You can use some of the devices we discussed in Chapter 7, such as comparisons, contrasts, and analogies. If, for example, you point out that divers in Acapulco, Mexico, astound tourists by diving into water from rocks 118 feet high, that statistic does not have much impact unless you point out that a 118-foot plunge is equal to a dive from the roof of an 11-story building.[5]

To give listeners a mental picture of what the inside of a tornado is like, student speaker Dale Higgins said: "A tornado's funnel is like the vortex you see when you let water go down a drain." Since everyone has seen the swirling action of water going down a drain, the comparison helped the audience visualize a tornado's vortex.

# Sample Informative Speech

The following classroom speech was delivered by a student who has given permission for it to be reprinted, but has requested that her name not be used (to protect the privacy of her family). The outline is presented first, followed by a transcript of the actual speech.

## *Outline*

### How to Help a Suicidal Person

*General Purpose:* To inform

*Specific Purpose:* To explain to my listeners how they can talk suicidal persons out of killing themselves.

*Central Idea:* You can persuade people not to commit suicide if you follow four steps: take their threats seriously, encourage them to talk, help them find solutions to their problems, and guide them toward a mental-health professional.

**INTRODUCTION**

I. Eleven years ago, my older brother, who was 15 years old, shot himself in the head with a .22-caliber rifle. He died the next day. My parents are haunted by the fact that my brother had threatened to kill himself many times, but they had failed to take his threats seriously. They thought he was just a rebellious teen-ager trying to get attention.

II. About 200,000 Americans attempt suicide every year; 28,000 of them succeed in killing themselves. The true total is probably much higher because some deaths, though probably suicides, are listed as accidents. The chances are great that at some point in your life, you will be around somebody who is threatening suicide. Will you know how to help that person? Will you know how to talk him or her out of committing suicide? Today I'd like to explain the four steps you should follow in order to deter people from suicide: first, take all their suicide threats seriously; second, encourage them to talk; third, help them find solutions to their problems; and fourth, guide them toward a mental-health professional.

(*Transition:* Let's start with my first suggestion.)

**BODY**

I. Take all suicide threats seriously.
   A. The U.S. Public Health Service estimates that eight out of ten people who kill themselves give some sort of warning within three months prior to the act.
   B. Any suicide threat is a cry for help.
   C. A suicidal person who is "improving" after a crisis is at great risk for killing himself because he or she now has the energy to carry out the threat.

(*Transition:* You take every threat seriously—now what?)

II. Encourage them to "talk it out," while you listen with empathy.
   A. Getting things off their chest will sometimes help relieve pain and depression.

B. Never try to minimize the person's problems.

C. Never ridicule the person.

(*Transition:* After you get the person talking, what next?)

III. Help the person find some way (other than suicide) out of his or her problems.

A. A depressed or angry person often cannot see things clearly.

B. Suggest possible solutions to the person's problems.

(*Transition:* Now let's look at my final suggestion.)

IV. Try to get professional help for the person.

A. Suggest calling the suicide hotline.

B. Try to arrange a meeting with a mental-health professional.

C. If the person won't go for counseling, extract a promise that he or she will not try to commit suicide without first talking to you again.

(*Transition:* I hope you never have to deal with a suicidal person, but if such a situation arises, I hope you'll remember what I've said today.)

**CONCLUSION**

I. My four suggestions are: first, take all suicide threats seriously; second, encourage the person to talk while you listen with empathy; third, try to help the person find a solution (other than suicide) to his or her problems; and fourth, try to steer him or her toward a mental-health professional.

II. These four steps give suicidal persons a powerful message—that you care. Sometimes that's all it takes to make them lay down the gun or the knife—knowing that another human being deeply and truly cares.

**BIBLIOGRAPHY**

Ellen Frank and David J. Kupfer, M.D., "The Battle Against the Blues," *Ladies' Home Journal,* March 1985, pp. 147–154.

Brana Lobel and Robert M. A. Hirschfeld, M.D., *Depression: What We Know* (Rockville, Md.: National Institute of Mental Health, 1985).

Donald H. McKnew, Jr., *et al., Why Isn't Johnny Crying?* (New York: Norton, 1983).

**VISUAL AIDS**

At the end, I will pass out cards listing the suicide hotline number.

Here is the transcript of the actual speech.

COMMENTARY                    SPEECH AS DELIVERED

## How to Help a Suicidal Person

This introduction is power-      Eleven years ago, when I was eight years old, my older brother took a
ful and provocative—a per-       .22-caliber rifle into our garage and shot himself in the head. He didn't
sonal narrative that imme-       aim straight because he was still alive when my mother found him. He

diately grabs the attention of every listener.

By courageously relating her own family's pain, the speaker prepares the audience for one of her main points—that all suicide threats must be taken seriously.

Background information helps the listeners see that they may need the speaker's tips in the future.

By saying "you," the speaker draws in every member of the audience.

The speaker previews the body of the speech by giving her central idea and main points.
Giving the source of her tips adds credibility to what follows.

Repetition of a point, though undesirable in a written essay, is a valuable and worthwhile technique in a speech because the listeners may fail to absorb a point the first time it is mentioned.

This hypothetical example helps reiterate the speaker's point and makes the listeners think, "Yes, this could happen to me."

The transition gives the speaker a chance to ham-

was taken to the hospital with massive brain injuries. He held on until the next day, when he died. He was only 15 years old.

Everyone in our family still grieves over the loss of my brother, but the thing that haunts my parents most of all is that my brother threatened to kill himself many times, but they didn't think he was really serious. They thought it was just a rebellious teen-ager's way of getting attention.

Suicide is one of the leading causes of death in our country. According to official estimates of the U.S. government, about 200,000 Americans attempt suicide every year; of that number, 28,000 succeed in killing themselves. The true number of fatalities is probably a lot higher than this official total of 28,000. Many people, for example, deliberately kill themselves by smashing their cars, but their deaths are listed as traffic fatalities rather than as suicides. Whatever the true figure, the chances are great that at some point in your life, you will be around someone who threatens suicide. It may be a friend, a relative, a neighbor, or a person you work with. If this happens, will you know how to talk that person out of committing suicide? Today I'd like to show that you can help prevent people from committing suicide if you follow four steps: first, take all their threats seriously; second, encourage them to talk; third, help them find solutions to their problems; and fourth, guide them toward a mental-health professional. My information comes from books written by suicide-prevention experts.

Let me explain my first suggestion: you must take *all* suicide threats seriously. The U.S. Public Health Service estimates that eight out of ten people who kill themselves give some sort of warning within three months prior to the act. Talk of suicide or threats of suicide should *always* be taken seriously. Any kind of talk about suicide is a cry for help. One of the biggest mistakes people make is to think that once a suicidal person has passed through a crisis and has shown improvement, everything's okay. For example, let's say you have a friend who has been deeply depressed and suicidal, and then he perks up and seems to be greatly improved physically and emotionally. Now when he talks about suicide, is he no longer at risk? No, believe it or not, since he has improved, he's at *greater* risk than he was when he was down at rock bottom. The Public Health Service says that most suicides occur within about three months following the beginning of so-called improvement. Why? Because that's when these people have enough energy to put their suicidal urges into effect.

Okay, you take every suicide threat seriously. Now what? My second suggestion is that you encourage the people to "talk it out" while you

mer at the first main point one more time.

Notice how direct and conversational the speaker's words are—very easy for listeners to understand and absorb.

Notice the smooth way in which the speaker goes from one point to another.

Once again, the speaker skillfully uses a hypothetical story to make the listeners feel as if her remarks are relevant to their lives.

Positive, specific suggestions are very helpful to the listeners.

At the end of her speech, the speaker passed out little cards with the suicide hotline number printed on it.

The speaker wisely anticipates a possible audience question, "What do you do if the person won't agree to go for professional help?"

The conclusion gives the speaker one last chance to drive home the central idea and the four main points.

The speaker ends gracefully—and on a note of hope.

listen with empathy. Sometimes, just getting things off their chest will give them relief from their depression and negativity. And when they talk about their problems, try to show that you understand the pain they're in. Never, never try to minimize their problems. In other words, don't say, "Oh, you don't really have a serious problem," or: "So you broke up with your boyfriend—big deal! You're better off without that bum." Maybe you're saying to yourself that the person has a silly or a flimsy problem, but don't say it out loud. To people who are hurting, their problems are very real and very painful. You just deepen their agony if you make light of their problems. And of course you should never ridicule the person. In other words, don't say, "Only a nut would want to kill himself."

After you get the person talking, what's the next step? My third suggestion is that you try to help the person find some way (other than suicide) out of his or her problems. A person who is depressed or angry sometimes can't see things very clearly. You should try to suggest solutions. For example, let's say you have a friend who's terribly depressed because she flunked a course. Now we all know that this is a trivial reason for killing yourself, but there are people who get real depressed over "minor" failures. Maybe there are a lot of other negative things going on in their lives and flunking a course is the final straw. Well, what can you do? You can suggest that she ask the instructor if she can do extra assignments to pull the grade up, or you can suggest that she take the course over and have a tutor help her through it. The suicidal person has narrowed vision during a crisis and oftentimes can't see solutions that are obvious to others. It's up to you to suggest these solutions.

My fourth, and final, suggestion is that you try to get these people hooked up to professional help. If they seem in imminent danger of committing suicide, try to persuade them to call the suicide hotline or go with you to see a professional—a campus counselor or a minister or a psychologist. These mental-health professionals are trained in dealing with suicidal cases. Once the crisis is past, urge them to see a counselor or a therapist on a regular basis to get some help for their underlying problems—in other words, whatever it is that's causing the depression or anger or unhappiness. If you can't get them to go see a professional, try to get them to at least promise you that they won't kill themselves before talking to you again.

I hope that you're never in a position of having to deal with suicidal persons, but if you are, you can persuade them not to kill themselves if you follow four steps: First, take all their threats seriously; second, encourage them to "talk it out" while you listen with empathy; third, try to help them find a solution (other than suicide) to their problems; and finally, try to steer them to a mental-health professional.

These four steps add up to one very important message to suicidal persons—that you really and truly care about them. And sometimes that's all it takes to cause them to lay down the gun—knowing that someone else cares.

## Summary

The informative speech is one of the most popular kinds of speeches given in the classroom and in the community. Your goal in this kind of speech is to give new information to your listeners and help them understand and remember it. Four subcategories of the informative speech are definition, description, process, and expository.

In developing an informative speech, you can draw from all of the techniques and methods discussed in the book so far, plus the following guidelines: (1) Relate the speech to the listeners' self-interest, if at all possible. Show them explicitly the connection between your material and their personal lives. (2) Do not overestimate what the listeners know. Define or explain any terms or concepts that some of the listeners might not know. (3) Use the known to explain the unknown. When you want to explain or describe something that is unfamiliar to your audience, relate it to something that is familiar.

## Review Questions

1. What is an *extended* definition? Why is it preferable in a speech to a dictionary definition?
2. What are the two kinds of process speeches?
3. List the five guidelines for preparing a process speech.
4. Why is it important to relate a speech, if possible, to the listeners' self-interest?

# TIPS *for your career*

### Tip 14: For Long Presentations, Plan a Variety of Activities

Your boss asks you to conduct a three-hour workshop Friday afternoon to explain important procedures to a group of new employees. What do you do? Do you spend three hours talking? No, not unless you want to put them to sleep.

For long presentations, you should provide a variety of activities to keep your audience awake and attentive. Here are some suggested activities:

1. *Invite audience participation.* At various intervals, or even throughout the entire presentation, you can encourage listeners to ask questions or make comments. By letting them take an active role, instead of sitting passively for three hours, you invigorate them and prevent them from daydreaming.

2. *Use visual aids whenever possible.* Visuals give variety and sparkle to the presentation.

3. *Give coffee or "stretch" breaks at various intervals.* A good rule of thumb for marathon sessions is to give a 15-minute break after every 45-minute period, even if the audience does not seem tired. In other words, don't wait until fatigue sets in. If you wait until the audience is nodding, you might lose their interest for the rest of the day. When you give a break, always announce the time for reassembly; when that time arrives, politely but firmly remind any stragglers that it is time to return to their seats. If you do not remind them, you will find that a 15-minute coffee break can stretch to 30 minutes.

4. *Call on people at random.* If your presentation is in the form of a lecture, you can use the teachers' technique of calling on people at random to answer questions. This causes every listener to perk up because he or she is thinking, "I'd better pay attention because my name might be called next, and I don't want to be caught daydreaming." An embellishment of this pedagogical ploy is to call the person's name *after* you ask the question. (If you call the name *before* the question, everyone in the audience except the designated person might breathe a sigh of relief and fail to pay close attention to the question.)

5. *Encourage the listeners to take notes.* Some business speakers pass out complimentary pens and pads at the beginning of their presentations in hopes that the listeners will use them to write down key points. There is, of course, a side benefit: taking notes helps the listeners to stay alert and listen intelligently.

## Chapter 15

# Speaking to Persuade

When Nancy Gibson, a dance instructor at a small college, asked the coach of the football team for permission to talk to the team, some people thought she was crazy, for her professed goal was to persuade the football players to sign up for her ballet class.

When the players assembled in front of her, their initial attitude was derisive glee. "Can you believe it?" one player snickered. "She wants us to learn that sissy ballet stuff." In her talk, Gibson told of certain well-known professional football players who had taken ballet lessons in college because it made them more agile and quick-footed on the playing field. Then she explained how the techniques learned in her class could help the students play football more effectively. So convincing was her speech that after she finished, there was a virtual stampede, led by the first-string players, to sign up.

This anecdote illustrates the art of persuasion—getting people to think or act a certain way. In your lifetime, you will be faced with many tasks that require persuasion, ranging from one-to-one situations (such as convincing a bank executive to give you a loan for a new car), to small groups (persuading your fellow employees to join with you in a grievance about working conditions), to large audiences (talking your club into holding its annual picnic at a particular site). In this chapter we will discuss the strategies that you can use in these many kinds of persuasion, with special emphasis on preparing persuasive speeches.

# Types of Persuasive Speeches

Persuasive speeches can be categorized in a variety of ways, but one of the most popular classification schemes divides them according to two objectives: (1) to influence thinking, and (2) to motivate action. While these categories sometimes overlap (for example, you often have to influence thinking before you can motivate action), they nevertheless provide a handy framework for developing the content of a persuasive speech.

## Speech to Influence Thinking

The speech to influence thinking is an effort to convince people to adopt your position on a particular subject. (If some listeners agree with your ideas even before you speak, your job is to reinforce what they already think.) In some cases, you may want to implant ideas that are completely new to the listeners; for example, you argue that we should experiment to see if tobacco can be used as a source of protein. In other cases, you may want to alter the audience's preexisting ideas; for example, let's say that from your audience analysis, you know that your listeners consider white-collar criminals to be rather harmless wrongdoers who do not deserve to be put behind bars. So, in your speech you show that white-collar criminals who steal from companies and banks hurt everyone in society—by jeopardizing the continued existence of those institutions and by causing prices to be raised—and, therefore, they deserve to be imprisoned.

Here are some samples of specific purpose statements for this kind of speech:

To convince my audience that dinosaurs became extinct because a rain of comets stirred up so much debris that sunlight was blocked from the earth for months.

To convince my listeners that the metric system is superior to the traditional American system of weights and measures.

To convince my audience that the President of the United States should be limited to one term lasting six years.

To convince my listeners that unchecked population growth is a threat to world peace.

In a speech to influence thinking, you may want to use the *statement-of-reasons* pattern of organization (which is a variation of the *topical* pattern discussed in Chapter 9), in which you state the reasons why your central idea has merit. Student speaker Frank Collins used the statement-of-reasons pattern in the following outline:

| | |
|---|---|
| *Specific Purpose:* | To persuade my audience that schools should stop using IQ tests. |
| *Central Idea:* | IQ tests should not be used to evaluate or place students. |
| *Main Points:* | |
| (Reason 1) | I. Because they reflect only a small part of human intelligence, IQ tests are not valid measurements. |
| (Reason 2) | II. Students who score poorly on IQ tests get unfairly labeled—and then treated—as slow or dumb. |

Frank's two main points are outgrowths of his central idea, giving good reasons why IQ tests should not be used.

Sometimes, the *problem-solution* pattern is the best way to organize a persuasive speech. You show that a problem exists, and then you present the solution. This pattern is especially effective when the audience does not know that a particular problem exists, or it does not know how serious it is. For example, student speaker Rebecca Carter gave a speech on frivolous lawsuits (such as children suing their mother and father for "malparenting," and patients suing their plastic surgeons for a belly-button left askew). Rebecca showed how these suits created a problem and then she presented her solution to the problem. Here is her outline:

| | |
|---|---|
| *Specific Purpose:* | To persuade my audience that frivolous lawsuits should be kept out of court. |

| | |
|---|---|
| *Central Idea:* | Settlement of frivolous lawsuits should be made not by the courts but by citizens acting as volunteer arbitrators. |
| *Main Points:* | |
| (Problem) | I. Frivolous lawsuits cost the taxpayers millions of dollars annually in court expenses. |
| (Solution) | II. Congress and state legislatures should pass laws that move settlement of frivolous disputes from the courts to nonprofit arbitration centers run by citizen volunteers. |

Under the first main point, Rebecca gave supporting details—statistics and examples—to back up her contention. Under the second main point, she discussed how arbitration centers could be established to handle frivolous disputes outside normal courtroom channels.

A subcategory of the speech to influence thinking is the *speech of refutation,* in which your main goal is to knock down arguments or ideas that you feel are false. In this kind of speech, you may want to attack what another speaker has said, or you might want to refute popularly held ideas or beliefs which you think are false. One student, for example, tried to explode the myth that mentally retarded people can contribute little to the work force.

Here are some sample specific purpose statements for speeches of refutation:

To convince my listeners that Christopher Columbus was not the first European to explore the New World.

To persuade my audience to reject the false picture of pigs as dirty, stupid animals.

To convince my audience that the present laws forbidding mercy killing are based on outdated concepts.

To persuade my listeners that dowsers (people who claim to find water by means of divining rods) are no more capable of locating underground water than a child with a stick.

Refuting an argument is easier when you are dealing with facts than when you are dealing with deeply held beliefs. Suppose, for example, that you want to demolish the commonly held idea that during the American Revolution, solid ranks of red-coated British soldiers marched to battle in open fields, while crafty American patriots hid behind nearby trees in guerrilla fashion and shot the unsuspecting British with ease. You could refute this idea by citing the works of scholars and by pointing out that the British army in North America had adapted to guerrilla-style warfare during decades of fighting the Indians—long before the American Revolution. All of this is a matter of historical record, so your persuasive task is easy. But suppose that you wanted to persuade an audience to reject the belief that children should be reared by their parents; instead, you argue, children should be reared by communes like the kibbutzim in Israel. Though you may win some respect for the value of your idea, you are highly unlikely to demolish the deeply held belief that children should grow up under the wings of their parents. Core beliefs are extremely difficult to change.

Let us turn now to an example of the right way to refute arguments. Jim Lawter heard a speech by a classmate who advocated state-operated gambling. Jim disagreed so strongly that he prepared a speech to try to refute some of the points made by the earlier speaker. Here is the gist of his speech:

*Specific Purpose:*  To convince my listeners that state and local governments should not sponsor gambling in any form.

*Central Idea:*  Government-sponsored gambling exploits the poor and corrupts society's work ethic.

*Main Points:*  I. The argument that "no one is hurt in legalized gambling" is erroneous.
   A. Studies show that poor people, who can least afford to gamble, are in fact the heaviest gamblers.
   B. In states that have legalized gambling, there has been a dramatic increase in the number of compulsive gamblers, who sometimes lose all their possessions in their obsessive desire to "strike it rich."
II. The argument that "gambling does not weaken society" is erroneous.
   A. Government-sponsored gambling whets the public's appetite for illegal gambling, which is usually controlled by organized crime.
   B. Heavy advertising for government-sponsored gambling creates a lust for quick riches that runs contrary to the work ethic needed for social stability.

Notice that Jim stuck to the issues; he wisely refrained from questioning the intelligence or morality of his opponent.

## Speech to Motivate Action

The speech to motivate action is like the above speech in that it tries to win people over to your way of thinking, but it also attempts one of the most challenging tasks of persuasion—getting people to take action. This action can be either positive or negative: you can urge people to *start* doing something (start using dental floss, start buying U.S. Savings bonds, start collecting stamps), or to *stop* doing certain things (stop smoking, stop tailgating, stop wasting time). Sometimes you want immediate action from your listeners ("Please vote for my candidate in today's election"); at other times, you simply want them to respond at any appropriate point in the future ("Whenever you see a child riding a bike, please slow down and drive very cautiously").

Here are some sample specific purpose statements for speeches to motivate action:

> To persuade my audience to walk three miles a day.
>
> To persuade my listeners to sign a petition aimed at outlawing corporal punishment in elementary schools.
>
> To persuade my audience to take a course in first aid.
>
> To persuade my listeners to stop buying merchandise on credit.

A popular way to organize a speech for motivating action is the *statement-of-reasons* pattern (discussed earlier in this chapter), as shown in this outline by student speaker Brett Clayton:

> *Specific Purpose:* To persuade my listeners to vote in all elections.
> *Central Idea:* Every citizen should vote in every general election.
> *Main Points:*
>   I. Universal voting would prevent small, special-interest groups from gaining power.
>   II. Since some elections are won by razor-thin margins, every vote counts.
>   III. In a democracy, it's important for all citizens to express their views via the election process.

The statement-of-reasons pattern was appropriate because Brett's strategy involved backing up his central idea with three good reasons.

Another way of organizing this kind of speech is the *motivated sequence*, a common-sense approach to persuasion that was developed by the late Alan Monroe.[1] There are five steps in this method.

1. *Attention.* Grab the audience's attention at the beginning of your introduction, as discussed in Chapter 10.

2. *Need.* Show your audience that there is a serious problem that needs action.

3. *Satisfaction.* Satisfy the need by presenting a solution, and show how your solution works.

4. *Visualization.* Paint a picture of results. Help the listeners visualize what will happen when your solution has been put into effect. If possible, show how they personally will benefit.

5. *Action.* Request action from the listeners. Be specific: "Sign this petition" or "Write your legislators today—here are their addresses" or "You can volunteer in Room 211 this afternoon."

**Citizens sign a petition concerning a neighborhood issue. A persuasive speaker often tries to move the audience to take such an action.** *(Bob Daemmrich/TexaStock)*

To see how the motivated sequence works, imagine that you want to persuade your audience to support expanded research on energy alternatives to oil. You could develop the following strategy:

1. *Attention.* To grab the listeners' attention, you could describe the disaster that would occur if America suddenly found itself without oil for cars, homes, and factories.

2. *Need.* To describe the problem and show the need for action, you could explain that a war in the Middle East would cut off much of our oil supply and strangle our economy, so we need to become independent of foreign oil.

3. *Satisfaction.* You can satisfy the need by presenting a solution: alternative energy sources such as solar, geothermal, and hydrogen can be developed.

4. *Visualization.* To help the audience visualize the results, you paint a picture of a future war that breaks out in the Middle East, disrupting oil

supplies to the West, but you describe the United States as serenely continuing to thrive, thanks to the alternative energy sources.

5. *Action.* You request that the audience take immediate action by writing legislators and asking them to support expanded research on energy alternatives.

Jennifer Wade, a student speaker, used the motivated sequence to create the following outline:

**INTRODUCTION**

**Attention**

I. You are driving down a steep road when suddenly your brakes fail. You try to gear down, and you try to steer your car to a safe spot, but there's not enough time. Your car goes out of control and smashes into a tree. You are thrown against the windshield. When the paramedics arrive on the scene, you are alive, but you're bleeding profusely. The paramedics quickly put you into an ambulance and race you to the hospital. Time is of the essence. If you don't get a blood transfusion in the next few minutes, you will die.

**Need**

II. Where is the blood going to come from? Obviously it must come from the blood bank, but will there be blood of your type in the bank? Will there be enough blood? Did you know that today our local blood bank has a critical shortage of blood? The Red Cross has issued an emergency appeal for people to donate blood.

**BODY**

**Satisfaction**
**Visualization**

I. The Bloodmobile will be on campus next week.
II. Blood donors save the lives of many people.
   A. Accident victims need blood transfusions.
   B. Leukemia and cancer patients need blood transfusions.
   C. Some new babies need a complete change of blood supply.
   D. Hemophiliacs will die without regular transfusions.

**CONCLUSION**

**Action**

I. Donating blood is giving the gift of life.
II. When the Bloodmobile comes to our campus next week, step forward and give the gift of life.

# Elements of Persuasion

As you prepare a persuasive speech, there are six questions that you should ask yourself about the listeners:

1. Who are my listeners?

2. How can I build credibility with the audience?

3. What evidence should I provide to convince this particular audience?

4. What form of reasoning would be most compelling to the audience?

5. How can I appeal to the listeners' motivations?

6. How can I arouse the listeners' emotions?

To help you answer these questions, let us examine each point in greater detail.

## Knowing Your Audience

Dr. Frank C. Laubach was an educator who launched a nationwide crusade in the 1950s to teach illiterate adults how to read. In the early days of his crusade, when he went to factories to try to recruit illiterates for his reading classes, he would make the following appeal: "Would any of you people like to learn how to read?" Much to Dr. Laubach's disappointment, only a few of the illiterates in each factory would sign up—even though the classes were free.

What was wrong? Didn't the illiterates know that their inability to read was a big handicap in an advanced industrial society such as ours? Yes, Dr. Laubach reasoned, these people were keenly aware that their illiteracy condemned them to spend their lives on the margins of society. Why, then, did they pass up a chance to take free classes to better themselves?

As Dr. Laubach analyzed his audiences, he realized that most illiterates were ashamed to admit in public that they could not read. So he altered his pitch. At a factory in Charlotte, North Carolina, he asked, "Would any of you people like to learn to improve your reading?" This time, scores of illiterates stepped forward. The new pitch was effective because it enabled the men and women to maintain their self-respect. Instead of embarrassing themselves with an open admission that they could not read, they could identify themselves as simply people wanting to improve a skill. Thenceforth, Dr. Laubach used the revised version for all his spiels, with the same good results.

This story, which I heard from a reading teacher who uses the still-popular Laubach teaching method, demonstrates that persuasion involves more than simply "giving the facts." To get people to think or act a certain way, you must know who they are. What are their backgrounds? What are their needs and desires? What are their fears? Though he had a fabulous free offer that he handed to each audience on a silver platter, Dr. Laubach was ineffective in his attempts at persuasion until he accurately analyzed and understood the listeners. (At first glance Dr. Laubach's change of words seems a bit deceitful, but it really was not; all of the illiterates certainly could have read their own names and a few other simple words, so it was not stretching the truth to talk of "improving" their reading.)

As Dr. Laubach discovered, the first step in persuasion is understanding your listeners. To truly understand them, you must find out where they are standing, then go over to that spot, stand inside their shoes, and see the world as they see it. Only after you have seen the world from their perspective will you have a ghost of a chance of leading them to where you want them to stand.

While you need to understand your listeners, it is important to realize that failure to win every listener to your way of thinking does not indicate failure as a speaker. You should *try* to persuade every listener, but it would be unrealistic to expect that you can succeed with all people at all times. If you were trying to get your audience to accept the theory that our solar system contains a mysterious, as-yet-undiscovered planet on its outer fringes, you would have a good chance of convincing all the listeners because that theory has some solid scientific support and, more importantly, your listeners would probably have no strong emotional commitment to a competing theory. But what if you were trying to convince your audience that private ownership of handguns should be outlawed? That is an issue that polarizes many Americans, with people on both sides strongly committed to their position. It would be unrealistic to hope that you could persuade every opponent to march over to your camp.

On controversial issues, you often have three "audiences" listening to you. First of all, you have the people who already agree with you. Your goal with them is to reinforce their belief and perhaps even give them new reasons for supporting your cause. On the other extreme, you have the people who oppose your views. While not compromising your integrity (by doing such things as watering down your beliefs), you should show respect for these people and their views. *Never* insult or belittle the opposition; sarcastic or belligerent remarks make people defensive and all the more committed to their side. Try to persuade these people, but if that fails, be content if you can move them a few inches toward your camp. Sometimes the best you can hope for is to plant some seeds of doubt about their position which might someday sprout into full-blown conversion to your side. Finally, your third "audience" consists of people in-between the two extremes, those who are neutral. This group is obviously your ripest field for converts, the group that you should try hardest to persuade. The tips in the rest of this chapter should help you reach them.

## *Building Credibility*

A few years ago I was looking for a good pair of running shoes. I was picky: I wanted a brand that would provide support for the peculiar contours of my feet. When I went to a sporting goods store and explained to a clerk what I was looking for, he grabbed a pair of shoes off the shelf and said, "Try these. They're perfect for your feet." I tried them on, and they seemed all right, but I had a vague uneasiness about the clerk's judgment. I decided to wait.

Later, I placed a long-distance call to an old Army friend who is a dedicated long-distance runner and frequently writes articles about running. When I explained my situation, my friend recommended a particular brand. The next day I went out and bought a pair of the kind that he suggested.

This story illustrates the nature of credibility. Whether you are selling shoes or selling ideas, you must have high credibility with your listeners. How do you achieve this? By showing that you are *trustworthy* and *competent*. In my search for the perfect shoe, I rejected the advice of the clerk because he had low credibility with me. I did not know him well enough to judge whether he was trustworthy (maybe he was just trying to make a sale and did not care what kind of shoe he sold me), and I had no way of knowing whether he was competent (maybe he knew nothing at all about runners and their special needs). My friend, on the other hand, had high credibility with me because I knew he was trustworthy and I knew he was competent to give advice on runners' foot problems.

Showing that you are trustworthy and competent is a process that goes on from the time you are called to speak until the time you sit down. You enhance your credibility if your delivery is enthusiastic and if your speech is clear, well-reasoned, and well-organized. In addition, you can build credibility through the following methods.

## Explain Your Competence

If you have special expertise, be sure to let your audience know about it—modestly, of course. Do not boast or brag, just give the facts. Telling about your special competence enhances your credibility because it shows that you are speaking from personal experience. It says, "I've been there— I know what I'm talking about." Here is how student speaker Lauren Shriver bolstered her credibility during a speech:

> Deep-sea diving is not dangerous—if you follow all the safety rules. I've made over 50 dives myself, and I feel very safe because I'm very careful each time. I never allow myself to get slack and overconfident.

Lauren's information about her dives was necessary to give credibility to her remarks. Notice how she inserted her personal background in a modest way.

If you do not have personal knowledge of a subject and therefore must rely on the authority of others, you can enhance your own credibility by showing that your sources are competent. For example, in arguing that computers in the future will be capable of humanlike thinking, Don Stafford knew that his ideas might sound far-fetched coming from a student, so he said:

> My information comes from the work of Dr. Patrick Winston, who for the past 10 years has been director of the Artificial Intelligence Laboratory at

the Massachusetts Institute of Technology. Let me explain an experiment that Dr. Winston carried out. . . .

By quoting from an eminent authority, Don was able to give his speech instant credibility.

## Be Honest and Careful with Speech Material

You must be careful in your research, and you must be honest and straightforward in your presentation of ideas. Otherwise, the audience will lose confidence in you.

If people are convinced that one part of your speech is erroneous, they often discount your entire speech. So check your facts carefully. In arguing against the Darwinian theory of evolution, one student gave an incorrect example of Charles Darwin's ideas:

> Darwin taught that giraffes have long necks because thousands of years ago they had to stretch their necks to reach food in trees. All this exercise made their necks longer, and when they reproduced, their offspring had long necks. This went on generation after generation until you got giraffes with very long necks. This is ridiculous. I can spend years and years stretching my neck and maybe make my neck a little bit longer than it is. But I can't pass on long-neck genes to my children.

There is nothing wrong with arguing against Darwin's theories, but in this excerpt, the student misrepresented Darwin's writings. As biology students in the audience quickly pointed out during the question-and-answer period, Darwin contended that as food became available only at high levels in trees, giraffes with short necks died off because they couldn't reach enough leaves to stay alive. Only giraffes with necks long enough to reach leaves were able to survive. That left only long-necked males and long-necked females for mating, and their offspring inherited the tendency to have long necks.

I don't think the student deliberately twisted Darwin's theory in an unethical attempt to disprove the theory of evolution. He simply had failed to do his homework. His blunder, however, probably caused his whole speech to be discredited in the eyes of many listeners.

## Show Your Open-Mindedness

"If you would convince others," Lord Chesterfield once said, "seem open to conviction yourself."[2] In other words, show that you are a reasonable person who is open-minded and receptive, and quite capable of being wrong. This approach is not only an ethical one, but it is also highly effective in building credibility. Audiences distrust fanatical know-it-alls who never admit that they might be mistaken.

In a classroom speech in which she argued against the use of lie detectors, Amy McGuffin showed her open-mindedness by conceding that some-times businesses do catch thieves by means of lie detectors. She said:

> A bakery in Southern California was close to going out of business because one of its 125 workers was tossing bits of glass and wire into the mixing drum. The damaged goods were being returned by outraged retailers. A polygrapher [lie detector specialist] hired by the company gave lie detector tests until he discovered the worker who was guilty—an employee who was angry at being passed over for promotion.

Was it stupid for Amy to tell a story that seemed to negate her central idea (that businesses should be prohibited from giving lie detector tests)? No, because she went on to say that there is a far greater chance of an innocent employee being falsely accused of lying and then being fired than there is of a guilty employee being caught. Here is how she expressed it:

> Controlled studies performed by psychologists in laboratory settings show that lie detector tests have an accuracy rate of about 80 percent. That means that 80 percent of the time, the machine is right, but it also means that 20 percent of the time, the machine is wrong. What if you are working for a corporation, and you are among the 20 percent who are erroneously iden-tified as liars and thieves? You would lose your job, and you would find it hard to get a job elsewhere—you would be branded as a liar and a thief. Though lie detectors sometimes smoke out the guilty (as in the bakery case), they are so unreliable that they endanger the innocent.

Rather than damaging her case, her concession strengthened it, for she showed herself to the audience as a fair-minded individual who could be trusted. If you were a listener, wouldn't you trust her more than you would someone who said, "Lie detectors are totally worthless; they never catch the guilty party"?

It is especially important to be reasonable and open-minded during the question-and-answer period. I have seen some speakers do a good job in their speech, but when they are asked questions by listeners, they become rigid and defensive, refusing to admit error, refusing to concede that a listener has a good point. These speakers severely damage their own credibility and undo much of the persuasiveness of the speech itself.

## Show Common Ground with Your Audience

When you are introduced to someone at a party, you try to find things that you have in common. You ask each other questions ("What is your major?") until you hit upon some interest that you share. Often a person introducing you will try to help you find common ground: "Bill, I'd like you to meet Susan. She's like you: loves to ski." We try to find common ground because it not only helps us to make conversation but it also helps us to feel comfortable with another person.

Likewise in a speech, listeners like and trust a speaker who is similar to themselves. Your job is to show that to some degree you are like your listeners. This does not mean compromising your beliefs; it means highlighting those characteristics you share with the audience. This is especially important if some of the listeners are hostile to your ideas. Say, for example, that you are speaking on gun control and you know that half the listeners are already against your position. Here is what you can say: "I'm talking on gun control today. I know that a lot of you are opposed to the position I'm going to take. I ask only that you hear me out and see if my arguments have any merit whatsoever. Though we may disagree on this subject, you and I have at least one thing in common: we want to see a reduction in the number of violent, gun-related crimes in our society." With this kind of statement, you not only pinpoint common ground (opposition to crime), but you also appeal to the audience's sense of fair play.

One of the best ways to build credibility is to show the listeners that you identify with them—that you share (or have shared) their ideas or feelings. For example, actress Carol Burnett made the following revelation in a talk on how relatives of an alcoholic should deal with the problem drinker in their lives:

> You may wonder why I'm here to talk about alcoholism. It's easy to explain: Both of my parents died when they were 46 years old because they were both drunks.[3]

Thus, Carol Burnett demonstrated that she was not an aloof, imperious star being paid to talk to the "lowly" masses about a problem that *they* had. She showed, by means of a revelation that must have been painful to make, that she shared the heartbreak of so many people in her audience—the heartbreak of being related to an alcoholic. Her revelation undoubtedly caused her audience to draw closer to her emotionally and to become especially receptive to the rest of her talk.

## Providing Evidence

When you make an assertion in a speech, it is not enough to say, "Trust me on this" or "I know I'm right." The audience wants *evidence*, or proof. Evidence can be presented in the forms we discussed in Chapter 7: narratives, statistics, examples, testimony, etc. For each main point in your speech, you should ask yourself, "What evidence is most likely to prove my point with this particular audience?"

Catherine Huseman, a student speaker, gave a talk in which she urged her listeners to cut down on their consumption of salt. Her first step was to prove that excessive salt intake was harmful to one's health. Here are some statistics (from a reliable source) that she used as evidence:

Salt is a combination of two chemical elements—sodium and chlorine. It's sodium that we need to worry about. The American Medical Association has concluded that too much sodium leads to hypertension (high blood pressure). Hypertension is known as the "silent killer" because one-fourth of all Americans suffer from the disease without knowing it—until one day they suddenly suffer heart or brain damage. The A.M.A. says that hypertension is a factor in one-half of all the deaths in the U.S. each year.

Catherine also used testimony from an eminent authority:

Dr. Mark Hegsted, head of the Human Nutrition Center of the U.S. Department of Agriculture, says, "If salt were a new food additive, it is doubtful that it would be classified as safe and certainly not at the level most of us consume."

Having argued that sodium was harmful, Catherine next had to convince her listeners that they probably use too much salt. She employed statistics that had been fashioned into an easily grasped contrast:

The body needs a small amount of sodium every day, but most Americans consume more than 20 times the amount of sodium that the body needs. A lot of people think that if they give up potato chips, pretzels, and crackers, they can forget about overconsumption of sodium. What they don't know is that sodium is found in lots of surprising places: Two slices of white bread have twice as much sodium as a small bag of potato chips. Cottage cheese has three times as much sodium as a comparable amount of salted peanuts. A one-half cup of instant chocolate pudding has more sodium than three slices of bacon.

Next, Catherine used some examples to drive home her point:

The following are just a few of the foods that are very high in sodium: bread, milk, cottage cheese, tomato soup, canned tuna, canned corn, margarine, and ham. Also, fast foods are very high in sodium: fried chicken, hamburgers, French fries. In other words, many of the foods we eat every day are loaded with sodium.

After giving all of this evidence, Catherine spent the rest of her speech telling the listeners how to cut down on salt in their daily meals. The audience should have been highly receptive to her suggestions because she had done such a good job in presenting evidence of salt's dangers.

Although a speaker should use a variety of supports, is there one type that is more persuasive than others? Yes, there is, but before we discuss the answer, imagine that you are planning a speech on drunk driving. If you want to convince your audience that they stand a chance of being victimized by a drunk driver, which of the following would be the more persuasive piece of evidence?

A. You relate the sad, shocking details of an automobile accident in which a drunk driver hit your car and killed one of your passengers.

B. You cite the fact that 25,000 people are killed in America each year in alcohol-related car accidents.

Though you would need to use both of these items in your speech, the more persuasive item for most listeners would be Item A. But, you might ask, how can one, solitary case be more persuasive than a statistic encompassing 25,000 people? Psychologists have conducted scores of experiments which indicate that one vivid narrative, told from the speaker's personal experience, is much more persuasive than its statistical status would imply.[4] "All other things being equal." writes social psychologist Eliot Aronson, "most people are more deeply influenced by one clear, vivid personal example than by an abundance of statistical data."[5]

So, use a variety of evidence in your persuasive speeches, remembering that your most powerful evidence might be found in your own pool of personal experiences.

## Reasoning

Reasoning is the act of reaching conclusions on the basis of logical thinking. While it is true that people are not always logical and rational, it is also true that they frequently can be persuaded by a message that appeals to their powers of reasoning.[6] Let us take a look at two major types of reasoning.

### Deduction

Imagine that you are driving a car on a highway at a speed about 15 miles per hour over the speed limit. Suddenly you see a police car parked behind a billboard; as you whiz past, you notice that a radar device is protruding from the police car. You slow down, but you know it is too late: you are certain to be stopped. Sure enough, you glance in your rear-view mirror and see a second police car with lights flashing; the officer motions you to pull over.

How did you know that you were going to be stopped? By using deduction—a chain of reasoning that carries you from a generalization to a specific conclusion. In formal logic, this chain of reasoning is expressed in the form of a syllogism:

| | |
|---|---|
| *Major premise (generalization):* | Motorists who are speeding when they pass a radar point are usually stopped by police. |
| *Minor premise (specific instance):* | I was speeding when I passed a radar point. |
| *Conclusion:* | Therefore, I will probably be stopped. |

In a speech, deductive reasoning is convincing *only if both premises are accepted by the audience as true.* Would an audience be likely to accept the following chain of reasoning?

*Major premise:*  Aerobic exercise improves eyesight.
*Minor premise:*  Jogging is a form of aerobic exercise.
*Conclusion:*  Therefore, jogging improves eyesight.

The minor premise is true, but the major premise is false, so the entire syllogism is flawed.

Placing your deductive reasoning in the form of a syllogism can sometimes help you prepare a persuasive speech. For example, if you plan to talk on the saguaro cactus, you might begin with this specific purpose statement:

*Specific Purpose:*  To persuade my listeners to support efforts to prevent the extinction of the saguaro cactus.

You are worried about how your listeners will react. You know that if you asked them to preserve the giant panda or some other cuddly, adorable-looking animal, they would respond favorably, but if you started off your speech with a plea for the salvation of the saguaro cactus, they might react by saying to themselves, "Who cares about a cactus?" Even if you describe the majestic grandeur of this giant plant and show pictures of it, your listeners still might be unmoved. "If all cacti disappear," they might say to themselves, "it's no skin off my back." So how can you persuade them? Creating a syllogism will give you a blueprint for building your argument:

*Major premise:*  Humans should try to keep all existing species of plants and animals from becoming extinct.
*Minor premise:*  The saguaro cactus is in danger of becoming extinct.
*Conclusion:*  Therefore, humans should strive to keep the saguaro cactus from becoming extinct.

Is the syllogism convincing? Not necessarily. A syllogism is convincing only if the audience accepts both of your premises. What if some of the listeners do not endorse the major premise? What if they do not care if seemingly useless species die out?

Thus, to make your syllogism work for your listeners, you must first win them over to your major premise—that *all* species, no matter how lowly and unglamorous, must be saved from extinction. How can you do this? The best way is to appeal to the listeners' self-interest—their attitude of "What's in it for me?" Show them how the extinction of species can have an impact on their personal lives:

Your life—or the life of someone close to you—may be saved someday because of what science derives from plants and animals. Many of us in this room have already benefited from the lowly bread mold, which gives us penicillin. The Antioch Dunes evening primrose—one of 3,000 plants in the United States close to extinction—has yielded a chemical that helps control heart disease and arthritis. The study of dolphins has given us valuable information about circulatory systems and heat-exchange mechanisms. Well, you may be thinking, why don't we just save the species that are valuable to medicine and science? The answer is: we have no way of knowing which ones may contribute. A plant or animal that seems "worthless" today might provide the breakthrough tomorrow to save humanity from the curse of cancer and other dreaded killers.

Upon hearing that they have a personal stake in the preservation of plant and animal species, the listeners should be willing to accept your major premise—that all species should be saved. Your next task is to convince them of the validity of your minor premise—that the saguaro cactus is in danger of extinction. This should be easy because you are dealing with a matter of public record:

> Because cactus rustlers and campers have been stealing rare cacti from the desert, the saguaro cactus has been declared an endangered species by the U.S. Department of the Interior. And the states of Arizona, California, Nevada, and New Mexico have passed laws forbidding the uprooting of saguaro and other rare cacti.

Now that your listeners have become convinced of your major and minor premises, they should be receptive to your conclusion:

> I urge you to join me in helping to preserve the saguaro cactus. If you go camping in the Western deserts, don't take any rare cacti as souvenirs. Don't buy rare cacti from florists, either, because the only way we can stop cactus rustling is to dry up the market. If people stop buying them, thieves will stop stealing them. And, finally, let's support the efforts of wildlife groups and law-enforcement officials to educate the public on the need to preserve these cacti, so that they can survive and flourish—an irreplaceable national treasure.

By leading your listeners through the process of deduction, you have made a convincing argument.

## Induction

While deductive reasoning moves from the general to the specific, inductive reasoning proceeds from the specific to the general. Assume, for example, that you are sitting in a windowless room in the library and you make the following observations:

☐ A student enters the room carrying an umbrella that is dripping.

☐ Another student walks into the room and appears to be wet on the head and shoulders.

☐ A third student enters and takes off a raincoat that glistens with water.

Based on what you have seen, you reason inductively that it has been raining outside. You use specific evidence to reach a general conclusion. In reaching this conclusion, however, you have to take an *inductive leap*. You cannot prove that it has been raining simply because of what you have seen. You are probably right, but your conclusion has to remain tentative (until you walk outside and see for yourself) because there is always the chance that some other explanation can account for the three students' wetness: perhaps they have just participated in a science experiment (involving water) that took place outside the library. Perhaps there has not been a drop of rain all day. The chances are overwhelming that rain *is* the explanation, of course, but the point is that induction, unlike deduction, never leads to a certain conclusion, only a very likely one.

To construct an inductive argument, you should follow these steps: (1) ask a question, (2) answer the question by collecting as much specific evidence as possible, and (3) reach a conclusion based on the evidence. Here is an example:

*Question:* Do air bags in cars save lives?

*Evidence:*

*Item 1:* Joan Baxter of San Diego survived a head-on crash because of the air bag in her car.

*Item 2:* Dr. Arnold Arms, a Kansas City physician, survived a 35-mile-per-hour crash into a city bus; the bus suffered $15,000 damage, while Dr. Arms was spared any injury because of the air bag in his car.

*Item 3:* Mrs. Mattie Lansing of Chicago was involved in a head-on collision at 50 miles per hour, but suffered no injuries because of the air bag in her car.

*Conclusion:* Air bags save lives.

Is this all you need for evidence? No, although the inductive reasoning is powerful, you would need to show that your examples are not isolated flukes. You could, for example, cite statistics from national authorities, such as: "The Department of Transportation estimates that 11,000 lives would be saved each year if air bags were used in all cars."

When you use inductive reasoning, you will convince an audience only if your evidence is strong. If you have weak evidence, your conclusion will be weak. In the preceding example, if you had used such vague statements as "The manufacturers of air bags assure us that the bags will save lives," your evidence would have been too flimsy to support the conclusion.

Earlier, we discussed the value of stating your central idea in the introduction of your speech; there are occasions, however, when this is not the best strategy. One such occasion is when you have an audience that is likely to be hostile or skeptical to your central idea. With such listeners, a wise strategy is to lead them through an inductive chain, saving your central idea for the latter part of the speech. Here's an example.

Student speaker Robert Burnham had the following as his central idea: "We could cut down on street crime in America if heroin addicts could legally get their daily 'fix' from government-sponsored clinics at no cost." If he had said this in the introduction, many of the listeners might have dismissed the idea as crazy and the speaker as a crackpot. But Robert used a smart approach. In his introduction, he made no mention of his central idea; he merely said, "I want to talk to you about one of America's worst drugs, heroin." Using the inductive approach, he built his case:

☐ He gave true accounts of heroin addicts robbing citizens in order to get money to support their expensive addiction.

☐ He told of an experiment in Great Britain where addicts were treated as patients rather than as criminals, and were given heroin in government-sponsored clinics so that they would not have to mug people on the street.

☐ He quoted a judge who said that if heroin were legally available to addicts, there would be a big drop in muggings and other street crimes.

Toward the end of his speech, having built a good case, Robert stated his argument: society should give addicts the heroin they crave so that they won't engage in street crimes. By then, the listeners were probably more open-minded about the idea than they would have been if they had heard it at the beginning of the speech. Even if they rejected the idea, they at least saw it as having some merit rather than being completely off-base.

### Fallacies in Reasoning

A fallacy is an error in reasoning that renders an argument false or unreliable. You should become adept at recognizing fallacies so that you can avoid using them in your own speeches and so that you can prevent yourself from being influenced by them when you listen to the speeches of others. Here are some of the more common fallacies.

1. *Hasty Generalization.* A hasty generalization is a conclusion that is reached on the basis of insufficient evidence. For example, "The mayor

was convicted of accepting bribes and a city council member was indicted for vote fraud. So we can conclude that all the politicians in this city are corrupt." The fact that two politicians are corrupt does not prove that all are. Make sure that you have ample evidence before you reach a conclusion.

2. *Sweeping Generalization.* A sweeping generalization is a statement that is so broad and so categorical that it ends up being unfair and inaccurate. It often includes words like *always, never, all,* and *none.* In a speech on America's neglect of old people, one student said, "America is the only country in the world that has no regard for its elderly family members. All other countries have great respect for the age and wisdom of the elderly."

The speaker had a good point to make—that we need to take better care of our elderly—but he damaged his credibility by indulging in such an outrageously unfair generalization. Is it true that *all* Americans have *no* regard for the elderly? Don't some Americans have high regard for old people? Even if his accusation were true, how can he say that America is the *only* country exhibiting such neglect? Has he researched the situation in such nations as Zaire, Luxembourg, and Sri Lanka?

To make his argument reasonable and accurate, the speaker would need to modify the generalization to say: "Some Americans do not give their elderly family members the honor and attention that they deserve." Now the generalization would be acceptable to most listeners.

3. *Attack on a Person.* Some speakers try to win an argument by attacking a person rather than the person's ideas. For example: "Rodney has lived in upper-class luxury all his life, so how can we believe anything he says about changing the welfare system for the poor? He obviously knows nothing about poverty." This tactic, sometimes known as *argumentum ad hominem* (argument against the man), is unfair and unethical. Rodney's arguments should be judged on how sound his ideas are, not on any aspect of his personal life.

Attacks on a person are often used in the courtroom to discredit a witness ("Ladies and gentlemen of the jury, this witness admits that he's an atheist, so how can we trust him to tell us the truth?") and in politics to discredit a foe ("My opponent has gambled in Las Vegas at least five times. Do you want such a person to manage your tax dollars?"). Though this tactic may be effective in the hands of such speakers, it should never be used by the ethical speaker, not only because it is dishonest and unfair, but also because it can backfire and cause careful listeners to lose respect for the speaker.

4. *False Cause.*    Beware of the fallacy of assuming that because events occur close together in time, they are necessarily related as cause and effect. A President takes office and four months later the unemployment

rate goes up 1 percent. Can we say that the President's policies caused the rise in unemployment? It is possible that they did, but there may be many other factors that caused the problem—for example, the economic policies of the previous administration.

The fallacy of false cause can also occur when a speaker oversimplifies the causes of complex problems. Take, for example, a speaker who said that *the* cause of cancer is negative thinking. That explanation is simple and understandable—and wrong. While negative thinking—and the stress and tension that go with it—may be implicated someday as contributing factors in cancer, medical researchers say that no one thing has been isolated as *the* cause of cancer. The disease is probably caused by an interaction of several factors, including genetic predisposition, susceptibility of the immune system, the presence of a carcinogenic virus, and environmental irritants. Cancer is too complex to be explained by a single causative factor.

5. *Begging the Question.* When speakers "beg the question," they act as if an assertion has been proved when in fact it has not. Suppose that a speaker made the following statement: "Since the Japanese never make a product that will last a long time, we should stop buying Japanese products and start buying American-made products." The speaker is acting as if the impermanence of Japanese products is an established fact, when in reality many listeners would probably disagree. An ethical speaker would first try to prove that Japanese products are less enduring than American products and then urge the audience not to buy Japanese-made goods.

When a speaker begs the question, careful listeners are resentful because they feel as if they are being tricked into giving assent to a proposition that they do not believe.

6. *False Analogy.* When speakers use a false analogy, they make the mistake of assuming that just because two things are alike in minor ways, they are also alike in major ways. For decades, some doomsayers have drawn an analogy between the Roman Empire and the United States, and then concluded that like Rome, the United States is destined to fall. There are indeed many parallels—establishment of far-flung military outposts, love of material things, intense interest in sports—but there are also vast differences. For example, unlike ancient Rome, the United States uses its overseas forces to defend itself, its commercial interests, and its allies, rather than to conquer and enslave smaller nations. Even if the two great civilizations were alike in most ways, this still would not mean that the United States is destined to share the fate of ancient Rome. History is not a series of predictable events that operate with the regularity of incoming and outgoing tides.

Here is another false analogy: "We can communicate effectively via satellite with people on the other side of the planet. Why, therefore, can't parents and children do a better job of communicating within the intimate environment of their own homes?" Upon close examination, this analogy falls apart. Satellite communication between nations is a purely technical matter of transmitting radio and television signals, whereas communication among family members involves psychological complexities and subtleties that are beyond the reach of technology.

7. *Either-Or Reasoning.* The either-or fallacy occurs when the speaker states that there are only two alternatives, when in fact there may be many. For example: "Either we wipe out our national deficit or we watch our economy die." Is there truly no other way? Is it not possible that we can trim the deficit, without totally eliminating it, and still preserve our economic health? Stating an argument in stark, either/or terms makes a speaker appear unreasonable and dogmatic.

Here is another example: "Intelligence is determined by either heredity or environment, and I say that heredity is the key. How smart you are is determined by your genes." Most psychologists would disagree with this statement because intelligence seems to be determined by a complex interplay of both genetic and environmental factors. People like Albert Einstein or Margaret Mead would never have thrived intellectually if their lives had been stunted by extreme poverty and malnutrition.

8. *Straw Man.* Some people try to win arguments by creating a straw man, a ridiculous caricature of what their opponents believe, and then beating it down with great ease. For example, one speaker, while arguing in favor of the death penalty for convicted murderers, said, "These people [who oppose the death penalty] say that a murderer is not really to blame for his crime. They say that society is to blame for not providing better educational and economic opportunities. So the murderer shouldn't be executed; he shouldn't even be sent to prison. We should simply say to him, 'Naughty boy, you did a no-no. Don't do it again.'"

Was this a fair summary of the belief of his opponents? Of course not. Most opponents of the death penalty favor long prison sentences for murderers. Speakers like this create a straw man in order to look like victors. Careful listeners, however, will spot the deception and lose confidence in them.

## Appealing to Motivations

Motivations are the needs, desires, or drives that impel a person toward a goal or away from some negative situation. People have hundreds of motivations, including love, happiness, health, social acceptance, financial security, adventure, and creativity.[7] If you show your listeners how your ideas can help them satisfy such needs and desires, you increase your chances of persuading them to adopt your point of view. Here are some examples of how student speakers appealed to the motivations of their audiences:

> To raise money to buy food for starving people in Africa, Lee Anne Washington appealed to the motivation that most Americans have to help those less fortunate than themselves.
>
> To try to persuade listeners to use seat belts at all times in a car, Jason Bradley appealed to the strong drive that people have to protect themselves from harm.
>
> To try to convince listeners to invest in real estate, Glenda Jorgensen tapped the public's desire for financial security and wealth.

Whenever possible, you should appeal to several motivations at the same time. Listeners who are not reached by one appeal can still be influenced by another. Suppose, for example, that you were trying to persuade your listeners to take up bicycling. Here are some of the motivations that you could identify, coupled with appropriate appeals:

| Motivation | Appeal |
|---|---|
| Feeling good | Bicycling works out tension and makes you feel energetic and happy. |
| Looking good | Bicycling burns lots of calories so it's ideal for weight control. It also tones up leg muscles. |
| Long-term health | Bicycling is excellent exercise for heart and lungs, thus helping prevent cardiovascular disease. |
| Friendship | Being on a bicycle is an instant passport to the world of cyclists. It's easy to strike up conversations with other riders, and you can often make new friends. Cycling also provides an enjoyable activity to share with old friends. |
| Adventure | With a bicycle you can explore out-of-the-way places, travel long distances in a single day, and experience the thrill of flying down a steep mountain road. |
| Competition | If you enjoy competing, there are bike races in almost every city or town. |

By appealing to more than one motivation, you increase your chances of persuading the audience. For example, the listener who is already in superb health may not be reached by the first three items, but might be swayed by one of the last three.

## Arousing Emotions

Emotions are "stirred up" feelings that can be either positive (amusement, love, joy) or negative (fear, anger, sadness). In a speech, emotional appeals can stir listeners and rouse them to action.

**It is ethical for a speaker to arouse strong emotions in listeners, but he or she should accompany emotional appeals with strong evidence and sound logic.** *(Alan Carey/The Image Works)*

To give an example of how emotion can be used effectively, here is an excerpt from a speech by a student, Stacey Brooks, who was arguing for a crackdown on divorced parents who kidnap their children and thereby deprive the other parent of seeing them:

One morning Martha Greer, a divorced woman, woke up her kids, Saman-tha, aged eight, and Bruce, aged six. She rubbed their backs to help them get awake, then she helped them find their school clothes. She made them a breakfast of orange juice, toast and jelly, bacon, hashed browns, and milk. Then she walked with them to the place where they caught the bus to school.

That was the last time Martha saw them. They were kidnapped by their father that afternoon as they left school. That was six months ago, and Martha has no idea where they are. The police have not been able to find them. Think how frantic Martha is, think how angry she is, as she wonders where her kids are and how they're getting along without their mother. Imagine how you would feel if your kids were suddenly snatched from your life.

This story was very effective in arousing anger and pity in the listeners.

A few words of caution: You should take care that emotion never becomes a substitute for well-reasoned arguments. A speaker who does nothing but tug on heart strings, completely neglecting the listeners' minds, will usually be less effective than the speaker who uses both emotional and rational appeals. In general, emotional appeals work best when they are used sparingly. Just as too much icing can cause a cake to change from sweet to sickening, too much emotion can cause a speech to change from effective to excessive. In her speech, Stacey relied upon sound evidence and logic in the rest of her speech, thus making sure that her emotional appeal was an accompaniment to her solid arguments, rather than a substitute for them.

# Sample Persuasive Speech

In a speech to motivate action, student Jeffrey Cordell argued for tougher laws against drunk driving. His outline is presented first, followed by the speech as delivered.[8] In the commentary alongside the outline, note the discussion of the five steps of the motivated sequence.

## *Outline*

### WHAT CAN WE DO ABOUT DRUNK DRIVERS?

**General Purpose:** To persuade

**Specific Purpose:** To persuade my audience to support tough legislation aimed at getting drunk drivers off our highways.

**Central Idea:** Tough new laws should be enacted to rid our highways of drunk drivers.

**Motivated Sequence**
**Attention**
Jeffrey grabs the listeners' attention with a tragic story.

**INTRODUCTION**

I. According to *Newsweek* magazine, a four-year-old boy in Memphis, Tennessee, David Gunderman, was run over by a car as he stood on the sidewalk waiting for an ice cream truck. His killer, a drunk driver who had eight prior convictions ranging from hit-and-run to drunk driving, was sentenced to five years in prison.

**Need**
Jeffrey shows the scope of
the problem and why ac-
tion must be taken.

II. David Gunderman's story is just one out of thousands. The FBI
estimates that 25,000 people are killed in alcohol-related traffic
accidents each year in the United States. The National Safety Council estimates that one-half of all Americans will be victimized by a
drunk driver in some way during their lifetimes—either in a serious
crash or a fender-bender. We, the public, do not have to put up
with this slaughter. We can—and we must—get drunk drivers off
our highways, permanently. We can do so if we pass tough new
laws that do two things—one, let police set up roadblocks, and two,
give drunk drivers harsh penalties.
(*Transition:* Let's start off by taking a look at what police can do.)

**BODY**
  I. Police should set up roadblocks at random sites every night of the
week to apprehend drunk drivers.
    A. Breathalyzers can be used to test blood alcohol level.
    B. Roadblocks in Sweden have apparently been successful.
(*Transition:* Now that we've talked about what police can do, let's turn
our attention to the courts.)
 II. Persons convicted of drunk driving should receive harsh penalties.
    A. They should get mandatory prison sentences.
    B. They should lose their licenses permanently.
    C. Though some experts doubt that jurors would convict under
such stern penalties, it's worthwhile to try harsh measures.
(*Transition:* Would tough new laws be likely to get drunks off the roads?)
III. States that have instituted tough policies have experienced a drop
in traffic fatalities.
    A. California saw a 14-percent drop in traffic deaths.
    B. Maine reported a 24-percent drop.
    C. Minnesota and Maryland had a 30-percent reduction.
(*Transition:* Let me review my two proposals)

**CONCLUSION**
  I. I have proposed police roadblocks and stronger punishment.
 II. All states should adopt these stringent new laws to get drunks off
the road—permanently.
III. At the end of class, I will have a petition for you to sign, urging our
state lawmakers to enact the proposals I've outlined for you today.
I hope you will sign. The life you save may be your own.

**Satisfaction**
Jeffrey presents his solution
to the problem.

**Visualization**
By showing what happened
in other states, he helps his
audience see what he be-
lieves will happen if his
proposals are adopted.

**Action**
Jeffrey makes a request for
immediate action by the
audience.

**BIBLIOGRAPHY**

"Drunken-driving laws vary across USA," *USA Today,* May 6, 1985, p.
4.

"One Less for the Road," *Time magazine,* May 20, 1985, pp. 76–78.

Shelley Patterson, exchange student, personal interview, April 1985.

Here is the transcript of Jeffrey Cordell's speech.

| COMMENTARY | SPEECH AS DELIVERED |
|---|---|

## What Can We Do About Drunk Drivers?

Notice that the speaker uses the ideas of his outline without using the exact wording. In an extemporaneous speech, the speaker does not read or memorize a speech, but speaks from brief notes.

David Gunderman was a four-year-old boy who lived with his parents in Memphis, Tennessee. One summer day, as David stood on the sidewalk waiting for an ice cream truck, he was run over and killed by a driver who had lost control of his car. According to *Newsweek* magazine, the driver was drunk. And it wasn't the first time he had been drunk behind the wheel. He had *eight* previous convictions ranging from hit-and-run to drunk driving. For killing David, he was sentenced to only five years in prison.

The story of the little boy is an effective device to arouse a well-justified emotion in the listeners—anger.

The story of David Gunderman is just one out of thousands. The FBI estimates that 25,000 Americans are killed each year in alcohol-related traffic accidents. The National Safety Council estimates that one-half of all drivers in the U.S. will become the victim of a drunk driver in some way during their lives. It might be a serious accident or it might be a fender-bender, but one-half of you will be victimized at some point in your lives. Is there anything we can do about this slaughter on our highways? I say that we can get drunk drivers off our roads and highways, and keep them off, if we pass tough new laws that do two things: one, let police set up roadblocks, and two, give drunk drivers strong punishment.

Notice that the speaker repeats the statistic and relates it directly to the listener. This drives home the point to the audience.

The speaker previews the body of the speech by giving his central idea.

First of all, let's see what police can do. I think that the police should be permitted—and encouraged—to set up roadblocks at random places every night of the week to catch drunk drivers. Breathalyzers could be used to test blood alcohol level. Some people say this is too drastic, this is too much like a police state, but I say that the law-abiding driver has nothing to worry about. The roadblocks would cause people to think twice before using a car on a night when they are planning to drink heavily. A friend of mine lived in Sweden for a year on a student-exchange program, and she said that Swedish police set up roadblocks at different places every night. She said that most Swedes are very reluctant to drink if they are planning to drive.

The speaker anticipates an objection that is likely to arise in the listeners and tries to rebut it.

The testimony of an observer can provide stronger support than a recital of dry statistics.

While the police can set up roadblocks, what can the courts do? My second recommendation is that we make the penalty for drunk driving much more severe than it is right now in most states. I believe that people who have been convicted of drunk driving should receive a mandatory prison sentence and should lose their driver's licenses permanently. Some legal experts say that if we have penalties that are real tough like this, some juries will be reluctant to convict. They may turn out to be right, but I believe that we at least ought to try it. If it proves

By admitting that his plan might have flaws, the speaker shows his moderation and open-mindedness, thus enhancing his credibility with the audience.

Statistics provide good support for the speaker's point.

The speaker summarizes his two key ideas.

If the speaker gets the audience to sign a petition, he increases their commitment to his cause.

to be unworkable, then we can modify the laws later. We have nothing to lose by trying tough sentencing and possibly many lives to gain.

Are tough new laws likely to get drunk drivers off the highways? Several states have already adopted stringent laws that include some or all of my proposals. What has happened in these states? Are the new laws working? Yes, most definitely they are. In the first year of their new laws, here's what happened, according to *Time* magazine: In California, the traffic death rate went down 14 percent; in Maine, it went down 24 percent; and in Minnesota and Maryland, it went down 30 percent. Those percentages translate of course into lives saved. Tough laws *do* work.

Today I have made two proposals—that police should set up frequent roadblocks at random places, and that a drunk driver who is convicted should lose his license permanently and be sent to jail. I believe that all states should put these proposals into law. These laws would be a giant step toward getting the drunks off the roads—permanently. At the end of class, I will have a petition at the table by the door. This petition urges our state legislators to pass the laws I've talked about. I hope you will sign the petition. The life you save may be your own.

## Summary

Persuasion—getting people to think or act in a certain way—is one of the most frequent tasks of the public speaker. There are many patterns that can be used for the persuasive speech, but one of the most effective is the *motivated sequence* in which you (1) gain the listeners' attention, (2) show them the need for action, (3) offer a solution that satisfies that need, (4) help them visualize what will happen if the solution is put into effect, and (5) request that they take action.

To be effective in persuasion, you should analyze your audience carefully, asking six key questions: (1) Exactly who are my listeners? (2) How can I build credibility with them? (3) What evidence should I provide to convince them? (4) What form of reasoning would be most compelling to them? (5) How can I appeal to their motivations? (6) How can I arouse their emotions?

In using logic, you must be careful to avoid these fallacies: *hasty generalization, sweeping generalization, attack on a person, false cause, begging the question, false analogy, either-or reasoning,* or *straw man attacks.*

## Review Questions

1. Why is it a good idea in many cases to tell the audience why you are competent to speak on your particular subject matter?
2. How is an audience likely to react if you are careless with your facts and ideas?

3. What is the difference between deduction and induction?
4. Why should a speaker never use the logical fallacy called "attack on a person"?
5. List at least five motivations that all listeners have.

# TIPS *for your career*

### Tip 15: Provide Supplementary Material at the End of a Speech

At the end of a speech, especially a persuasive talk to a community or business audience, it is sometimes effective to offer the listeners supplementary materials that support or elaborate your message. Here are some possibilities:

☐ Pass out a brief written summary of your key ideas. This reinforces your message and gives the listeners, many of whom probably did not take notes, an accurate record of what you said. A summary is especially helpful for technical presentations that include complex ideas and detailed statistics.

☐ Pass out a supplementary reading list. If you get your listeners interested or excited about a particular subject, they will appreciate receiving a list of books and articles that they can read to delve further into the subject.

☐ Offer written documentation of your sources. You might say, for example, "I don't have time to name all the books and articles from which I got my information, but I have a bibliography which I'll place on the table at the front, and you're welcome to pick this up after I finish." Such a list is not only helpful to listeners who want to pursue your subject further, but it also suggests to the audience that you are a careful researcher who is concerned about getting the facts correct.

## Chapter 16

# Special Types of Speeches

**Entertaining (or After-Dinner) Speech**

**Speech of Introduction**

**Speech of Acceptance**

**Speech of Tribute**

**Speech of Inspiration**

Though most of the speeches that you will give in your lifetime will probably be informative or persuasive, there are occasions when you may be called upon to give other kinds—an entertaining speech at a banquet, a brief speech introducing the main speaker at a convention, a eulogy at a funeral to honor a close friend, an acceptance speech to thank an organization for giving you an award, or an inspirational speech to lift the morale of your fellow employees. In this chapter, we will take a look at these special types of speeches.

# Entertaining (or After-Dinner) Speech

An entertaining speech provides amusement or diversion for the audience. It should be light and enjoyable, and easy to listen to. There should be no lecturing, no preaching, no doomsaying.

An entertaining speech can be given in a variety of circumstances, but it is most often delivered at meetings such as conventions and annual club dinners. It is frequently referred to as an "after-dinner speech" because it is usually given after luncheon or dinner. People who have just eaten a big meal want to sit back, relax, and enjoy a talk. They don't want to work hard mentally; they don't want to be given anything negative and gloomy. So if you are an after-dinner speaker, do not challenge their beliefs or pump them with statistics. Strive to entertain them.

An entertaining speech can consist of a series of jokes, but joke telling is a difficult and risky business (see Tip 16 at the end of this chapter); besides, an entertaining speech does not have to be humorous to be effective. In other words, to entertain you do not have to elicit belly laughs, shrieks of glee, or deep chuckles. You can entertain an audience with stories and word pictures; for example, a well-told story about the calamities that occurred on your first date, a dramatic account of Sir Edmund Hillary's conquest of Mt. Everest, a description of the weird behavior of the South American sloth, or an imaginative forecast of life in America 100 years from now. All of these speeches could be given without thigh-slapping jokes, but they nevertheless would be highly entertaining.

Students have given entertaining speeches on such topics as these:

My first piano recital—a total disaster

Hitchhiking from East Coast to West Coast

My grandfather's favorite ghost stories

The wit and wisdom of Mark Twain

The best rock concert I ever attended

While entertaining the audience is the general purpose of this kind of speech, this does not mean that you cannot include a few elements of persuasion, information, or inspiration; it just means that you should weave them unobtrusively and gracefully into the cloth of entertainment. To see how one speaker dispensed information in a light, entertaining manner, read the speech "Blue Beans and Purple Potatoes" in Appendix B.

# Speech of Introduction

☐ At a meeting of her civic club, Paula Moreno spoke briefly on why she was supporting a particular candidate for Congress and then turned the lectern over to the candidate.

☐ Theodore Lansing, a university librarian, stood up in front of 1,500 delegates at a national librarians' convention and introduced the keynote speaker, a renowned writer of science fiction.

These are examples of speeches of introduction. When you introduce one friend to another, you want them to get interested in each other and to like each other. When you introduce a speaker to an audience, you want to achieve the same goal. You want speaker and audience to be interested in each other and to feel warmth and friendliness.

An introduction should mention the speaker's name several times (so that everyone can catch it), and it should give background information to enhance the speaker's credibility with the audience. Your tone of voice and facial expression should convey enthusiasm for the speech to come.

Here are some guidelines for speeches of introduction.

1. *Ask the speaker ahead of time what kind of introduction he or she would like.* Some speakers will write out their introduction and send it to you in advance. While you should not actually read the document (because this would be boring to the audience), you should use it as the basis for your remarks. If the speaker provides you with a lengthy résumé or list of accomplishments, select those items that would be most appropriate for the audience and the occasion. Also, the speaker may want you to establish ground rules about questions; for example, "John will take questions at the end of the speech."

2. *Be sure to pronounce the speaker's name correctly.* If you have any doubt about how to pronounce the speaker's name, verify the pronunciation beforehand. If the name is difficult to pronounce, practice saying it in advance so that you do not stumble during the introduction.

3. *Use the name the speaker prefers.* If you are scheduled to introduce Dr. Elizabeth Wilson, find out beforehand what she wants to be called. Do not assume that she prefers to be called "Dr. Wilson." It could be that

for this particular audience she prefers the informality of "Elizabeth" or even her nickname, "Liz."

4. *Set the proper tone.* When you introduce someone, you help set the tone for the speech to follow. Be careful to set the right tone—a humorous tone for a humorous speech, a serious tone for a serious speech. Consulting with the speaker in advance will insure that you understand the tone he or she wants you to set.

5. *Avoid long introductions.* A good rule of thumb is to keep an introduction under three minutes. After all, an audience wants to hear the speaker, not the introducer.

6. *Avoid exaggeration.* If you exaggerate the speaker's abilities or credentials, you build up unrealistic expectations in the audience. Consider this kind of introduction: "Our speaker tonight is a funny person who will have you laughing so hard you'll have to clutch your sides." Or: "The speaker will give us insights that are wise and brilliant." Such statements raise expectations that are very difficult for the speaker to meet. If the listeners are expecting one of the world's funniest speakers, or one of the wisest, they are likely to be disappointed. Overpraising a speaker also puts enormous pressure on him or her. This introduction, "Our speaker is a dynamic personality who is known far and wide for her flawless platform technique," not only will cause the audience to focus on the speaker's delivery rather than on the message, but will also place great pressure on the speaker to perform perfectly.

7. *Discuss the topic only after coordinating your remarks with the speaker's.* Some speakers will want you to discuss the significance of their topic (to help prepare the audience for the speech); other speakers prefer to save all discussion of the topic until *they* step to the lectern. If a speaker wants you to discuss the topic, tell him or her exactly what you plan to say, and then make sure to get his or her approval. This is more than a matter of courtesy; it prevents you from spoiling the speaker's speech (as we will see in the next paragraph).

8. *Never steal the speaker's material.* Let us say that you are being introduced to an audience of 1,000 people. You feel nervous, but you also feel confident because you have spent weeks preparing and practicing your speech. As the introducer talks, you suddenly realize with a sinking heart that he is telling the anecdote that you planned to begin your speech with. A few moments later, he relates the story you were planning to tell as a conclusion for your speech. How in the world are you going to begin and end your speech?

Though it sounds like a nightmare, this scenario (or a variation of it) has actually happened to some speakers. When you are an introducer, stay away from speakers' material unless authorized by the speaker. If you delve too deeply into the topic or try to summarize the speech, you put the speakers at a severe disadvantage. You might "give away" some of their anecdotes, or even worse, you might give a wrong interpretation of what they are going to say. As an introducer, your task is to set the stage, not steal it.

The following introduction of professional speaker Danny Cox was delivered at a national convention of a professional organization:

> Danny Cox is a graduate of Southern Illinois University and spent ten years in the United States Air Force flying all-weather supersonic fighters . . . Upon leaving the Air Force, he joined one of the nation's largest real-estate corporations as a salesperson. One year later he was promoted to branch manager, followed by another promotion to first vice president and district manager of eight offices and 143 salespeople. After teaching the same people-building techniques to the managers assigned to his district that he had used as a branch manager, their offices doubled, tripled, and quadrupled all previous records. In a five and one-half year period, those offices sold over two-third billion dollars' worth of real estate, increasing production an incredible 25.6 percent per year—and that included two so-called recession years. This was the proof he needed that a leadership style that takes into consideration the worth and importance of each individual can help break down self-imposed barriers and can be taught to others. He packed his bags in early 1977, and has scarcely unpacked them since. Due to the wide acceptance of both his material and easy-to-listen-to style, Danny spends an average of 28 hours per week on platforms throughout the United States and Canada. Would you help me welcome . . . Danny Cox![1]

This introduction helps give background on the speaker and establishes his credibility. When Cox rises and tells his listeners how they can motivate people to boost productivity and increase profits, they know that he speaks from experience—his methods have been tried, and they work.

# Speech of Acceptance

If you are ever given an award, a promotion or some other sort of public recognition, you may be called upon to "say a few words." Giving a speech of acceptance is difficult because you want to sound appreciative without being syrupy; you want to sound deserving without being egotistical. Here are some guidelines to follow.

1. *Thank those who played a part in your achieving the honor.* If a few individuals made your recognition possible, mention them by name; if a lot of people did, mention the most important contributors to your success and say something like this, "There are many others but they are too numerous to name. Nevertheless, I am grateful to all of them."

**A speaker who receives an award is often asked to "say a few words" to the group presenting the award.** *(Kolvoord/TexaStock)*

2. *Thank the organization giving you the award and recognize the work they are doing.* If, for example, you are cited by the United Way as top fundraiser of the year, spend a few moments extolling the great work that United Way does in helping the unfortunate and needy.

3. *Do not exaggerate.* If you receive an award for perfect attendance at

your club's meetings, do not say, "This is the greatest honor I've ever received or ever hope to receive," unless, of course, you mean it. Exaggeration makes you seem insincere.

4. *Be brief.* I have seen some ceremonies marred because an award recipient viewed the acceptance speech as a chance to expound on his or her pet ideas. If you deliver a lengthy oration, the people who gave you the honor might regret that they did. Make a few sincere remarks—and then sit down.

A sample acceptance speech is the one given by Rita Goldberg, who was honored by a chapter of the Lions Club for her work with the handicapped:

> I want to thank you for choosing me to receive your Distinguished Service Award. In the past year I couldn't have accomplished half of what I did without the help of Henry and Judith Fletcher. I am grateful to them for their valuable assistance. And I am grateful to you Lions for setting up programs for the visually handicapped. Because of your compassion and your work, you have made it easy for volunteers like me to help the handicapped. Again, thank you for this honor.

# Speech of Tribute

A speech of tribute praises or celebrates a person, a group, an institution, or an event. For example, the leader of a veterans' organization might pay tribute on Memorial Day to comrades who had died on the field of battle. At a ground-breaking ceremony for a new building, the president of a college might give a speech honoring the individual for whom the building will be named.

A speech of tribute should be completely positive. It is not appropriate to point out faults or dredge up old disputes. Concentrate all remarks on the praiseworthy and noble.

The kind of tribute speech that you are most likely to make is a eulogy—a speech of praise for a friend or colleague who has died. A eulogy should be somber and dignified, without exaggerated sentimentality. It should focus on the *significance* of the person's life and deeds, rather than on a mere recital of biographical facts. In other words, how did this man or woman enrich our lives? What inspiration or lessons can we draw from this person's life?

In the U. S. House of Representatives, Congresswoman Olympia J. Snowe of Maine delivered the following eulogy to E. B. White, author of *Charlotte's Web* and coauthor of *Elements of Style*. (In keeping with the tradition of the House of Representatives, she addressed her remarks to the Speaker of the House, though she was actually speaking to the entire House.)

## E. B. WHITE

Mr. Speaker, in the foreward to his "Essays" in 1977, E. B. White wrote that an essayist is one who "can pull on any sort of shirt, be any sort of person, according to his mood or his subject matter—philosopher, scold, jester, raconteur, confidant, pundit, devil's advocate, enthusiast." With the passing of this great craftsman yesterday, we have lost all of those and more.

While E. B. White's death finally stilled a voice that has spoken to America since the 1920s, he has left behind a rich landscape of essays, letters, stories, and poems which will attract readers for generations yet to come. As J. Russell Wiggins, a longtime friend of White's and now head of the *Ellsworth American,* said: "He left a lot of himself around us." White's writing reflected the concerns of everyday life in our country, yet managed to impart the perspective and outlook, uniquely his, of a man who was thinking about things just a bit more clearly than the rest of us.

The style of E. B. White's prose, in many ways, had its mirror in the lives along the Maine coast which he had adopted as his home: Clear and clean, pointed and concise, indulging in little nonsense but always maintaining a soft touch of humor. As Henry Mitchell writes in this morning's *Washington Post:*

> *E. B. White took pains not to be grand and all for naught; he wound up grand for all his avoidance of grandeur, and the more he avoided noble and elevated style the more convinced his readers were that he was noble—a word not always trotted out for writers of short and casual pieces.*

Mr. Speaker, generations have tried, usually without success, to live up to the dictum expressed by William Strunk and championed by E. B. White: "Omit needless words." The words of E. B. White will never be omitted by that standard. I would only like to express, for myself and for his neighbors in the state of Maine, a great sorrow for his death, but a profound gratitude for his life and noble works.[2]

Congresswoman Snowe points out the significance of White's life for her audience: "He has left behind a rich landscape of essays, letters, stories, and poems which will attract readers for generations yet to come." Notice, too, that she avoids gushy, maudlin sentimentality. She speaks of White's accomplishments in a straightforward and dignified manner, using the kind of simple, clear prose that White himself would have approved of.

# Speech of Inspiration

The goal of the inspirational speech is to stir positive emotions—to cause people to feel excited, uplifted, encouraged. You may need to give inspi-

**At commencement exercises, it is traditional for speeches to be inspirational and upbeat.** *(Owen Franken/Stock, Boston)*

rational speeches at various times in your life. Let us say, for example, that you are manager of an office or department, and you give your staff an upbeat, "you-can-do-it" speech to get them fired up to do good work. Or let us say you coach a children's softball team and you give the boys and girls a "pep talk" before a game to make them feel confident that they can win.

The inspirational speech is similar to the persuasive speech, with the two purposes often overlapping. The main difference is that in the inspirational speech, you devote yourself almost solely to stirring emotions, while in the persuasive speech, you use emotional appeals as just one of many techniques.

Delivery is an important dimension of inspirational speaking. To get other people fired up, you must be "on fire" yourself. Your facial expression, your posture, your tone of voice—everything about you must convey zest and enthusiasm.

An inspirational speech should tap the emotional power of vivid language. An example of effective language can be found in a speech by Benjamin L. Hooks, executive director of the National Association for the Advancement of Colored People (NAACP), to the annual convention of the group. In the early part of his speech, Hooks lamented the limited educational and job opportunities for many blacks. Then, in a style reminiscent of the oratory of Dr. Martin Luther King, Hooks closed with an emotional plea for the delegates to "struggle on" in the fight to gain equality for blacks in America:

> My brother and sisters . . . I want you to know that the struggle that we will face through the remaining period of the eighties and on through the twenty-first century will not be an easy one. It is fraught with pitfalls and plagued with setbacks, but we as a people have developed a resiliency which has made it possible for us to survive slavery and vicious discrimination. We must never tire or become frustrated by difficulties. We must transform stumbling blocks into stepping stones and march on with the determination that we will make America a better nation . . .
>
> Struggle on: We want more schoolhouses and less jail houses,
> Struggle on: We want more books and less weapons,
> Struggle on: We want more learning and less vice,
> Struggle on: We want more employment and less crime in our communities,
> Struggle on: We want more justice and less vengeance,
> Struggle on: We want more of our children to graduate from high school able to read and write, not more on unemployment lines,
> Struggle on: We want more statesmen and less politicians,
> Struggle on: We want more workers in our ranks and less cynics,
> Struggle on: We want more hope and less dope,
> Struggle on: We want more faith and less despair . . . .[3]

Hooks made effective use of the techniques of *repetition* and *parallel structure* (which we discussed in Chapter 12), causing his speech to grow in power and intensity.

## Summary

While informative and persuasive speeches are the most frequent types, there are speeches when other purposes must be served. When you need to entertain an audience, as in an after-dinner talk, your remarks should be light and diverting; any elements of information or persuasion should be gracefully interwoven into the fabric of entertainment. When you are asked to introduce a speaker, you should convey enthusiasm for the speaker and the topic, and you should give whatever background information is necessary to enhance the speaker's credibility. When you are called upon to "say a few words" in acceptance of an award or promotion, you should thank the people who gave you the honor and acknowledge the help of those who made your success possible. When you give a speech of tribute, you should praise the person, group, institution, or event being honored, avoiding any negativity. When you speak to inspire an audience, you should devote yourself to stirring emotions, using a dynamic delivery to convey your zest and enthusiasm.

## Review Questions

1. Why would an informative speech on a difficult, highly technical subject usually be inappropriate for an after-dinner audience?
2. If you are asked to introduce a speaker, why should you coordinate your remarks with those of the speaker?
3. Name four guidelines for the speech of acceptance.
4. What is the difference between an inspirational speech and a persuasive speech?

# TIPS *for your career*

### Tip 16: Inject Humor—If It Is Appropriate

If you can use humor effectively, it is a good way to keep an audience interested in your speech. It creates a bond of friendship between you and the listeners, and it puts them into a receptive, trusting mood. You should use humor only when it is appropriate; a speech about a solemn subject such as euthanasia would not lend itself to an injection of humor.

One kind of humor is of course the joke, a funny story that depends upon a punch line for its success. I do not recommend that any novice speaker use jokes, for these reasons: (1) jokes usually do not tie in smoothly with the rest of the speech; (2) most speakers (both inexperienced and experienced) cannot tell jokes well; and (3) the audience may have already heard the joke.

I have seen speakers tell a joke that no one laughed at. And I mean *no one*. Maybe the audience had heard the joke before, or maybe it was too early in the morning or too late in the evening. Whatever the reason, a joke that fizzles can be devastating to the speaker's morale. "But it looks so easy on TV," some students say. It looks easy and *is* easy because TV joketellers have advantages that most speakers lack: They have studio audiences that are predisposed to laugh at virtually any joke the comedians tell (your audiences will probably not be *poised* for laughter in this way). They have a supporting cast of gag writers who test the jokes out before they are used. Most important of all, they have years of joke telling experience before they appear on national TV.

You can use other kinds of humor beside jokes. A mildly amusing story, quotation, or observation can be as effective as a side-splitting joke. The best thing about low-key humor is that it's safe. While the success of a joke depends upon the audience laughing immediately after the punch line, the success of a light story or witty observation does not depend on laughter or even smiles. Sometimes the only audience response is an inner delight. In a speech urging his listeners to exercise regularly, student speaker Jerry Cohen began with a humorous quotation:

> The late Robert Maynard Hutchins, president of the University of Chicago, once said, "Whenever I feel like exercising, I lie down until the feeling passes." Is this your attitude toward exercise? Do you think of exercise as an odious chore to be avoided if possible?

Notice that Jerry's quotation was the kind of wry humor that does not depend on belly laughs; also notice that he tied the humor in with the purpose of his speech. This is an example of how you can sneak humor in, so that the audience sees it as part of your speech, not as a "joke." If they laugh or smile, fine; if they don't, no harm has been done. It's still enjoyable and relevant. If you use humor, here are some points to remember.

1. *Humor must always relate to the subject matter.* In other words, never tell an amusing story about a farmer unless your speech is about farming and the story ties in with the rest of the speech.

2. *Never use humor that might be offensive to any person in the audience.* You should avoid humor that is obscene or that ridicules members of any group in society (racial, ethnic, religious, political, gender, etc.). Even if the audience contains no members of the group being ridiculed, you run the risk of alienating listeners who disapprove of such humor.

3. *Never let your face show that you expect laughter or smiles.* Let us say that you cleverly insert a delicious piece of ironic humor into your introduction. After you make your humorous remark, do not stand there with an expectant grin on your face. If no one smiles back or laughs, you will feel very foolish. By the way, if you do fail to get any smiles or laughs, this does not mean that the listeners did not appreciate your humor. As I mentioned previously, some kinds of humor elicit only an inner delight.

4. *If you use jokes, use self-deprecating ones.* Although jokes are inappropriate in classroom speeches and are risky in community addresses (as discussed previously), you may decide someday that you want to tell a joke to your audience. You can minimize the risks if you make *yourself* the target of your humor. Professional speaker Hope Mihalap says, "I always try to start with a line that will get a laugh, usually something about myself (slightly derogatory, of course)."[4] And former Olympic Gold Medalist John Naber says: "I always begin with a cute joke *at my expense*."[5] Poking fun at yourself is fairly safe because you escape the possibility of telling a joke the audience has already heard, and you avoid offending anyone (as long as you don't resort to vulgarity or obscenity).

# Chapter 17

# Speaking in Groups

**Responsibilities of Leaders**

**Responsibilities of Participants**

**The Reflective-Thinking Method**

Define the Problem

Analyze the Problem

Establish Criteria for Evaluating Solutions

Suggest Possible Solutions

Choose the Best Solution

Decide How to Implement the Solution

Decide How to Test the Solution

Sample Discussion

**Team Presentations**

Symposium

Panel Discussion

Small groups do much of the work of our society, at all levels of government, education, business, and industry. For example, NASA (National Aeronautics and Space Administration) uses small task forces to develop space programs. Colleges and universities use committees to set policy and develop new curricula. Businesses use small sales teams to sell their products.

The value of small groups is even recognized by giant corporations. After studying 43 successful American companies for their best-seller *In Search of Excellence,* management consultants Thomas J. Peters and Robert H. Waterman wrote, "Small groups are, quite simply, the basic organizational building blocks of excellent companies." The most effective groups, they say, range from four to ten members.[1]

Here are some of the examples that Peters and Waterman cite:

☐ 3M Corporation has several hundred four- to ten-person "venture teams" that design and develop new products.[2]

☐ Texas Instruments has 9,000 teams "zipping about looking for small productivity improvements."[3]

☐ To solve problems quickly and effectively, many corporations such as General Motors and IBM bypass the chain of command—the formal organizational structure—and instead, form task forces made up of "champions"—a few key employees who are known for their creativity and dedication.[4]

For creativity and problem solving, small groups have obvious advantages over individuals: they provide a pooling of resources, ideas, and labor. Errors can be caught and corrected. Small groups also have advantages over large conglomerations of people: they act with greater quickness and flexibility. In this chapter, we will focus on meetings, the means by which small groups do their collective work. If carried out properly, meetings give group members a chance to discuss ideas, solve problems, reach decisions, resolve differences, and reduce tensions. Meetings provide close eye-to-eye contact with lively interaction between participants.

To perform well in meetings, groups should (1) have a purpose, (2) secure the cooperation of all members, and (3) have effective leadership. Everyone in the meeting should possess a spirit of good will or, to use the term of etiquette expert Letitia Baldrige, good manners. "I have observed," says Baldrige, "that every well-run meeting invariably has a combination of a chairman with good manners and participants with good manners—it is like an excellent symphony conductor who needs an excellent corps of musicians in order to make truly beautiful music."[5]

Let us take a closer look at the roles of the leader and the participants.

**The Society of Seamen's Children on Staten Island, New York, provides services for families and children of sailors. Much of the work of American society is done in small groups such as this.** *(Catherine Ursillo/ Photo Researchers)*

# Responsibilities of Leaders

Meg Slubiski, head of the sales force at a car dealership, called a meeting of salespersons to try to work out a problem that was causing hard feelings among the staff: whenever a potential customer walked into the automobile showroom, the salespersons would elbow each other aside in an effort to be the one to greet the person (and possibly make a sale). Patiently, Meg listened to the complaints and accusations, and then shepherded the group toward a compromise that everyone seemed happy with: the staff would use a rotating system for greeting potential customers so that each salesperson got the same number of contacts as everyone else.

Meg demonstrated the importance of firm, but friendly leadership in small groups. When you are the leader of a small group, here are some guidelines for planning and conducting a meeting.

1. *Establish an agenda.* An agenda is a list of items that need to be covered in a meeting. When there is no agenda, groups often fail to work efficiently and productively. They waste time pursuing irrelevant matters,

or they spend all their time and energy on minor items and never get around to the major issues. When you are leader of a group, decide in advance what issues should be discussed (be sure to consult the participants on what topics they want to discuss), then write out an agenda, ranking items from most important to least important. Be sure the group members receive the agenda well before the meeting so that they can prepare themselves. At the beginning of the meeting, ask the participants if they want to add items to the agenda or make alterations in the order of priorities. If circumstances prevent you from preparing an agenda in advance, take a few moments at the beginning of the meeting to establish the agenda, asking group members for their suggestions and then rank-ordering the items on a chalkboard for everyone to see. Though setting the agenda may take a few minutes, it is time well spent, for it will help the group stick to the relevant and important issues. If your group is working against a deadline, you may need to establish a timetable for the agenda—for example, allotting 10 minutes for discussion of Item A, 15 minutes for Item B, and so on. (A special kind of agenda, using the reflective-thinking method, will be discussed in detail later in this chapter.)

2. *Start the meeting on time.* If some group members fail to arrive at the designated time, you may be tempted to delay the start of the meeting in hopes that they will soon appear. This is a mistake for two reasons: (1) You are being discourteous to the group members who were punctual; their time is valuable and should not be wasted. (2) You are setting a bad precedent for future meetings. If the people who arrived on time see you wait for latecomers, they will have no incentive to show up on time for the next meeting; thus, as time goes by, they will arrive later and later for meetings.

3. *Set a friendly tone.* Start off with a friendly, upbeat welcome. If some of the participants do not know each other, introduce all the members of the group, one at a time, or let them introduce themselves.

4. *Make sure that minutes are kept.* If the group is not a formal committee with a previously designated secretary, the leader should appoint someone to take notes and later prepare minutes of the meeting. Minutes are a record of what was discussed and accomplished during a meeting. They should be circulated to group members as soon after the meeting as possible. While minutes are obviously valuable for absentees who need to get caught up on events, they are also important for people who were present—to remind them of their responsibilities for the next meeting. Minutes should consist of five elements: (1) agenda item, (2) decision reached, (3) action required, (4) person(s) responsible for taking action,

and (5) target date for completion of action.[6] At each meeting, the minutes of the previous session should be briefly reviewed to make sure that tasks have been completed.

5. *Make sure all participants know the purpose of the meeting and the scope of the group's power.* Even if you have circulated an agenda in advance, you should still review the purpose of the meeting. Some of the participants may have failed to read the agenda carefully or correctly, while others may have forgotten what it contained. Refresh their memories; make sure everyone knows the task that the group faces. Also review the scope of the group's power, so that participants do not labor under false ideas of what the group can or cannot do. Group members need to know the following: Does the group have the power to make a decision, or is it being asked simply to recommend a decision? Will the group reach a decision and then carry it out, or will someone else actually carry out the decision? Is the group's decision subject to revision by a higher authority?

6. *Encourage participation.* In some groups, especially ones led by a boss, group members say nothing while the leader does all the talking. Such groups are little more than rubber stamps for whatever the leader wants—the meetings are really a waste of time. When you are a leader, do not be dictatorial or directive. Guide the discussion, but do not dominate it. Encourage the free flow of ideas from all members of the group. This is more than a mere matter of politeness: group-created decisions are usually better than leader-dictated decisions because people tend to support what they have helped create. If, for example, you are the manager of five employees and you call them together and dictate a policy, there may be grumbling behind your back and passive resistance in implementing the policy, but if you call your people together and spend a few hours letting *them* hammer out the same policy, they will feel a strong commitment to it—now it is *their* idea, *their* policy.

7. *Guide the discussion.* As leader, you should move the discussion along from point to point on the agenda. If participants go off on tangents, you should diplomatically pull them back to the task at hand. (You can say something like, "That's an interesting point, but let's stick to our agenda; if we have any time left over, we can come back to your idea.") If a participant talks too much, not giving others a chance to speak, you should gently but firmly intervene. (You can say, for example, "Good point; if I may interrupt, I would like to hear how the others are reacting to what you just said.") If a participant is shy or unusually quiet, you can try to elicit comments. Do not ask a "yes or no" question such as, "Do you have anything you would like to say?" Instead, ask open-ended ques-

tions such as, "How do you think we can solve this problem?" If the person says, "I don't know," do not press any further. Thus you avoid badgering or embarrassing the person. It may be that he or she truly has no particular contribution to make on the issue. If participants become hostile toward each other, try to mediate by finding common ground and by helping the participants stick to issues rather than resorting to personal attacks.

8. *Discourage side conversations.* Meetings can be marred if two or more people break off from the group's activities and hold a private discussion. This, of course, is rude to the other group members, and it prevents the group from staying together as a unified team. As leader, you should gently shepherd the wayward group back into the fold; for example, if two members are carrying on a private conversation, you can say, "It looks as if you've come up with something interesting. Could you share it with the group?" This technique usually has one of two results: the offenders share their comments with the group, or (if they have been chatting about unrelated matters) they grin sheepishly, decline to reveal the content of their discussion, and return to participation with the group.

9. *Summarize periodically.* Since you are playing the role of guide, you should occasionally let the participants know where they are on their journey toward the group's goal. Summarize what has been accomplished, and indicate work that still needs to be done. For example: "Let's see where we stand. We have decided that Item A and Item B should be recommended to the board of directors. But we still need to tackle Problem C . . . ." Keep your summaries brief—just say enough to help the participants gain their bearings.

10. *Keep meetings short.* Most small-group meetings should last no longer than one hour. Anything longer will cause fatigue and a drop-off in the group's effectiveness. If one hour is not enough time to handle the group's work, a series of one-hour meetings should be set up. If, for some reason, the group is obliged to conduct all of its business in one day or during an afternoon, one-hour sessions should be interspersed with coffee or "stretch" breaks.

11. *End the meeting.* At the end of a meeting, summarize what the group has accomplished, make sure that all participants know their assignments for the next meeting, and express appreciation for the work that the group has done.

12. *Follow up.* After the meeting, make sure that the minutes are written and distributed to each participant and that all participants carry out their assignments.

# Responsibilities of Participants

In one community, a committee was formed to plan and finance the construction of a new swimming pool for a YMCA. The committee included a cross-section of community talent—for example, a financier who was experienced at fund-raising, an engineer who was knowledgeable about pool construction, and a swimming instructor who knew what kind of pool the public wanted. When the committee met, it was effective in overseeing the design and construction of an excellent pool because the participants were able to share their ideas and expertise.

This story illustrates that while leadership of a small group is important, the participants themselves play a vital role. When you are a participant in a small group, here are some guidelines to keep in mind.

1. *Prepare for every meeting.* Find out in advance what is going to be discussed at the meeting and then decide what contributions you can make. Jot down items that you think need to be discussed. Do whatever research, background reading, and interviewing that might be necessary to make you well-informed or to bolster your position on an issue. If documentation is likely to be requested for some of your data, bring notes to the meeting so that you can cite your sources.

2. *Arrive on time.* Meetings cannot work effectively if some participants straggle in late. Make sure that you arrive at the appointed time. Even better, arrive a bit early; this will give you a chance to chat informally with your fellow participants and create a mood of friendliness.

3. *Participate in group discussions.* Do not sit back and let others carry on the work of the group. Throw yourself wholeheartedly into the discussion, contributing your ideas and opinions. This does not necessarily mean giving a brief speech or saying something brilliant. You can enter the discussion by asking questions, especially when points need to be clarified, by expressing support for ideas that you like, and by paraphrasing other members' ideas to determine if you are understanding them correctly.

4. *If possible, speak up early in the meeting.* If you have the opportunity to make a contribution to the group, do so at the earliest possible time. This serves as an "icebreaker," causing you to draw closer (psychologically) to the other members of the group and making you more attentive to the discussion. The longer you wait to speak, the harder it becomes to enter the discussion. This does not mean that you should blurt out the first thing that pops into your head; you should never speak impulsively or aimlessly. But when a chance to make a genuine contribution arises, take advantage of it.

5. *Exhibit positive nonverbal behavior.* Nonverbal cues, such as clothes, facial expression, posture, and eye contact, speak as powerfully as words. In a meeting, you should avoid slumping in your chair because that conveys boredom, negativity, or lack of confidence. Instead, sit in an alert but relaxed posture that shows you are both comfortable and confident. Whether you are playing the role of speaker or listener, look people in the eye. Your facial expression should convey openness and friendliness.

6. *Do not treat your own ideas as beyond criticism.* Some group members act as if criticism of their ideas is an attack upon themselves, so they fight ferociously to defend their position. What they are really defending is not their ideas, but their ego. Unfortunately when people are busy defending their ego, they refuse to listen to what their critics are saying, they refuse to budge an inch from their position, and they sometimes prevent a group from making progress. When you present your ideas to a group, you should recognize that no human is perfect and that a wise and mature person readily admits the possibility of being in error.

7. *Do not monopolize the meeting.* Give others a fair chance to state their views.

8. *Stick to the point.* A common problem in meetings is for participants to stray off the subject and get bogged down in irrelevant matters. Before speaking, ask yourself if what you plan to say is truly related to the purpose of the meeting.

9. *Treat all group members fairly.* All too often, some group members form coalitions with people who already agree with them and then freeze out the rest of the group (by not listening carefully to what they say, by not giving them sufficient eye contact, by not soliciting and respecting their ideas). Aside from being rude, this cold-shoulder treatment cripples the effectiveness of the group; members who feel frozen out tend to contribute little. You should treat each person in the group with dignity and respect, offering a friendly ear and an open mind to his or her ideas.

10. *Express dissenting views.* Some group members never raise objections or express views contrary to the majority. There are a number of reasons for this timidity: fear of being ridiculed, fear of antagonizing others, or fear of displeasing the leader (especially if he or she is the person's boss). When you disagree with an idea being discussed by the group, it is a mistake to remain silent. Group decisions that are made in a mood of pseudo-unanimity are often poor decisions.

11. *Avoid personal attacks.* Conflict—a clash of ideas or opinions—is healthy in group discussion. It helps the group see weaknesses in plans, to separate the workable from the unworkable. While conflict is desirable,

it should always be centered on *issues*, not on personalities. In other words, disagree without being disagreeable.

12. *Whenever possible, express objections in the form of a question.* While you should certainly speak up when you think an idea is poor, there is a diplomatic way to offer criticism. If you blurt out, "Oh no, that will never work," you might deflate the person who suggested the idea, and even provoke hostility. A better approach is to ask a question such as: "How could we make this work?" As the group members try to answer the question, there is a spirit of cooperation, and often they come to the conclusion you hoped they would reach—the idea *is* unworkable—without hostility or bad feelings.

13. *Do not work from a hidden agenda.* A group's work can be sabotaged if some members pretend to be committed to the goals of the group, but in reality have hidden agendas—that is, unannounced private goals that conflict with the group's goals. Examples of hidden agendas are a desire to gain personal power over other participants, a striving to impress a superior, and a secret wish to see the group fail.

14. *Do not carry on private conversations.* Group unity can be undermined if two or three participants engage in a whispered conversation, which is rude and insulting to the speaker; it is also damaging to the work of the group since it cuts off teamwork and a spirit of cooperation.

# The Reflective-Thinking Method

When a group must solve a problem, one of the most effective techniques is the *reflective-thinking* method derived from the writings of the American philosopher John Dewey.[7] To illustrate the steps of this method, imagine that you and I and several other people are joint owners of a restaurant, and suppose that we have a problem that must be solved: many customers have been complaining about slow service.

## Define the Problem

A group will sputter and falter unless everyone has a clear idea of exactly what the problem is. Sometimes a problem is obvious (for example, what prices to set for each item on the menu at our restaurant). But sometimes a problem is vague; for example, "We need to improve our restaurant." This statement is so vague that it would probably mean different things to each of the owners. To one, it might mean that we need to improve the food; to another, it might mean that we need to improve the skills of our waiters and waitresses. One of the best ways to define a problem is to

**When small groups meet, the leader must make sure that all partici-
pants get a fair chance to speak and that the group stays on track in its
discussion.** *(Michael Weisbrot & Family)*

phrase it in the form of a question. In the case of our restaurant's problem,
we could ask, "What steps can be taken to improve the service in our
restaurant?"

## Analyze the Problem

A problem-solving group should scrutinize the problem in order to learn
as much as it can. Some of the questions that should be asked are: What
is the nature of the problem? How severe is the problem? What are the
causes?

   In our restaurant, we need to focus on causes so that we can correct
the situation. Is slow service caused by the waiters and waitresses? If so,
is it because they are lazy or inefficient, or is it because they are forced
to serve too many tables? Or can the slow service be blamed solely on the
kitchen staff? Are *they* the lazy or inefficient ones? Are *they* understaffed?
At this point, if we cannot get a clear picture of the cause of the problem,
we need to stop the problem-solving process and get answers to these

questions before continuing. Let us assume that we ascertain the cause of the problem: the kitchen staff is slow in getting items into the hands of our waiters and waitresses.

## Establish Criteria for Evaluating Solutions

Suppose that you are asked by a friend to pick up "a good movie" for her while you are visiting a videotape store. What should you do? Grab the first videocassette you see? No, before going to the shop, you would need to find out your friend's tastes—her criteria for what constitutes a good movie. For example, does she enjoy comedy? If so, does she lean toward subtle British humor or slapstick Hollywood farces? Armed with the answers to such questions, you can choose a movie likely to appeal to her.

The same strategy works well for problem-solving groups. Instead of rushing to find a solution, a group should first decide the criteria—the standards or conditions—by which to judge a solution. To establish criteria, a group should ask: What must a proposed solution do? What must it avoid? What restrictions of time, money, and space must be considered? If there are more than one criteria, they should be rank-ordered in terms of importance.

In our restaurant example, the most obvious solution might be to hire more cooks, but what if we simply cannot afford to hire any new people? If at this stage we establish criteria, we can avoid pursuing solutions that are ultimately impossible. For our restaurant's problem, let us set the following standards, rank-ordered from most important to least important: (1) Orders need to be taken to tables 10 minutes quicker than at present; (2) We must take action immediately; (3) We must not lower the quality of food; and (4) Whatever solution we come up with must cost no more than $1,000.

## Suggest Possible Solutions

It is important for groups to show patience and avoid leaping at the first solution that comes along. Getting out on the table a wide variety of possible solutions can enhance the chances of the group arriving at a sound decision. One of the best techniques for generating these potential solutions is *brainstorming*, wherein participants rapidly throw out ideas and the group leader writes them on a chalkboard. For brainstorming to work effectively, there should be an atmosphere of total acceptance—no one analyzes, judges, ridicules, or rejects any of the ideas. Let us say that for our restaurant, we generate a dozen potential solutions, ranging from "use frozen (instead of fresh) foods" to "hire an efficiency consultant to teach the kitchen staff to work faster."

## Choose the Best Solution

After the brainstorming session, a group should analyze, weigh, and discuss the various ideas in order to come up with the best solution (or solutions). Each possibility should be measured against the criteria previously established. In our restaurant example, let us say that the idea of using frozen foods is examined. Since the chef tells us that frozen food is not as tasty as fresh, we would now reject the idea because it would violate our criterion about not compromising the quality of our food. The idea about hiring an efficiency expert would be rejected because one of our criteria stipulates immediate action. Let's say that another idea is to buy two more microwave ovens to speed up the kitchen's work. The two ovens would cost a total of $750; this would permit us to meet the under $1,000 requirement, and the chef assures us that two ovens would help get the food out to the customers quickly, without lowering the quality. So we choose this option.

## Decide How to Implement the Solution

A solution may sound fine at the talking stage, but can it be realistically implemented? Our next step is to decide how to put the solution into action. In our restaurant's case, we authorize our bookkeeper to write the necessary check and we verify that a certain restaurant-supply store can send us the ovens within 24 hours.

## Decide How to Test the Solution

Many groups hammer out a solution to a problem, but never follow it up to determine whether their solution really solved the problem. The last task of the problem-solving group is to decide how to find out if the solution, when put into effect, really works. In our restaurant's case, we can create customer response cards to be placed at each table. The customers are asked to rate, among other things, whether the service was fast enough to suit them. We decide that if 99 percent of our customers express satisfaction with the service, then our solution has indeed worked. (We aim for 99 percent rather than 100 percent because we know from our studies of restaurant management that there is always an irritable 1 percent of customers who are never happy with the service—no matter how fast it may be.)

## Sample Discussion

A group of students was assigned to use the reflective-thinking method to suggest solutions to a troubling social problem in America: the plight of mentally ill patients who roam the streets of many American cities without adequate food, shelter, or medical treatment. Here is a summary of the group's work:

*Define the Problem:* The first matter the group discussed was, "Is there really a problem?" If mentally ill people are happy roaming the streets rather than being confined to institutions, isn't this their right in a free society? After doing research on this issue, the group agreed that while some mentally ill persons adapt to society, thousands of them are too disoriented to cope effectively with life on the streets. They go hungry, their psychiatric problems worsen, they are exploited by others, and some even freeze to death.

After concluding that a just and humane society should intervene and care for these people, the group defined the problem by phrasing it in the form of a question, "What should be done with the mentally ill who live on the streets?"

*Analyze the Problem:* Group members carried out research to answer two key questions:

*How severe is the problem?* One student quoted an American Psychiatric Association's report that between 250,000 and 3 million Americans are homeless, with as many as 50 percent suffering from serious mental disorders, such as schizophrenia. From this, the group concluded that the problem is quite severe.

*What are the causes of the problem?* The students discovered that thousands of patients once confined to the back wards of state mental institutions have been released because (1) powerful antipsychotic drugs are available to control patients' hallucinations, (2) it is believed by many mental health experts that the mentally ill fare better in their own communities than in institutions, and (3) many states cut back on mental health services to save money.

*Establish Criteria for Evaluating Solutions:* The group decided that a solution would be unacceptable unless it met two criteria: (1) It must provide food, shelter, and psychiatric treatment, and (2) it must preserve the dignity and self-respect of the patients.

*Suggest Possible Solutions:* The group held a brainstorming session, and came up with 14 potential solutions, ranging from "return the patients to state hospitals" to "set up more soup kitchens and hostels for the homeless."

| | |
|---|---|
| *Choose the Best Solution:* | Using its two criteria as yardsticks, the group rejected many solutions. For example, the idea of returning patients to large, understaffed state hospitals was rejected because it could mean a loss of dignity and self-respect. Finally, the group decided that the best solution would be to commit the patients to "group homes" in residential settings. The first criterion would be met by requiring the homes to provide psychiatric treatment in addition to basic amenities. The second criterion would be met by requiring the homes to treat the patients as full-fledged members of the community. |
| *Decide How to Implement the Solution:* | To put the solution into action, the group recommended that state legislatures pass laws mandating quality psychiatric care for the mentally ill in group homes. Each home would be assigned a psychiatrist to care for the patients' mental disorders and a social worker to help the patients integrate themselves into the mainstream of society. To make sure that the patients receive quality care in a dignified setting, the group recommended that a state board of examiners be formed to monitor the homes and revoke the charters of any homes that fail to provide adequate care. |
| *Decide How to Test the Solution:* | To determine whether the plan truly solved the problem, the group recommended that each state create a review panel, made up of mental health professionals, to assess the group homes after one year of operation by inspecting facilities, interviewing patients, and conducting public hearings. The panel could then decide whether the plan had been successful. |

# Team Presentations

While most group work is done in private, there are some occasions when you may act as part of a team in making a presentation to an audience. Two of the most popular forms of team presentations are the symposium and the panel discussion.

## *Symposium*

A symposium is a series of brief speeches on a common topic, each usually discussing a different aspect of the topic. In some cases, the speakers might be members of a problem-solving group who present their ideas and conclusions to a larger group. A symposium usually features a question-and-answer period after the speeches, and sometimes includes a panel discussion.

When you prepare and deliver a speech as part of a symposium, you should use the same skills and techniques of solo speechmaking, but you should work in advance with other members of your team to avoid duplication of material.

# Panel Discussion

A panel is usually made up of three to eight members and is led by a moderator. Though there are many different methods of conducting panel discussions, a common pattern is to have the panelists give a brief opening statement, then permit them to discuss the subject among themselves, with the moderator serving as referee. At the end of the discussion, the audience is usually invited to ask questions.

Because of the variety of viewpoints and the liveliness of informed conversation, audiences enjoy a good panel discussion.

## Guidelines for the Moderator

Much of the success (or failure) of a panel discussion is determined by the moderator. He or she must keep the discussion moving along smoothly, restrain the long-winded or domineering panelist from hogging the show, draw out the reticent panelist, and field questions from the audience. Here are some guidelines to follow when you are a moderator.

1. *Arrange the setting.* You and the panelists can be seated at a table facing the audience. Or, even better, you can be seated in a semicircle so that all members of the panel can see each other, while still remaining visible to the audience. A large name card should be placed in front of each panelist so that the audience will know the participants' names.

2. *Brief panel members in advance.* Well before the meeting, give panel members clear instructions on exactly what they are expected to cover in their opening remarks. Are they supposed to argue the "pro" or "con" position? Are they supposed to speak on only one aspect of the topic? (For information-giving discussions, you may want to assign each panel member a subtopic, according to his or her area of expertise, so that there is not much overlap among speakers.) Instruct the panelists not to bring and read written statements because this would kill the spontaneity that is desired in a panel discussion, but tell them that they are free to bring notes.

3. *Before the meeting, prepare a list of items that you think should be discussed.* By so doing, you can make sure that no important issues are inadvertently omitted. If the discussion begins to lag or go off into irrelevancies, you will then have meaningful questions at your fingertips.

4. *Prepare and deliver an introduction.* At the beginning of the program, introduce the topic and the speakers, and explain the ground rules for the discussion; be sure to let listeners know if and when they will be permitted to ask questions.

5. *Moderate the discussion.* Give each panelist a chance to make opening statements (within the time constraints previously announced) and then encourage the panelists to question each other or comment upon each other's remarks. Be neutral in the discussion but be prepared to ask questions if there is an awkward lull or if a panelist says something confusing or leaves out important information. Listen carefully to what each panelist says so that you do not embarrass yourself by asking questions on subjects that have already been discussed.

6. *Maintain friendly, but firm control.* Do not let a panelist lead everyone off on a tangent that is far afield of the speech topic. During the question-and-answer session, do not let a member of the audience make a long-winded speech; interrupt kindly but firmly and say, "We need to give other people a chance to ask questions." If a panelist exceeds the time limit for opening remarks or monopolizes the discussion time, gently break in and say, "I'm sorry to interrupt, but let's hear from other members of the panel on their ideas concerning . . . ." If a panelist is reticent and says very little, draw him or her out with specific, pertinent questions.

7. *Be respectful of all panelists, including those with whom you disagree.* Think of yourself not as a district attorney who must interrogate and skewer criminal defendants, but as a gracious host or hostess who stimulates guests to engage in lively conversation.

8. *Ask open-ended questions, ones that require elaboration, rather than questions that elicit a simple "yes" or "no."* For example, "How can we make sure our homes are safe from burglars?" rather than "Is burglary on the increase in our community?"

9. *End the program at the agreed-upon time.* Wrap up the proceedings on time and in a prearranged way, perhaps by letting each panelist summarize briefly his or her position. Another option is for you to summarize the key points made during the discussion (to do this, you would need to take notes throughout the program). Thank the panelists and the audience for their participation. If some members of the audience are still interested in continuing the discussion, you may want to invite them to talk to the panelists individually after the program is over.

## Guidelines for Panelists

If you are a member of a panel, here are some guidelines to keep in mind.

1. *Prepare for the discussion in the same way you prepare for a speech.* Find out all that you can about the audience and the occasion: What particular aspect of the topic are you expected to speak on? Who are the other panelists and what will they cover? Will there be questions from the audience? What are the time constraints?

2. *Prepare notes for the panel, but not a written statement.* If you write out your remarks, you may be tempted to read them and thereby spoil the spontaneity that is desired in a panel discussion. In addition to notes, you may want to bring supporting data (such as bibliographical sources or statistics) to draw from in case you are asked for substantiation of a point.

3. *Respect the time limits set by the moderator.* If, for example, you are asked to keep your opening remarks under two minutes, be careful to do so.

4. *In the give-and-take of the discussion, be brief.* If the other panelists or listeners want to hear more from you, they will ask.

5. *Stay on the subject.* Resist the temptation to ramble off into extraneous matters.

6. *Be respectful and considerate of your fellow panelists.* Do not squelch them with sarcasm, ridicule, or an overbearing attitude. Do not upstage them by trying to be the one to answer all the questions from the audience.

7. *Listen carefully to the comments of other panelists and members of the audience.* If any of them disagree with you, try to understand and appreciate their position instead of hastily launching a counterattack. Then be prepared to follow the next guideline.

8. *Be willing to alter your position.* If you listen with an open mind, you may see merit in others' views, and you may decide that you need to modify your original position. Though such a shift may seem like an embarrassing loss of face, it actually causes the audience to have greater respect for you. It shows you are a person who possesses intellectual courage, flexibility, and integrity.

## Summary

Small groups are important elements in business and professional life, and much of the work of small groups is done in meetings. To lead a meeting, you should establish an agenda and make sure that it is followed; you should encourage all members to participate in group discussions, and you should guide the discussion to make sure that it stays on the subject. When you are a participant in a small-group meeting, you should enter the discussion with a positive attitude and an open mind.

One of the most effective agendas for problem solving is known as the reflective-thinking method. It involves seven steps: defining the problem; analyzing it; establishing criteria for evaluating solutions; suggesting possible solutions; choosing the best solution; deciding how to implement the solution; and deciding how to test the solution.

Sometimes groups appear in public to discuss or debate an issue. Two popular formats for team presentations are the symposium (a series of brief speeches on a common topic) and the panel discussion (an informal presentation involving a moderator and panelists).

## Review Questions

1. Why is an agenda necessary for a meeting?
2. Why should a participant speak up, if possible, early in a meeting?
3. If you disagree with what everyone else in the group is saying, what should you do?
4. What is the best way to express objections to an idea?
5. What are the seven steps of the reflective-thinking method?
6. What are the duties of the moderator in a panel discussion?

# TIPS *for your career*

### Tip 17: Strive to Improve Your Communication Skills Throughout Your Career

If you watch professional football on television, you have probably seen Dr. Jim Tunney, a National Football League referee, who has officiated at three Super Bowls. Dr. Tunney, formerly a superintendent of schools in Southern California, is also a leading professional speaker, giving motivational talks to business and professional groups throughout America. When I asked Dr. Tunney to explain his success as a speaker, he said that one of the main factors is "*always* trying to improve, watching other speakers, constantly searching for new ideas, new materials." One of the biggest mistakes some speakers make, Dr. Tunney says, is failing to develop and sharpen their skills. "They just do what comes easiest instead of working to improve."[8]

How can you continue to improve your speaking skills? Here are some suggestions.

1. *Get a lot of practice in front of real audiences.* Bob Murphey, a humorist

who was named by *Texas Monthly* magazine as Texas' Best "Good Ole Boy," advises novice speakers to "get out and speak. Speak to the civic clubs, the PTA, the dog lovers' society, the farm bureau, the garden clubs, or any group of as many as three people who will sit still long enough to listen to you. There [is] no substitute for getting up and speaking. Speaking to a mirror or in the privacy of your living room won't hack it."[9] An excellent place to practice is in a Toastmasters club, where your speaking skills will be critiqued in a friendly, supportive atmosphere. For the name and phone number of the club nearest you, write: Toastmasters International, P.O. Box 10400, Santa Ana, California 92711. You may also want to have yourself videotaped while giving a speech and then analyze the tape to spot areas in which you need to improve.

*2. Read books and articles on public speaking.* Reading the advice of other speakers is a good way to garner new ideas and to sharpen your skills. Here are a few good sources.

- ☐ Toastmasters magazine, a monthly publication of Toastmasters International, features good tips for speakers. You do not have to be a member of a Toastmasters club to subscribe. For a sample copy and subscription information, write to the address above.

- ☐ *Decker Communications Report* and *Communication Briefings* are both monthly newsletters on all aspects of communication, with special emphasis on business and professional life. For sample copies and subscription information, write to *Decker Communications Report,* 607 N. Sherman Ave., Madison, Wisconsin 53704, and *Communication Briefings,* P.O. Box 587, Glassboro, New Jersey 08028.

- ☐ *Public Speaking for Private People,* by Art Linkletter (Indianapolis: Bobbs-Merrill, 1980). A seasoned professional shares some of his secrets of the platform.

- ☐ *The Overnight Guide to Public Speaking,* by Ed Wohlmuth (Philadelphia: Running Press, 1983). Snappy, a delight to read.

- ☐ *Speak Easy,* by Sandy Linver (New York: Summit Books, 1978). A wise and friendly guide to handling all kinds of communication problems.

# Notes

## Chapter 1

1. "A Spunky Tycoon Turned Superstar," *Time* Magazine, April 1, 1985, p. 33.

2. *Ibid.*

3. Barbara A. Magill, Roger P. Murphy, and Lilian O. Feinberg, "Industrial Administration Survey Shows Need for Communication Study," *American Business Communication Association Bulletin* (1975), 31–33.

4. Teresa L. Thompson, "The Invisible Helping Hand: The Role of Communication in the Health and Social Service Professions," *Communication Quarterly* 32 (Spring, 1984), 148–163; Thomas E. Harris and T. Dean Thomlison, "Career-Bound Communication Education: A Needs Analysis," *Central States Speech Journal* 34 (Winter, 1983), 260–267.

5. Garda W. Bowman, "What Helps or Harms Promotability?" *Harvard Business Review* (January-February, 1964), 14; Edward Foster, *et al.*, *A Market Study for the College of Business Administration, University of Minnesota, Twin Cities* (Minneapolis: College of Business Administration, University of Minnesota, 1978); *Instruction in Communication at Colorado State University* (Fort Collins, Co.: College of Engineering, Colorado State University, 1979).

6. William R. Kimel and Melford E. Monsees, "Engineering Graduates: How Good Are They?" *Engineering Education* (November, 1979), 210–212.

7. *Ibid.*, p. 211.

8. Edward Foster, op. cit.

9. Frank S. Endicott, *The Endicott Report: Trends in the Employment of College and University Graduates in Business and Industry 1980* (Evanston, Il.: Placement Center, Northwestern University, 1980).

10. Stewart L. Tubbs and K. J. Gritzmacher, "Supervisory Communication as a Contributor to Organizational Success," paper presented at the annual convention of the Speech Communication Association (Minneapolis, Minn., November, 1978), p. 6.

11. Jack Valenti, *Speak up with Confidence* (New York: William Morrow, 1982), 99.

12. John F. Kikoski, "Communication: Understanding It, Improving It," *Personnel Journal* 59 (February, 1980), 126–131.

13. David W. Richardson, professional speaker (see Acknowledgments), in reply to author's survey, November, 1984.

14. Nido R. Qubein, *Communicate Like a Pro* (Englewood Cliffs, N.J.: Prentice-Hall, 1983), p. 67.

15. James "Doc" Blakely, professional speaker (see Acknowledgments), in audiotape, "Anatomy of a Bomb, Analysis of Success," copyright 1983 by Blakely.

16. Michael McGuire, "The Ethics of Rhetoric: The Morality of Knowledge," *Southern Speech Communication Journal* 45 (Winter, 1980), 133–149.

17. Philip D. Steffen, professional speaker (see Acknowledgments), in response to author's survey, November, 1984.

18. *Ibid.*

19. Roy Fenstermaker, professional speaker (see Acknowledgments), in response to author's survey, November, 1984.

20. Arnold "Nick" Carter, professional speaker (see Acknowledgments), in response to author's survey, November, 1984.

21. Hope Mihalap, professional speaker (see Acknowledgments), in response to author's survey, November, 1984.

22. Rosita Perez, professional speaker (see Acknowledgments), in response to author's survey, November, 1984.

## Chapter 2

1. Paul B. Thornton and Paul J. LeVarge, "Avoid Communication Breakdowns," *Toastmaster* magazine, March, 1985, p. 18.

2. D. A. Roach, "State of the Art in Listening Compre-

hension: A Compendium of Measures," paper presented at the International Listening Association Convention, Denver, 1981.

3. Lyman K. Steil, "Your Personal Listening Profile," booklet published by Sperry Corporation, undated, p. 5.

4. Lyman K. Steil, interview in *U.S. News & World Report,* May 26, 1980, p. 65.

5. M. Scott Peck, *The Road Less Traveled* (New York: Simon & Schuster, 1978), p. 128.

6. Jeremy Main, "How to Sell by Listening," *Fortune,* February 4, 1985, p. 52.

7. *Ibid.*, p. 54

8. Gary T. Hunt, *Communication Skills in the Organization* (Englewood Cliffs, N.J.: Prentice-Hall, 1980), p. 63.

9. Robert Bostrom and Carol Bryant, "Factors in the Retention of Information Presented Orally: The Role of Short-Term Listening," *Western Journal of Speech Communication* 44 (Spring, 1980), 137–145.

10. Margaret Lane, "Are You *Really* Listening?" *Reader's Digest,* November, 1980, p. 183.

11. M. Scott Peck, *op. cit.*, p. 122.

12. Ralph G. Nichols, "Listening Is a 10-Part Skill," in James I. Brown, ed., *Efficient Reading* (Boston: D.C. Heath, 1962), p. 101.

13. *Ibid.*, pp. 101–102.

14. Enid S. Waldhart and Robert N. Bostrom, "Note-taking, Listening, and Modes of Retention," paper presented to the International Listening Association, Washington, D.C., 1981; Francis J. Divesta and G. Susan Gray, "Listening and Note Taking II: Immediate and Delayed Recall as Functions of Variations in Thematic Continuity, Note Taking, and Length of Listening Review Intervals," *Journal of Educational Psychology* 64 (1973), 278–287.

15. Wayne Austin Shrope, *Speaking & Listening* (New York: Harcourt Brace Jovanovich, 1970), p. 232.

16. Lyman K. Steil, "Ten Keys to Effective Listening," undated pamphlet published by Sperry Corporation, p. 10.

17. Anonymous speaker quoted by Ronald B. Adler, *Communicating at Work,* 2/e (New York: Random House, 1986), p. 88.

## Chapter 3

1. Cleveland Amory, 'The Loves and Hates of George C. Scott," *Parade* magazine, October 27, 1985, p. 4.

2. George C. Scott, interview in *Playboy,* December 1980, p. 126.

3. "What Are Americans Afraid of?" *The Bruskin Report* 53 (July, 1973); Susan R. Glaser, "Oral Communication Apprehension and Avoidance: The Current Status of Treatment Research," *Communication Education* (October, 1981), 321–341; James C. McCroskey and Lawrence R. Wheeless, *Introduction to Human Communication* (Boston: Allyn & Bacon, 1976).

4. Reggie Jackson, interview during an ABC sports telecast, October 2, 1984.

5. Don Beveridge, professional speaker (see Acknowledgments), in response to author's survey, November, 1984.

6. Elayne Snyder, *Speak for Yourself—with Confidence* (New York: New American Library, 1983), p. 113.

7. I. A. R. Wylie, quoted in Bert E. Bradley, *Fundamentals of Speech Communication: The Credibility of Ideas,* 4th ed. (Dubuque, Ia.: Brown, 1984) p. 385.

8. The term *stage fright* originated in the world of theater, but it is used today to designate the nervousness or fear experienced by a person before or during an appearance in front of any kind of audience. Other terms that are sometimes used to describe this condition are *speech fright, speech anxiety,* and *communication apprehension.*

9. Joel Weldon, professional speaker (see Acknowledgments), in response to author's survey, November, 1984.

10. Joel Weldon, in audiotape, "Elephants Don't Bite: Joel Weldon Live," copyright 1984 by Joel H. Weldon & Associates, Scottsdale, Arizona.

11. Ali MacGraw, quoted in James Link, "Dealing with Stage Fright," *Cosmopolitan,* October 1982, p. 112.

12. James "Doc" Blakely, professional speaker (see Acknowledgments), in response to author's survey, November, 1984.

13. Steve Allen, *How to Make a Speech* (New York: McGraw-Hill, 1986), p. 9.

14. *Ibid.*, p. 9.

15. Philip Zimbardo, *Psychology and Life,* 11th ed. (Glenview, Ill.: Scott, Foresman, 1985), p. 448.

16. Joe W. Boyd, professional speaker (see Acknowledgments), in response to author's survey, November, 1984.

17. "Tarantula from Cabin Creek," *Time* magazine, February 8, 1960, p. 49.

18. Ali MacGraw, quoted in James Link, *op. cit.*, p. 112.

19. Hugh Downs, quoted in Max D. Isaacson, *How to Conquer the Fear of Public Speaking* (Rockville Centre, N.Y.: Farnsworth Publishing, 1984), pp. 70–71.

20. Theodore Clevenger, Jr. "A Synthesis of Experimental Research in Stage Fright," *Quarterly Journal of Speech* 45 (April, 1959), 135–136.

21. Dick Cavett, as quoted in Steve Allen, *op. cit.*, pp. 9–10.

22. Dr. Henry Heimlich, professional speaker (see Acknowledgments), in reply to author's survey, November, 1984.

23. Danielle Kennedy, professional speaker (see Acknowledgments), in reply in author's survey, November, 1984.

24. Maggie Paley, "Modern Image Signal: Voice," *Vogue,* August 1984, p. 412.

25. Associated Press news dispatch, July 31, 1981.

## Chapter 4

1. Adapted from Sandy Linver, *Speak Easy* (New York: Summit Books, 1978), pp. 42–45.

2. Carl Sagan, *Cosmos* (New York: Random House, 1980), p. 196.

3. Thomas Leech, *How to Prepare, Stage, and Deliver Winning Presentations* (New York: American Management Associations, 1982), p. 38.

4. Karen Carlson and Alan Meyers *Speaking with Confidence* (Glenview, Ill.: Scott, Foresman, 1977), p. 73.

5. Fred Ebel, "Know Your Audience," *Toastmaster* magazine, June, 1985, p. 20.

6. Leech, *op. cit.*, pp. 37–38.

7. Paul Gillin, "Sparse Attendance May Turn out to Be the Kiss of Dearth [*sic*] for Softcon Shows," *PC Week*, April 9, 1985, p. 18.

8. John Naber, professional speaker (see Acknowledgments), in reply to author's survey, November, 1984.

9. Earl Nightingale, *Communicate What You Think* (Chicago: Nightingale-Conant Corp., 1976), Audio cassette #11.

10. Rosita Perez, professional speaker (see Acknowledgments), in response to author's survey, November, 1984.

11. *Ibid.*

## Chapter 5

1. Danielle Kennedy, professional speaker (see Acknowledgments), in reply to author's survey, November, 1984.

2. Arnold "Nick" Carter, professional speaker (see Acknowledgments), in response to author's survey, November, 1984.

## Chapter 6

1. Stewart Brand, Editor in chief, *Whole Earth Software Catalog* (New York: Quantum Press/Doubleday, 1984), p. 143.

## Chapter 7

1. Jon M. Shepard, *Sociology*, 2nd ed. (St. Paul, Minn.: West Publishing Company, 1984), p. 164.

2. News article distributed by The Associated Press, July 8, 1984.

3. Report cited by Shepard, *op. cit.*, p. 164.

4. Lewis Thomas, *The Lives of a Cell* (New York: Viking Press, 1974), pp. 11–12.

5. Robert R. Updegraff, "The Conscious Use of the Subconscious Mind," in Barry M. Smith and Betty Hamilton Pryce, *Reading for Power* (Providence, Rhode Island: P.A.R., Inc., 1982), p. 241.

6. Joe W. Boyd, professional speaker (see Acknowledgments), in response to author's survey, November, 1984.

## Chapter 8

1. Anita Taylor, *Speaking in Public* (Englewood Cliffs, N.J.: Prentice-Hall, 1984), p. 174.

2. William J. Seiler, "The Effects of Visual Materials on Attitudes, Credibility, and Retention," *Speech Monographs* 38 (November, 1971), pp. 331–334.

3. George L. Gropper, "Learning from Visuals: Some Behavioral Considerations," *AV Communication Review XI* (Summer, 1963), pp. 75–95.

4. Hower J. Hsia, "On Channel Effectiveness," *AV Communication Review* (Fall, 1968), pp. 248–250.

5. Bill Crider, "Professional Presentations," *PC World* (August, 1984), pp. 248–254.

## Chapter 9

1. Shelly Chaiken and Alice Eagly, "Communication Modality as a Determinant of Message Persuasiveness and Message Comprehensibility," *Journal of Personality and Social Psychology* 34 (1976), pp. 605–614.

2. John P. Houston, *et al.*, *Essentials of Psychology*, 2nd edition. (Orlando, Fla.: Academic Press, 1985), p. 185.

3. Harry Sharp, Jr., and Thomas McClung, "Effect of Organization on the Speaker's Ethos," *Speech Monographs* 33 (1966), pp. 182–184.

## Chapter 10

1. Joel Weldon, in audiotape "Elephants Don't Bite: Joel Weldon Live," copyright 1984 by Joel H. Weldon & Associates, Scottsdale, Arizona.

2. John E. Baird, "The Effects of Speech Summaries upon Audience Comprehension of Expository Speeches of Varying Quality and Complexity," *Central States Speech Journal* 25 (1974), pp. 124–125.

3. Edward L. Friedman, *The Speechmaker's Complete Handbook* (New York: Harper & Row, 1955), p. 16.

4. Martin Luther King, Jr., "I Have a Dream," reproduced in Lewis Copeland and Lawrence W. Lamm, eds., *The World's Great Speeches* (New York: Dover Publications, 1973), p. 754.

5. Introduction and conclusion printed with the permission of Amy McGuffin.

## Chapter 11

1. Stan Lee, *The Best of the Worst* (New York, Harper & Row, 1979), p. 51.

2. Outline, notes, and classroom speech by Laura Garcia used with her permission.

3. "American Preaching: A Dying Art?" *Time* magazine, Dec. 31, 1979, p. 64.

## Chapter 12

1. Julian L. Simon, *How to Start and Operate a Mail-Order Business* (New York: McGraw-Hill, 1981), p. 196.

2. *Ibid.*, p. 216.

3. Thomas Leech, *How to Prepare, Stage, and Deliver Winning Presentations* (New York: American Management Associations, 1982), p. 253.

4. Kenneth McFarland, *Eloquence in Public Speaking* (Englewood Cliffs, N.J.: Prentice-Hall, 1961), p. 186.

5. Roy Fenstermaker, professional speaker, in response to author's survey (see Acknowledgments).

6. Edward T. Thompson, "How to Write Clearly," reprint of advertisement by International Paper Company, undated.

7. "What Do You Mean by That?" *Decker Communications Report*, July, 1985, p. 8.

8. Theodore Solotaroff, quoted in Frederick Crews, *The Random House Handbook*, 4th ed. (New York: Random House, 1984), p. 128.

9. Winston Churchill, as quoted in William Safire and Leonard Safir, *Good Advice* (New York: Times Books, 1982), p. 253.

10. *Ibid.*, p. 294.

11. Dave Johnson, as quoted in *The Nido Qubein Letter: A Confidential Report for Speakers, Trainers, and Consultants,* P.O. Box 6008, High Point, NC, 27262, undated, p. 59.

12. Frederick Crews, *The Random House Handbook*, 4th ed. (New York: Random House, 1984), p. 220.

## Chapter 13

1. R.T. Kingman, quoted in Thomas Leech, *How to Prepare, Stage, and Deliver Winning Presentations* (New York: American Management Associations, 1982), p. 223.

2. Arnold "Nick" Carter, professional speaker (see Acknowledgments), in response to author's survey, November, 1984.

3. Robert Rosenthal and Bella M. DePaulo, "Expectations, Discrepancies, and Courtesies in Nonverbal Communication," *Western Journal of Speech Communication* 43 (Spring, 1979), pp. 76–95.

4. Janet Stone and Jane Bachner, *Speaking Up* (New York: McGraw-Hill, 1977), p. 55.

5. Jack Valenti, *Speak Up with Confidence* (New York: William Morrow, 1982), pp. 74–75.

6. James "Doc" Blakely, professional speaker (see Acknowledgments), in response to author's survey, November, 1984.

7. Danny Cox, professional speaker (see Acknowledgments), in audiotape of entitled "Perils of the Platform," delivered to a National Speakers Association convention and provided in response to author's query, November, 1984.

8. Rosita Perez, professional speaker (see Acknowledgments), in response to author's survey, November, 1984.

9. Sandy Linver, *Speak Easy* (New York: Summit Books, 1978), p. 121.

10. Steve Allen, *How to Make a Speech* (New York: McGraw-Hill, 1986), p. 120.

## Chapter 14

1. This and the other data in the paragraph came from a Gallup Poll, as reported to the U.S. Senate by Senator George McGovern, *The Congressional Record*, Jan. 31, 1979, p. S835.

2. "Harper's Index," *Harper's* magazine (August, 1985), p. 11.

3. "Harper's Index," *Harper's* magazine (May, 1985), p. 13.

4. Dorothy Sarnoff, *Make the Most of Your Best* (New York: Doubleday, 1981), p. 51.

5. The Diagram Group, *Comparisons* (New York: St. Martin's Press, 1980), p. 22.

## Chapter 15

1. Douglas Ehninger, Bruce Gronbeck, and Alan Monroe, *Principles of Speech Communication*, 9th brief ed. (Glenview, Ill.: Scott, Foresman, 1984), pp. 249–259.

2. Lord Chesterfield, quoted by William Safire and Leonard Safir, *Good Advice* (New York: Times Books, 1982), p. 60.

3. Carol Burnett, as filmed in the video program "Drink, Drank, Drunk," KQED-TV, Pittsburgh, 1974.

4. Eliot Aronson, *The Social Animal*, 4th ed. (New York: W. H. Freeman & Co., 1984), p. 87.

5. *Ibid.*

6. Jeanne Fahnestock and Marie Secor, "Teaching Argument: A Theory of Types," *College Composition and Communication* 34 (February, 1983), pp. 20–30.

7. Abraham H. Maslow, *Motivation and Personality* (New York: Harper & Row, 1970).

8. Outline and speech reprinted by permission of Jeffrey Cordell.

## Chapter 16

1. Introduction of Danny Cox on audiotape, "Perils of the Platform," a speech delivered to a convention of the National Speakers Association. Audiotape furnished to the author in response to survey of professional speakers (see Acknowledgments).

2. Congresswoman Olympia J. Snowe, eulogy delivered in the U.S. House of Representatives, October 2, 1985, as printed in the *Congressional Record* (Oct. 2, 1985), p. E4319.

3. Excerpted from Benjamin L. Hook's speech, "Struggle On," in Owen Peterson, *Representative American Speech 1983–1984* (New York: H. W. Wilson, 1984), pp. 90–91.

4. Hope Mihalap, professional speaker (see Acknowledgments), in response to author's query, November, 1984.

5. John Naber, professional speaker (see Acknowledgments), in response to author's query, November, 1984.

## Chapter 17

1. Thomas J. Peters and Robert H. Waterman, Jr., *In Search of Excellence* (New York: Warner Books, 1982), p. 126.

2. *Ibid.*, p. 127.

3. *Ibid.*

4. *Ibid.*

5. Letitia Baldrige, *Complete Guide to Executive Manners* (New York: Rawson Associates, 1985), pp. 191–192.

6. Adapted from Harold Tyler, as quoted in *Decker Communications Report* (March, 1984), p. 1.

7. John Dewey, *How We Think* (Boston: Heath, 1933), pp. 106–115.

8. Dr. Jim Tunney, professional speaker (see Acknowledgments), in response to author's query, November, 1984.

9. Bob Murphey, professional speaker (see Acknowledgments), in response to author's query, November, 1984.

# Appendix A

# Speaking in Front of a Camera

The next time you go for a job interview, you might find yourself sitting in front of a video camera, because more and more businesses are using videotapes to select their employees. "The video interview has some advantages over the face-to-face chat," says *Time* magazine. "The tape can be passed around to several executives for review, crucial parts of the interview can be watched more than once, and if a candidate looks hopeless in the first five minutes, the employer can hit fast forward and move to the next applicant."[1]

Once you have a job, you may appear again on television. Many companies communicate by means of teleconferences—video hookups that enable employees in different parts of the country to talk to each other on-screen (the way national network TV anchors interview people in other cities during news broadcasts). Each year almost one million business meetings are conducted in the United States by means of teleconferences.[2]

A growing number of firms also use videocassettes for in-house communication and training. For example, instead of using a company newsletter, Sonoco Corporation sends news to its plants throughout the world by means of a monthly videocassette that features interviews with executives, human interest stories about workers, safety tips from engineers, and footage of new equipment in operation. "The beauty of a videocassette 'newsletter,'" said one Sonoco official, "is that you can show it to every shift and it builds a team spirit. Our people are thrilled to see themselves and their fellow workers on television."

There is also a chance, of course, that you will appear someday on regular television. You might be asked by a local TV station, for example, to give comments related to your job, your club, your church or synagogue, or your neighborhood. Or you might be asked to participate in a debate over some local controversy.

Since the chances are great that you will appear in front of a video camera at least once in your life, here are some tips to help you.

1. *Find out in advance the production "rules."* The director or interviewer can tell you how the program will be produced. He or she should explain any hand signals that you need to know—such as the signal for "Fifteen seconds left" or "Stop speaking—time is up." In all programs, the camera that has a red light on is the one operating at the moment.

2. *Find out in advance whether the program involves direct or indirect TV.* There

are two distinct types of television programs.[3] *Direct* TV means that you look straight into the camera and speak directly to the viewers. This kind of program is used for news reports and teleconferences. *Indirect* TV means that you converse with an interviewer or with fellow panel members while the TV camera looks on. Indirect TV is the more popular type; it is used for talk shows, interviews, and many documentaries. It is important for you to know which type of TV program you are on so that you can prepare yourself psychologically and so that you can observe the next two guidelines.

3. *For direct TV, always look at the camera.* If you fail to look steadily at the camera in a direct-TV program, you come across to viewers as evasive, untrustworthy, or unprepared. The only exception to this rule would be glancing down at notes occasionally and briefly. In some cases you may want to look at cue cards or a teleprompter placed next to the camera's lens; the virtue of using these aids is that you give the viewer the impression that you are looking directly into the camera (the newscasters you see on TV appear to be talking straight into the camera, but they are actually reading the news from a teleprompter).

4. *For indirect TV, never look at the camera.* One of the reasons for the popularity of indirect TV is that it creates the illusion that the viewer is eavesdropping on a conversation. Thus you must never look into the camera because you might destroy this illusion. Give your full attention to the interviewer or other participants.

5. *If possible, practice in the studio.* Being ushered into a TV studio, with its bright lights, huge pieces of equipment, and bustling technicians, can be unnerving for the person who has never had television experience. If possible, practice sitting and speaking in the studio a few days before the production. If your program will be a *direct* show, practice looking at the camera lens. If you are not able to use the actual studio, you might be able to practice in front of a video camera operated by a friend. If you are able to have a videotape made of your practice session, you should watch yourself in playback to correct any problems in your delivery.

6. *Dress conservatively.* The colors that show up best on TV are the medium hues—pink, green, tan, and gray. Avoid extremely bright colors such as red and extremely dark colors such as black. Because it reflects other colors, white is a poor choice. Also, stay away from fine prints such as checks or plaids—they can cause visual distractions. Likewise, avoid sparkling or noisy jewelry. Both men and women sometimes need make-up—such as powder to cut down on shininess and glare.[4]

7. *Always keep your "real" audience in mind.* Let us say that you take part in a videotaped program about your company's new product. If you are interviewed by a colleague about the product, you real audience is not the colleague but the people who will be watching the program. So while you are ostensibly chatting with your colleague, you need to fashion your remarks to reach your true viewers. What are their needs and interests? How can you entice them into buying the product?

8. *Speak conversationally.* Jack Valenti, president of the Motion Picture Association of America, makes frequent appearances on TV in programs such as the Academy Awards presentations. "The indispensable element of television speaking," he says, "is [to be] conversational, as if you were in a living room talking to a half-dozen people." But how can you be conversational if you are on a *direct* TV program, needing to speak straight into the unblinking gaze of a camera? "I think it useful," says Valenti, "to have someone (preferably two or three people), either friends of yours or studio technicians, stand slightly behind and around the

camera. When your cue comes, and the red light [goes on], talk to them. If they are grouped closely around the camera, you will not be diverting your own gaze too far to the left or right of the lens but will be able to talk to living people rather than that robotlike, sterile companion." If no one is available to stand near the camera, says Valenti, "imagine the camera eye to be a window through which you are speaking to the cameraman on the other side of the lens" or "pretend that someone you trust is sitting in front of you. Speak to that imaginary friend."[5]

9. *Be yourself.* Try to be relaxed and natural. Do not paste a smile on your face and wear it throughout the program; smile only when it is appropriate. Do not feel that you must be an expert on everything discussed. If the interviewer asks a question and you do not know the answer, simply say so.

10. *Project warmth.* How can you project your humanity and warmth via a machine to an audience that you cannot see? The trick is to imagine your audience—the people who will be watching you in their homes or offices. Imagine that you are talking directly to them and that the camera is merely a channel through which you are making contact. Think of the machine as your messenger, your interpreter.

11. *Never assume that the eye of the camera is no longer on you.* During interviews, many people assume that because another person on the show is talking, the camera is no longer focused on them; so they scratch their heads or look around at the TV studio or grin at someone off camera. Meanwhile, the TV camera may be mercilessly televising this rudeness and inattentiveness, the camera operator having broadened the focus to include all participants. You should always assume that you are being televised—not only to avoid making a fool of yourself but also to keep from distracting viewers from the content of the program.

12. *Scale down movement and gestures.* The kind of vigorous movement and powerful gestures that are excellent in a speech to an auditorium of 500 people will make you look like a buffoon if repeated in front of the TV camera. In the language of TV, these actions are "too hot" for the medium. Any gestures you make should be small and low key. Jack Valenti says, "It is fine to express passion in your cause, but without flailing of arms and head. On television, passionate belief is better expressed by a gaze or an emotional inflection of a phrase than by an outthrust fist or jaw."[6] Avoid sudden, swift movements such as crossing your legs rapidly; this can have a jarring effect on the viewers. If you must make such movements, make them very slowly.

13. *Sit in a relaxed, confident posture.* Do not sit in a rigid position that suggests nervousness and anxiety. But do not go to the opposite extreme and slouch in a casual position that suggests boredom and lack of interest. Try to make yourself comfortable, yet alert—they way you would sit if you were carrying on an animated conversation with your best friend.

14. *Use the microphone correctly.* There are two facts about microphones that you need to know: (1) A microphone picks up *all* sounds, not just your words. Avoid coughing, rustling papers, whispering side comments to someone off camera, and brushing against the microphone. (2) A microphone works best if you do not put your mouth right next to it. Some people think that they must almost eat the mike in order to get their words picked up. In reality, today's microphones are engineered so that they work best when you speak at some distance from them. The best advice is simply to speak in your normal voice and forget all about the microphone. (If, however, you are required to hold a microphone, hold it about one foot below your mouth and speak over it, instead of into it.)

15. *Ignore distractions.* When the red light goes on, concentrate all your attention on reaching your audience. Ignore the crew members and the machinery.

16. *Speak briefly.* If you are long-winded, rambling, or tedious, your viewers will tune you out—of their minds or their TV screens. Be brief. Be concise. Do not use ten words when one will do.

NOTES

1. "Video Headhunting," *Time*, January 13, 1986, p. 52.
2. John F. Budd, "Video: A Corporate Communications Tool," *Vital Speeches of the Day*, July 15, 1983, p. 593.
3. "The Media and the Message: The Executive on Television," a supplement to the *Decker Communications Report* (November 1985), p. 2.
4. *Ibid.*, p. 3.
5. Jack Valenti, *Speak Up with Confidence* (New York: Morrow, 1982), p. 101.
6. Valenti, p. 122.

# Appendix B

# Sample Speeches

## Humans to Mars—Why? *James M. Beggs*

Will humans explore Mars within the next 60 years? Yes, predicts James M. Beggs, who was Administrator of NASA (National Aeronautics and Space Administration) when he delivered this speech at the National Air and Space Museum in Washington, D.C., on July 16, 1985. Beggs's speech is primarily *informative* (he tells his listeners what is likely to happen in future space exploration), but it is also *persuasive* (he tries to convince the audience that sending humans to Mars is a sensible idea), and *inspirational* (he challenges the listener to reach for the stars). The speech is reprinted with permission from *Vital Speeches of the Day* (November 1, 1985).

1   Mark Twain once said: "Predictions are very difficult to make, especially when they deal with the future."

2   I won't quarrel with that. But even if the immediate future is uncertain, I have no doubts about the more distant years. So I'll make a prediction. It is that some day human beings will rove the surface of Mars. They will crate up those wonderful Viking machines, return them to earth and send them here to this museum. And future generations of children will come here and stand before not merely one, but three Viking landers, and imagine their journeys and the adventures of the people that replaced them.

3   It is fitting that we should be discussing the question of human journeys to Mars on this tenth anniversary of the Apollo-Soyuz docking in space. That mission was the last to employ a manned Apollo spacecraft.

4   Apollo opened the floodgates of the human imagination to the exciting possibilities of people exploring the universe. Science fiction became fact because we demonstrated conclusively that humans could, indeed, leave earth, land on another world and return safely to their mother planet.

5   Now that we have opened those gates, humankind will never be the same. We will take many more steps on many more worlds before we're through. And one of those worlds, most likely the first we will go to, will be Mars.

6   Indeed, we could be en route to Mars before the middle of the next century. By then, using as our springboard the Space Station and its infrastructure, which will include an interorbital transportation system, we may very well have estab-

lished a manned lunar base. Mars would be the next logical niche for human expansion in the universe.

7    Why Mars? Clearly, Mars will have priority in any manned solar system exploration program because it offers the least severe environment for humans. Due to its atmosphere, its accessible surface, its probable availability of water, and its relatively moderate temperatures—they range from − 120° C to + 20° C— it is the most habitable of all the planets other than earth.

8    Moreover, Mars' resources include materials that could be adapted to support human life, including air, fuels, fertilizers, building materials, and an environment that could grow food.

9    There is a truism, but one that bears repeating, that the universe doesn't care who explores it. It is we who care. And because we do, this epochal step in human exploration to a planet which could become the first self-sufficient home for human beings should be a cooperative international effort.

10    Indeed, given the enormous scope of such an effort, the resources required and its benefits to all mankind, it is tempting to say outright that it should not be done unilaterally. Nevertheless, if the commitment and the resources were forthcoming, nothing would preclude a technologically sophisticated and dedicated nation from going it alone.

11    But whether a manned Mars mission should turn out to be a unilateral or a multilateral undertaking, one thing is clear. To make any sense, such a program must be viewed as a long-term commitment. It cannot focus merely on landing humans on the planet and returning them safely to earth. A Mars landing must also include planning for subsequent sustaining operations. The first Mars explorers probably will not become permanent residents. Rather, they will set the stage for others to come. For others will come—to build, to live, to work, to learn and above all, to explore with their own hands and eyes and tools this exciting and unknown world.

12    Mars has a special meaning as we look out into the universe to plan our next steps in space in the post–Space Station era. It is attainable. It is livable. And its major mysteries remain unsolved. Space-age exploration of the planet has revealed it as a kind of "halfway world," in part like earth and in part like the moon and Mercury. What caused its climate changes? How did its surface features—the great rifts and huge volcanoes—form? Is the whole planet really lifeless? If so, why, given that next to earth, Mars has the best environment to sustain life in the solar system?

13    Mars has a thin atmosphere, climate, weather, and apparently, huge reservoirs of frozen water. Like the moon and Mercury, the ancient, cratered surface of its southern hemisphere is little changed over billions of years. It probably bears evidence of the solar system's formation.

14    In Mars' northern hemisphere, huge volcanic mountains climb as high as 25 kilometers—three times higher than Mt. Everest and up to six times higher than any volcano on earth. Elsewhere on this younger half of Mars, there is a 2800-mile-long canyon stretching three times deeper and seven times longer than the Grand Canyon of the Colorado. In that canyon is probably locked the whole geological history of Mars, and, perhaps, equally important, clues to the history of our own star, the sun.

15    So Mars is geologically interesting. But we can study planetary geology with unmanned spacecraft. Indeed, we have done so on Mars with several unmanned spacecraft. Some have flown by the planet. Others have orbited it. And two have landed on it. We will continue to explore the planet with unmanned spacecraft.

16   In 1990, for example, we expect to launch the Mars Observer, which will do global mapping of Mars for a full Martian year, which is equal to two earth years. We will focus on geoscience and climatology.

17   Later, unmanned spacecraft will surely focus on other science missions—such as the planet's upper atmosphere, its magnetic field, its seismology. And more ambitious unmanned [craft] would, most likely, return Mars samples to earth. We have already demonstrated the ability to learn about other worlds from the moon rocks, from meteorites and from cosmic dust. We can now apply proven techniques to determine the nature and history of Mars from its own rocks.

18   Indeed, by studying Martian rocks and soil in a laboratory right here on earth, we may even settle the question of whether there is or ever has been Martian life.

19   If we can learn so much about Mars with our robot spacecraft, why would we want to go there ourselves? Would we go for the same reason we climb a mountain—because it is there? I doubt it. We would need broader reasons than that. Consider Bernard Shaw's line from "Methuselah": "Some men see things as they are and say, why; I dream things that never were and say, why not."

20   Why not go to Mars to advance the human presence in space?

21   Why not go to Mars to build a permanent gateway to the Asteroid Belt and the other planets?

22   Why not go to Mars to use human judgment, human abilities, and human intelligence to explore an exciting new world? Why not go there to recognize, to describe, to organize, to correlate, and to solve problems as only humans can solve them, using all our experience and skill?

23   On Mars, we could unleash all the richness and subtlety—all the variety and versatility of the human mind and spirit—to plumb the mysteries of who we are, how we came to be and what our destiny might be. So why not go to Mars to better understand ourselves and our earth, our ice ages, the effects of atmospheric changes on our weather and climate? And, in T. S. Eliot's words: "The end of all our exploring will be to arrive where we started and know the place for the first time."

24   Why not go to Mars to stimulate progress in our own space capabilities, to develop new cutting edge technologies—propulsion, life support, habitation, non-terrestrial resource use? These will not only get us to Mars, but also leave their benefits on earth.

25   And, finally, why not go to Mars to build on the framework for international cooperation the Space Station will have begun and, perhaps, a manned lunar base will have continued?

26   An immensely challenging program such as a manned Mars mission could be a strong force for peace in the world. It could redirect creative human brains from the prospects of dealing with armed conflicts to the prospects of planning and carrying out a peaceful, stimulating and ultimately more valuable program of unprecedented scope and magnitude. Ironically, Mars, the primitive symbol of the God of War, could become a powerful instrument for peace.

27   "Humanity is just a work in progress," wrote Tennessee Williams. Indeed we are. And as we evolve and grow, I believe we will demonstrate that there are no limits to our future in the universe.

28   Shakespeare understood that well. And, as usual, he put it best.

> Man is master of his liberty . . .
> There's nothing situate under heaven's eye
> But hath his bound, in earth, in sea and sky.

29   I believe that. There truly are no limits to what we can do if we have faith in the promise of the future.

30   Humans to Mars? Indeed, why not!

31   Thank you very much.

# Two Persuasive Appeals

The following speeches, delivered in the United States House of Representatives by two congresswomen, illustrate a form of public address—the short persuasive appeal—that is popular in such media as television. The first (delivered August 14, 1985) is by Congresswoman Cardiss Collins, a Democrat from Illinois who is treasurer of the Congressional Black Caucus; the second (delivered December 16, 1985) is by Congresswoman Marge Roukema, a Republican from New Jersey. Although both legislators address their remarks to the Speaker of the House, this is merely a traditional formula; they are in reality speaking to the entire House.

One speaker uses the problem-solution pattern, whereas the other uses the motivated sequence. Can you identify which speaker uses which pattern?

# Smokeless Tobacco *Cardiss Collins*

1   Mr. Speaker, the prevalance of alcohol and illicit drugs in our society and their attraction to our children are well known. In recent months, public attention has been drawn to a new fad sweeping the country, one that has invaded our school playgrounds and college campuses. Although an age-old custom, smokeless tobacco, which refers to chewing tobacco and snuff, is the "in thing" among our nation's youth, and its use is increasing at an alarming rate.

2   Over 22 million Americans are said to be using smokeless tobacco. Conservative estimates are that 8 to 10 percent of teenagers and preteens have taken up the pinch, chew, or dip habit. Individual state surveys have found even higher rates of use, up to one-third and higher among students in junior and senior high schools and in college.

3   One reason for this new-found appeal is the increased fear over the dangers of cigarette smoking. Another is the Madison Avenue type advertising by producers of smokeless tobacco which features national sports stars and music celebrities aimed at enticing young, prospective users to "go smokeless."

4   A number of studies have found that smokeless tobacco is not a risk-free product. Oral cancer, dental disease, high blood pressure, and addiction are some of the findings researers have uncovered. And while the volume of scientific information for smokeless tobacco products may not equal that compiled for cigarettes, it has raised a "red flag," prompting a number of major health organizations to voice strong concern and a call for action.

5   Only a handful of states have addressed this problem, however, either through product warning labels or minimum sales age limits. At the federal level, the Federal Trade Commission has punted to the HHS [Health and Human Services], whose office of Smoking and Health is now studying the issue. But because groups like the American Cancer Society, the American Medical Association, the American Dental Association, the National Cancer Institute, and even the U.S. Surgeon General have pronounced smokeless tobacco as detrimental to human health, we cannot afford to hold off action.

6   What is needed in my view is a comprehensive legislative solution. On July

25, I introduced the Smokeless Tobacco Control Act of 1985—H.R. 3078—which will not only make people more aware of the hazards associated with smokeless tobacco, but of the utmost importance, will make it more difficult for young people to get their hands on these potentially deadly products.

7   My three-part proposal will deal with this problem by requiring HHS to develop educational programs on the health risks of smokeless tobacco for use in our school systems and by health agencies. Grants to states will be authorized as an incentive to enlist help from the states in distributing these educational materials and in setting minimum sales age limits. My bill will also reinstate a federal excise tax and will earmark the new revenues for the state grants and for cancer research. Lastly, my bill will prohibit producers of smokeless tobacco from deducting advertising expenses from their income taxes.

8   I believe my legislation will well serve the public health. It will meet the twin goals of making sure that those who wish to use these products are well informed about the inherent dangers, and it will discourage our nation's children from engaging in an activity that might later result in serious health problems.

9   I would urge my colleagues on both sides of the aisle to join me in working for the passage of this important and timely legislation.

[Postscript: Collins's bill was passed by both houses of Congress and signed into law by the President in February, 1986.]

## Universal Immunization *Marge Roukema*

1   Mr. Speaker, last month I joined 12 of my colleagues as an original cosponsor of House Concurrent Resolution 211. This resolution calls upon the President to direct the Agency for International Development to work with international health organizations in achieving the goal of universal access to childhood immunization by the year 1990. The efforts of world health officials will concentrate on the eradication of six dangerous childhood diseases: tuberculosis, diphtheria, tetanus, whooping cough, polio, and measles.

2   A year ago this month I traveled to Ethiopia as a member of a congressional fact-finding delegation, with a number of members of the Select Committee on Hunger. The shock of seeing miasmic men, women, and children in the grip of starvation was a soul-searing experience. We could not prevent this tragedy, which was due in large part to history, civil strife, and drought. But there is another tragedy continuing this very day, a malevolent and insidious one. Millions of children die each year from diseases that are entirely preventable. It is this needless human suffering that is the greater tragedy, because we have the immunizational know-how to stop these diseases right now.

3   The statistics on the six childhood diseases I mentioned and their effects on Third World children are well known, but I would like to reiterate just a few for the record. Only 2 children in every 10,000 die of measles in the United States, yet this affliction kills 3 of every 100 children in lesser developed countries. The percentage of children immunized against all six diseases in industrialized nations is more than twice as high as for those in the developing world. In 1984, less than 20 percent of the developing world's children were protected against all or most of these infections. Measles is a disease that kills 2 million children a year, tetanus 800,000, and whooping cough 600,000. These numbers are appalling and very discouraging. We must employ every means possible to reduce these numbers significantly.

4   This is a formidable challenge and raises specific questions. First, we must know what the needs are in developing countries, in terms of vaccines, medical personnel, logistics, and education. Second, we need to ask how we can implement a program that is sustainable, especially in the poorest countries, so that generation after generation can enjoy the benefits of immunization. And finally, we must ask what resources and efforts are necessary to reach our goal.

5   The costs of immunizing a child are small when you consider that the results pay huge dividends in terms of reduced future health-care costs, reduced infant mortality, and healthier children. High level political support is essential if we are to make progress in immunizing all the world's children. If other countries, international organizations, and private voluntary organizations maintain a commitment to work with the United States, we can save these children. A redoubling of efforts by all the parties involved will set us on the road to reaching our goal—universal immunization.

## Blue Beans and Purple Potatoes *Cecelia Miller*

One of the things all of us humans have in common, someone once said, is that we grew up in the same faraway village—childhood. As you read the following, you will probably remember some of your own eating habits in that village. This speech, delivered in a class at Asheville-Buncombe Technical College in Asheville, North Carolina, is a good example of an entertaining speech, sometimes called an after-dinner speech. Notice that Cecelia Miller's talk is simple and light—a tasty snack rather than a heavy meal. Note, too, that it entertains without resorting to comic one-liners.

1   Imagine that you are visiting with a friend you haven't seen in several years, and you receive a last minute invitation to dinner. Of course you accept and everything is fine until you sit down to eat. There on the plate in front of you are blue beans, purple potatoes and orange meatloaf. What would your reaction be? Would you think your friend is a color-blind artist who takes out her frustrations in the kitchen? Or would you think she was ready for the loony bin?

2   Maybe the answer is much simpler. She probably has a nine-year-old son who is into "space food" and the only way she can get him to eat a well-balanced meal is to serve "Martian" cuisine. This is just one of the sneaky, devious tricks parents use to get their finicky children to eat what they should. As the experienced mother of two very picky eaters, I'd like to let you in on some other tricks.

3   When children are small, say between the ages of one and four, getting them to eat is fairly simple. We're all familiar with the old "here comes the train—open the tunnel" game. That takes care of half the problem—it gets the food into their mouths. You'll have to find your own way to get them to swallow it. If your toddler doesn't want to eat eggs, try boiling the eggs and then draw faces on the shell. You can use wax crayons or food colors. If that doesn't work, you can fall back on that old favorite, Dr. Seuss. Put green food coloring into scrambled eggs and pretend they are the green eggs that Dr. Seuss made famous in his children's classic. You can also make bunny-rabbit salads out of cottage cheese. Use carrot sticks for ears and raisins for eyes.

4   For children aged nine or ten you may need a little more imagination. Try dyeing food weird colors and telling the children it's space food—fresh from Pluto this morning. You can also put good wholesome food into a pie shape. I believe

this is why quiche is so popular—children will eat anything pie-shaped without argument. On some mornings you will wake up to find several boxes of cereal on the shelf with only one or two inches of cereal left in them. The children will not eat these rejects. One way to dispose of them—other than to just throwing them away—is to pour them all into one big box, cover with aluminum foil, and paint "Venetian Surprise" on the front. It will be gone in no time.

5   Teenagers are sophisticated, cool, and too smart to be fooled by anyone as dumb as a parent. Anyway, that's what they think. But getting teenagers to eat is really not that hard—it just takes a little trickery. I used to save the containers from fast-food places and refill them at home. The food was always eaten and enjoyed, and the kids didn't know the difference. (At least not until they heard me rehearse this speech.) Another trick is to make everything into pizza. Teenagers will eat pizza hot, cold, or even lukewarm. Mine usually eat it cold in the morning for breakfast. If you want them to eat a more conventional breakfast, put tomato sauce and cheese on a tortilla over the top of eggs and sausage. It's just a Mexican omelette upside down. If all else fails, try using the old trick my mother used on us. Tell them it's not good for them. A teenager will decide that spinach is his favorite food if he thinks it isn't good for him to eat much of it.

6   I hope these ideas help you when your own children become picky eaters. But let me inject one word of caution. Unless you can stomach green eggs for breakfast, don't eat with your four-year-old. Whatever you feed him, you'll have to eat, too.

# Diploma Mills Versus Responsible Training: Sending Degrees to the Dogs *Sandra D. Lindquist*

A student at St. Olaf College in Minnesota, Sandra D. Lindquist delivered this speech at the 112th annual contest of the Interstate Oratorical Association at Peoria, Illinois, in 1985. It is reprinted with permission from *Winning Orations 1985.*

1   Sassafras Herbert proudly displays her handsome diploma, which entitles her to a listing in the "Official Directory of Nutrition and Dietary Consultants" and special rates for malpractice insurance. The latter benefit is a good thing because dietician Sassafras is an 11-year-old poodle. Victor Herbert, a New York City physician and proud owner of Sassafras, stated in *Time* magazine, April 2, 1984, that he bought the diploma for $50 to prove a point. "Something that looks like a diploma doesn't mean that somebody has responsible training." According to *Harper's* magazine, Spring, 1985, "Every day 40 people in the United States add false credentials to their resumes."

2   *U.S. News & World Report*, August 6, 1984, reports the case of Gary Robinson, who went to work for a respected Florida psychiatrist. He boasted an impressive resume: bachelor of science and doctor of medicine degrees from Columbia, and a doctorate in biochemistry from Stanford. He obtained staff privileges at two hospitals and gave psychiatric treatment to at least eight patients. Then one of the hospitals checked his record, and the bubble burst. Robinson held none of the degrees he claimed.

3   In order to gain a deeper understanding of the escalating problem of fraudulent credentials, it is first necessary to understand the major cause of this problem: diploma mills which sell degrees to anyone with the money to buy them.

Then we need to explore a course of action that must be taken in order to stop diploma mills and expose those people with fradulent credentials.

4  Lying about credentials is reaching epidemic proportions as pressure to acquire advanced degrees grows. "It occurs in 10 to 15 percent of the people who submit resumes," says Carl Menk, chairman of an executive-search firm in New York, in an article in *U.S. News & World Report*, August 6, 1984.

5  The most common method of padding credentials is the purchase of degrees from diploma mills. The business of selling fake degrees to people seeking to boost their egos or, more likely, their job prospects is growing. The FBI, in *Time*'s April 2, 1984, issue, estimated that there are at least 100 diploma mills in the United States. John Bear, who has worked with the FBI in its investigation of diploma mills, estimates the number of phony sheepskins distributed worldwide to be "hundreds of thousands and quite possibly over a million." In their investigation named Dipscam, the FBI has uncovered only five fictitious schools over the past four years. Currently, in most states and many foreign countries, it is legal for anyone to set up offices, motel rooms, or post office boxes as campuses. Without faculty or curriculum, they may begin mailing out any kind of degree you would like for a price. No cracking books, attending classes, or taking stiff exams is required. In fact, most of these counterfeit colleges demand only a few hundred dollars for a B.A. and up to $5,000 for a Ph.D.

6  The April 1982 edition of *Phi Delta Kappa* summarizes the problem. Diploma mills are frauds—not against students, but against society. The students get what they want, what they expect, and what they pay for. Employers who rely on the empty credentials are cheated, and so are those who become patients, clients, or colleagues of these people. Worst of all, these frauds include teachers, preachers, medical practitioners, and others who violate the trust we should be able to place in those committed to socially constructive occupations.

7  In the December 7, 1984, *New York Times*, a House subcommittee estimated that upwards of 10,000 United States doctors have phony degrees from foreign medical schools. Rep. Claude Pepper, chairman of the House subcommittee, said, "This data indicates the largest medical scandal in recent memory."

8  The most widely publicized exposure of a foreign diploma mill occurred in the Dominican Republic. Pedro de Mesones was found guilty of mail fraud and conspiracy and sentenced to three years in federal prison for operating two diploma mills in the Caribbean. He collected over $1.5 million from 165 United States residents seeking medical degrees. Of those receiving degrees, at least 13 had obtained medical licenses in the United States and 36 were working in hospital residency programs when they were discovered, according to the February 8, 1984, *Chronicle of Higher Education*.

9  However, the problem is not confined to the medical field. The legal profession is also affected by falsified credentials. The state bar of Michigan gets roughly 40 complaints a year of people passing themselves off as lawyers.

10  Those who use fake credentials are not only troublesome, but they can be life-threatening as well. A 45-year-old man was able to impersonate a doctor and give anesthesia improperly during surgery to remove a bladder tumor. The patient lapsed into a coma and remains brain dead, according to the August 6, 1984, issue of *U.S. News & World Report*. Bogus doctors have this same power of life and death over patients as real ones.

11  At the core of the diploma mill problem is the federal government's stand on the question of education. As stated in the April 1982, issue of *Phi Delta Kappan*, at least two major federal laws prevent federal officials from interfering in the

internal affairs of colleges. All that the U.S. Office of Education says on the matter is that "in the United States, no reputable institution of higher education confers degrees solely on the basis of correspondence study." The staff of the Office of Education found it almost impossible to draw a line between those who should be run out of town on a rail and those fringe operators who could sue for libel, slander, and federal interference in the internal affairs of their institutions.

12   Charles Alfred Durham of Seneca, South Carolina, who has been charged with mail fraud in connection with three diploma mills, has a clever defense: that the diplomas, costing up to $940 for a doctorate, were only "expensive novelties." Says Durham's lawyer, Daniel Day, in *Time* magazine, April 2, 1984: "People who bought these diplomas knew exactly what they were getting, and I don't think the FBI can show otherwise."

13   Since the federal government does not want to interfere in the internal affairs of colleges, diploma mills must be dealt with on a state level. The first change must be made in state laws so that diploma mills can at least be defined in a workable manner. New York presently has appropriate legislation. Their code, as reproduced in *A Comprehensive Guide to Alternative Degree Programs* by John Bear, states that "no individual not holding university, college or similar degree conferring powers granted by the state legislature, or the Board of Regents shall confer any degree or transact any business under the name of college or university or a similar title without the written consent of the Board of Regents under their seal." A small step in overcoming this problem would be for each state to adopt laws similar to those of New York. The next step would be for each state to adopt mandatory laws stating that each school must receive recognition from an appropriate accrediting association.

14   Currently accreditation is only desirable, so many colleges choose not to apply for accreditation. Each state association should have consistent guidelines for accrediting all degree granting institutions. This would serve as a safeguard against diploma mills because all properly accredited United States institutions are listed in the Handbook of Accredited Post-Secondary Education published by the American Council on Education. Because we are not familiar with foreign schools, and there has been evidence of foreign diploma mills, the American Council on Education should check on the authenticity of those schools and keep a similar list of legitimate foreign schools.

15   But the American Council on Education and state government can only go so far in giving out information. Then the responsibility of solving this problem falls to employers and consumers. Because 10 to 15 percent of the resumes currently submitted have phony credentials in them, employers need to be more stringent in verifying the credentials of prospective employees. More outside services that verify credentials such as the National Credential Verification Service in Minneapolis must be developed and used by employers and consumers. As an added precaution, employers should never accept any credential verification information directly from the individual applying.

16   We need to be more aware consumers. How often do we stop to examine the diploma of a doctor or a lawyer hanging on the wall? We usually only see the examining room, but we do have a right to see the diploma hanging in the doctor's office. Most legitimate doctors will share their credentials with you. If you are in doubt about the authenticity of any alternative degree program or any degree, write the U.S. Office of Education, because as Victor Herbert pointed out, "Something that looks like a diploma doesn't mean that someone has had responsible training." If we follow these steps, we can go a long way toward stopping diploma mills and exposing those people with fraudulent credentials.

17   In our fast paced society, the easy way is often lauded as the best, but in the area of diploma mills, it is obvious that this is not the case. None of us can afford to become the unknowing victim of a diploma mill's unqualified graduate because short-cut graduates short change everybody.

## Amusement Park Safety *Robert Rager*

How safe are the rides in amusement parks? This question is answered by Robert Rager, a student at Prince George's Community College in Maryland, in a speech delivered at the 112th annual contest of the Interstate Oratorical Association at Peoria, Illinois, in 1985. It is reprinted with permission from *Winning Orations 1985*.

1   It was another beautiful day at the amusement park. Warm sunshine, the smell of cotton candy, the kids. And the rides. The roller coaster's whooshing 60-mile-per-hour speed was accompanied by the familiar screams of delight from kids of all ages. Another ride, the comet, was flying gracefully through the heavens when suddenly a chain broke, flinging one of the gondolas 75 feet into the air before it crashed, killing a man and seriously injuring his son.

2   This accident, on May 26 in Pontiac, Illinois, was just one of many in 1984—one of many that could have been avoided.

3   Most of us don't think about accidents while we're having fun, and if there's one place where danger is farthest from one's mind, it would be at a carnival or amusement park.

4   But in 1983 the Consumer Product Safety Commission reported nearly 10,000 hospital emergency room treated injuries from amusement rides. All in the name of fun. When you get on an amusement or thrill ride, is safety your primary concern? Probably not. Well, maybe it's time you were told the truth—that these thrill rides aren't all fun and games.

5   Today I want to direct your attention to the lack of safety on amusement rides by examining how widespread this problem is, why it continues to be a problem, and what can be done about it.

6   In the last ten years there have been 89 consumer deaths at amusement parks and carnivals throughout the United States, 49 of the 89 deaths at fixed-site parks.

7   While the total number of deaths and injuries constitutes only a small percentage of the millions of parkgoers each year, consider that many of these people are children—innocent, fun-loving children who board these rides seeking thrills and adventure in a secure environment—not danger. But the danger is there, and all too often it becomes a reality, as we shall see in the following examples of injuries.

8   According to the August 4, 1984, *Washington Post*, a roller coaster at Six Flags over Georgia came to an abrupt stop when a pull chain failed. Four riders were taken to the hospital. One week before at the same park a computer malfunction caused simulated airplanes to collide in the air. Thirty-three riders were injured.

9   The July 9, 1984, *Chicago Sun-Times* reported that a nine-year-old boy who fell 30 feet to his death at the North Dakota State Fair may not have been strapped in properly.

10   The Railblazer, a new stand-up roller coaster at Six Flags over Mid-America in Missouri, had been open for just three weeks when, according to the July 30, 1984, *Oakland Tribune*, a woman fell 50 feet to her death from the last compartment of the ride.

11   These incidents exemplify the two major reasons for amusement ride accidents—mechanical failure and safety neglect. But why do these accidents continue to happen?

12   In 1981 the Consumer Product Safety Commission (CPCS) was stripped of its power to regulate the nation's more than 600 permanent amusement parks. This left the commission jurisdiction only over carnival rides that are moved from town to town.

13   This action was the result of a budget-slashing Congress, with assurance from industry experts that the states were doing a good job of ensuring that rides were safe.

14   Does the federal government not know that little more than half of the states have safety programs of any kind? Within the 27 states that do have some type of safety program, there is very little consistency. Inspections that are made daily in one state may be made only once a month in another. Some of the states don't even require inspections at all—they require only that the rides be insured. In these states, according to commentary in the August 27, 1984, *St. Louis Post-Dispatch*, insurance companies usually send out their own inspector just prior to issuing a new policy. Perhaps just once, before the fair opens for the season.

15   But in Gurnee, Illinois, a state that requires only that the rides be insured, three youths were injured on a ride called The Edge when, after being stranded 60 feet above the ground for 10 minutes, their car plunged straight down onto the ride's loading platform. It was later learned that the same ride had malfunctioned only two days early, but it was not closed down.

16   Unfortunately, the problem doesn't end here, as evidenced by CPSC commissioner Stuart Statler, in his August 6, 1984, testimony before the Subcommittee on Health and the Environment.

17   According to Statler, the Enterprise is one of the most popular rides in the country; there are 19 of them across the land. Because a fatal accident at the Texas State Fair in October 1983 involved an Enterprise ride which was moved from place to place (that is, a carnival ride), the CPSC was authorized to investigate the incident and determine the probable cause for this tragedy. "Our inquiry," says Statler, "pointed out alarming design and structural concerns that were apparent in many versions of the ride, both fixed and mobile. For the seven Enterprise rides that were transported from one locale to another, because we had jurisdiction, we could require an upgrading of safety features and monitor their maintenance. But we had no authority to require such changes in 123 parks around the country where the Enterprise was set in concrete—fixed in its site, but not fixed in its design or maintenance."

18   "This just doesn't make sense," continues Statler. "Our inspectors found a problem, yet we were powerless to include more than half of the affected rides in our corrective action plans. Perhaps these owners and operators will take up our suggestions, but we don't know that they will and can't even find out. And neither does the public who may board those Enterprise rides."

19   "The bottom line," says former CPSC chairperson Nancy Steorts, "is that the American consumer has no way of knowing the level of safety on a particular ride at a particular location. In effect, we are forcing the consumer to play amusement ride roulette with his or her family's safety."

20   In an effort to solve the problem, Senator Simon from Illinois and Representative Waxman from California have introduced a bill that is currently being reviewed by Congress. This bill, if passed, would give the CPSC the power to investigate serious accidents, require immediate reports when any owner, manufacturer, or operator suspects a potential hazard, and to issue corrective action plans pertaining to safety changes that are needed. This would be done for all amusement rides, including the fixed-site rides that the CPSC currently cannot investigate.

21   But most park owners and amusement company executives are lobbying hard against the bill, saying that the rides are safe enough and that such a bill would only mean more red tape for them.

22   If the rides are safe, though, then why are these people still being injured? And while there would be more paperwork, is there one life or one preventable injury that isn't worth the filling out of a few more forms?

23   A similar bill failed last year in the Senate due to the intense lobbying of these parks owners. This bill was reintroduced on March 20, 1985, as Bill S-702 in the Senate and HT-1596 in the House. It is due to be voted on in late spring or early summer of 1985, before the height of the park season. Don't let this bill fail again. We need to have the CPSC investigating these accidents and regulating these rides, but there's more that can be done.

24   In addition to federal controls, every state should have a mandatory safety inspection program. The state of Maryland, for example, has one of the most rigorous inspection codes in the country. Maryland applies a checklist of 53 safety items to each ride covering such areas as support structures, safety stops, chain axles, belts, lighting, and much more. These inspections are made daily at every carnival and amusement park by experienced owners and operators.

25   As a result, Maryland has one of the best safety records in the country, and it is essential that all states adopt and consistently enforce the same thorough regulations. As CPSC commissioner Statler puts its, "In states without safety inspections, the prevailing attitude is: let the rider beware."

26   So, before you get on that favorite ride of yours, check the credentials of the carnival or park where it's located. And be sure that the rides are inspected. And when you do get on, your primary concern will still probably be to have fun. But until these proposed solutions become realities we all have to live with the sad fact that the old saying, "A little fun never hurt anybody," just isn't true.

# Acknowledgments

The following professional speakers responded to the author's survey and generously gave advice from their experience on the public platform:

Sheila Murray Bethel, 1390 Market St., Suite 908, San Francisco, CA 94102
Don Beveridge Jr., P.O. Box 223, Barrington, IL 60010
Dr. James "Doc" Blakely, 3404 Fairway Dr., Wharton, TX 77488
Joe W. Boyd, 3534 Riley St., Bellingham, WA 98226
Arnold "Nick" Carter, Nightingale-Conant Corp., 7300 N. Lehigh Ave., Chicago, IL 60648
Danny Cox, 17381 Bonner Dr., Tustin, CA 92680
Lyle Crist, 2550 Belleflower, Alliance, OH 44601
Dr. Charles B. Dygert, 6314 Oakhurst Dr., Grove City, OH 43123
Ruth Duskin Feldman, 935 Fairview Rd., Highland Park, IL 60035
Roy Fenstermaker, 4223 Hackett Ave., Lakewood, CA 90713
Bonnie Gordon Flickinger, 31 Nottingham Terrace, Buffalo, NY 14216
Ed Foreman, 2995 LBJ Freeway, Suite 115, Dallas, TX 75234
D. Michael Frank, Box 27225, Columbus, OH 43227
Patricia Fripp, 527 Hugo St., San Francisco, CA 94122
Ira M. Hayes, 326 Meadowlark Court, Marco Island, FL 33937
Christopher Hegarty, P.O. Box 1152, Novato, CA 94948
Henry Heimlich, M.D., Xavier University, Cincinnati, OH 45207
Tom Hopkins, 7531 E. 2nd St., Scottsdale, AZ 85252
Robert William Hunt, 4106 N. State Rd. 269, Bellevue, OH 44811
E. Ray Jerkins, 307 Doctor's Pavilion, 1916 Patterson St., Nashville, TN 37203
Danielle Kennedy, P.O. Box 4382, San Clemente, CA 92672
Hope Mihalap, 1316 Graydon Ave., Norfolk, VA 23507
E. Larry Moles, 1940 Elida Rd., Lima, OH 48505
Bob Murphey, Attorney, P.O. Box 854, Nacogdoches, TX 75961
John Naber, P.O. Box 50107, Pasadena, CA 91105
Thom Norman, P.O. Box 536, Scottsdale, AZ 85252
Rosita Perez, 756 Fortuna Dr., Brandon, FL 33511
David W. Richardson, 36 Old Redding Rd., Weston, CT 06883
Jeanne Robertson, 2905 Forestdale Dr., Burlington, NC 27215
Dick Semaan, 20214 Lake Sherwood, Katy, TX 77450
Philip D. Steffen, 3217 Fox Tail Ct., N.E., Marietta, GA 30062
Dr. Jim Tunney, P.O. Box 189, Lakewood, CA 90714
Joel Weldon, 7975 N. Hayden Rd., Suite D-261, Scottsdale, AZ 85258
Dave Yoho, 10803 West Main St., Fairfax, VA 22030

# Index